S0-AXW-246

CONFESSIONS OF AN ENRON EXECUTIVE

A WHISTLEBLOWER'S STORY

BY
LYNN BREWER

WITH
MATTHEW SCOTT HANSEN

1663 LIBERTY DRIVE, SUITE 200
BLOOMINGTON, INDIANA 47403
(800) 839-8640
WWW.AUTHORHOUSE.COM

*Some of the names of persons involved in this account have been changed to protect their identity. Those are indicated with an * at the first reference. If no * appears, the name has not been changed. Anecdotal passages are based upon the Author's recollection of the events as they occurred. Every allegation, instance and event detailed by the Author is based upon either personal experience, documentation she has retained, public records, and/or conversations with individuals as referenced in this book.*

First published by AuthorHouse 09/29/04

ISBN: 1-4184-8537-3 (e)
ISBN: 1-4184-8536-5 (sc)
ISBN: 1-4184-8535-7 (dj)

Library of Congress Control Number: 2004097034

Printed in the United States of America
Bloomington, Indiana

This book is printed on acid-free paper.

To The Little Guy

TABLE OF CONTENTS

I believe in God and I believe in free markets. That's the fairest way to allocate and price resources. It does create more wealth and a higher standard of living for people than any other alternative. That ought to be the conclusive statement on markets. Certainly Jesus attempted to take care of the people around him, attempted to make their lives better. He also was a freedom lover. He wanted people to have the freedom to make choices. The freer the country in terms of its market and political system, the higher the standard of living of the people.

Kenneth L. Lay,
son of a Baptist minister,
former Chairman and CEO, Enron Corp.

PROLOGUE

No single raindrop ever considers itself responsible for the flood.

Unknown

I am a former Enron executive. During my tenure with Enron I called to the attention of senior management such things as bank fraud, espionage, manipulation of power prices, and ultimately the overstatement of Enron's financial condition to the media and analysts.

After leaving Enron, I discovered I had not been alone. In a presentation made to Enron's Board of Directors in early 2001, the board members would learn that between 2000 and 2001, there had been a 300% increase in whistleblowing reports to Enron's Office of the Chairman. "Whistleblowing" reports, via Enron's internal hotline, went from 2 per month in early 2000 to 2 per day in early 2001, of which 33% were reports of criminal activity, of which 75% were reports of fraud. These same board members would deny before Congress they had any knowledge that members of Enron's staff were committing fraud.

Before leaving the Company, nearly a year before the implosion, I telephoned Enron's employee assistance hotline from my company-issued cell phone, and laid out the details of what I had discovered, only to be told, "Inasmuch as our fees are paid by Enron, I can't take your call. You'll have to hire a private lawyer." Based upon Enron's unwillingness to investigate the death threat I had received, I decided to force the company to lay me off from Enron Broadband Services in order to take advantage of Enron's Severance Plan.

In February, 2001, I received my final severance check and then watched my entire 401(k) dissolve as I remained blindly faithful to the same company I was secretly blowing the whistle on. Long before Sherron Watkins had ever considered writing her memo to

Ken Lay, I was in confidential discussions with class action lawyer, Charlie Gastineau, sharing the details of my knowledge with him. Although I am qualified as a class member in the lawsuits pending against Enron, like Watkins and the other Enron employees, I personally have never actively participated in the lawsuits to seek financial reimbursement.

In December, 2001, long before the investigative committees inadvertently came across Watkins' internal memo in a box of subpoenaed files produced by Enron to the FBI, I telephoned the head of the Energy Commerce Committee, Senator Byron Dorgan (D-North Dakota). Moments after getting off the phone with one of his staff, I sent the following e-mail at their request.

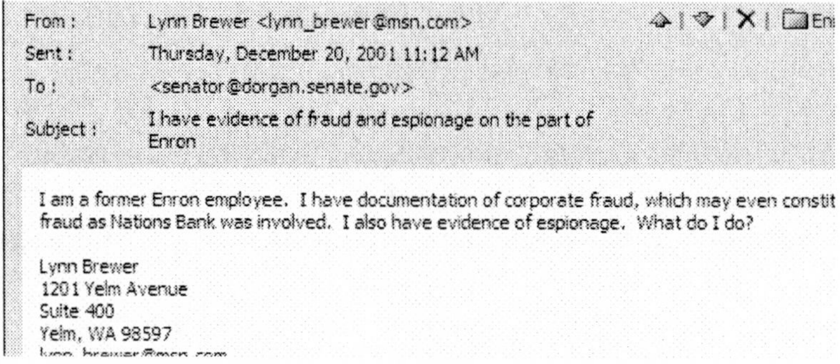
From : Lynn Brewer <lynn_brewer@msn.com>
Sent : Thursday, December 20, 2001 11:12 AM
To : <senator@dorgan.senate.gov>
Subject : I have evidence of fraud and espionage on the part of Enron

I am a former Enron employee. I have documentation of corporate fraud, which may even constit
fraud as Nations Bank was involved. I also have evidence of espionage. What do I do?

Lynn Brewer
1201 Yelm Avenue
Suite 400
Yelm, WA 98597

Yet, today, despite my phone and e-mail records, the Senator's office "has no record" of my contact.

While the world has hailed Sherron Watkins as "Enron's Whistleblower," her critics, like Dan Ackman of *Forbes* Magazine, have understandably said "A whistle-blower, literally speaking, is someone who spots a criminal robbing a bank and blows a whistle, alerting the police. That's not Sherron Watkins."

Watkins sent an internal memo – intended to remain internal – to Enron CEO Ken Lay, which was inadvertently discovered by the investigative committee and released to the public without her knowledge six weeks after the filing of Enron's bankruptcy. The company's stock was already trading at a mere 25¢ per share.

Despite serving in 2000 on an internal audit committee, created to detect internal fraud, Watkins never voiced her concerns that Enron had "become a risky place to work." Rather, in an e-mail to Chief

Risk Officer, Rick Buy, produced to the Federal Energy Regulatory Commission (FERC), Watkins expressed her real motives:

> *"I sure hope we make good use of the bad news about Skilling's resignation and do some house cleaning – can we write down some problem assets and unwind Raptor? I've been horribly uncomfortable about some of our accounting in the past few years and with the number of 'redeployments' up, I'm concerned some disgruntled employee will tattle."*

Ms. Watkins spent eight years at Enron before she spoke up and did so only when her personal financial security was in jeopardy. As she wrote in her memo "For those of us who didn't get rich over the last few years, can we afford to stay?"

In 1999, Watkins neglected to raise any red flags when she worked hard to sell Enron's stake in a Caribbean power plant to one of Andy Fastow's phony off-the-balance sheet partnerships. Although the deal would ultimately fall through, it was "not due to any lack of effort on her part", according to *BusinessWeek*. Perhaps Watkins had good reason to fear that "Enron will implode in a wave of accounting scandals" because she was actively involved in putting those transactions together and knew how fraudulent they were.

Charles Ganske of *The Washington Times* points out that Watkins herself has admitted that she was involved in the very sham deals at the focus of Enron's implosion for at least 18 months before she wrote her memo. She sold $48,000 in Enron stock and options in the two months following the writing of her memo. However, because she kept her memo secret, other Enron investors, including employees, who worked right alongside Watkins, did not have the good fortune of selling Enron's stock before the company imploded.

While Martha Stewart has been convicted for lying to investigators about selling stock based upon inside information, Watkins received a $400,000 advance for a book and negotiated a lucrative television movie deal. Meanwhile, according to Mr. Ganske, she receives $25,000 per speech on the lecture circuit, as a "self-styled expert on corporate ethics."

After her 2002 naming by *Time* magazine as one of three "Persons of the Year," I can only hope this laid to rest Watkins' concerns about her future career as expressed in her infamous memo to Ken Lay that "my 8 years of Enron work history will be worth nothing on my resume." In a survey of more than 4,434,495 participants, 67.8% said they disagreed with *Time's* choice for "Persons of the Year."

While Watkins' real motivation for writing her memo to Ken Lay may have been, as Robert Bryce suggests in his book *Pipe Dreams: Greed, Ego and the Death of Enron*, an effort to convince Ken Lay to fire Andy Fastow and promote Sherron to the position of CFO, it matters not.

What does matter is this – by Watkins gracefully accepting *Time's* "Person of the Year" as Enron's whistleblower, implying that she single-handedly is responsible for standing up against the establishment, as though she was the first to declare the Emperor had no clothes, is a disgrace to the hundreds of Enron employees who blew the whistle, like Margaret Ceconi. Ceconi, who first went anonymously to the SEC in July 2001, then publicly to Jeff Skilling on August 3, and then, unlike Watkins, ultimately to the analysts and the board of directors, had far more to lose as a manager than Watkins ever did as a vice president.

As Cora Daniels of *Fortune* Magazine points out "For every Sherron Watkins, there are 200 to 300 whistleblowers you never hear about who don't fare so well." Countless Enron employees made heroic attempts to voice their concerns, including Cliff Baxter, who lost his life because of what he knew.

Advised by my legal counsel to remain silent, I realized I could be silent no more – silence serves no one except those who have something to lose. I have been scared, threatened, criticized, my documents subpoenaed, and I have testified in the government's case against Enron. I have nothing to lose and everything to gain by telling my story.

Enron is not a story of one woman who blew the whistle but hundreds if not thousands who were never heard and will never be named *Time's* "Person of the Year" – my story is for those brave souls.

CHAPTER ONE

Display profits to entice them.
Create disorder in their forces and take them.

Sun-Tzu
The Art of War

BEFORE THE STORM

A few weeks before I was to escape Enron Capital & Trade Resources for a position in Enron's new water division, Azurix, I arrived at work and logged on to my computer to check e-mails. Plowing through the usual spam and correspondence, I noticed a screen name I didn't recognize, RipcordHouston@webtv.net (Chuck Drake). I clicked on the mail and as I read, I felt my face flush and my heart begin to race.

> *good luck you no good fat ass fucking whore bitch.... you will NOT be missed as you know the entire company of ECT hates your fucking guts and fucking laughs at your nasty big tittied ass every fucking day. so try and figure out who I am you fucking disgusting big-tongued lizard!!! Fuck you forever and ever with a big nasty aids ridden dildo!!!! YES THE WICKED WITCH HAS MOVED AWAY!!!*

There was no signature and I had never heard of Chuck Drake. As I read, then reread the message, my first reaction was to laugh. But through my laughter my mind began analyzing the message on several levels. The acronym "ECT" told me it was an insider, since no one but an insider used that to refer to Enron Capital & Trade Resources. And whoever it was knew I was leaving. I was also taken aback by the viciousness of the invective. Whoever it was absolutely hated me.

As that revelation sank in, my laughter faded. This was someone I knew, and probably pretty well. I spun out a list of perpetrators in my head and arranged them in order of motivation. I had tried hard to be liked, but Enron's world was a hard one, unsentimental and sometimes heartless. I had seen crimes committed from afar and been involved in misdeeds up close. I had been pushed to attack people I didn't know and had made enemies simply by being in the wrong place at the wrong time. My intense workload had caused an injury that might very well limit my career. I was physically and mentally exhausted. Now I felt trapped. Bound to this company by the most money I had ever made, I also had a desperate need to try to make a bad situation better, as I had done with the all too many dysfunctional men in my life.

All of these thoughts rushed through my head as I analyzed that vile message. I parsed the words to determine whether this was an actual threat. If so, to whom would I take it? The police? Human Resources? A lawyer? Through all of my mental games, one overwhelming thought began to supersede all others: this was about failure.

I had come to Enron with the highest hopes and greatest expectations. In the beginning, Enron offered me safety and stability and, more than anything else, the home I had always wanted. But my dreams had dissolved into a nightmare. Now, just a year and a half later, circumstances had me mired in a company that I found to be not only dishonest, but evil. And I was working among people who apparently despised me. Tears began to well.

My boss, Kathy Simpson*, passed my desk and out of instinct I called it to her attention. She glanced at the screen impassively. As she read it, I knew it was a mistake showing it to her. I had been harassed in her department for the past nine months and believed that much of it was by her order. She finished reading, seemingly unaffected. I wondered for a split second if she already knew about it. As she walked away, she looked back over her shoulder and casually asked me to forward it to her. In shock, I saved the e-mail, forwarded it to her, and then stood. I didn't know where I was going, but I just had to get out of there. Fighting tears, I walked out.

I was going to be a champion figure skater. Growing up in Tacoma, Washington, I never knew my real father. He left shortly after I was born and my mom got remarried to an alcoholic when I was six. He adopted me two years later when my brother, Rick, was born. That was about the time I took up figure skating. Like everything else I've ever done, I approached skating with total intensity. Life wasn't perfect at home, but for those six hours each day on the ice, I created my own little version of perfection.

When I was sixteen, and at the height of my competitive career and Olympic aspirations, my life began to fall apart. I came home one afternoon and found my mother cheating on my step-father. I became hysterical and my mother slapped me so hard she broke my nose. Soon after, I lapsed into anorexia as a way of dealing with stress. But I held onto my dreams and continued to skate. One night on my way home from practice, a drunk driver slammed into my car. I was severely injured and my hopes of an Olympic medal were dead.

I finished high school and recovered enough to spend the next year skating with Shipstad and Johnson's *Ice Follies/Holiday on Ice*. After discovering my mother was having an affair with a young man I was dating, I took up with Wayne Peterson*, eight years my senior, and moved in with him. I wanted children, Wayne didn't. I went to work for a law firm, and although I had no legal training, I learned quickly and the attorneys were soon giving me work usually assigned to second year attorneys. The discipline of my years on the ice and my desire to succeed served me well in the business world. Wayne and I married, but after several fruitless years of trying to convince him to start a family, we got divorced.

Now serving as a trial assistant and maritime financing specialist, my law firm began shuttling me between our Portland and Seattle offices. When I discovered one of the partners committing malpractice, I quit and went to work for a huge Seattle law firm.

In 1989, during the Final Four basketball tournament, I met a man named Brian* at a local restaurant. Although intuition warned me he was no good, I was blinded by the hope he offered of finally starting a family. After six months of dating, I quit my job and moved to St. Louis to be near him. With my stomach twisted in knots, we married in December of 1990. The marriage was doomed from the get-go. Brian was a jealous, controlling, rampant womanizer.

I was now working for medical industry giant Johnson & Johnson as a pharmaceutical rep. In February of 1991, J&J planned a big rollout of a new antibiotic and I flew out to Palm Springs for the event. The very first night, my roommate took up with our married boss. He got me stinking drunk on 13 shots of tequila, hoping I would pass out. When we returned to our room I did…sort of. Yet I was conscious enough to witness the two of them writhing naked in the next bed. He must have suspected I had seen him *flagrante delicto*, because he made my life at work a living hell for the next year.

Meanwhile, Brian had become increasingly violent towards me. He had some twisted sexual issues with his mother that seemed to torture him, and one night in an explosion of madness, Brian forced himself on me. I was absolutely traumatized. Had it been any state other than the judicially backward State of Missouri, it would have been called rape. Two weeks later, I underwent emergency surgery to repair a bleeding ovary. I never reported the attack and soon sank into a deep depression. By the middle of summer I decided the only solution was suicide.

One night, while Brian was catting about the town, I decided to end my life. Then I made a fateful decision by calling a girlfriend in North Carolina and telling her what I was about to do. After a moment of panic she spoke very firmly to me.

"Oh my Gawd, Lynn? I want you to hang up and call the suicide hotline *right away*. Do you hear me? Will you do that?"

I told her I would, mostly because I wanted to see if some stranger could find at least one reason why I should continue living. I looked up the number and dialed.

"Suicide Hotline, can I help you?" came the cheery voice.

"Yes. I think I'm going to commit suicide."

"Oh, okay. Can I put you on hold?"

I was taken aback. "Uh, okay."

So I listened to Barry Manilow for the next few minutes. When "Mandy" ended, Simply Red's "Holding Back the Years" began. I couldn't believe they would keep a potential suicide waiting so long. After a few minutes it seemed downright comical. I started snickering. Pretty soon I was laughing so hard I had tears in my eyes. I hung up. Laughter was just the shock treatment I needed. Somewhere between being put on hold, Barry Manilow, and a sophisti-pop group from the 80s, I was saved.

Back at the office, the gorilla who ravished my roommate in Palm Springs, then terrorized me for a solid year, was finally fired. I took a leave of absence from work and flew out to Canyon Springs Ranch in Palm Springs to get help. When I returned, I asked Brian for a divorce, which he refused to grant for nearly a year. I extended my absence from J&J and wrote a book about sports visualization, using my experiences and training as a competitive ice skater to help people push through barriers.

I eventually quit J&J and returned to law, specializing in complex litigation. A few months later I was offered a great opportunity at Ralston Purina, where I was swept into the middle of some major deals, including performing due diligence on one of the largest mergers in corporate history. I was a vital member of a powerful team assisting both the CFO and General Counsel in corporate development and investment banking.

My divorce from Brian was final and my career was back on track.

My path to Houston, and then Enron, had been an 18-year arc. Desperate to leave St. Louis and the ghosts of my personal life, I began to explore my options, but couldn't settle on a new town. I half-heartedly sent resumes to nearby Indianapolis, but wasn't particularly enthused about moving there. Several months later I attended a conference in San Diego, organized by a company based in Houston. Many of those present were from Houston and couldn't say enough wonderful things about all the opportunity awaiting me there.

Back in St. Louis, I did some research on Houston and what I found intrigued me. A big, busy city. Still, it wasn't so big that I'd be lost, like in L.A. or New York. I began a campaign to see what I could earn in Houston, then expanded my search to include Dallas. Of the forty or so resumes I mailed, I got a number of invitations to interview. One was from a woman named Shelly Wilson*.

Shelly was young, ambitious and had luxuriously flowing locks like Lady Godiva. As the owner of Wilson & Associates, a recruiting firm in Dallas, she fawned over me during our initial lunch meeting and immediately offered me a fabulous position expanding her business with a second office in Houston. When the recruiter recruits you, it's quite an honor. Or so I thought.

I gave notice to my boss at Ralston Purina, the General Counsel and CFO, who wished me luck. Then I went home and started packing. My house had been for sale since Brian's attack, but I figured the salary Shelly was going to pay would cover my expenses as well as my $2,200-per-month mortgage, at least until I could rent or sell it. After cutting ties with Ralston Purina, I packed up my house and sat back, waiting for the formal offer letter from Shelly. I waited and waited. When I realized Shelly's offer wasn't going to materialize, I was in a really tight spot. Ralston Purina had already replaced me and it was either stay in St. Louis or follow through on my move to Houston.

As I labored over my decision, fate made it for me. I got a call from Ted Tetzloff, General Counsel for Tenneco in Houston. He was responding to one of the resumes I sent out.

"Are you still coming to Houston?" he asked.

I considered my dilemma for about half a second. "Yes."

And with that Houston would become my new home. Tenneco was selling their energy division and Ted needed help preparing their due diligence. The position would be with Tenneco's in-house consulting firm, Peterson Consulting. Peterson was a huge firm, with roots in Arthur Andersen. Tenneco had a legal department, but outsourced their financial and damage analysis of complex litigation matters, as well as their legal support, to Peterson. I would be responsible for running the daily operations of the project. Over the next few days, we worked out the details of my job and salary and I made arrangements to move. A few weeks later, I packed up my car and left the ice and snow for the 22-hour drive to Houston. I was pleased while passing through at least two or three successively warmer climates during the drive.

As a newly-imported Texan, I discovered some givens about my adopted home. First, Texas is less a state than it is a state of mind. Fanaticism about all things Texan is required. Secondly, Texans loathe the meek, the puny, and the indistinct. Everything in Texas, whether or not it really is, is BIG. Texans do not suffer small. Boots, ranches, hair, it's all big. In my research I had uncovered a bit of trivia: Houstonians utilize more hairspray than any other city on Earth. By the flair of the architectural marvels perched atop many a Houston matron's head, I understood the relevance of that fact. Despite Houston's outsized ambitions, I liked the town and the people. I took my first week getting the lay of the land so I could choose a good neighborhood.

The place to live was River Oaks, but the five million dollar average price was a bit beyond my means. Instead, I rented a bungalow in a lovely and stylish area called West University, adjacent to Rice University, "the Yale of the South". I found that Houstonians' social ranking placed you either "inside the loop" or "outside the loop", that is, within or outside the boundaries of the 610 freeway that ringed the inner city. Outside was déclassé. I also found that in addition, Houston had a caste system that was based upon birth or marriage, and the only way to be considered a "real Houstonian" was either to be born there or to marry in.

It was all a lot to absorb my first week in town, but I wanted to peel back as many layers of the onion skin that comprised Houston culture so I could operate and thrive within the system. I enjoyed my work at Peterson and quickly made a solid core group of friends. One of them was a handsome young man named Aaron Whitehurst*.

At 24, Aaron was ten years my junior, but we hit it off and were soon good friends. Aaron was an analyst with Peterson, but had plans to leave work and go to law school the following September. As we drew closer, he mentioned his family and their little brick business in East Texas, but was evasive when I asked about them. After Aaron left Peterson he made it clear he wanted to pursue me by inquiring whether it would surprise me that someone his age would be interested in me. I couldn't help but chuckle as I said "not as much as it would your probably surprise your parents." I began falling in love with him, and as our relationship became more serious he asked me to attend his church. In Texas, the two major religions are Baptist and football. The Second Baptist Church had a following no less fervent than an NFL franchise and practiced in a facility no less grand than a stadium. Nicknamed the Baptidome, Second Baptist's church was necessarily spacious for a parish with 20,000 congregants.

I jumped into church activities only to find a slightly cold shoulder. Despite my relationship with Aaron, I was viewed with some skepticism – a woman with questionable virtues. To many I was seen warily as a single working woman from the north trying to insinuate herself into church functions. Nevertheless, I continued to attend Sunday classes, despite the judgmental "good Christian folk" around me.

As Aaron attended to his family business in east Texas, he told me he was temporarily putting off plans to attend law school. He assured me it would not affect our relationship, since he would be spending most of his time in Houston studying to retake his CPA exam. Not long after, we had a serious conversation about our future. Aaron and I talked about marriage, and though he was a lot younger, I adored him, he loved me, and I felt he was mature enough to be a good husband and father. Then something came up that changed the whole tone of our love affair.

"Of course you'll have to sign a prenuptial agreement," he said, one evening after discussing our future together. "My family will require that."

I thought he was kidding. "Yeah, right," I laughed. All along I had envisioned putting him through law school.

"No, you will. It's not really my idea. My mother won't let me marry anyone without a signed agreement. It's to protect the family money."

Family money indeed. It turned out the young executive with whom I had fallen in love, and assumed was just "scraping by", would, three years hence, fall heir to a portion of the $320 million fortune his grandfather reaped from selling his oil reserves to Arco. You could have knocked me over with a rolled up oil lease.

"And you're going to need to meet my mother," he added.

And I did. But it took Aaron three agonizing months to convince her to meet me. Every week I would ask and he'd get this hangdog expression. Momma hadn't relented. Finally, either Aaron's wheedling paid off or her heart had thawed, because she agreed to an audience with me. With that sort of build up, I was expecting just about anything. I drove up to Henderson, a small town not far from the Louisiana border and Shreveport. Mrs. Whitehurst was icily cordial and had all the arrogant entitlement of the nouveau riche Southerner who felt her wallet and *her* God made her just that much better than the rest of us. I could see her meager hospitality was in deference to Aaron, whom she unwittingly demeaned as her "Tittee Baby."

During our afternoon together, I tried very hard to like her and tried picturing her as my next mother-in-law. What deeply concerned me was the interaction between her and Aaron. It was like they were intimate, and not in the mother and son sense. In horror, I realized it was a ghastly déjà vu of my ex-husband Brian and his "loving" mother. As I was trying to come to terms with all the weirdness, Mrs. Whitehurst made several offhanded, virulently racist remarks and I immediately wrote her off.

Back in Houston I hoped I would see her as little as possible. I needn't have worried. Apparently she had dug around and found out I was divorced. Aaron already knew, and I had made no secret of it, but that was it. Her Tittee Baby was going to have no part of that carpet-bagging harlot who was trying to take her place. And as simple as that, Aaron was out of my life. I was devastated and sought refuge in the church Aaron had introduced me to.

When I phoned and told the receptionist I needed to speak with the pastor for counseling, she couldn't help but let out a little chuckle. I was so naive. Apparently my request was like phoning the White House and asking to talk to the president.

"I can try and set up a meeting with one of the full-time assistant pastors. There are thirty so we should be able to find you one."

I started counseling with one of the pastors, but was made to feel like I was to blame. As an outsider, I was daring to claim that an insider might be the cause of my problems. After the pastor dismissed my grief, I never went back for counseling. Instead, I threw myself into work and tried to forget Aaron. At Peterson we were finalizing a huge merger between our client, Tenneco, and El Paso Energy. When the dust settled, El Paso was now our client and Tenneco's energy division had been absorbed.

My house in St. Louis finally sold and I contemplated buying a home in Houston. In June of 1997, Jimmy Rich*, a man I had befriended at church, called me.

"Lynn," he said, his voice distressed, "I'm about to lose my house. They're gonna foreclose in less than three weeks if I don't get them some money. Could I borrow a little to bail myself out? It would save my life."

"How much do you need, Jimmy?"

"Well, fifteen hundred would be great. It'd be a life saver. I'll pay you back as soon as I can."

I was hardly made of money, but had done well the past year, salting away a small savings account. Jimmy had his share of trouble from a recent divorce, and I couldn't stand by and watch a friend suffer such a fate.

"I'd be happy to help you."

I gave a grateful Jimmy the check. Two weeks later I got another phone call.

"Lynn," said a nearly tearful Jimmy, "I'm really hurting financially. I had to use the money you loaned me to pay off some other bills. I have a huge favor to ask. I have a great deal of equity in my house, which I'll lose if they foreclose. How about you buy my house?"

I was taken aback. "Buy your house?"

"Right. If you buy it I won't lose my equity and you'll make some money, too."

Buying a house was a big commitment, particularly since it had taken three years to sell my last one. More importantly, I didn't really like his house. But it was a decent deal and would help Jimmy out. Our agreement was that he would stay in the house until he could find another place to live. He would also make the payments as long as he occupied the place. Once I moved in, if Jimmy was still living there, we would split the mortgage, but I would legally own it. At closing I would also receive the fifteen hundred he owed me. I didn't mention interest. After considering it for a few days, I consented. We had a vague discussion about a real estate partnership, but never came to an agreement. Within the next few days, I entered into escrow to purchase the house. Since I didn't want to lay out any cash, Jimmy used his equity as collateral and gave me a promissory note for five percent of the value of the house, which I gave to the loan officer as my down payment.

In late August we closed escrow and I owned a new home. Almost immediately, Jimmy's attitude changed. Though balding, paunchy, and at around five-seven hardly a big man, when Jimmy was provoked he would exhibit a frightening persona. His pale face turned beet red, sweat poured off his bald head and his rat eyes darkened with fury. As I began moving my stuff in, he began acting like I was imposing on his privacy. He would not allow me to move any of his kitchen items to make way for my own. He also expressed irritation that my belongings "cluttered" the garage, even though they were there because he wouldn't allow me to unpack them. Then he came to me with an odd, and what I considered an unreasonable, demand. Prior to closing some construction workers had allegedly stolen a few items, including a gun, and now he wanted me to pay half of the insurance deductible. He also expected me to pay half of his monthly storage facility fee because I had "displaced" some of his household goods.

Relations between us became increasingly strained as I tried to settle into the house I owned, yet was clearly not welcome in. On October 3, since Jimmy was obviously making no effort to find another place to live, I reluctantly left him a notice on his bed to vacate the property. I was closing a $100 million acquisition early the next morning, so I retired to my bedroom at around 8:30 p.m.

At 2:00 a.m. the door exploded open as he charged into my room and flipped on the lights. He was drunk as a skunk and raging.

"You fucking bitch!" he screamed. "You chicken-shit, fucking bitch! You think you can throw me out of MY house?"

He scared the wits out of me, but I held my ground. "This is MY house. If you don't get the hell out of my room, I'll call the cops and have you thrown out!"

He got in my face and I was terrified. "There's no fucking way you'll evict me, bitch!"

Then he backed off and seemed to calm down. He walked to my doorway then turned back to me. Wiping the slobber off his chin, he glared, "Don't fuck with me. You hear me? Don't you dare fuck with me."

That didn't seem to get the response he was looking for, so he tried what any obscenity-spewing, psychotic "Christian" would: invoke the Almighty.

"God will never bless you financially!"

"I think I'll let God tell me that directly."

I couldn't sleep the rest of the night, but it wasn't because I was worried about God striking my wallet. I knew Jimmy had a large gun collection and I worried he might be planning to use one on me. The eviction threat had provoked him. I got up and slid my dresser in front of the door, as if trying to keep a vampire at bay. The next morning I tried hurrying out the door to work, but Jimmy stopped me. He was in a foul mood and looked hung-over.

"I have a lien on this house. My promissory note says I still own it and there's nothin' you can do to get rid o' me, goddammit."

I immediately consulted a real estate lawyer who told me I couldn't sell the house until I got rid of the liens, which meant I had to get Jimmy to agree to let me sell the house and that wasn't going to happen. Catch 22. She said there wasn't much I could do, other than offer to sell him back the house. I was incredulous.

Over the next two weeks, I consulted literally ten more attorneys and they all told me the same thing: declare bankruptcy, move out and leave Jimmy holding the bag. As my frustrating legal dilemma continued, the problems with Jimmy escalated. I heard through the grapevine that he was bad-

mouthing me at church. One night, while I sat worrying about my reputation, he burst into my room.

"I went to see a judge in Fort Bend County and he told me I had no right to stay if you try to evict me. But if you do, well...be careful," he said with maximum menace.

I quickly packed, cancelled the homeowner's insurance, filed for bankruptcy, and walked away from the house and that madman.

My first brush with anything to do with Enron came in April 1997. While I was at Peterson I volunteered for the MS150, a charity bike ride from Houston to Austin to benefit the Multiple Sclerosis foundation. Although the distance was 175 miles, the ride was named after the minimum $150 in donations needed to enter. On the first day of the ride I rode behind a guy wearing an Enron shirt. He had a wiry build and thinning blond hair. I had been following him for a few miles when we reached the halfway point. The rest area included several tents, including a large white one with an Enron logo on it. We would spend the night there then hit the road bright and early.

Moments after I arrived, I heard a car horn honking and looked up to see a sparkling Range Rover bullying its way into the area reserved only for bikers. Shoving people aside, the SUV zoomed right next to the tent, to everyone's dismay. Out climbed a hard-bitten brunette in biking shorts, which was pretty ironic given how she got there. She walked over and gave the balding blond guy a kiss. My only reaction was that she was uncouth and arrogant. I went looking for water and didn't give the two another thought until a year later when our paths crossed again.

It was in late January 1998 when I got a phone call at my desk at Peterson Consulting.

"Lynn? Ronda Maze* at Prescott Legal. Mary Rye* suggested I give you a call."

Prescott Legal was a legal recruiting firm and Mary Rye was a partner. Mary had also been a friend since my arrival in Houston. We met during my initial job search. She took an immediate liking to me and offered me a job with her company as a recruiter. Unfortunately for her, I was offered the Peterson job at the same time and reluctantly turned her down, using the excuse that Peterson offered a salary, versus a commission at Prescott Legal. The real reason was I was emotionally depleted and needed stability. The choice was simple – use my legal skills, something I could do on autopilot, or expend enormous mental and physical effort to flex my people skills. I just couldn't face a job at that time that required me to be "up" the entire working day. Though Mary knew I was fairly happy at Peterson, I knew Ronda's call concerned a job offer.

"I have an opening and Mary said you'd be perfect."

"Well Ronda, I have a job."

"I know, I know, but this one's really good."

"What's the position?" I asked.

"Contract administrator."

Slightly insulted, I tried to smile, knowing Mary had my best interests at heart.

"My job here is well above a contract administrator. That'd be a step backward for me."

"True," she persisted, "but then again you don't work at Enron." Despite having been in Houston nearly two years I knew little about Enron.

"That energy company?"

"No," she corrected, "*the* energy company."

Enron was one of the city's biggest employers, but big companies were a dime-a-dozen in Houston. Mary had bragged during one of our lunches that a friend inside Enron had helped her land the account, but the particulars of her conquest had gone in one ear and out the other.

Having planted the idea, Ronda realized I needed to be sold on the notion, as I was probably one of four people in the greater Houston area who didn't genuflect when they heard the name Enron.

"What's the salary range?" I asked with some indifference.

"I'll tell you what, I'll have Mary call you with the details."

We hung up and a few minutes later Mary called. Without trying to pitch me we agreed to have lunch at the Galleria.

After some small talk, we got down to business.

"Okay, so why should I take a contract administrator job?"

Mary smiled slyly. "The base is sixty-eight."

I was surprised. That was more than a twenty percent increase over the fifty-five thousand I made at Peterson, despite being a lesser position. "Okay, I'm listening."

"And," she continued, "that's just the beginning. Enron is a very, very hot company and they pay extremely well. The benefits will likely mean you'll be over a hundred within a year, especially when you consider the stock options."

Stock options were two magic words. My father had retired early on the few million he accumulated from stock options over the course of his career. At thirty-five, and given the horrors and battles of the past ten years, I had fantasized about financial stability for a long time. Mary knew enough about my history to understand that a solid economic foundation was a huge priority. She also understood something else about me.

"You could spend the rest of your career at Enron," she continued. "It's like a family."

That hit me. I had experienced many jobs in my career, but I had never felt the real warmth and camaraderie that I knew some companies offered. Like finding a good man, I just figured it wasn't for me. Suddenly the possibilities were intriguing.

Mary had worked at Enron. "Tell me why I should work there," I said.

"You could make more money than you've ever seen."

"Where do I sign?" I laughed.

Mary's laugh evolved into a matter-of-fact expression. "You're gonna work hard."

"Look, I'm working sixty hours a week at Peterson."

"You'll work more at Enron. Sometimes eighty."

She saw my eyes widen.

"But," she continued, "your medical and benefit package is second to none, they'll pay for you to go back to school, they'll pay for travel, and you'll get regular, generous raises. There isn't a more generous company in Houston. And that stock in your pocket? Well, it's made a lot of people filthy rich. You could put in five years, quit, retire."

Mary paused to take a bite of her salad. "I won't lie to you. Enron is a sweatshop. But Harvard is a tough school. It's really hard to get in to Enron. They have lots of contractors inside who have been contractors for ten years or more, but this job is as a fully-vested employee. Big difference."

We sat in silence for a moment.

"You worked at Enron," I stated. "What did you do there?"

"I was in Origination. Putting together huge energy deals."

"Why did you leave?"

She looked down at her lunch. "As a single mom, I wanted to get of the rat race."

"So you want to put me in the rat race?" I asked with a grin.

She smiled back. "Yeah, but you'll be a really rich rat and the guys are real eye-candy."

We both laughed. "Okay, I'm hooked."

"Good. I'll have the woman hiring you, Kathy Simpson, call you for an introductory interview."

The next day my phone rang. It was Kathy Simpson. Her voice was pleasant but tentative.

"Mary sent me your resume and letters of recommendation. I'm impressed."

I demurred. "Thanks." I had never been comfortable with self-promotion.

"You've got a lot of experience, maybe even too much for our job. Do you get bored easily?"

"Oh no," I came back, finding myself selling harder than I'd expected.

The day before I wouldn't have given Enron a second thought, and now I was fighting to get those mythical stock options. "As you can see, I've had a wide range of experience and I've always given a hundred percent to each."

Kathy seemed satisfied I'd sucked up enough. "Good. Let me tell you a little about the job opening and a little about Enron. I have two openings for contract administrators. Now I know that's below what you're doing now, but we'll start you at sixty-eight thousand. That's your base. From there we'll give you regular raises at regular intervals. We'll also encourage you with what we call 'Personal Best Awards'. Believe me, there's a lot of low-hanging fruit to be had in this company."

I was struck by the term "low-hanging fruit". It was a phrase I had never heard and it created a strong, jungle-like visual in my mind. I quickly refocused, lest I miss the rest of the details as to how I was going to get wealthy.

"With your bonuses and those awards, you could easily see an extra twenty thousand a year. And that doesn't include your options. Mary mentioned stock options? Did she tell you how that worked?"

I shook my head even though we were on the phone. "Uh, no, she didn't."

"The company gives you two percent of your salary every year in stock options, based on the value of the Enron stock when the options are granted. Once the options vest, you can take possession of the stock, sell it, whatever. We're currently trading in the mid-thirties, but Jeff Skilling says it's worth a hundred."

I quickly scribbled some numbers on the legal pad in front of me and concluded the job that was "a step down" was going to pay me nearly double what I was making at Peterson. I didn't bother to ask how that was possible.

We concluded our conversation with pleasantries and her promise that she'd "let me know ASAP".

A little later Mary called. She had just spoken to Kathy.

"You charmed her. She wants you to come in for an interview. You'll be meeting with Kathy and Emma Toombs*. Emma oversees the contract administration under Kathy."

I was excited at the possibility of doubling my income. "How can they afford to pay so much?" I asked.

"It's Enron, honey." She said in her sweet sappy Texan accent.

After we got off the phone, I walked down to the office of Raeanne Ford*, a contractor I hired for a due diligence project. Raeanne had worked at Enron.

"Raeanne," I said, "I'm interviewing with Enron. Can you tell me a little bit about the company?"

Raeanne stared thoughtfully at me. "I left Enron," she began, "because I wanted to spend more time with my kids."

"I hear it's a sweatshop."

"And then some," added Raeanne. "Sixty hours a week is common.

But the money is great. And the environment is good if you get with the right group. But I won't sugar-coat it, the place can be brutal. They have forced ranking. They call it 'Rank and Yank'."

"Rank and Yank? How does that work?"

"It's survival of the fittest, and if not the fittest, then the luckiest or even the most blood-thirsty."

"Seriously?" I asked with a slight chill.

"Twice a year you go through a review that's more like a cross between a police line-up and the Spanish Inquisition. It's Skilling's contribution to the corporate culture at Enron."

"Who?"

"Jeff Skilling. He's the president and one of Ken Lay's golden boys. You'll meet him. Some think he's very handsome. Don't be fooled by his looks and don't ever, ever cross him."

I'd heard of Ken Lay. His face was always on the local news for a charity event or some such thing. But this guy Skilling sounded downright frightening.

"You'll meet all those guys. Skilling, Ken Rice, Kevin Hannon, Andy Fastow. They're sort of like the A-Team meets the Mafia; smart, ruthless. That's what makes Enron's world go 'round. Skilling and Rice are downright womanizers while Hannon and Fastow keep the dollars flowing in the door."

Raeanne's comments both intrigued and concerned me. I had gotten mixed signals as to what Enron was, either a dreamlike environment where money grew on trees and employees had practically unlimited benefits and opportunity, or a big, shadowy monster that ground people under its wheels. Given my history and where I wanted to be, both personally and financially, I wanted to believe the former.

I was also surprised by the reaction of my colleagues at Peterson Consulting. When word got around that Enron was after me they buzzed about my desk like I was being considered to ride on the space shuttle. They were well aware of something I was just learning – that Enron was a deity in the culture of Houston. I was finding that, true to Mary's words, the perception of getting into Enron was regarded as something akin to winning the lottery. I marveled at how a company could generate so much fervor among people. My interview with Kathy Simpson and Emma Toombs was two days away, but I was already getting butterflies. Now, more than ever, I really wanted this job.

I had seen the huge, gleaming tower on Smith Street but, not being a devotee of architecture, hadn't paid much attention. Now, as I was to enter the portal at 1400 Smith Street, I was suddenly intimidated. I had learned regarding Enron that a little well-placed awe was in order. Having risen from a nondescript oil and gas company, they had endured some rocky times along the way, but in ten years had become a titan in the energy field, branching out from their early roots into such disparate areas as power plants, energy and global finance.

As I walked in the front doors I could feel the pulse of the place. It was electric. Crisp-shirted execs scurried about, folders under arms, conversations buzzing about their latest financial triumphs, and on every face I scanned, the steely, confident shine of success. Checking in with the front desk, I sat down on one of the leather sofas to wait for Kathy Simpson. Taking a deep breath, I told myself that if I didn't get this job it was okay, that I would be okay because I already had a decent job, and prior to a week ago had never even thought about Enron. After suffering so much disappointment in my life, I had developed little safeguards to protect myself and this mantra was one of them.

The place stunk of money. I had seen many lobbies, but this one exuded a special power. Ten immense banners proclaimed Enron's Vision and Values. I began to understand why Houstonians spoke so reverentially about these people: their meteoric success came *despite* their lofty ideals, such as respecting one another and playing fairly. I was deeply impressed that such an enormous, thriving organization had avoided the pitfalls that occur when naked ambition and almighty dollars were mixed.

Across the lobby my eyes were drawn to an anomaly as she exited the elevator. An alien among these gym-buffed acolytes in their Armani and DKNY, she was a truck of a woman swaddled in a generous khaki skirt snatched from a Target hanger. Stalking in my direction, I realized this bruiser had made eye contact and was heading right for me. Seconds later she extended a Christmas ham-sized paw and forced a smile that jiggled her suety jowls.

"Lynn? Kathy Simpson."

We shook hands. As we walked to the elevator, I glanced sideward and was alarmed at the length of her arms. I remembered the queer use of her term "low-hanging fruit" and couldn't help but now relate it to her in a simian way. I pictured Kathy swinging from a tree, grabbing a tasty mango. Kathy punched the twenty-sixth floor.

"Your first time here?" she asked.

"Yes. It's very impressive."

Kathy nodded. "We're growing exponentially. I've reserved a conference room. Emma Toombs, who works for me, will be joining us."

We went to a conference room where I found a plush leather swivel chair and sat. As I leaned back, the chair offered no resistance and I almost fell out of it, my legs nearly flying over my head before I recovered. Kathy gave me an odd look before asking if I was alright. I righted myself, tried to smile and kissed off my career at Enron before it had even started. But things went better as Kathy and I chatted. Soon Emma Toombs joined us. Emma was the antithesis of Kathy. Tall, slim, and attractive, with a touch of severity, she was dressed to the nines in contrast to Kathy's ones or twos.

"So you don't think you'd be bored?" Emma asked in a syrupy, little girl voice. "Given your current responsibilities at Peterson?"

"No. Although I'm running the project for Peterson, I'm interested in having more hands-on experience with gas contracts. Besides, I don't see this as being my last job inside Enron."

That answer elicited knowing nods from both women. I think they appreciated my confidence. The rest of the interview went well, then Kathy shuffled through my file and noted that I had lived in Portland. Almost offhandedly she threw out, "You know, we just closed on the purchase of Portland General Electric. Would you consider moving back there?"

I laughed. Enron *and* Portland seemed too good to be true. "When do I move?"

That signaled a natural end to a good meeting. We shook hands and Kathy escorted me out. I returned my temporary ID badge and we shook hands again. As I turned to walk out I saw the big stock ticker proudly displaying Enron's current share price in the high thirties. I mentally owned some of that stock already and calculated my earnings while walking the five blocks back to El Paso Energy's office.

Before I could get back to my desk, I was stopped by several colleagues.

"How'd it go?" asked my best friend at Peterson, Lori Cortez*.

"I don't know. The interview went really well, but I really don't know."

My only concern was that I was overqualified for the job, but what seemed like genuine concern from Kathy and Emma now seemed like plain old pragmatism in the light of day. I realized they just wanted an employee who wouldn't bolt in terror after three months of training; money and benefits be damned. That night I went home and started unraveling the history of Enron. I wanted to understand this company. I had learned all too well from relationships with bad men that a bad company could be just as deadly. I decided some due diligence was in order, despite how wonderful Enron sounded.

CHAPTER TWO

We treat others as we would like to be treated ourselves.
We do not tolerate abusive or disrespectful treatment.
Ruthlessness, callousness, and arrogance don't belong here.

from Enron's Vision and Values statement

VISION AND VALUES

By the mid-1980s, an old-time vacuum salesman and former government economist named Ken Lay had formed a small empire in the oil and natural gas business. In July 1985, Lay merged his company, Houston Natural Gas, into an Omaha company, InterNorth. I was more than a little surprised to find that the bankroll came from junk bond guru Michael Milken. After pocketing Milken's contribution, Lay's company took off, despite sizable debt. In 1986, the company was proudly christened Enteron. Not long after that, someone's head must have rolled when it was discovered "Enteron" was the anatomical term for intestines. Runner-up name Enron then quickly succeeded Enteron as the name of the new venture.

The next year Enron discovered that oil traders in their New York office had embezzled hand-over-fist and run the company a billion dollars in debt (clever accounting, I was to find later, reduced the billion to the more bite-sized $142 million). At that point, Lay ordered the development of systems to ensure that such losses would not happen again, and that there would be failsafe mechanisms to prevent future internal corruption.

During the 1980s, the climate in the energy industry began to change as companies lobbied Washington hard to deregulate their field. Soon, as the government lifted controls, competition heated up and the market was suddenly exciting, but wildly volatile. With the energy industry ripe with opportunity in 1989, a Harvard MBA in his mid-thirties working at the prestigious McKinsey consultancy firm presented Ken Lay with his vision for the future of Enron. His plan was for Enron to become an energy middleman by trading in gas futures between suppliers and utilities, thus creating seeming stability for buyers and sellers in a potentially unbridled market. He promised Ken they would laugh all the way to the bank. It was audacious, but Ken Lay loved the smell of the man's smoke and promptly made Jeff Skilling the CEO of Enron Capital & Trade Resources (ECT), the power center under which Enron would build its future.

As I investigated Enron in early 1998, it was already a gigantic company, branching into areas outside its core energy mien. While Enron Corp. functioned basically as a holding company, it was divided into a handful of operating business units. To the outside world, ECT was comprised of Enron's merchant or trading business, where commodities were marketed or traded like stock. ECT, led by Ken Rice as Chairman and CEO, and Kevin Hannon as CFO, was the largest employer within Enron's groups. Enron International (EI), chaired by powerhouse Rebecca Mark, was responsible for the development of international assets. ECT was asset-light and operated in a market where supply outweighed demand, while EI was asset-heavy and operated in the foreign markets where demand outweighed supply. These two units made up the Wholesale Energy Operations and Services and bought and sold energy to wholesale customers while residential deregulation was still moving at a snail's pace.

Enron also had a vast network of natural gas pipelines, spanning the United States and Canada, which represented the lion's share of Enron's domestic assets. The Gas Pipeline Group, or GPG, handled the transportation and distribution of natural gas. Meanwhile, Enron had interests in two other entities, both publicly traded. Enron Oil and Gas (EOG) derived its revenue from the exploration and production of crude oil and gas, and EOTT Partners, LP was a major marketer of crude oil in the United States and Canada and a domestic marketer of refined products.

As Enron moved to become the "World's Largest Energy Company", they put all groups under one umbrella so all the companies would be known to the outside world simply as Enron. Internally, the groups were still differentiated. Enron Wholesale Services would identify those businesses which served the wholesale marketplace and would be divided into Enron North America (ENA, formerly ECT), Enron Europe, Enron Japan, and Enron Australia. EnronOnline (EOL) would eventually fall within this business unit. The new markets Enron had entered were metals, credit, coal, weather, crude oil, liquefied natural gas (LNG), forest products and steel. While under the control of Jeff Skilling, Enron sought to rid itself of assets. Enron Global Assets and Enron Wind Corp. represented a small portion of Enron's diversified asset portfolio.

The retail side of the energy business consisted of medium-sized companies, as well as residential customers. To serve that market, Enron created Enron Energy Services (EES), whose major business was in energy outsourcing to assist companies in reducing their costs, managing risks of energy price volatility, and improving energy infrastructures.

Enron Transportation Services represented Enron's remaining pipelines, having sold Houston Pipe Line Company (HPL) to American Electric Power (AEP) in 2000. Transwestern Pipeline operated 2,500 miles of natural gas pipeline from the San Juan, Permian and Anadarko Basins to the California border. Florida Gas Transmission, with 4,795 miles of pipeline serving the Florida peninsula, was connected to 10 major pipelines. Enron, as the largest general partner in Northern Border Partners, LP, held an interest in Northern Border Pipeline, which consisted of 1,214 miles of pipeline from Illinois to the Canadian border through Montana. Northern Border Partners, LP, was publicly traded on the NYSE. And finally, Portland General Electric Company (PGE) was Oregon's major electricity-utility.

Although it would appear to the outside world that Enron had wrapped its business into nice neat little packages, consisting of a few consolidated operations, the truth was that Enron had more than 2,300 subsidiaries, of which a majority were offshore for tax reasons. I was stunned when I uncovered that number.

I had been solely responsible for the administration of Ralston Purina's domestic and international subsidiaries, which consisted of approximately 250 companies. While working for one of Enron's largest competitors, El Paso Energy, I dealt with a mere 300 subsidiaries. I was well aware of what a reasonable number of subsidiaries would constitute and 2,300 raised some questions for me. I wondered if Enron was a labyrinth or, worse, a hologram. I put my fears aside and chose to believe this was just one big company with Napoleonic dreams and pockets deep enough to see them to reality. I was excited.

I went to their Web site and poked around. I found the page proclaiming their lofty Vision and Values. The following is what I read:

Statement of Human Rights Principles

As a partner in the communities in which we operate, Enron believes it has a responsibility to conduct itself according to certain basic principles that transcend industries, cultures, economies, and local, regional and national boundaries.

Because we take this responsibility as an international employer and global corporate citizen seriously, we have developed the following principles on human rights. Enron's Vision and Values comprise the platform upon which our human rights principles are built:

Vision –

Enron's vision is to become the world's leading energy company –creating innovative and efficient energy solutions for growing economies and a better environment worldwide.

Values –

Respect: *We treat others as we would like to be treated ourselves. We do not tolerate abusive or disrespectful treatment. Ruthlessness, callousness and arrogance don't belong here.*

Integrity: *We work with customers and prospects openly, honestly and sincerely. When we say we will do something, we will do it; when we say we cannot or will not do something, then we won't do it.*

Communication: *We have an obligation to communicate. Here, we take the time to talk with one another...and to listen. We believe that information is meant to move and that information moves people.*

Excellence: *We are satisfied with nothing less than the very best in everything we do. We will continue to raise the bar for everyone. The great fun here will be for all of us to discover just how good we can really be.*

Principles of Human Rights –

Enron stands on the foundation of its Vision and Values. Every employee is educated about the company's Vision and Values and is expected to conduct business with other employees, partners, contractors, suppliers, vendors and customers keeping in mind respect, integrity, communication and excellence. Everything we do evolves from Enron's Vision and Values statements.

At Enron, we treat others as we expect to be treated ourselves. We believe in respect for the rights of all individuals and are committed to promoting an environment characterized by dignity and mutual respect for employees, customers, contractors, suppliers, partners, community members and representatives of all levels of Government.

We do not and will not tolerate mistreatment or human rights abuses of any kind by our employees or contractors.

We believe in treating all employees fairly, regardless of gender, race, color, language, religion, age, ethnic background, political or other opinion, national origin, or physical limitation.

We are dedicated to conducting business according to all applicable local and international laws and regulations, including but not limited to, the U.S. Foreign Corrupt Practices Act, and with the highest professional and ethical standards.

We are committed to operating safely and conducting business worldwide in compliance with all applicable environmental, health, and safety laws and regulations and strive to improve the lives of the people in the regions in which we operate. These laws, regulations, and standards are designed to safeguard the environment, human health, wildlife, and natural resources. Our commitment to observe them faithfully is an integral part of our business and of our values.

We believe that playing an active role in every community in which we operate fosters a long-term partnership with the people with whom we come into daily contact. Strengthening the communities where our employees live and work is a priority. We focus community relations activities on several areas, with particular emphasis on education, the environment, and promoting healthy families.

We believe in offering our employees fair compensation through wages and other benefits.

We believe that our employees and the employees of our contractors working in our facilities are entitled to safe and healthy working conditions.

Education and Communication –

Because we take our responsibilities to our fellow citizens seriously, we act decisively to ensure that all those with whom we do business understand our policies and standards.

Providing clearly written guidelines reinforces our principles and business ethics. Enron employees at all levels are expected to be active proponents of our principles and are trained to report without retribution anything they observe or discover that indicates our standards are not being met.

Compliance with the law and ethical standards are conditions of employment, and violations will result in disciplinary action, which may include termination. New employees are asked to sign a statement indicating that they have read, understand and will comply with this statement, and employees are periodically asked to reaffirm their commitment to these principles.

Furthermore, Enron seeks to require its contractors, suppliers, and vendors to uphold the same respect for human rights that we require of ourselves, and to include appropriate provisions in every new contract entered with these parties. When we are joint venture partners with other companies, we will work to gain board approval for similar measures in joint venture contracts with contractors, suppliers and vendors.

The truth in the end would reveal these principles were either written by someone outside Enron who hadn't a clue about the Company's principles or someone inside Enron who obviously had a propensity for smoking crack cocaine. The high-flying philosophy behind the statements reminded me of the scene in *Citizen Kane* when Orson Welles, as Kane, proudly posts his "declaration of principles". Of course, by the end of the film, Joe Cotton's character points out that Kane has gone against everything he believed in. I was hoping this would not replay itself at Enron, but was a little disquieted when I found that Jeff Skilling didn't give a crap about the Vision and Values manifesto until he learned the stock of companies with such statements did better than the companies without them.

Now that I knew Enron's basic story, I dug into their financials for the previous year, 1997. Everything was looking good until I found an alarming after-tax, non-recurring charge of $537 million over "settlement of the J-Block contracts". Slightly reassured that it appeared to be a onetime loss, I was nevertheless troubled by the staggering amount and probed further into what J-Block was.

In 1990, Enron, through its subsidiary British Teeside Power Ltd., entered into a contract to purchase gas from a field in the North Sea. The gas would be delivered through a 36-inch diameter, 255-mile pipeline, to be constructed between 1990 and 1993. Known as The Central Area Transmission System (CATS), the pipeline would be owned by a consortium consisting of Amoco UK Exploration, Ltd. (30% ownership), British Gas North Sea Holdings and British Gas Exploration and Production (51%), Amareda Hess, Ltd. (17.5%), Phillips Petroleum United Kingdom, Ltd. (.66%), Fina Exploration Company (.54%), and AGIPE (UK), Ltd. at .3% ownership. It was to be operated solely by Amoco (UK) Exploration.

The first use of the pipeline was to specifically carry gas from the Everest and adjacent Lomond fields, also owned by the pipeline consortium, to a power station at Teeside owned by Enron. The Teeside complex is a massive oil and gas hub on the northeast coast of England, near the city of Middlesbrough. Much of the oil and gas in the North Sea goes through Teeside before it is routed to the rest of the world.

After it was determined that the pipeline's capacity would exceed the amount necessary for Enron to operate its power station, Enron entered into a separate agreement through its subsidiary, Teeside Gas Transportation, Ltd. (TGTL) to capitalize on a portion of the excess capacity. On September 10, 1990, well before the pipeline had been built, TGTL entered into an agreement called a Capacity Reservation and Transportation Agreement (CRTA). The agreement was, in essence, a "take or pay" agreement guaranteed by Enron from April 1, 1993 through October 1, 2018, requiring quarterly payments in the amount of £8m through October 1, 2013.

Two and a half years later, on March 26, 1993, another Enron subsidiary, Enron Europe, Ltd. (EEL) entered into a Gas Sales Agreement whereby it purchased all gas within the gas field known as J-Block, which was scheduled to come on stream within the CATS pipeline in late 1995 or early 1996, and would be commingled with the gas for the Teeside Power Plant. This, too, was a "take or pay" contract, which called for the purchase of 260 million cubic feet of gas per day at a net price of 19 pence per therm. By 1994, gas was trading at 22 pence per therm so this was looking like a damn good deal. However, by 1995, well before the time Enron was to take delivery of any gas, prices in the region tanked to 10 pence per therm and remained depressed.

With a fifty percent price drop in the previous one-year period, by 1996 Enron was desperate to get out of J-Block's "take or pay" contract. Marshaling their legal forces, the edict was given to peruse the contracts with a magnifying glass and find an escape route. Enron's open window came through terms of the agreement regarding the definition of the Commencement Date of gas delivery. Among other things, the proposed physical tie-in to the TGTL pipeline from the J-Block fields, which had been built by the consortium, was, from an engineering standpoint, considered "not satisfactory".

Ultimately, Enron reached a settlement with the J-Block suppliers in 1997, requiring Enron to make a cash payment of $440 million to get out of the contract, which is why there had been a "non-recurring" charge taken.

It wouldn't be until much later that I would learn that, thanks to J-Block, I was being considered for the position at Enron. Jeff Skilling, with an iron-willed determination to never take another bath on Enron's stock value, demanded the entire company become globally integrated with historical and future pricing available at the finger tips of every trader and originator. Hence the purpose for the birth of the Global Systems Group as well as numerous other work groups. Their single-minded focus was to turn Enron into the world's largest energy company.

I had mixed feelings from my investigation. I was no Pollyanna, understanding that to achieve such lofty goals in the dog-eat-exec world of global business, one had to play by rules that were often dictated by situational ethics. Every firm I had worked for had, at some level, played fast and loose with ethical and moral standards that, in one's personal life, would be considered sacrosanct. Why did people check their principles at the door when they went to work? Or did they have any to begin with? Was I just naive, expecting people to be good all the time, except when it involved a merger, an off-the-books loss, a shaky transaction? I guess I hazily equated it with a form of warfare. Lives and countries might not be at stake, but the financial lives and futures of people were at stake. I remembered a phrase put forth by a boss of mine from many years past that stuck in my head, *"If you're not winning, you're losing."* Enron was winning and I decided I wanted to be part of that.

A few days later, I got a call from Mary at Prescott Legal that rendered my aspirations moot.

"They gave the jobs to two other applicants," she reported.

I was shaken, partly because of the rejection, but also because I had done my due diligence and made my own decision about Enron and to have it taken away was crushing.

"If it makes you feel any better, Kathy really liked you and just thought you were overqualified. They actually brought in a lawyer from El Paso Energy for one of the positions, so you should feel good that you're considered overqualified when a lawyer isn't."

I didn't. "Is it Elaine Small*?"

Mary sounded surprised. "Yes. How did you know?"

"I'd heard she was also talking to Enron. I just didn't know about which job."

Elaine had come to El Paso Energy out of law school and worked there on a contract basis because she had been unable to get a permanent offer. Elaine was morbidly obese and perhaps some bitterness over her compromised physical state caused her to be a terminal gossip. I was glad to see her go, despite having taken *my* job. That she was a lawyer and considered beneath me in qualifications did offer me some consolation.

I thanked Mary then settled in to answering questions around the office about why I hadn't been accepted into the Enron priesthood. About ten days later, on March 6, after the wounds had healed somewhat, Mary called again. We made some small talk and I figured she was calling to arrange lunch.

"They want you," she said.

"Who does?"

"Enron. I just got off the phone with Kathy Simpson. Another position has opened up and they want you."

I was wary. "They want to interview me again?"

"No. They want to hire you. The job's yours if you want it. It's managing the contract briefing group although the money's about the same. But will include international travel to do training abroad."

Slightly dazed, I hesitated a moment. Mary jumped back in.

"Honey, it's Enron. Take it!"

"Okay, sure. When do I start?"

It was agreed I would begin at Enron on March 20, 1998. As news of my departure got around the ranks at Peterson, people began dropping by my desk to offer congratulations and advice. One of my colleagues, Mike Shively*, ambled up one afternoon. "I heard you got stock options."

"I did. Pretty cool, huh?"

"Yeah," he nodded, "you lucky dog."

Soon after committing to the 3/20 start date, I realized my duties at Peterson required me to stay an extra week to complete a large tax ruling project. I technically owed them only two weeks' notice, but

I'd never walked out on a job unfinished. I phoned Kathy Simpson, explained the situation and asked for an extra week. Kathy was disappointed but respected my loyalty and granted me the extra week.

On March 14, I received my formal offer by mail from Enron and marveled at the laundry list of benefits and potential income streams. In addition to my salary, which was $13,000 more than I was making at Peterson (with few benefits), I would be getting the fabled stock options, performance awards, participation in an annual bonus pool, which purportedly paid some mid-level executives as much as $5 million, comprehensive health and dental, long-term disability, travel disability for myself as an executive, a health club membership, subsidized parking, subsidized meals, and topped off with the icing of a 10% to 20% salary bump every year. I'd worked at many firms but had never heard of rank-and-file employees getting some of these benefits. I was bowled over.

Then, as if Enron sprang from thin air, I was noticing the company everywhere from local TV stations and newspapers to charity events. It was similar to buying a blue Ford, and then suddenly noticing every blue Ford on the road. I was filled with pride whenever I saw the logo, the now famous angled, block lettered "E" over the smaller-cased "enron". For the first time in my life I had the strong sense that I was entering a very special time. Enron's success was now my success. That they wanted me gave me a feeling of accomplishment and self-validation like nothing before.

On March 28, 1998, I began working for Enron. Stout Kathy met me at the front desk, got me checked in with security, then sent me to New Employee Training with the promise we'd meet later for lunch. The training was simply an orientation. Sitting with around 30 other new hires in a small auditorium, we were told about Enron's myriad benefits and employee perks. They explained how Enron's in-house concierge service worked, how to charge your subsidized meals at the company cafeteria, the services and benefits of the company credit union, mailing services for holiday packages (something I'd never heard of), on-site massage therapists for my weekly massage (that was too good to be true), an onsite medical center, and that live bands would often play in the park just outside the tower during the summer. They even had a store where you could buy clothing, coffee mugs and other paraphernalia, all adorned with Enron logos. It was sounding more like Disneyland than a job.

It seemed as though everything could simply be charged using your employee badge, with the monthly balance being deducted from your pay check. Coffee at Starbucks – no problem. Clothing for the gym – not a problem. Birthday cards for the relatives – "charge-it". It was like having your own American Express card with no spending limits with all of the charges simply and easily deducted from your paycheck – all with a simple swipe of the old employee badge. Of course, all of this purchasing power it would turn out was not for our benefit but rather for "Big Brother" to track our every move – and boy did they – everything from whether I ate salad or deep fried southern chicken. Enron tracked it all.

After the orientation, the parade of the Business Group Heads began. One after the other, they made their pitches to us. Although we were all bound by company policy to our respective groups for one year, I was more than a little impressed that these people were laying the groundwork to interest us, in case some of us turned out to be desirable employees if not superstars. And I was beginning to see that "desirable" meant "profitable", and that it didn't just pertain to those in traditional profit roles, such as sales staff, traders or execs who made earth-shaking decisions affecting the company's bottom line; rather, it meant *everyone* at Enron. The old expression, "if you're not part of the solution, you're part of the problem" for Enron could be translated to "if you're not making money, you're costing us."

The blatant courting by the business group honchos was heady and exciting, and gave me the dizzying yet thrilling rush that this was a game with stakes like nothing else I'd experienced. Having participated in sports, then authored a book about the psychology of winning and competition, it struck me that for the first time I was not only on a major league team, I was finally going to be a starter.

For lunch, Kathy and I were joined by a pudgy, nondescript, balding exec named Lance Schultz*, whom I had replaced after he was transferred to head another group within Kathy's organization. Lance and I followed Kathy down to the parking garage to her brand spanking-new Jeep Grand Cherokee. As Kathy clicked her remote and it chirped to indicate the doors were unlocked, she looked at me and raised an eyebrow.

"Bought this with my last bonus. It was great to pay cash."

Lance nodded knowingly as if he had bought one too. With the leather, fancy wheels and all the trimmings, I figured her bonus had to have been more than the $35,000 sticker. We piled in.

"You're gonna have to watch it when you cash in your stock options," she noted as she backed out.

"Yeah," Lance chimed in, "tax problems if you sell too early."

"Right," continued Kathy. "If you sell too soon that can cause capital gains consequences, so you'd better get some good tax advice – you're going to need it."

Lance chuckled knowingly. Kathy joined in on the laugh and I giggled along though not quite sure what was so funny.

When Lance composed himself he decided to underline the joke for the newcomer. "Yeah, I heard people at Microsoft had problems." And with that punch line he and Kathy guffawed. That I understood. Anyone who had gotten in on Microsoft early was rich, regardless of whether you had invested in a hundred shares or a hundred thousand. They were telling me that the biggest problem in my future would be whether or not I'd decide to incur capital gains.

Settling in at our table in the restaurant, a glance passed between Kathy and Lance indicating that the "meeting" was about to begin.

"Let's talk about your mission," she said.

"My mission?" Suddenly I felt like I had signed onto the CIA, not Enron.

Lance opened his mouth to speak, but Kathy raised her hand.

"We know your abilities, Lynn," she began. "What we're more concerned about is how you'll be handling the members of your team. The people under you."

Lance relaxed slightly as if Kathy had read his mind.

His face took on a serious set. "You've got some, uh, situations, within your team and we just wanted to bring you up to speed, so to speak."

Suddenly our friendly little get-acquainted lunch had taken a dark turn.

"What kind of situations?" I asked.

"You'll have three people under you," said Kathy.

"...and two of them are deadwood," finished Lance.

Kathy nodded. "Ronnie Jones* is your first problem."

"A total slacker," spat Lance.

"And he's always late," said Kathy.

"Thirty years old," added Lance, "looks like a Sumo wrestler and he's, excuse my French, a big pussy. And he collects Beanie Babies," he threw in with a measure of contempt.

"Spends all of his money on 'em." said Kathy matter-of-factly. "Has 'em all over his desk."

"I hate that little faggot," grated Lance.

Kathy sighed. "Then there's Sherlynn."

Lance nodded vigorously as he tasted the blood in the water.

"Sherlynn Jessup*," he said to me. "Morbid alcoholic. Morbid."

Kathy sighed again. "Sherlynn never met a bottle she didn't like."

Lance jumped in. "Now Sherlynn has the most knowledge about gas in the unit. She claims to have been a trader. But she's a drunk and she's unreliable. Plus," he added with a look to Kathy, "she's probably going to be a real problem for you."

Kathy nodded ruefully. "I passed her over and gave you the job, Lance's old job. Sherlynn is pissed so she'll probably be gunning for you. Just watch your back and you'll be okay. Oh, and it wouldn't hurt to keep your file drawers locked and watch what papers you leave around."

My stomach was starting to churn. I laughed inwardly that I was already in need of that free company massage and I hadn't even started yet.

"The only saving grace in the department is Faith Randall*", said Kathy. "She'll never give you any grief. As a matter of fact, if you need it, she can carry the whole group. She's completely underrated at her current level."

"We want her promoted," noted Lance.

"Which brings us around to your mission," said Kathy.

I was beginning to understand that my "mission" was probably not going to be related to contracts.

"We want you," she continued, "to get rid of Ronnie and Sherlynn. And you have only two months."

"Come review time in June," said Lance with a bit of relish, "you'll rank and yank those two."

Kathy smiled, now that my mission was out in the open. I smiled too, but felt the blood drain from my face. All I could think of was the Mafia. I had been wooed inside with the promise of stock options and free gift wrapping and now I was being told, "Oh, by the way, you gotta whack these two guys you don't even know." My job title should have been "Hitman".

I was too stunned to really say anything. I couldn't believe my ears and I was suddenly paranoid that this was some kind of malevolent new hire screening technique where management tries to goad you into agreeing to "assassinate" fellow employees you'd never even met. Maybe acquiescing too easily and agreeing to railroad these two people was their way of winnowing out the bad eggs and the morally-weak because, after all, this was not the Enron way. It just couldn't be, not after seeing those fabulous Vision and Values banners waving proudly in the lobby.

To protect myself I merely nodded but never actually agreed to get rid of my targets. My next worry was that if Kathy or Lance had a secret little tape recorder and I agreed to their plan they'd have the evidence and I'd be out. I grinned like an idiot during the rest of lunch but never actually said yes or incriminated myself. They didn't seem to notice. I went home that afternoon with a sinking feeling.

The next morning, I arrived for my first real day at work. Kathy greeted me at my desk, giving no indication anything was wrong. The good news was that as soon as she introduced me to Ronnie Jones, I realized everything she and Lance had told me the previous day was absolutely straightforward and not a ruse to test my integrity. The bad news was that they apparently assumed I had no integrity.

The image of Ronnie as a Beanie Baby-clutching Sumo wrestler was so accurate as to be disarming. I even did a slight double-take when Kathy introduced me to the chunky young man in the wrinkled golf shirt. My eyes fell on his desk, a playground littered with little stuffed animals. It evoked the feeling of a teenage girl's bedroom, not a businessman's work station. Then Kathy walked me over to another desk, behind which sat a sullen, middle-aged frump with ruddy circles rimming her slightly bloodshot eyes. I almost blurted out "So you're the wino" to Sherlynn Jessup, but managed to keep my cool. The only warm face in the group was that of Faith Randall. Neatly pressed in a suit, Faith, a soft-spoken African-American, resonated good vibes. If I took everything I had been told at face value, then Faith was my go-to girl in the group.

As the day wore on and I interacted with Ronnie and Sherlynn, I realized why Kathy and Lance wanted them gone, but I resented having been put in the position of doing their dirty work. I also remembered their warnings about Sherlynn, and in the short few conversations I had with her, I understood what they meant. Alcoholic or not, this woman was canny, and her eyes told me conniving as well. She liked working at Enron as much as the next guy and had more to lose now that she had been made a "permanent" employee after starting out as a contractor. It sickened me, but by the end of the day I was already scheming how I could jettison the two "anchors". After all, I had been given the very solid impression it was either me or them, and I wanted to stay.

As the first week ended, I had a pretty good take on the shortcomings of my team. Ronnie was chronically late and unreliable in his assignments. Sherlynn spent hours indulging in personal phone calls. Neither really seemed to care about their actual jobs. Faith, as billed, was the one carrying the majority of the workload. By Friday I looked at lazy, late Ronnie, his desk crowded with overpriced stuffed caricatures and photos of his beloved miniature pugs, and then at that bloodshot old souse, her breath reeking of the previous evening's cheap Merlot, and I embraced my charge. No longer did I feel guilty. I had met the enemy and the enemy had to be vanquished. Firing these two would be like shooting fish in a barrel.

Before I had completed my first month at Enron, Kathy took it upon herself to indirectly instruct me on the finer points of the fast termination. Kathy ordered a subordinate named Dave Paisley*, a manager of the pipeline facilities group, to her office.

I listened and watched through Kathy's window as they yelled at each other for a few volleys, then escalated into screaming, which ended in Kathy's offer to have security escort him from the building. With a good thirty or forty seconds to gather his belongings from his desk, Dave was gone. I had watched Kathy belittle Dave in management meetings but this was vicious. Faith appeared and tarried by my desk for a second, ostensibly on her way to the copy machine, but really to impart some of the back story.

"Dave's been with the company for years, but in Kathy's group only a short time," she whispered. "He did a good job. Kathy just didn't like him."

The surprises just kept coming.

A few minutes after Paisley stormed out, Kathy waved me over to her office. I went in, sat down and Kathy handed me a file folder. I looked at the label and realized it was Dave Paisley's personnel file. I was shocked and started to hand it back, but Kathy held up a hand, stopping me.

"Did you see all that?" she asked.

I was embarrassed to answer but felt she had wanted me to hear it. "Yes."

"Take a look in there," she said, indicating the file.

Reluctantly I opened it. I knew that personnel files were highly private and should not be seen by anyone except Human Resources or top management, and only if there was just cause. Having only recently been introduced to Enron's lofty Vision and Values, I felt her giving me access to his file was flying in the face of all that. I felt dirty opening it, but I was already developing a healthy fear of my boss. Kathy waddled around her desk and flipped through some of the file's pages.

"See?" she asked, eagerly indicating file entries. "This was a write up, and this, too. He didn't do his job. And on top of that, he was an asshole. Did you hear him yelling at me?"

I wanted to say *"yeah, and I heard you yelling at him"*, but Dave Paisley wasn't holding my future at Enron in his hands. I nodded meekly.

"He deserved to be let go. I can't have that kind of insubordination in my department. Understand?"

"Yes," I said, now unsure whether this was meant to scare me. It did. Kathy leaned in close and lowered her voice. "If either of those two...and you know who I mean. If either of them act-up, well, then do what I did to Paisley. Are we clear? Otherwise we're going to have to get rid of them during reviews."

"Yes," I said again, but far from certain I could even come close to Kathy's blood-thirsty style. I also didn't understand how you could just fire someone. I was under the impression that Enron's review process was generally the accepted path to getting rid of an employee.

Kathy smiled and laid a meaty paw on my shoulder. Barely a month and my training was complete. The actual job part of my job, I realized, had never been the issue. What Kathy had now was what she wanted all along, someone to pull the trigger when she gave the thumbs down.

Later that day, Faith passed my desk. "Big meeting tomorrow. Hear about it?"

"No," I said, "what meeting?"

"Across the street. Everybody goes. You'll see."

The next day there was a buzz through the office about the companywide meeting. With fanfare similar to the product launches I had seen at Johnson & Johnson, this event sounded like a major production. At the appointed hour, the entire company more or less shut down as employees filed across the street into the voluminous main ballroom at the Hyatt.

As I entered the hotel, I knew this was going to be nothing like the stuffy, boring presentations at J&J. To warm up the crowd, management hired artist Denny Dent, a wild eyed, bushy haired painter who blended what amounted to a seeming Native-American rain-dance with oil painting. His two-fisted art attack fascinated me as he danced about on stage to the Beatles and literally threw paint at a massive canvas. I watched in amazement while this madman in a tuxedo leaped around, brandishing a couple of brushes in each hand, and from this chaos of creation a familiar six-foot face began to take shape. Within a few moments of his rendering the hair and jaw-line, everyone in the room recognized Albert Einstein. As he put the finishing touch on his creation, a big yellow hand print, he stood back, bowed, and the crowd went wild.

I smiled to myself, appreciating that the people who ran this company were part of a new wave. Not the stodgy dinosaurs of yesteryear, but cutting-edge visionaries who understood that for a company to achieve success on the scale to which they aspired, they needed to lift the spirits of their people and allow them to soar in inspiration. Choosing Denny Dent over the traditional motivational speaker spoke volumes about their own vision. I looked around at every face beaming with enthusiasm. I knew I could take the petty in-fighting in my own group because I was a part of this great company's strength and high-minded mission. Dent's minute-masterpiece still hangs in the main lobby of the Human Resources Department.

In March 1998, Enron had been named Most Innovative Company by *Fortune* magazine for the third year in a row. Its stock was on the rise and the company was expanding far beyond the original confines of oil and gas. These were Enron's halcyon days. After Denny Dent's presentation, the crowd settled in for the first speaker, eyes glued to the single microphone on the stage.

Within moments the crowd began screaming as a man who could have been a Ralph Lauren model, muscles rippling under a crisp white t-shirt and exquisitely packed into a perfectly faded pair of Levis, strode across the stage on lizard-skin Tony Lamas. I was back in high school again and he was the captain of the football team. In those ten seconds before he reached the microphone, I pictured him astride a thundering Harley with the wind in his hair and me clinging to his chiseled abs. My insides had gone to mush.

I turned to Faith. "My God, who is that guy?"

"Ken Rice. He's CEO of ECT."

My heart fluttered as he spoke. When I first heard rumors that many women flocked to Enron less for the stock options and more in hopes of finding a husband or a sugar daddy, I had found it trivial at best and repugnant at worst. That was until I saw Ken Rice. In ten seconds, I was on board. I wanted him.

He told some jokes to which I laughed uproariously. Then he introduced the next speaker, Kevin Hannon. In contrast to Ken Rice's "James Dean", Hannon looked like a product of a union between "Lyle Lovett" and "Ben Stein". Hannon narrated a slide show with all the wit of an accountant expounding the conquests of ECT while Rice hammed it up to the side, mimicking Denny Dent by using paint, a huge easel and his hands to finger-paint his own presentation, complete with improvised "graphs and charts". As they interacted, I saw them as the numbers guy, the tight-assed Type A, and the salesman, an amiable clown – the perfect combo. At the end of their show, Rice left a big green handprint, à la Denny Dent, in the middle of his "charts". The crowd screamed.

Next we watched a video presentation on a fifty-foot OmniMax screen of various executives in action at Enron. I paid particular attention to see if I could match up faces with the names I had been hearing. As dynamic shots of the different moguls within Enron flickered by I was making mental notes of who was who. I marveled at how attractive everyone was, almost as if they had been cast, not hired. Then came poor Gene Humphrey.

During the filming of his sequence, no one had alerted him to wipe his nose before the camera began rolling. As the president and CEO of Enron Economic Development Corporation talked earnestly to the camera, occasional titters began to issue forth from the crowd. Soon, the chuckles evolved into shocked and embarrassed silence, for there, clinging to Gene's left nostril, magnified 10,000-fold by the grandeur of OmniVision, was a booger the size of an armadillo.

I was impressed that although none of the 7,000 employees in the ballroom missed it, few were crass enough to cackle out loud. Mercifully, Gene's visage disappeared but returned a moment later. This time he jabbered away and no one paid attention. I glanced around to see dozens of employees wiping their noses, as if that action would somehow clear the wad of congealed snot from Gene's beak. I pictured the local videographer – who had probably bragged to friends and family about landing Enron – and how he would be looking for new clients after this incident.

Following the unpleasantness with Gene Humphrey's dried mucus came "The Ken and Jeff Show". Much like Ken Rice and Kevin Hannon, Ken Lay and Jeff Skilling were a study in contrasts. Ken Lay was the kindly father figure, a "Ward Cleaver", soothing his team with a warm and fuzzy pep talk. Then came his team captain, the purposeful Jeff Skilling, a slight man with thinning blonde hair. Skilling took control and transformed Ken's emotional brushstrokes into hard numbers on the big screen. I recognized Skilling the moment I saw him, but couldn't place the face. Then I recalled as I saw the back of his balding head shinning under the lights, it was Skilling I had followed in the MS bike ride the previous year, and wondered who the obnoxious woman in the Range Rover had been.

Three things stood out during Skilling's speech. One was the mention of J-Block in relation to the 1997 financial report. The second would turn out to be a mantra for Jeff and Enron management.

"The analysts just don't get it," he said, with more than a touch of bitterness. "We have to sell them on our story, which we will continue to do until they are singing our tune."

After Jeff railed at the shortsighted Wall Streeters, he punched his remote control, bringing up a map of the world on the giant screen. As colored dots appeared at specific locations, Jeff ticked off Enron's steps toward the creation of price volatility and global domination. The map, the screen, and Jeff's passionate commentary about what Enron would control next smacked a bit of a rally in a certain Munich beer hall, but perhaps more so, a scene from *Dr. Strangelove*. This was not simply the main ballroom at the Hyatt – it was a war room.

In the popular business buzz lexicon, Jeff Skilling had dubbed Enron a "risk management" company. This was a polite way of saying Enron juggled flaming hatchets to make a buck. Such a term was wholly appropriate and a more genteel description for analysts to describe a major company delving more and more into financial derivatives.

Warren E. Buffett, chairman of Berkshire Hathaway has described them as "Weapons of Mass Destruction". Financial guru Martin Weiss perhaps gives the best description of how derivatives work.

"I bet you that, in the next 15 days, the Thai baht is going to plunge against the Indian rupiah more quickly than the Swiss franc is going to rise against the Japanese yen."

"You don't take the bet, but someone else does. Again, a deal is cut. A customized contract is negotiated and signed. Everybody's happy."

"You buy one instrument, while you sell another; and the two instruments are similar in some way. So instead of simply betting on the market going up or down, you're often betting just on the DIFFERENCE or "spread" between one market and the other." "Multiply this by thousands of financial institutions, hedge funds and pension funds – hundreds of instruments – countless permutations and situations – and it all adds up to the $71 trillion in commitments on the books of U.S. banks as of December 31, 2003."

At Enron the value of those contracts were put on the books, the minute they were entered into even though they may not be worth anything until the year 2010. Using "mark-to-market" or should I say "market-to-myth" accounting, Enron would have been willing to write a contract speculating anything, including as Buffett would say "the number of twins to be born in Nebraska in 2020".

There is enormous incentive and the ability to cheat in accounting for the value of derivative contracts, which is why Enron loved them. There is marginal business sense behind entering into a derivatives contract, but in practice, derivatives have more in common to off-track betting. The fate of Barings Bank, the seemingly unsinkable British financial giant, was on the minds of more than a few members of the business community during that time. Only a few years earlier, Barings was mortally wounded by young Nick Leeson of their Singapore office, after he experimented with derivatives like a kid with a chemistry set.

Skilling knew that the labeling of Enron as a risk management intensive company would tend to limit embarrassing questions by pesky analysts, so he embraced it. He did so because they supposedly understood and accepted that risk management was just that – risky. I found it ironic that as Jeff's map filled with yellow and red circles, representing power stations and natural gas facilities, his explanation of them also became circular.

The third thing that would strike me to the core, and haunted me for the rest of my career at Enron, was Jeff's launch of Enron's "new" Vision and Values statement intended to define the core of Enron's values – Respect, Integrity, Communications and Excellence.

"We have found that companies that have a written vision and values statement have a far greater return on investment than those that don't." Skilling proclaimed without a blink of an eye.

I, on the other hand, blinked in astonishment. *Certainly he didn't just say what I think he said – did he?* His blatant arrogance clearly demonstrated that the leadership at Enron, or at least Skilling, was nothing more than self-serving individuals with empty values. That it was okay to mislead investors "as long as we sell them on our story".

I watched as Jeff introduced the film that was apparently nothing more than propaganda.

The big crooked "E" filled the screen as I heard Ken Lay's voice open the five minute film.

"We're strong believers in competition. We have the people and the skill base and experience to win in a competitive marketplace. Virtually every industry that's opened up for competition sees tremendous innovation, almost immediately."

I had already seen the competition inside Enron on my first day. I could only imagine if Kathy Simpson was willing to cut the arms and legs off employees like something out of a Monty Python movie, I can only imagine what they would be willing to do "win in a competitive marketplace."

As I watched the movie, I began to realize this really was propaganda as Jeff Skilling would be shown testifying.

"Reducing electricity cost is only one benefit from choice and competition."

Three minutes into the film entitled "Vision and Values", we finally get a glimpse of Enron's values.

"We have a lot of very aggressive people in the company. A lot of people have a point of view on what they should be doing and how the company ought to evolve and that's great, because that's what you want. You want the organization to move as people find opportunities. You may disagree with someone and that's fine, let's get the disagreement out on the table and let's resolve it. But let's do it with mutual respect."

"It's a tough world out there. It's very competitive world and there probably are times that there's a desire to cut corners. We can't have that at Enron."

Wasn't having a <u>*written*</u> *vision and values statement for the sole purpose of pumping Enron's stock value – cutting corners* I thought.

Skilling was on a roll now. I could begin to hear the words of William Shakespeare echo in my years. "Doth protest too much, me thinks."

Ken Lay would soon follow with his own idea of values.

"Enron is a company that deals with everyone with absolute integrity. We play by all of the rules. We stand by our word. We mean what we say, and we say what we mean. We want people to leave a transaction with Enron *thinking* that they have been dealt with in the highest possible way, as far as integrity and truthfulness and really doing our business right. We really do want to be excellent in everything we do. Excellence hopefully in the ideas that we have; excellence in the people we have; excellence in how we treat our people, how we operate our plants, deal with our customers, and protect the environment. In fact, everything we do, we kind of set the standard."

Five minutes in all, and I was on board – motivated to play fair with others, bound by no limits. Perhaps I should have taken Jeff Skilling more seriously when he said "It's a wild ride" as the screen faded to black.

I listened closely as Skilling continued with his presentation. I realized he might be a number-crunching business grad on the one hand, but he was just as good a salesman as Ken Lay, except he was either far, far smoother or a mild sociopath. I had encountered many execs in my time, but few impressed me with the intellect Skilling demonstrated, and even fewer did I trust less than him. As the meeting ended and we filed out, I couldn't help but have a wishful sense that within Enron's management Ken Lay somehow represented the greater good and Skilling the lesser evil. Perhaps it was such chemistry, like a person's dastardly alter ego, or Mr. Hyde, that made them complete, even strong. Perhaps I was grasping for justification that Enron, and my decision to work there, was going to be okay.

Upon returning to my desk, I found my computer displaying a screen saver that had not been there before the meeting. "What will you do to change the world today?" circled a spinning globe. Next to the keyboard was a new mouse pad and Swatch watch with the same words inscribed on them. Little did I know when I put on the watch how prophetic those words would become as Enron would indeed change the world, robbing us of our innocent trust, perhaps as much as Osama bin Laden did on September 11th. But at the time, I thought, maybe I was wrong about Jeff Skilling. But I did know two things for sure: Enron knew how to impress me, and I wanted to meet Ken Rice.

CHAPTER THREE

We don't want anyone to know what's on those books.
We don't want to tell anyone where we're making money.

Andrew Fastow, Chief Financial Officer
Enron Corp.

THINK BIG, STEAL BIG

My Contract Administration Briefing Group was located on the 38th floor within the legal department. It was our responsibility to brief the legal aspects of all contracts as to the terms and conditions before they were disseminated. The information was then entered into a database by Ronnie or Faith to provide the basis for the entire trading operations system integration, created as a result of J-Block.

The day after the company meeting I phoned Mary Rye to set up a lunch as my thank you to her for recruiting me for the job. Just as we were saying our goodbyes, I remembered something.

"Hey, do you know a guy named Ken Rice?" I asked, my crush not having subsided a bit. "He's the CEO of Enron Capital & Trade."

"Wow," she exclaimed, "I didn't know he was so high up." Then she giggled. "Ken and I are really close friends. We started at Enron in the same department at the same time."

"Get outta here!" I gasped.

"Yeah. You know, you really have him to thank for your new job."

"Oh my God! He's gorgeous," I blurted.

"Honey, he's married."

That stopped me cold. "Damn."

"But that hasn't stopped most of the women at Enron," she added slyly.

I wouldn't go after a married man, but I was curious. "Really? What do you mean?"

"You'll find out soon enough," she said knowingly. "I've heard there's a gentlemen's club right down the street that keeps a special room in the back open just for the Enron boys. They drop thousands in there. And the top two floors of the Enron building are called the Bachelor Pad, even though most of the guys are married. The secretaries look like Dallas Cowboy cheerleaders or Playboy Bunnies, and apparently few are over twenty-five. How do you think Linda Lay met Ken?"

I wondered what kind of vision and values that expressed? After so many revelations already, I saw this as just another layer of the onion. "Well," I said with resignation, "I'm not getting involved with a married man. I guess I'll just admire him from afar."

I heard Ken Rice's hot-headed partner, Kevin Hannon, had a temper rivaling that of Jeff Skilling. I got to see him in action a few days later. I was riding the elevator down with two other people and it stopped at the 33rd floor, ECT's executive offices. The door opened and two more people stepped on, followed by Hannon. Looking slightly disheveled and wearing a scowl, he punched his floor then made it clear to all of us with his body language that he was far too important to fritter away those few precious seconds between floors. When the lift stopped on 28 and two of the people hesitated ever so slightly before stepping out, Hannon shoved through them screaming, "Get the fuck moving!" As he vanished around the corner I heard an angry, "Jesus Christ! I'm in a hurry." I made it a point from that day forth not to get in his path.

I soon became aware Enron had less to do with being a natural gas company than an investment banking and brokerage firm. The commodities we dealt in were anything Enron considered energy-related, which broadly included either energy used directly or any product that required energy for its manufacture. This allowed us to trade in everything from natural gas, oil, power, wind, weather, and water, to paper, pulp, steel, and wood products. As I came to terms with the nearly limitless scope of Enron's business, I wondered why they hadn't harnessed pigs and cows to machines to gather and sell their flatulent emissions.

I oversaw the briefing of the Contract Administration for ECT on a daily basis. My staff was responsible for pulling out the significant details of the commodity contracts for gas and power entered into by all of Enron's subsidiaries, as well as all of Enron's financial derivatives. Initially, I believed this was an effort to manage our risk by understanding at any given time what our exposure was. However, as time passed I began to get the big picture. It appeared to be little more than a shell game as we moved contracts, entered into by one Enron entity with another, from one subsidiary to another.

Having worked in corporate development at Ralston Purina, and been responsible for the administration of all of the domestic and international subsidiaries and actively involved in a huge merger there, I was fully aware that any move a corporation makes on its books is done for tax or revenue purposes, which is ultimately designed to increase, maintain, or limit a drop in the stock price. My first real suspicions about Enron's business practices came the first time we assigned more than 10,000 gas contracts from Enron's subsidiary, Houston Pipe Line Company (HPL), to HPL Resources (HPLR), the marketing arm of their pipeline business. I'd been around the corporate block a few times and was immediately suspicious of the timing, which just happened to fall at the end of a financial quarter. I was even more surprised when, at the end of the next quarter, we moved the same contracts over to ECT.

This exercise of contract assignments (or more accurately kiting) kept an entire group of eight people busy for weeks at a time as the contract administration group headed by Emma Toombs entered the details into two separate systems. That was another thing I found quite strange. We used two different systems, one that was Y2K compliant and one that was not. I would later wonder whether the systems were Enron's way of having two sets of books or whether those in charge were hoping for a millennial computer meltdown, thus being another method to cover their massive losses.

While contract ownership and assets were being transferred from one entity to another, it was my responsibility, because of the depth of detail, to handle briefing the off-the-balance sheet transactions and financial derivative contracts of Andy Fastow for senior management. Swimming in a jungle of details, I was getting my first long look at how Enron transacted its business. What quickly became obvious to me was that Enron was creating partnerships for no apparent reason other than to move debt off the books.

Although I wasn't working directly with them, I noticed the dealings of Enron with some large partnerships, Jedi and Chewco. These entities were involved in a joint venture between Enron and the California Public Employees Retirement System (CalPERS). The partnership names seemed to ring a bell, but I couldn't put my finger on it until one day during a conversation with Sandy James*, a legal assistant.

Looking around conspiratorially she asked, "So, have you noticed Jedi and Chewco?"

I wasn't sure what she meant. "Yeah, why?"

"Andy Fastow is a big fan of *Star Wars*. His wife's name is even Lea, as in 'Princess Leia,'" she said with a wink.

"That's cute", I observed, then remembered the companies were supposedly outside partnerships. "Oh."

Sandy smiled. "Yeah. 'Oh' is right," she said walking away.

Working late one night I passed an office, and as I glanced in the shadows the face of a huge ape-like creature caused me to drop my files and scream, "Holy shit!"

Looking more closely I realized it was just a big costume head. The next morning I asked one of the legal secretaries about it.

"It's a Wookie."

"Huh?"

"Chewbacca the Wookie. From *Star Wars*? Everybody who worked on Jedi and Chewco got one from Andy."

By all appearances, the involvement of Jedi and Chewco gave me no indication they had any connection to Enron, other than to do business with us. But if what Sandy alleged was true, that they were under Fastow's control, the implications were sinister. It meant that Enron was either using, or worse – *inventing* – legal entities for the express purpose of faking the appearance that Enron was engaging in commerce. Fake companies, that is, companies created solely for accounting purposes, which could be used to hide profits or shield losses. In this case, it was easy to guess which they were doing.

My baptism in the mechanics of Enron's deals began soon after I settled into the office routine. One day a guy from the records department showed up with a hand truck loaded with three file boxes, asking for me. Kathy approached as the guy unloaded the boxes.

"This is Bammel," she said, as if that meant something. She headed back to her office. I stared at the boxes and she turned, à la Columbo, adding offhandedly, "I'll need you to write a business brief for senior management."

Kathy rarely came up to the 38th floor, which seemed odd. Why hadn't she sent an e-mail or called me? I took her personal appearance as an indication that the brief on this particular deal had obviously been at the direction of someone higher up.

A brief is more or less a summary of the particulars of a deal, giving senior management an overview. I looked at the three boxes knowing the brief would probably be very lengthy, but I was undaunted since I'd written so many myself over my legal profession. I opened the first box.

On New Year's Eve, 1997, an Enron subsidiary, HPL, pledged 80,000,000 MMBtu's [million Btu's] of natural gas in a deal. The gas was stored as both a recoverable cushion and working gas in the Bammel Storage Facility. Bammel Storage is the largest natural gas storage facility outside Houston, Texas, a massive natural container created from an underground aquifer. Enron had used the stored gas as collateral against a very large loan – a $232,000,000 loan.

The first thing that seemed fishy to me was the date of the transaction. Having closed the deal that resulted in the first-ever reversal of a publicly-traded targeted stock while at Ralston Purina, I knew how long it would take to finalize a deal of this magnitude. The deal had been made on the last day of 1997 and accounted for as such, but it was only now that we were looking closely at it. In ten minutes I saw it had all the earmarks of a tax dodge. It troubled me that the collateralized gas was to be marketed, which meant revenue to offset the debt for accounting purposes.

The particulars of the transaction called for the Trustee, Bank of New York, to issue notes to an entity known as Kitty Hawk Funding

Corporation. The notes were then sold to NationsBank, now known as Bank of America, and none other than Andy Fastow's group, Enron Finance Corp., as lenders in a loan, collateralized by both the 80,000,000 MMBtu's of gas and a guarantee from Enron Corp.

As I skimmed through the massive stack of papers, I realized it was going to be difficult to brief senior management on the overly convoluted terms of the agreement. The Bammel deal was the first of many I worked on simultaneously, and it took me nearly six months to complete, due primarily to the difficulties in unraveling the maze of details of the partnerships involved.

When I had stacked the contents of the boxes next to my desk, they made a tidy pile three feet high. As I examined the pages and pages of agreements, memos, and specs, I felt a slight sense of panic. With all my experience I had never seen anything like this. Almost every deal I had been involved in had clear lines of delineation: a buyer or buyers, sellers, and the product or service.

This deal was different because I honestly could not discern who the actual buyers and sellers were. The deal seemed to go in a circle, with the end result being Enron, or rather one of its subsidiaries, received nearly a quarter billion dollars in a loan that would probably never show up as a debt on their books. As I looked at the deal terms, I wondered why these outside partnerships were agreeing to such terms with Enron, since they didn't seem to benefit them in any conventional way. I began to wonder if these partnerships had a similar genesis as Chewco and Jedi and that they were actually in-house. All I knew for sure was that Enron had pledged a lot of gas and gotten a big loan off the value of that gas, and on top of that, would be marketing the gas as revenue, at a significantly inflated price at that. What I couldn't begin to understand was why the deal was so ridiculously complicated.

After spending several fruitless days struggling to get an overview on the Bammel deal, I decided the most efficient way to untangle this mess was to go to the source. Although Enron had many in-house accountants, Arthur Andersen was Enron's official accounting firm and had 143 full time accountants and consultants permanently located in our building. I would get some answers from them, thus saving time, which translated into saving the company's money.

I wandered about the Andersen floor, inquiring as to whom I should speak with but got only vague responses. The more I asked about Bammel, the less anyone seemed willing to answer my questions, or even tell me who might know. I became more aggressive in my attempts to find a person at Andersen knowledgeable about the Bammel Storage Deal, and who could also help explain many of the issues with the partnerships. As the days passed, I was staggered that a deal of this magnitude had just slipped through the cracks. After repeatedly being stonewalled by not only Andersen but our own accountants, I decided to launch my own covert investigation into Bammel. I had been working on the deal for the better part of a month and had, maddeningly, accomplished very little except to accumulate a giant pile of documents at the end of my desk.

With 15 years of legal experience in private practice, and five years in corporate law, I could brief a document with my eyes closed, making even the most complicated details simple to understand. Legalese is a language (and an art form) all its own, but what was contained within the Bammel contracts was utterly confusing, even to the most accomplished lawyers. I could smell something wrong. The way these contracts were worded clearly indicated that the people who wrote them didn't want anyone to actually understand them.

As I worked desperately to make sense of the Bammel mess and its maze of financing structures, I learned that Enron had just financed the creation of a Masters program in Energy Finance at the University of Texas at Austin. Believing this might help me better understand these complicated energy financing deals, I contacted Beth Tilney, Enron's Senior Vice President of Corporate Marketing and Administration, to find out how to apply. My application was accepted and now my only hurdle was convincing Kathy Simpson to allow my absences on Monday, Wednesday and Friday afternoons in order to make the two-and-a-half hour drive to Austin for the 3:00-5:00 p.m. class.

I discussed the matter with Kathy and she gave me approval to attend. Then I realized that upon completion of the twc-year program,

I would almost certainly end up in the clutches of Enron's Darth Vader of finance, Andy Fastow, so I opted out of the course. Otherwise, I might find myself personally involved in these partnerships that from all appearances were nothing more than a sham and appeared to violate logic as well as the guidelines established by the Generally Accepted Accounting Principles.

With growing concern I was uncovering Enron's hidden alter ego. There was Jekyll and Hyde, Lay and Skilling, and now I was seeing the two faces of Enron – the public face, the one Skilling was selling to investors and new employees, and this one.

Just as Jeff had predicted, now that Enron had launched its new "written" vision and values statement – the stock was on the rise. The goose had laid its golden egg – all we had to do was wait for it to hatch. And hatch it did. The stock had a rapid rise from $38.50 to $46.00 in less than two months.

By mid-March, 1998, a couple of weeks before I arrived, the stock had risen to $48.00 and we could hear the cheers clear down the street at El Paso Energy. As plans got underway to mark the momentous occasion of Enron's stock hitting the $50.00 mark, shock hit when the stock unexpectedly dropped nearly 10% to $44.00.

By the time I arrived, the stock was trading back up at $46.00, and plans were back on schedule to throw a huge block party. I could only imagine if Enron was willing to celebrate the launch of its "written" vision and values in grand style, what would be planned when the entire purpose for the vision and values statement was fulfilled. As the stock continued to rise, elation filled the building when it hit $47.00 and was climbing. The dancing bears were waiting on cue for the celebration to begin and the tchotkes were ordered with the date inscribed and then suddenly without warning, the stock dropped again.

Walking the tight rope between hitting the $50.00 mark in time for the planned celebration and having to throw away 20,000 tchotkes was cause for great concern. Certainly I had witnessed first hand at the Ralston Purina board meeting how stock prices can literally be changed with a mere call to the exchange on which the stock is traded, but raising Enron's stock $3.00 in three days would take a miracle.

This was the point at which I truly came to appreciate Enron's tag line "Endless Possibilities". In typical Enron fashion, on April 14th, Ken Lay pulled a rabbit out of his hat and the stock reached its $50.00 mark at the 11th hour just long enough to pass out the gifts. But even Ken Lay could not keep the stock artificially inflated for more than a day and once again it dropped back to $47.50 in a matter of minutes.

On April 15th, everyone at Enron received a crisp new $100 bill in commemoration of Enron's stock hitting $50.00. Given we had almost 20,000 employees I quickly calculated that little gesture cost the company a cool two million, but their return from the morale boost was priceless. Even in moments of generosity Enron was all about returns.

Later that day, we all received a blank Enron stock certificate encased in Lucite with the inscription "A Memento in Appreciation of your Commitment to Enron's Success" "In Commemoration of Enron's Common Stock Closing at $50.00/share." Also inscribed on the front was the date April 14, 1998 and on the back was a capsule of Enron's Vision and Values: "Respect, Integrity, Communication, and Excellence". I had been at Enron long enough to smile at the irony that Enron's stock value was commemorated on the front of the memento while its Vision and Values were seen only when you turned the miniature stock certificate over. Jeff was right...our written Vision and Values statement had caused a greater ROI; however, he had conveniently left out the part about the accounting shenanigans that would be required.

Because Enron had grown so explosively, office space with real walls was at a premium and, at least in the legal department, reserved for in-house counsel. The rest of us were given cubicles, which created great frustration. Executives like me were used to the privacy and stature of literal offices with walls and doors. Although Skilling's spin was this would create a team environment, the reality was Enron had more room to cram in bodies as the walls gave way to "pits" similar to those at the New York Stock Exchange.

With the nearly exponential growth in Enron's stock price, that rising number was on the minds and lips of everyone in the company. In fact, it was nearly a company-wide obsession. My desk was situated underneath one of two big television monitors mounted from the ceiling on the legal floor, each displaying information like a brokerage firm, one showing the forward gas and power prices at the New York Mercantile Exchange (NYMEX), and the other keeping vigilance on Enron's current stock price.

Employees lingered near my desk, eyes glued to the ticker monitor as Enron's stock climbed virtually minute to minute. It was like sitting next to the old-fashioned water cooler, only instead of chattering about movies or sex or the latest restaurant they'd discovered, the talk was serious and about one thing only: money. I learned much about the company by eavesdropping. I was particularly impressed with snatches of info gleaned from people who had been with the company long enough to have accumulated small fortunes in stock options. With money and financial stability such an issue for me, it was like they had already won the lottery and I would too, if I were simply patient. I knew that if I could hang in at Enron I would one day be a millionaire like many who passed by my desk.

Ryan Hyatt* was one of my favorite visitors. A quiet man with a warm smile and kind but careworn eyes, he had the look of an old roughneck who had done time on a drilling rig before heading to law school. Ryan had been with Enron a long while and spent a lot more time calculating his earnings than preparing the gas contracts assigned to him. I didn't begrudge him that, since he was always willing to share his extensive knowledge about the company's dealings. Whenever I had a technical question, Ryan Hyatt was always my source. While happy to have received the $100 cash and the Lucite tchotke, I watched with some alarm as the stock value went up dramatically over a short period of time. As a new hire, the strike price of my stock options had not yet been set. Because of that, I was in a vulnerable position. As long as Enron's stock price rose, so too would my strike price, and until then every dollar it went up meant a dollar out of my pocket.

Within a few months, my strike price was settled at $57.0625 per share and I was informed I had been granted 465 shares. Now, like all the others who tarried at my desk, I found myself staring longingly at the monitor above me. The perpetual question among everyone was: could Enron sustain its current growth and continue to rise? I knew it would require more than a written vision and values statement. It would require no missteps and making major inroads in a high-risk arena far outside the focus of Enron's business model – it would require an e-commerce presence.

While stock options were the popular topic of conversation among employees, my options would not vest for more than a year, so I decided it would do little good expending any more energy on discussing the "what ifs" with my colleagues. I refocused on my work on the Bammel deal and continued to make waves to get answers while doing some "extracurricular" investigations.

One of the names that kept cropping up in the Bammel deal was Emily Welk*. Welk was a lawyer with the company but had decided to leave the field to become a first-grade teacher. She was in transition to her new job when I began my nosing into Bammel. Once I had her name, I got her phone number and left several voicemail messages. She never returned my calls, which I assumed was because she was fulfilling her student teaching requirements. I would soon learn I was wrong. She was dodging my calls alright not because she didn't have time, but because she was purposely avoiding me. One day she appeared before me at my desk. A diminutive woman, she was obviously irritated.

"You were looking for me?"

I assumed, by her attitude, this was the elusive Emily Welk "Yes."

"You wanted to talk to me about the Bammel deal?" Before I could open my mouth she raised her hands in disgust. "I don't want to talk about it. We're already in default. We were in default the day we entered into the deal."

"How can that be? The deal was just closed."

Of all of the names in the Bammel Storage deal, Emily Welk's was particularly prominent. She had been involved in all of the partnership deals. Her provocative comment that Enron was in default since day-one confirmed that I wasn't losing my mind. I knew there was something wrong with the deal and now I wanted to know how Enron was in default. Defaults by their nature require some performance under the terms of the contract, which Enron had none yet, except for the assignment of the gas to secure the loan.

She leaned in close and dropped her bomb in a hushed but forceful voice. "The gas isn't there." she said angrily. "And what is there, is either not ours or must stay there to keep the pressure level sufficient to inject and withdraw gas – can't ever be marketed."

"You mean the gas that collateralized the loan?" I said as my eyes widened in shock and amazement.

"That's right." She turned abruptly and walked away.

My mouth fell open. I was momentarily stunned. I had assumed many improprieties with this deal, but the idea that the gas didn't exist had never occurred to me. If Enron had really pulled this off, it would be like they secured a home equity loan on their non-existent mansion by using their neighbor's mobile home as collateral. And if they had pulled this off, it also meant I had just discovered bank fraud. As I ran details of the deal in my head I realized Emily Welk's secret was the puzzle piece that had been missing. Yet I was in denial because my future was now tied to Enron. I thought about Tom Cruise's character in *The Firm* when he discovers his law firm is working for the Mob. It was a sick, dirty feeling. I tried to clear the emotion from my mind and think clearly. How could I confirm Welk's accusation? I had been in Texas long enough to know there was probably one place that would confirm or deny her claim – the Texas Railroad Commission where gas inventories were recorded.

Sorting through the records filed with the Texas Railroad Commission, it took me about 15 minutes to find what I was looking for. There in black and white were the numbers that told the story. According to documents filed by Enron, the total amount of working gas in Bammel Storage on 12/31/97 was 22,163,540 MMBtu's, not 80 million pledged by Enron in the deal. Additionally, most of the gas in storage was there on behalf of other producers and marketers, and Enron had no right, title, or interest in it. What Enron actually owned was a mere fraction of the gas they committed as collateral. I was dazzled no one had called them on it. Then I realized everyone involved, from the gas administrators to the bankers, must have known about it.

But even more stunning was not only was the gas not Enron's, but the price Enron represented it could market the now apparently mythical collateralized gas pledged for was almost 50% higher than the going rate. By simultaneously entering into an agreement to market the gas pledged, Enron could "book" the projected revenue from the future sale of the gas. By structuring the deal this way, Enron considered the loan "prepaid" so felt they didn't need to book the loan as a debt because – like the gas – it didn't exist. This meant that the revenue booked for the gas – had it even existed – was inflated by more than $72,000,000. So when you consider the shortfall, represented by the difference between the 80,000,000 MMBtu's pledged and the actual inventory of 22,163,540 MMBtu's of mostly other people's gas, it represented fraud by Enron of nearly $168 million. Given that most of the gas in Bammel wasn't Enron's, you could safely pronounce that pretty much the whole $232 million had been secured fraudulently and illegally booked as revenue.

At first I was stupefied, then I got scared. This deal required a lot of time to conceive and would certainly have been reviewed by Bank of New York and NationsBank's in-house lawyers and outside counsel. Enron's in-house counsel and outside counsel would have had to review it. I had to assume the deal was devised by those higher-ups in the company, but had the banks and lawyers been paid to somehow look the other way? How could this "minor" little detail have been missed? If this was an indication of how Enron operated, then perhaps it was symptomatic. Bammel was an enormous deal and if a group of people within the company had conspired to pull this off, then what else had they, or were they, doing?

I thought about Enron's boy money genius, Andy Fastow, the keeper of Enron's funnel of cash. It suddenly seemed opportune for Enron to have made the Bammel deal during the year they would have had to offset the J-Block loss. It was either that or suffer a big hit, and Enron's climbing stock value told a sunny story. I had noticed Fastow from time to time in the legal department. He was always in the office of, Carol St. Clair, the attorney with the giant Chewbacca head that had scared the crap out me. I thought about the Chewco partnerships and pondered what else Mr. Fastow had done to manipulate Enron's worth. Now that I understood what Fastow was capable of, I was free to speculate on what possible maze of dealings he had going. What concerned me was that if Bammel was a fraud, then what other deals had been faked or doctored? And what really terrified me was if the corruption extended beyond Bammel, and I had no reason to suspect it was isolated, then Enron was, in fact, a house of cards or worse yet, a weapon of mass destruction.

While my background was primarily in the law, with some accounting thrown in, I was nevertheless amazed at the impenetrable jungle created by the terms of the Bammel agreements. This was put-a-bag-over-their-head-and-spin-'em-round-til-they're-dizzy financing at its best, and it really had Emily Welk, if not other lawyers, furious. After my discovery, I decided to settle in and write the business brief on the deal, then figure out what to do as I got closer to handing it in. I had several options. I could keep my mouth shut. I could tell my boss. Or I could go to the authorities.

Bound by a confidentiality agreement as well as legal ethics, if I did the latter I'd be on the street inside of twenty seconds. Though I might then be perceived as some kind of ethical heroine, I would lose my place, belongings, and credit because no one in Houston would touch me with a ten-foot pole. I also visualized a scenario that my life could be in jeopardy given the kind of money and power involved. But keeping my mouth shut went against my grain so I screwed up my courage and went to Kathy Simpson. I sat down at her desk and assumed the properly somber expression.

"What's wrong?" She turned from her computer.

I whispered to imply the gravity of the situation. "It has to do with Bammel."

Her expression was neutral.

"The gas we used for collateral to get the loan?" I asked rhetorically.

"Yeah?"

"It isn't there. There's no collateral. No gas. At least not ours."

Her expression blew my mind. *No change*. She looked back to her computer.

"Just leave that out of your brief." she said, as casually as if she was asking me to overlook her putting a company pen in her purse.

After a moment she looked up at my stunned face. "Anything else?"

I went back to my desk. Was I insane? Had I lost my mind? Was I the only one that thought this was a huge crime? Then I remembered Emily Welk's reaction and took comfort that she seemed to know it was wrong. I replayed the previous three minutes in my mind and explained to myself that I had just been asked to cover up a quarter *billion* dollar scam.

After regaining my composure I began writing my brief. A dozen times I wrote the details of the bank fraud in my memo to senior management, but then deleted the paragraphs. I had watched too many employees stabbed like shish kabobs at the end of Kathy Simpson's sword – and knew I would easily be the next if I ignored the edict.

Thoughts began flooding my mind as to the lesser of two evils. On one hand, if I remained silent, would I be contributing to a "cover-up"? Certainly I couldn't be held accountable or culpable – I wasn't even at Enron in 1997 and had not been on the legal team that put the deal together. On the other hand, if I refused to comply with her instructions, I would be quickly eliminated from the "team".

I thought back to the look of disgust on Emily Welk's face when I had discussed the deal with her. Obviously she had alerted someone hadn't she? If so, no one had apparently done anything to resolve the discrepancy. If she had not said anything, she would lose far greater than I. Unfortunately, I realized Emily and I were both bound by attorney-client privilege and a legal code of ethics so going outside the company and blowing the whistle was not an option. It would cost us not only our jobs but our careers. And what if I were wrong? And besides who could I trust? This would remain, for now the first of many Enron secrets.

Somehow in my mind, rather than adopt some outlandish conspiracy theory, I reconciled the problem as just a simple oversight of details that slipped through the cracks at closing. Although I had negotiated and closed multi-billion dollar deals and from time to time a few documents would be missed in closing, I had never "overlooked" the issue of whether the assets securing a quarter of a billion loan were missing. Why hadn't the banks caught the minor missing detail? Or had they too been wooed by the promises of Enron's Yellow Brick Road the same way I had.

I quickly dismissed my theory of a "cover-up" realizing that while it might make for a great John Grisham novel – it's certainly not the sort of thing the "world's largest energy company" would engage in. I would eventually learn at Enron, choosing to "look the other way" was a mandatory requirement for continued employment.

In the end, I did as I was told and created a brief to deliver to the Director of Communications for HPL, Rob Schwepper*. Per my instructions from Kathy Simpson, I left out certain minor details, such as there was no real collateral. However, my conscious would not allow me to leave my speculation that bank fraud had been committed out of Kathy's copy of my memo. Besides Kathy was a director and was in a position to let senior management know of the bank fraud if she chose to.

I completed my brief, adding an additional page to Kathy's copy, setting forth the details of the bank fraud, and confirmed her request that I "leave the details out" of my brief to senior management. In retrospect, perhaps I would have been far better off if I'd gone to Andy Fastow directly. While there is no doubt in my mind he would have fired me, nothing could compare to the torture I would ultimately suffer at the hands of Kathy Simpson. She was now, as a result of my memo, holding the bag of information that Enron had been engaged in a bank fraud and she had chose to cover it up. My only hope was that it would be her career – not mine.

Now that I had been formally introduced to large-scale corruption on the part of at least one group at Enron, I looked around for other forms of impropriety. One thing that stood out from the beginning was the large number of attractive young women working in the executive offices. After Mary mentioned that phenomena, I kept my eyes open. I'd been at many large corporations and had seen secretarial pools but none had stood out – that is until Enron.

When I would go to the upper floors on business I would take a visual inventory and sure enough, most of the women were young, particularly attractive, and clad in form fitting and/or low-cut clothing. Even if Mary hadn't mentioned it, I still would have noticed, because the effect was so pronounced. I didn't care what someone looked like as long as they did their job well, but the cookie cutter babes I saw in the executive suites told me many had been hired on sight, so to speak.

I had been at Enron long enough to accept the boy's club atmosphere, but once in a while my tolerance for unbusiness-like behavior was severely tested. It was about this time I met a legal assistant named Jennifer Hampton*. A small, very cute brunette in her mid-thirties, Jennifer epitomized Enron's obsession with good-looking women. Her appearance, charming smile and almost overly solicitous demeanor smacked of an aging pageant queen. Although she didn't seem to be well liked in the department, after several conversations we struck up a friendship. I often worked late, as did Jennifer, but for different reasons. I had an abnormal work load, but she stayed after hours to finish work she neglected during the day due to her frequent and lengthy personal phone calls. We would often engage in enlightening discussions late into the night. While I was working on briefing financial derivative contracts, Jennifer was often my source of information, whether it was official or otherwise. Jennifer was responsible for preparing contracts for the traders of financial derivatives, which included calls, puts, collars, and swaps.

Swap options allow you to exchange or "swap" specific price risk exposures over a predetermined period of time. Swaps are privately-negotiated financial contracts between two parties. Premiums are not charged on swaps, which are settled against an indexed price. Swaps are an effective way to create "new" terms for a fixed contract. In financing, interest rates swaps allow you to substitute floating interest rates for a fixed rate and vice versa. Enron could assume the fixed price obligation while its customer or counterparty could profit from floating rates. A swap allows the contract holder to create new terms for the contract.

Price Caps (Call Options) are options or the "right to buy" a commodity at a predetermined price (strike price) before a present deadline in exchange for a premium. Call options are often referred to as "caps", because they can set a maximum price for the commodity. With call options, buyers can protect themselves from rising prices.

Price Floors (Put Options) are options or the "right to sell" a commodity at a predetermined price (strike price) by a certain date in exchange for a premium. Put options are often referred to as "floors", because they can set a minimum price for the commodity. With put options, sellers can protect themselves against falling prices.

Collars are contracts to limit extreme market moves by limiting price exposure to a defined range. Collars are often referred to as a "cashless collar", because they can set a minimum price in exchange for surplus revenue when prices exceed a certain level. There is no premium charged for this protection.

Swaptions are simply a combination of a swap and an option.

Jennifer would get the contracts ready and I would then brief them. She often complained bitterly that she was underpaid, comparing her salary to someone making more who she felt was undeserving.

I make fifty-five and so and so makes sixty-two and I work a lot harder. I should be making at least seventy was her pre-recorded whine that I heard over and over. Part of Jennifer's frustration came from her thwarted efforts to sleep her way to the top. She seemed to work much harder at that than her actual job and, to her dismay, it had not yet paid off. Recently divorced, Jennifer was a desperate social climber within Enron and freely shared her game plan with me, including her successes and failures. One of her mixed successes came with her relationship to Hunter Green*, a limited partner with Enron's investment banking firm, Goldman Sachs. A Redfordishly handsome man, Hunter and Jennifer would take weekend jaunts to places like the King Ranch, an 825,000-acre ranch in South Texas.

Hunter and his wife, Leslie*, enjoyed separate lives. He maintained his home and lifestyle in Houston, and she lived in the Southwest on a ranch training horses. Jennifer described how wife Leslie had caught Hunter in a torrid affair with another woman who would later date Jeff Skilling and it nearly ruined their marriage.

Apparently the near loss of his beloved pushed Hunter to make sacrifices in his personal life. He put his foot down and gave Jennifer the bad news that he would never leave his wife. Have an affair, yes, but leave her, no.

Jennifer was informed she would have to settle for premiere theater tickets and arms-length invitations to exclusive barbecues in Austin, but she'd never, ever get a rock from him. Jennifer bit the bullet and kissed marriage to Hunter goodbye, seeking comfort over her loss in such things as exclusive artworks, a collection of exquisite Ralph Lauren picture frames from England, and sixty-five hundred bucks cash for a boob job.

As I listened to stories about how she would slip over to Hunter's for an *affaire d'amour* by his pool, a picture of the social culture at Enron was coming into clear relief. Many of the women at Enron were not only looking for powerful men to shower them with gifts, but many, Jennifer included, hoped that some of that success mojo would trickle down to them and improve their lot with the company. Her close personal friendship with a married man connected to the company was commonplace among Enron's senior management with whom Jennifer socialized.

Jennifer was becoming increasingly frustrated with the cold shoulders turned toward her in the legal department. Many of the women had sized her up as a gold-digging slacker, so she sought my company partly out of loneliness. But while her peers were shunning her, she was cementing bonds with women much higher up who either understood the mechanics of Jennifer's scramble to move up in the ranks at all costs, or just didn't care. Jennifer had aligned herself with the Houston Junior League, a clan of right wing, God-fearing Martha Stewarts who found charity the next best thing to networking. Jennifer's goal through Junior League was to find a man, but instead it turned out to be a savvy career move. It was either through Jennifer's previous position in commercial real estate or through the Junior League, Jennifer met Jeannine Turner*, a commercial escrow agent. Jeannine, in turn, introduced Jennifer to a critical contact, Amanda Martin, President of Enron's North American Markets.

Through Jeannine, Jennifer then made the acquaintance of an even bigger Enron fish, a tall brunette who would sometimes stop by Jennifer's desk and visit. Equipped with a voice raspier than the cartoon sitcom character, Marge Simpson's sister, this woman sounded like a plaintiff in a tobacco litigation case. Not unattractive but appearing seasoned enough to roller skate on, she walked hard, as if her shoes were made of cement, and always wore her hair greased back in a long ponytail. Her attire was top-notch, at least Ann Taylor, yet was chronically black with slacks and a long jacket. Something seemed familiar about her and by her third or fourth visit I recalled she was the lunatic in the Range Rover who had nearly bowled over all the hapless bikers during the MS bike-a-thon. I also remembered her leaping out in her biking shorts and bussing Jeff Skilling on the lips.

One day I asked Jennifer. "Who's the tall brunette who frequently stops by your desk? She looks familiar."

Jennifer couldn't help but puff up her saline implanted chest as she snidely replied, "You mean, Rebecca Carter? She's Jeff Skilling's girlfriend."

Suddenly my respect for Jennifer's game plan grew. I knew Rebecca Carter by reputation. An exec with Arthur Andersen before joining Enron, Carter worked her way up through the ranks at Enron and right into Jeff Skilling's bedroom. Or maybe it was the other way around. If Jennifer counted Rebecca Carter and Amanda Martin as pals, her strategy was far better devised than I had given her credit for. I began to see it as a two-pronged approach; sleep with the powerful men, but befriend the powerful women as back-up. I figured Jennifer was using Rebecca and Amanda as confidantes, just as she did with me.

We continued our lengthy after-hours conversations, which had gotten very personal. Mostly it was me listening to Jennifer vent about her never-ending men trouble. Despite what I saw as huge positives in her life, her health, a great job, benefits, and a decent circle of friends, she was miserable, often falling victim to profound bouts of depression. I told her to get help, both therapy and some course of anti-depressants, but she brushed it off, seeming to prefer wallowing in her misery.

Jennifer once described to me in great detail an odd habit of hers. As a sort of twisted sport, she would get roaring drunk, pick up the phone well after civilized hours, and telephonically berate old beaus. She jokingly referred to them as her "daffy dialing" episodes, but after listening to her accounts of giving guys a verbal shellacking at three in the morning, I knew this girl was a powder keg looking for a spark.

As Jennifer constantly meowed about bad men, I thought of how great it would be to have a nice, stable relationship. My thoughts turned to the ever-dreamy Ken Rice and Mary's buzz-killing statement that Ken was hitched. Since I figured I'd eventually run into him in the course of business, as a diversion I visualized what I might say to him. I didn't have much time to work out my routine because the next day I got my wish.

I was riding an elevator to my floor when my crush himself climbed aboard. It was just the two of us. I smiled, he smiled, and then I did my best to conceal a double-take. Allow me to explain that I am neither a snob nor an elitist, but in such a high-powered corporate shark cage, one has to conform to certain givens, such as a wardrobe commensurate to your standing in a company of Enron's stature. First, let me say Ken did not quite possess the fashion magazine looks I had visualized from afar – less Calvin Klein and more Skoal tobacco or Chevy Trucks. But that didn't really drop my heart rate too much. The deal breaker was his clothing. Here he was in public wearing a twelve dollar shirt with a marginal design that had JCPenney written all over it. His artless tie was one of those thick, early-seventies brocade looking things that winds up with an obnoxious knot the size of a codpiece. But his biggest fashion crime was his footwear. Ken's smaller-than-expected feet were sporting something from the bargain rack at Shoes 'R Us, truly heinous Vibram-soled, Indonesian knockoffs of penny loafers. I'm afraid Ken looked more like the assistant manager of a Jiffy Lube than a guy who raked in seven figures at one of America's commercial giants. I was appalled.

I reached my floor, smiled at him again then raced to Jennifer's desk for counseling. I described Ken's hayseed motif and Jennifer shrugged.

"Oh well," she sighed, "it's Amanda's problem."

"Amanda? Martin?

Jennifer nodded.

"But he's married, right?" I asked.

"Yeah," admitted Jennifer. "That's pissed Amanda off for a long time."

"His being married?" I asked as the conversation took a surreal turn.

"Uh huh. Ken had an affair with his wife and she got pregnant and Amanda broke it off."

"Amanda broke it off because he had sex with his own wife?" I could hear the *Twilight Zone* theme.

Jennifer nodded seriously, unable to recognize the absurdity. "Ken's wife is a doctor – a pediatrician, I think. Anyway, he and his wife are on again, off again, just like him and Amanda."

This was more information than I had planned on. Between the disheartening elevator encounter with dream guy, the bizarre account of Ken's infidelity with his own wife, and Jennifer's desperate mission to hook a man, I accepted that being single wasn't so bad.

Despite Jennifer's eccentricities and naked quest to scale the Enron ladder, I liked her. She had a sweet charisma and, except for droning on about bad relationships, she never mistreated me. However, I would never turn my back on her as I had witnessed her brutal retaliations not only against men she'd been "in love with" the week before, but colleagues who had crossed her. I was also becoming wise to the ways of the company and understood that being Jennifer's friend couldn't hurt, especially since she hung with the top brass at Enron.

Jennifer's proximity to Jeff Skilling gave me the idea that if I could get close enough to him I might be able to tell him of the wrongdoing I had seen and garner some Brownie points. On the other hand, he might be behind it. I needed to get to know Skilling, to look in his eyes and see whether Enron had a future or was just a big scam. Although every employee had encountered Ken Lay at some point, whether in the cafeteria or holding the elevator for you, I didn't think Lay was necessarily the guy to get close to if I wanted to figure out Enron's nature. Although Lay founded the company, I felt it was the younger capos like Fastow and Skilling who were calling the shots.

Some Fridays, I would join Jennifer and we would make the social rounds. In downtown Houston's business world, that generally meant starting at Carrabbas, an Italian restaurant. The first time we ran into Jeff and Rebecca, although I was impressed with his stature in the company, he was much smaller than he appeared on stage. Since I had first seen him and his bald head reflecting the bright stage lights, he had undergone laser surgery to correct his vision.

Up close, I realized Jeff's glasses had obviously done a good job of hiding his rather cynical eyes. His teeth were particularly crooked, which surprised me given that most of the women execs at Enron adorned veneers. I was astonished quite frankly that Jennifer had not dismissed Jeff as a friend based upon his physical appearance. It was then that I realized the rules for men and women at Enron differed tremendously. Obviously, for women to climb Enron's corporate ladder, it was more about beauty than brains while, at least in the case of Jeff, brains came before beauty.

I must admit that what Jeff lacked in physical attributes he made up for in brain power. As I laughed at his witticisms and acerbic comments, I studied his every move and quickly concluded he was extremely smart, possessing both an exceptional intellect and a storehouse of knowledge. I heard rumors of his tantrums, of his obsessively detailed nature and his bull-in-the-china-shop style of hands-on management, but sitting there and interacting with him, I began to get a real sense of what kind of person he was.

Skilling was wickedly articulate, but I was disappointed that he squandered his gift, using it to spit poison, eviscerating both those around us and fellow employees in absentia. His cruel comments seemed to stem from an arrogance that those he mocked were inferior because he had so much more going for him in terms of money, brains and power. What he didn't have was any warmth, compassion or joy. As Rebecca fawned over him, I got a queasy feeling and felt oddly sorry for her. I quietly thanked God I was not her. He reminded me of my ex-husband. I was surprised to find Jeff Skilling someone to be pitied, because in many ways he was missing the point of life. Like Jennifer, only on a much grander scale, he had myriad blessings and yet chose a low road. Skilling gave me the creeps and I found it hard to believe that the women of Enron had gotten there by purportedly knowing Jeff on an intimate level – something that repulsed me when I momentarily visualized it.

When Jeff and Rebecca moved on, Jennifer turned excitedly to me. "Isn't Jeff great? Gawd he's smart!"

"Yeah, he's that."

I didn't want to get into a character debate on Jeff Skilling. Jennifer was enamored with him because he represented all that she felt was lacking in her life, some fuzzy notion that success was measured by the best office, the mansion in River Oaks, and the greatest number of people who smooched your ass. In the weeks to come, as we ran into Jeff and Rebecca on a few more occasions, I spent less time talking to Enron's Chief Operating Officer and got to know Rebecca a little better. I concluded that my first impression of her, the power-crazed socialite who almost ran down those innocent MS bikers, had perhaps been harsh. As I warmed to her personality, I rationalized that she had probably been having a bad day. I suppose everyone deserves at least one pass for nearly grinding a group of charity riders under their wheels. Perhaps she had learned that move from Jeff. I had heard the horror stories of Skilling screeching his car through the parking lot to cut in line, and flipping off anyone bold enough to resist.

One evening after the office had cleared out, Jennifer came over to my desk. She was upset. "I hate Lyle Garrett*", she began.

Garrett, an attorney, was her boss in the department.

"I think he's trying to screw me over," she stated.

Almost in a tone of paranoia, Jennifer told me she thought Garrett had enlisted the aid of one of her peers within the department, a woman named Veronica Miller*, to undermine her.

"It's because I'm cute, I'm smart, and I know people," she spat.

And she was right. But what she failed to take into account was the animosity those qualities engendered. In combination with her sense of entitlement, which brought about a carefree, even lazy attitude, I wouldn't have been surprised if her colleagues had risen up one day and crushed her to death with office equipment. Jennifer felt that at $55,000 she was underpaid, but I didn't have the heart to tell my friend she was lucky to be making that much, given the amount of time she actually worked. I also wouldn't comment on what I had observed about Enron: if a woman wanted to get to the top she almost invariably had to be blonde.

"I'm going to Amanda," she said emphatically.

That would not be the first time she went to her powerful friend to back her up against Garrett. Amanda Martin outranked Lyle Garrett, which was both good and bad for Jennifer. At Jennifer's behest, Amanda would occasionally slap Lyle's wrist for his "treatment" of her, but when the dust settled and Amanda left the playground, Lyle's resentment against Jennifer would only have been stoked. Jennifer claimed that documents she had prepared were either missing or altered to make her look bad. She also bemoaned her treatment in her group, claiming no one would talk to her about anything but business, and that she often heard whispers behind her back. She couldn't understand why an underpaid, highly attractive and nice person with such powerful connections would be resented. I swallowed hard and merely nodded sympathetically. I knew Jennifer's reputation with the traders was a lost cause, and it sounded like her colleagues, possibly under the direction of Garrett, had moved from simply ostracizing her to trying to set her up.

She sighed and changed the subject.

"Have you met Melanie St. James*? She's the new attorney and she's the only one in the group I can talk to. I think she's someone I could be friends with."

St. James was a lawyer brought in from Europe who had been counsel with a bank in the U.K. Melanie St. James was named Senior Counsel under Garrett. Although Jennifer claimed to have a growing personal bond with Melanie, I saw her survival skills surfacing, and I'm certain she saw her friendship with Melanie as an opportunity to develop an ally. Despite my friendship with Jennifer, we both knew I was of no practical use in getting her to the top of Enron. Melanie, on the other hand, was higher on the food chain and could provide a friendly face in her own group, and her credibility as a Senior Counsel might help Jennifer by association.

Jennifer called Amanda the next day, complaining bitterly of the conspiracy against her and, true to form, Amanda spoke to Lyle Garrett. Jennifer noticed a difference right away, but within a few days it was business as usual, with Jennifer pretty much shunned among her fellow group members. Lyle, apparently not too fearful of the wrath of Amanda Martin, continued to make Jennifer's life miserable. But now Jennifer had a new, powerful friend in the group and decided to bide her time. She now pinned her future in the company to Melanie's rising star.

After spending weekends over the previous few months socializing with Jennifer – beginning after work on Friday and ending late Sunday night – I grew tired of the social whirl and began begging off on the sorties to clubs and restaurants. Jennifer didn't miss a beat though, as she had a new buddy in Melanie St. James. Melanie St. James's motivation in hanging out with Jennifer was to make a friend in a new place as well as to find a guide to Enron's power structure. Melanie quickly discovered that her new companion, although fraught with bad relationships, insecure, and alarmingly scheming, did know where the bodies were buried, and in some cases had even slept with them.

Part of scaling back on my time with Jennifer came from concern that she was becoming increasingly desperate to make her move upward. Jennifer was experiencing deep frustration and a growing feeling of betrayal. Her career was stalled despite having made, as she saw it, all the right moves. She had sex with the right men, looked good, and aligned herself with as many of Enron's strong women. *What more can I do?* she'd complain. I found it hard to believe she overlooked hard work as a path to promotion, but understood how Enron's culture sent mixed messages to their employees, particularly attractive women. From Jennifer's viewpoint, she had done all Enron had asked and had gotten screwed, in more than one way.

I still felt a slight twinge when Jennifer would recount her adventures on Monday with her new pal Melanie St. James, but I was relieved not to have to maintain such a pace. Jennifer trolled the local haunts in the hopes she would hook a big fish from Enron. My reason was simply companionship with Jennifer – I knew my success at Enron would be tied directly to my abilities.

One Friday night, my friend Lori Cortez and I were out on the town and dropped in for happy hour at America's, a nice restaurant in Houston's River Oaks area near the Galleria. As we walked in, we saw Jennifer and a female friend at a table in the bar. We said hello and Jennifer told us they were waiting for the son of a prominent Houstonian. Jennifer had met the lad in Aspen, a frequent hangout of hers. Thirteen years her junior, the kid had gotten the immediate "hots" for sexy little Jennifer, but she had told me she was far more interested in getting close to his powerful daddy. Though his father did not work for Enron, he was wealthy and that was good enough for Jennifer. Unfortunately, there was only one problem with that plan, the man was dating her friend Jeannine Turner. In most cases Jennifer would have cut her friend's throat to get the man...but this would have surely been the end of her Enron career had Jeannine told Amanda Martin. But I'm sure Jennifer weighed her options.

We talked with Jennifer and her friend for a moment and, not wanting to interrupt the flow with her new potential squeeze, we excused ourselves and found seats across room at the bar. Our table was located underneath the stairway to the restaurant and restrooms. The steps were open between the risers affording those sitting at the bar a worm's eye view of anyone walking up the stairs.

During the night, Jennifer crossed the room on her way to the stairs, waved, then headed up the steps. I had my back to the risers, but Lori had an unobstructed view.

Lori's eyes widened. "Holy shit!" she said in a whisper.

"What? What's wrong?" I asked.

She took a long pull off her straw then her astonishment became a wry smile. "Wait'll your buddy Jennifer comes back. I'll tell you when to look."

"Look at what?" I wondered.

"You'll see," was all she'd say.

A few moments later Lori's eyes caught Jennifer returning and, trying not to move her lips, muttered, "Okay. Look up."

I turned and gazed up into the open staircase. I saw black pumps and shapely tan legs. My eyes trailed upward to find a very short skirt framing a gynecologist's view of my friend Jennifer. I almost did a spit take.

"Holy shit!" I gasped, trying to whisper. "She's got no underwear on!"

I'd heard of suiting up for the game, but this was ridiculous. With the abbreviated length of her skirt I wondered aloud to Lori what Jennifer must be thinking. Having heard about Jennifer's reputation, Lori shrugged her shoulders. "Hey, she just wants to be ready to close a deal."

We giggled and made a few suggestive jokes at Jennifer's expense, but I was worried this outrageous behavior was a last ditch effort to get attention. After ordering our second drink and speculating on Jennifer's mental state, a rather scrawny balding man approached us.

"May I join you ladies?" he asked.

He looked like Mr. Whipple from the Charmin ads of the 90s, even though he was probably not quite fifty. Though Lori was married and I wasn't really looking, we were often hit on by men. Rarely did a lone man try to join us, so I assumed he was just some poor loser looking for company. He looked harmless enough, so we invited him to sit.

He shook our hands. "Hi. My name's Steve. Steve Naeve."

"Your name sounds familiar," said Lori. She had been moving in Houston's circles a lot longer than I had. "Where do you work?"

"Houston Lighting and Power," said our new friend Steve.

"What do you do there?" inquired Lori.

"I work for Don Jordon."

Okay, so he was a really well-to-do lonely loser looking for anyone to tell his woe-is-me tale. As it turned out, Houston Lighting & Power (HL&P, now known as Reliant), was Enron's arch enemy and Don Jordon was its very well known CEO. When I mentioned I was with Enron, Steve took that as an opportunity to go off on a tangent about how much his boss Jordon hated Ken Lay.

"He'd do just about anything to outdo that son-of-a-bitch," he admitted to us. After going on and on about Lay – and never inquiring if we knew or liked him – he then began relating a sordid tale about his own affair a few years earlier with a woman in his organization. Too caught up in himself to care whether we wanted to hear such a story, he explained how he had left his wife to be with this woman, who then refused to be a part of breaking up his marriage. Reading between the lines, I figured she was repelled by his clingy behavior. I remember thinking, *Look you idiot, she just wants to move up the corporate ladder, she doesn't want to marry you!*

Although Steve was a boring putz, we figured he was innocuous enough and good for a laugh or two. Plus Lori was intrigued by the possibilities HL&P might offer her as a consultant, hoping to use Steve as an in for business development. As he rattled on, I knew it was a wild long-shot, but HL&P just might offer me an escape route from Enron. At that point, I was open to any possibilities.

Steve mentioned a corporate development position that would soon be opening up.

"I'm gettin' ready to fire the bozo in there now," he said. Then he threw a change-up.

"You ladies know Jeff Skilling?" Lori didn't, but I admitted to it.

"What do you think of him?" he asked.

I wasn't sure if Jeff was friend or foe so I turned it back to Steve. "I don't know," I said vaguely. "What do you think?"

Steve took a big swig of his cocktail for emphasis. "I hate the scumbag."

"Don't mince words, Steve. What do you really think of him?" deadpanned Lori.

"He and I were at McKinsey together," he said, referring to the consulting firm. "Nobody could stand him over there. Ken Lay believed his bullshit. Skilling says he created the gas bank. That's total horseshit. An employee – just some clown in the trenches – came up with the idea and 'ol Jeff Boy just stole it and took credit. The guy's a weasel."

He fished something out of his pocket. "Hey, check this out." It was a piece of paper.

"Fax from my dealer telling me my new Porsche is on the way. Jeff would throw a baby under a steam roller to have this. Only a few like it in the country. Jeff wanted this one bad. His name was on the list, but I scooped it. Next time you see him, tell that asshole I got the last one in Texas."

Steve, Lori and I held our bar stools until 12:30 a.m. when Steve offered, "You two want to go get something to eat?" Normally we would have declined, but I thought this guy with his corporate development position actually could be my way to cut myself loose from Enron's golden handcuffs so I thought why not.

Steve made a last trip to the men's room and Lori asked, "Do you like him?"

"Are you crazy?" I said, half laughing, half irritated. "Him? He looks like Ichabod Crane. God no! I think I'm about ready to pack it in."

Then Lori reminded me, "This guy runs one of Enron's biggest competitors. I mean what could it hurt, having dinner with him once in a while? Who knows, it could mean bailing from Enron without getting hurt."

She had a point, but I wasn't going to lead Steve on. If he hired me at some point in the future it would be on my merits. After all, I wasn't Jennifer – I wore underwear.

We accompanied Steve to the valet stand and when Lori's car pulled up he held out his claim check and ten bucks to give to the valet.

"You go with Steve." Lori insisted.

Always the matchmaker she jumped in her car as a little white Mercedes SLK purred up. Steve handed me the keys. "Here, you drive."

I grabbed the cash and the claim check and looked at Lori with a look of disbelief. "Really?"

He climbed into the passenger's side. "Oh, we just have to stop by my wife's place and feed her goldfish." Then they were off.

Feed her goldfish? I thought he was kidding, but I drove as Lori followed for 45 minutes to a suburban section of Houston called Friendswood where we pulled in front of the Fiesta all-night grocery store. Steve jumped out and motioned for Lori to come over.

"We're gonna get something here to make at his wife's place," she said to me as I sat behind the wheel of the Mercedes.

I was disappointed that such a big-shot was now expecting us to cook for him instead of feting us to a decent late night snack. She explained that Steve's estranged wife was out of town and he had agreed to take care of her fish. She followed him inside and, after waiting in Steve's lovely new car for at least fifteen minutes, I decided to go in too. I tried to remove the key, but couldn't get it out. After consulting the owner's manual I eventually figured out the intricacies of a Mercedes key and joined them inside.

We finished shopping and hit the road. My cell phone rang. It was Lori calling to give me special instructions. If Steve's wife, Vivian*, had not gone out of town, her car would be in the driveway and we would just continue on. We got to the place in Friendswood, a surprisingly modest Mediterranean-style bungalow, at least compared to the outsized dwellings back in ritzy River Oaks. I parked Steve's car, vowing to never again be at the mercy of my friend, as dear as she was. Once Lori got the cooking underway, I stepped back and marveled at how I'd ended up an hour away from my place, in another woman's home, with her middle-aged dweeb estranged husband and my girlfriend making dinner at 2:30 in the morning. I pictured this as the fate of all of us in our mid-to-late thirties who refused to leave the sorority/fraternity merry-go-round of college and the pursuit of adventure.

I left the kitchen and headed to the living room to acquaint myself with the large exotic bird that was capable of carrying on more scintillating conversation than Steve. I imagined what the bird would tell Vivian when she returned. While the food simmered, Steve appeared and demonstrated to us his pride and joy, a $35,000 stereo system that, he claimed, required the floor to be reinforced to support the gigantic speakers. When he fired up the Doors and cranked the volume to ear bleed territory, I saw why Viv had booted his ass.

Now that Jim Morrison and the boys had exacerbated my migraine, I took Lori aside and explained to her that if listening to this was what it took to succeed in Houston, then in the words of Samuel Goldwyn, "include me out" and I'd happily stay at Enron. With that we bid Steve baby adieu and left. As we drove away we noticed the name of his street, "Cowards Creek", and laughed so hard Lori nearly crashed the car. From that encounter I knew with absolute certainty that as a climber I wasn't even close to Jennifer's league.

Come Monday morning, Jennifer and I exchanged our usual "how was your weekend" stories. I carefully omitted the part where I'd viewed her giblets on the stairway and eagerly asked about the new flame. Jennifer had recently broken up with a guy named Mark, who had fallen victim to a late night daffy-dialing session. If the new boy toy turned out to have staying power (that is, his ability to put up with her), I knew it would have a positive effect on Jennifer. She had been divorced a little over a year and, between that and having her career stall at Enron, I felt she was on the edge as she began to remind me more and more of Glenn Close's character in *Fatal Attraction* after being rejected by Michael Douglas. I took it as a good sign that she was beginning the process of changing her name back from Hampton to her maiden name, Wellsley*. It was a cleansing break from the past, but her recent behavior had me worried. I saw the new fling as a diversion from her single-and not-moving-up-the-ladder funk.

Then in June 1998, fortune smiled on Jennifer. Enron's Origination group was responsible for the largest wholesale gas deals. Gary Donohue* was the group's vice president, a blue jeans and starched shirt good 'ol boy I would often see on the trading floor. One of the guys in charge of Enron's most profitable division, Gary was considered the top salesman in the company. It befell Gary's group to create a company-wide intranet, an internal Internet for use within Enron.

Luckily for Jennifer, Gary worked for her good friend Amanda Martin. Jennifer's constant buzzing in Amanda's ear finally paid off when Jennifer got the call from Gary. The next day, Gary and Jennifer had dinner to talk about moving over to his new intranet group. He told her, "If you help me get this project off the ground, I'll take care of you." At the conclusion of the meal Jennifer walked away with a new gig, a salary increase from $55,000 to $80,000 and, after her first review, a very large bonus and promotion to manager. She was ecstatic. Now she felt she'd broken the ice and her career was on the move. Jennifer was riding high, with a new job and her shiny new boyfriend, Rich* – after dumping the kid. All she needed to feel complete would be a new Porsche Boxter.

Rich, originally from Indianapolis, was a sales manager for a software company in Dallas. Their relationship deteriorated very quickly from honeymoon to tempestuous. One day it was up, the next day down. Soon after they began dating, Jennifer came to me glowing that Rich had just asked her to marry him. I was thrilled for her. A week later she approached my desk in tears and informed me the engagement was off. From that time on I never knew what the day would bring for Jennifer and Rich.

One Friday night they were having dinner at a restaurant in downtown Houston, when the subject of her friendship with Hunter Green came up. Rich jealously accused her of sleeping with Hunter then moved on to the subject of her relationship with her new boss, Gary Donohue. Apparently Rich questioned the appropriateness of Gary having accompanied Jennifer to her breast augmentation surgery. The discussion quickly grew heated and, deciding he'd had enough, he stormed away from the table. Jennifer followed him outside to the valet stand and, as they waited for their car, she struck up a conversation with a friend she bumped into. When she turned around, her fiancé was speeding off in the car, leaving her stranded with no way home.

She hitched a ride with her friend and arrived home to find that Rich had let himself in to her apartment and was asleep in her bed. She furiously demanded he leave at once.

"I'm not going anywhere!" he said.

To which she retorted, "Oh yes you are!"

And with that, she called the police. The vision of a soft, rich young thang thrown in, overnight, with the hardcore riff-raff in the Houston pokey scared the bejabbers out of Rich, and he skedaddled before the police arrived.

Having endured more than my share of troubled relationships, I felt it was time to open my mouth and give Jennifer the benefit of my wisdom. I strongly suggested that she end the relationship and begin seeing the value in herself.

"Any guy who would abandon his fiancé with no way home and no money on her is a real jerk," I said as forcefully as she could take. "And going back to your house as if nothing happened? Well, he's stupid to boot."

Jennifer's new position in Gary's group had her reporting to Sullivan "Sully" Graas*. Sully was a broad-shouldered black man in his fifties. He was also close friends with fellow South African, and Jennifer's friend, Amanda Martin. Sully was charismatic, with a deliciously rich Afrikaans accent and the air and demeanor of a GQ cover model. Once I got to know him I realized he too suffered from the belief as a director he was undervalued by Enron's management. He'd gotten where he was by politics and relationships, not knowledge of the field, of which he had very little. But I respected him nevertheless.

Once Jennifer was ensconced in the department, I asked her to pass on my résumé to Sully. I had writing experience and they needed people in her new group who could create content for the intranet. Sully got my résumé but never responded. I later found out Sully deeply resented Gary's dropping Jennifer into his department without his knowledge, much less his approval. He felt she was unqualified and was paid far too much money for what she did. Sully was particularly infuriated by the $60,000 bonus Jennifer was promised after her first review. That was more than Sully had ever received. So Sully secretly dug in his heels when it had to do with anything regarding Jennifer. I did not know it at the time, but using Jennifer as my entrée guaranteed I would never get into the intranet group.

Sully Graas and his small group were charged with developing Enron's internal Web site for employees as part of Enron's Knowledge Management. The idea was to make more efficient communications not only within departments, but between them. It would also allow the company to clarify its views, policies, and news to employees, as well as allow employees a cross-company forum to express their thoughts. Management felt that increased communications would mean increased profits. Joining Jennifer in the worker's pool was Elizabeth Wright* and Colleen Lawrence*. Elizabeth and Colleen were dedicated workers and quickly developed a close working relationship. Jennifer was the odd man out. She didn't have any history with her colleagues and had a rep as a goof-off and gold-digger. While Elizabeth and Colleen would be trying to get their work done, they would also be listening to Jennifer's never-ending stories about her ups and downs with Rich and the cash and trinkets she was copping off Hunter Green.

Elizabeth and Colleen had gotten an earful from Sully that Jennifer was not only a bitch on wheels, but that she was now having regular sexual encounters with the group's major domo, Gary himself. And all three resented Jennifer's relatively absurd compensation, which was far more than Elizabeth and Colleen were making and almost as much as Sully was pulling down. As they were conspiring to find a way to eliminate her, Jennifer took a personal blow. She learned that her drinking buddy and confidante Melanie St. James had been bad-mouthing her all over the department. Jennifer was crushed when she discovered Melanie's betrayal.

Unbeknownst to Jennifer, Melanie had apparently been spreading the news about her for some time. She'd been sharing some very juicy details of Jennifer's corporate game plan, from her numerous sexual liaisons to her habit of forgetting to don panties with her tiny skirts. Jennifer was outraged, but since she had made her latest upward move without any help from her alliance with Melanie, she got over it quickly. Melanie, on the other hand, had probably decided to distance herself from Jennifer to maintain her own credibility.

Not long after she reported to Sully's group, Jennifer and I attended the company seminar entitled "Understanding ECT", which was designed to give those on the executive management track a complete understanding of all aspects of Enron's trading business. It was then that I learned just how big her raise had been. We broke for lunch and she suggested a place down the street and offered to drive. When we got to her new car I did a double take. Jennifer's nice but well-used BMW had been replaced by a brand new fifty-thousand dollar Porsche Boxster with all the options.

"Wow, Jennifer! It's gorgeous," I gushed.

She nodded. "Yeah, and so's my new place. You'll have to stop over."

Jennifer had gone hog wild with her new salary, not only springing for an expensive new sports car, but also moving up to fancy new digs near downtown.

As we came back from lunch she made an announcement. "Sully is sending me to a conference in New York. It's my consolation prize."

"What do you mean?"

"Oh, two weeks ago he sent Elizabeth to London on a project she didn't know shit about and I did. I was so pissed at him he offered me the New York trip. Probably to shut me up," she added with a laugh. "Hey, at least I can get in some shopping."

A few days later Jennifer asked me to drop her off at the airport for the trip to New York. Before I left the office, she called from home.

"Hey, before you leave," she said, "I forgot a book that Rebecca's got. Would you mind getting it from her and bringing it? She said it would be good for me to try and understand Rich."

I wanted to say *understand he's a loser*, but I bit my tongue and said I'd pick it up. During a break I went up to the 50th floor executive suites to Rebecca Carter's office.

Rebecca was glad to see me and warmly invited me to sit down. We talked for quite a while, chatting like schoolgirls. I asked about the book and she handed it to me. The title was *Too Good to Leave; Too Bad to Stay*. I looked at the book then questioningly at her. She and Jeff seemed to have a good relationship. Her smile was slightly embarrassed. She got up and closed the door.

"I hope this helps her," she said. "God knows she needs it with that Rich."

My eyes again asked the question that had caused her to close the door.

She sighed, "Jeff and I, well, we've talked about getting married. We will, I think, but we have...uh, problems. He wants me to stay at home once we get married. Give up my career and hang around the kitchen," she joked, but I could tell she didn't think it was that funny.

"So what are you going to do? Is he flexible?" I asked innocently.

Her eyes flared and she guffawed, "Jeff? Flexible? That's too hilarious! No, he's not, so that's the problem. The big problem. He wants me to stay home, run the household and entertain. I'm Chief Control Officer and Corporate Secretary for Enron," she suddenly blurted angrily. "What does he think I'm gonna stay home and be a fucking June Cleaver? That's not gonna happen?"

We talked a while longer, and Rebecca calmed down. She seemed at a loss in her own relationship, but was obviously hoping the book would help Jennifer. I returned to my desk and had another of those rare moments when I was delighted to not be involved with anyone.

Shortly after the "Understanding ECT" seminar, I met with a man named Steven Grant* to explore life after Bammel. I wanted out of Kathy's group and thought a little networking couldn't hurt. Steven had been a food wholesaler in his native England when he flew over to join his wife Mackenzie* at Enron. Now he traded one of the most arcane financial instruments in existence: weather derivatives. The interview was more informational than anything as I sought to understand Enron's most obscure commodity.

According to former US Secretary of Commerce William Daley, at least $1 trillion of the US economy is affected by weather. The European and Japanese economies are also exposed to weather risks to the tune of $1.25 trillion and $700 billion, respectively.

To further their reputation as a risk management company, in August 1997, Enron created the first weather-indexed commodity transaction with a utility company. The following month they completed their first financial transaction in the weather risk management market. By September 1998, Enron completed its first international financial weather transaction.

Headed by Lynda Clemmons, Enron's Wonder Woman of Weather, the weather desk was a small, asset-light group. Lynda had started her career in the investment banking division of NationsBank prior to coming to Enron in 1992. Initially, Lynda had managed the emissions allowance trading until she became a vice president at the age of 27 and traded her first weather derivative transaction in 1997. With her background, Lynda was certainly qualified to trade air – hot or otherwise.

Steven explained that weather trades are generally based upon cooling degree days (CDDs) or heating degree days (HDDs) to describe the variances from 65°F, which is the temperature that either the heat is turned on if it is below 65°F, or the air conditioner is turned on if it is above 65°F. And of course in Europe, Australia and Canada, centigrade calculations are based on 18°C, while the Nordic regions are based upon 16°C.

Most trades were done as swaps, collars and options, and like other markets, swaps and collars required no cash outlay until the expiration of the contract. On the other hand, options required the purchaser to pay an up-front premium.

To clarify how it worked, let's use the example of a snowmobile manufacturer that relies heavily on pre-sales in the springtime for the following winter in order to know how many machines should be built. However, come the following winter when the snowmobiles have been made and delivered, if no snow exists, sales will be in the dumper. By covering his position with the purchase of a weather derivative, the manufacturer could offer a cash rebate of, say $500, if the snowfall did not average at least 50% of the norm in the customer's local area – based upon a three-year historic average – over the next winter season.

The weather information was based upon the National Weather Service data. Through his weather derivative, the snowmobile manufacturer is able to cash in by requiring Enron to pay if the snowfall is less than anticipated. The money from Enron would cover the cash rebate he paid the consumer. In the event that the snowfall was above average, the bounty reaped from his extra sale of snowmobiles paid for the cost of the weather derivative.

What I liked best about the concept of trading weather was that no one was standing over you to define what you could and could not do. By utilizing the weather as its measuring stick based upon temperature extremes, snowfall, rainfall, stream-flow, storm activity or perceived temperature, like wind chill or heat index, this was more fun than making snow angels. There was just one problem. Storms were brewing in the group and it was rumored that Lynda Clemmons felt, as did every other 27-year-old vice president, that she was not appreciated. I heard she was about to pack her bags and take Steven with her. If she did, it could leave the group in chaos and that's exactly what I didn't need. Since I was seeking refuge and stability, Kathy's group suddenly didn't look as awful as it had the day before so I opted to stay put.

The doors at the point of entry to each of Enron's floors were secured. To enter, one needed a magnetized security card that, when swiped across the magnetic "Enron" sign, would give you access to the floor. From the other side you had to press a round button the size of a silver dollar, releasing the magnetic lock, allowing you to exit. There was a delay of perhaps a second or so from the time you pushed the button to the release of the magnet.

One afternoon, I was slogging though financial derivative contracts when I heard someone screaming.

"OPEN, you fucking thing!"

A nice-looking man in his mid-thirties, wearing a gray suit that matched his full head of hair, was pounding the exit button like a chimp in an anthropology experiment. He brutally pummeled the button but paused long enough before the next attack to allow it to open. He made off a like a jack rabbit and I turned to a legal secretary walking by my desk.

"Who the heck was that?"

"Oh, that was Andy Fastow." She said it with a slight roll of the eyes, implying that such behavior was not unusual.

Fastow had been appointed CFO on March 18, 1998, a couple of weeks prior to my arrival at Enron. Finally, I had caught a glimpse of the man who had caused this three-foot wall of recycled trees to appear on my desk. Fastow came to Enron in 1990. Prior to becoming CFO, he had been the senior vice president of Enron Capital Management, which encompassed Enron's treasury and corporate risk management functions, as well as ECT's funding, capital pricing and management activities.

While I had been charged with "dumbing-down" the details of transactions involving the off-the-balance-sheet partnership's financial derivatives for senior management, I had heard Skilling often saying "the devil is in the details." While I am not an accountant, I had come to understand that Fastow was responsible for this means of accounting innovation through the creation of SPEs (Special Purpose Entities). Technically speaking, SPEs are legitimate and used to generate cash or revenue for the company to operate. By transferring assets to an SPE, an outside partnership, Enron was able to keep any debt associated with the asset off its balance sheet. In exchange for the asset, the SPE then gave Enron a wad of cash to finance its business operations, hence the reason it was called "Off-the-Balance-Sheet Financing". In order to meet SPE rules, the law required outside partners in the SPE to have made a substantive capital investment, which amounted to owning at least 3% of the partnership. The outside partners also had to maintain independent control over the SPE in order for Enron to keep the debt off the books.

In order to sweeten the pie, Fastow had Enron guarantee these financing arrangements by ensuring that the partners would not lose any money. The loans were backed with Enron shares of stock. As long as the value of the transferred asset remained elevated, Enron would eventually repay the loan and everything would be fine. In the event that the value of the asset fell, the Enron stock could be cashed in to cover the shortfall.

However, Andy, Jeff and the gang either hadn't accounted for, or ignored, the Nuclear Winter scenario. In that worst of worse cases, the value of the asset would fall and Enron's stock would also fall and then...well, you'd have a bit of a problem. In that frightening picture there would not be enough value in the pledged Enron stock to cover the loss, so more devalued stock would need to be issued, thus diluting the value of Enron stock for all investors even further. It had the potential for catastrophe.

By keeping debt off its books, Enron would be able to appear more profitable than it actually was, which was desperately important to Enron for two reasons. First, they needed to attract a constant crop of investors to buy Enron stock to keep its value up. Secondly, they needed to protect their credit rating.

In order to borrow money, as Enron had done in the Bammel case, it needed to have a superior credit rating, which required – just as with any individual consumer – a reduced debt load. In the event the credit rating were to fall, Enron would suddenly be required to pay the entire loan under what is called a Material Adverse Change, or MAC, clause. Were that to happen, it would set off an old-fashioned run on the bank. All of Enron's creditors would demand their money at the same time leaving no cash to operate their business. Ultimately, this is what happened.

By 1998, Enron had $31 billion of assets on the balance sheet, and $50 million off the balance sheet. While conventional financing techniques would have jeopardized Enron's BBB+ rating from Standard & Poor's, by issuing additional Enron shares, Skilling and the rest of senior management knew they would be diluting the share-price. As Ron Barone, a director at New York based Standard & Poor's stated at the time, "Cash is King and Andy knows that."

Andy had a reputation for squeezing a nickel. I had heard the story of a cab ride in Chicago in 1985. He paid the fare and waited for seventy cents change. When the cabbie got pissed, Andy grabbed a buck back from the driver and replaced it with the thirty cents owed. The cab driver in exchange punched Andy.

To aid him in his schemes, Andy recruited a guy named Michael J. Kopper, who looked a bit like Pee Wee Herman. He was also a buddy of Jeff Skilling's. Kopper was a guy from Finance, and because he was low ranking enough, Enron could legally avoid having to put his name on any proxy statement disclosure, thus avoiding embarrassing questions from shareholders about who he answered to, or actually worked for. This left Kopper open to run any of Andy's off-the-balance-sheet partnerships with impunity. As Kopper played both sides of the fence – working for Enron while playing the role of "independent" manager of the SPEs – I heard grumblings by employees who were angry that he was making a fortune as Andy's puppet. For a figurehead, Kopper did well by knowing Andy. For the modest $125,000 investment in Chewco that he and his domestic partner, William Dodson, ponied up, they made a respectable return of $10,500,000. Between 1997 and 2000, Kopper also hauled in $2 million in "consulting" fees. Additionally, for his grueling dual roles, he would receive a lump sum severance of $905,000 on July 23, 2001. It was really, really good to be friends with Jeff and Andy.

Meanwhile, as Jennifer enjoyed her bounty while barely cracking a sweat to get the intranet going, I continued to work on contractual issues. After I finished the Bammel brief, my next big project was to provide an analysis of Enron's 10,000 gas contracts. My job was to determine which contracts allowed for excessive amounts of carbon dioxide (CO^2).

The principal greenhouse gas thought to cause global warming is carbon dioxide. By its nature, natural gas contains carbon dioxide; sometimes in older gas fields high concentrations exist and, if so, the mixture is very corrosive to the physical pipelines. Because of the standards regulating what goes through a pipeline, natural gas containing elevated chemical impurities such as CO^2 is considered "sour" or "bad" gas. Over time, the corrosive nature of such gas can actually have a devastating impact on the structural integrity of a natural gas pipeline, including a thinning of the walls of the pipe and degradation of valves and joints.

For this reason, if levels of CO^2 are excessive, the gas must be processed or "treated" to meet the gas product guidelines established for each pipeline.

"Otherwise," said Pamela James*, the attorney with whom I worked on the project, "the life of your asset could be cut in half. So rather than a pipeline being viable for 30 years, it could potentially rupture in 15 years, causing a huge liability for the company if the bad gas has not been monitored."

Pam is a brilliant woman, a lawyer and gifted natural teacher. From her, I learned a great deal about the pipeline business and became her close friend in the process.

One day, Pam confided to me. "You're going to see things in these contracts that don't make sense. Don't try to make sense by assuming you don't know the gas business. You know business and your instincts will probably be correct. Just keep in mind Enron's prime directive: Get the deal done at all costs."

I had an inkling of just what that philosophy entailed, but when I soon uncovered what Jane Gray* had perpetrated, Pam's words took on a new, more powerful meaning. Relatively new to the trading floor, having been promoted from a contract administrator to gas trader, once Jane Gray got the lay of the land she saw an enormous opportunity to make some good money and generate herself a really fat bonus.

A gas producer had approached Jane with a problem. They had a lot of sour gas, which they needed to unload it or take a loss. The gas was contained in old wells in a concentrated area of south central Texas. The wells were so elderly that the pressure was diminished to the point it could not be extracted by the normal means of sticking in a pipe and letting the gas flow. An aging gas field like that required special extraction or "lifting" agreements. Lifting agreements allowed for pure, untainted natural gas to be sold to the producer then injected back into the well to create sufficient pressure to raise the gas to the surface.

Initially, Enron was going to sell the producer the good gas. Then the gas producer floated out the idea that Enron was so big it could take their bad gas for a song, figure out some way to clean it up, then resell it at a big profit. Jane jumped on the idea and Enron purchased the sour gas at way under market value. So Enron ended up with a lot of gas for cheap and Jane Gray got her huge bonus. The only problem was what to do with the crummy gas.

Enron's brilliant solution, which no doubt earned some other Enron employees big money, was to build a treatment facility. I was stunned that Enron would buy gas at a low price, seemingly for the purposes of making a profit, but then turn around and construct a multi-million dollar facility to clean it up, thus negating any possible profit. As I read through the documents I couldn't see any scenario other than a loss in the $10 to $20 million range for Enron. And Jane Gray would get a bonus for this that was several times my annual salary. Enron was beginning to look far less like the towering symbol of world energy and more like the Mad Hatter's Tea Party. I couldn't help but think of an idiot's version of the underlying goal of commerce – buy high and sell low, which had been a costly experiment with the J-Block deal. Of course, no one would be the wiser if Enron needed to cover up the loss – they could pledge the gas inventories in Bammel to secure another loan!

As I performed my risk analysis, I discovered that the number of contracts Enron had that allowed for high levels of carbon dioxide was alarming, particularly when you considered that all the wells were located in a concentrated area. That meant it was likely all of the gas in the field would be of a diminished quality. I learned that while sour gas was not desirable, an acceptable level of CO^2 was allowed, and that level determined the worth of the gas. The contracts, depending upon where each well was, allowed for certain levels of CO^2. Higher contamination would reduce the value of the gas and thus the cost of the gas if you're the buyer. Early on I realized that without performing specific gas analysis of each well, it would be virtually impossible to accurately determine the extent of the risk.

I did some homework and found that all natural gas is subject to "stringent requirements of custody transfer" under a computerized system of measurement called Supervisory Control and Data Acquisition, or SCADA. As large pipelines connect with each other and gas from various sources flow together, the system of quality conformity they devised was called SCADA. Since all gas was not created equal, SCADA measured a number of parameters such as pressure and chemical content, thus grading the gas and establishing a means of valuing it.

SCADA monitored and controlled the EFM measurement points (Electronic Flow Measurement for Custody Transfer) installed in Enron's 38,000 miles of gas pipelines. A Server collected EFM historical records (both daily and hourly records), events (stuff that went wrong) and alarms (stuff that went really wrong) from the field devices, and then interfaced them into a database. In other words, at any given moment, one could nearly verify the precise quality of the gas running through any part of the maze of pipelines that were longer than a transcontinental highway.

I located the SCADA records to determine the actual levels of CO^2 that were coming out of the wells covered under the specific contracts. Generally, the gas contracts allowed for CO^2 levels between 4% and 8%. While CO^2 of 8% is considered a relatively elevated level, I was amazed to find many of the Enron wells exhibiting extremely high levels of CO^2, in some cases on the order of 12% to even 25%. I learned that Enron was betting that the gas would be commingled enough downstream that the elevated levels of CO^2 would go unnoticed. It was like a bank finding out that a large percentage of their deposits were counterfeit and sending the cash to the Federal Reserve, hoping no one would catch it.

I went to Dana Reasoner*, someone I knew to be very knowledgeable about gas. She had worked in Enron's gas control group and I thought she might be sympathetic, as she was often critical of Kathy Simpson's seek and destroy methods. I had also heard her on more than one occasion voice criticism of the company's behavior. I explained my findings regarding the gas contracts. I was hoping she had some kernel of inside information that might help me.

"Dana, is it possible that the company has just made a mistake concerning the CO^2 levels? I mean, how easy is it to keep track of gas?" Dana smiled as if to say *you are so naive*. "You got ten minutes?"

"Sure."

She stood and gestured for me to follow. "I'm going to show you something that not many people see. When you see it you can decide whether you think anything is left to chance at Enron, *particularly* with gas."

We rode the elevator to the 42nd floor. As the doors opened, I realized this was nothing like any of the other floors in the Enron building. Not like the usual, inviting, wide open spaces on other floors, this was austere and featured a long sloping ramp leading to a robust security door with no indication of what was on the other side. Dana had a key card and opened the heavy door. We took a few steps, turned right and entered a darkened conference room. The opposite wall consisted of panes of floor to ceiling glass, but the glass was dark as if in covered by a curtain. Dana poised by a wall switch.

"Watch the windows."

She pushed the button and miraculously the windows began to clear. I realized they were filled with a gas that had rendered them opaque. In a second or two the gas dissipated, revealing a sight that took my breath away. On the other side of the glass was a room out of a science fiction movie – or nearby NASA's Mission Control. About a dozen men sat in a row, facing massive banks of digital readouts, colored and flashing lights, electronic graphs, and buttons and switches, perhaps thousands of them. My mouth dropped open.

Dana began, "Like the guys in a missile silo waiting for World War III, this place is manned 24/7."

She pointed at the exterior wall. "That's double-reinforced concrete. Everything around them is bullet or bomb proof. In this room, Enron controls every inch of a gas pipeline grid that criss-crosses 38,000 miles over the US and Canada."

I was awestruck. "Holy crap!"

Dana chuckled. "You're not the first person to say that when they've walked in here."

With no illumination but the wall of instruments, the men went quietly about their business, switching off the occasional enunciator and rerouting gas from one pipeline to another. Whether in Illinois or Louisiana or Northern Canada, it was all accomplished with the touch of a button.

"If CO^2 levels get too high, an alarm sounds at the local compressor station and also here at Gas Control. Then Gas Control can either shut it down or reroute it. Those red phones?" she indicated. "Those are hotlines to the compressor stations."

I recognized that Enron had invested many tens of millions to create this room and the effortless management it exerted over its gigantic web of gas lines.

"And this isn't the only control. There's a redundant control room, just like this one, in case something happened to this building like a hurricane or nuclear attack. Some of us think it's in Omaha. They keep it a secret. It's kind of Enron's Area 51."

Dana turned to me and joked, "It's ten o'clock. Do you know where your gas is?" Then she waved a hand at the men and the dazzling bank of lights and readouts. "So, did they make a mistake on your gas contracts? You be the judge."

Certainly at some point the words "Houston we have a problem" had to have been uttered from this room.

I was aware that on November 21, 1996, an Enron gas line in San Juan, Puerto Rico ruptured and exploded, killing 33 people and injuring 69 others. Although the NTSB attributed the disaster to a construction excavation crew, the report also noted that *"Enron*

Corporation had known since 1985 that the [pipeline] operations did not comply with pipeline safety requirements and industry practices, and it failed to require the gas company to comply with those requirements and practices." I couldn't help but wonder if the pipe had been weakened by corrosive gas.

I decided the best way to assess the risk to the assets, meaning the pipelines involved in Jane Gray's deals, was to get an idea of how long the gas with the high concentration of CO^2 had been passing through them. To do so I created maps, comparing the gas content from the various producers in the area and the details of the contracts relative to those producers. What alarmed me was that while Jane Gray was blithely purchasing corrosive gas from one producer, so were a number of other Enron traders purchasing equally corrosive gas in the same area and blending it with good gas. I believed this created a demonstrable devaluation of the asset, because the longevity of the pipe had been compromised based on CO^2 levels that were in excess of 60% of the standard contractual rate. It went without saying that the diminished value of the assets was nothing, compared to the possible loss of life should the line corrode to the point of rupturing, but I would soon learn my concerns would be diminished by senior management at the same rate as the value of the pipeline.

CHAPTER FOUR

They will stab you in the back simply because you have one.

Sullivan Graas, Vice President,
Enron Broadband Services

RANK AND YANK

A few days later, I was to attend a luncheon with many of the bigwigs of the company and decided to make known my concerns at that time. Although it crossed my mind that I might be making waves with the wrong people, I prayed that this company would not coldly risk lives to turn a buck. I assumed the company was big enough and, as organized, somewhat compartmentalized. I thought it possible that there were rogues working toward their own ends, and against the better judgment of the company. I prayed that such shoddy and dangerous business practices were not endemic to Enron, but were isolated instances of greedy traders trying to make a buck, no matter what the cost. The problem was that by now I knew Enron, from the top down, encouraged such "creative" business practices. What I still didn't want to believe was that Enron would make money and knowingly put people in mortal danger.

As the luncheon speakers were announced, I saw Jeff Skilling was on the docket. I decided it would be Jeff who would get my question. In the contact I had with him, I knew he was exceptionally smart. I deduced that as a smart person, how could he allow this type of fraud? No matter what the crime or how smart you are you will always be caught, and in Enron's case, being caught would mean one thing: promotion or utter destruction. I could not imagine Jeff would allow that to happen.

We took our seats at large round tables and waiters began serving the food. Sitting next to Jennifer, I speculated on the subjects to be covered when Jeff came over and sat down at our table. We exchanged pleasantries.

"Jeff," I said, "are you riding in the MS150 again this year?" I had the previous year's 175-mile ride in mind.

His eyes lit up. "Enron's goal is to raise $700,000 this year. I have to be in it," he said, his small chest puffing. "With a little help from my friends," he said, as he elbowed Jennifer, "and my assistant Sherri, I expect to raise $50,000 personally this year – I'd say that should put me in the top money earner's seat again this year."

We all talked about the charity ride and Jeff went on and on about how he'd managed to ace everyone with the top money. I found it telling that for him it was not about sparing people the ravages of multiple sclerosis, but rather beating everyone else. I thought he needed something to take his mind off that track.

"I had drinks recently with an old friend of yours, Jeff."

"Oh? Who would that be?"

"Steve Naeve."

The mention of the name caused Jeff to blink. He then regained his composure. I noticed his jaw take an almost imperceptible set.

"What were you doing with Naeve? Slumming?" he asked snidely.

I could see his brain cells working on overdrive wondering, why I had been drinking with such a prominent Houstonian who was an arch rival of Enron.

"He said you guys were at McKinsey together."

"Yeah. And I recall he could barely find his ass with both hands."

The table chuckled at Jeff's snappy put-down.

"He said to tell you he'd glommed onto your Porsche."

Jeff's face clouded in annoyance.

"He wishes. I'll get mine before he does."

"Well, actually, he was just about to pick it up."

Jeff's face turned to stone and he abruptly changed the subject. A few of my tablemates made discreet eye contact to register surprise that I had made Jeff squirm. I took a deep breath, knowing the fireworks hadn't really started. I knew this was make or break for me. How Jeff answered my next few questions would tell me whether, as top dog, he knew of the games going on.

After lunch Jeff took center stage and began his brief "State of the Union" address. He began with glowing generalities about the rock-solid future of Enron. Then he got into what I realized was the reason for this whole meeting: internal spin control as to why in the hell Enron had gotten into the water business. He explained that with the growing privatization of water resources in Europe, Enron wanted to be in the $400 billion a year industry so they bought a British water company, Wessex Water. I had heard about the purchase, as had everyone else, and we'd also heard that Enron overpaid. Jeff labored to scotch that ugly rumor and explained how Enron, by such bold moves, earned *Fortune's* label as the "Most Innovative Company". I also found it ironic that Jeff was having to rationalize an asset while I knew he was vehemently anti-asset.

When Jeff finished making his points as to why Enron was really smart, as opposed to the dirt many analysts were spreading about us, he opened the discussion up to Q&A. I sat back and patiently listened to various apple-cheeked recent college grads gush about what an honor it was to ask Jeff himself about our projected P/E ratio for next year. Jeff was certainly a wizard with numbers, and perhaps an even more talented alchemist with words, as he eruditely explained to the junior Enronites how the company was heading into the stratosphere.

Then came my turn.

"Jeff," raising my voice to be heard, "I'm currently working on a project that clearly indicates that HPL is accepting elevated levels of CO^2 into its system. Now obviously CO^2 is corrosive and will ultimately damage the asset...."

Before I could finish, Jeff was trying to dismiss my question.

"Well, Enron has state-of-the-art pipeline safety controls in place, which are guaranteed to prevent any problems."

Although I had agreed to remain quiet about the bank fraud – not this time I thought. And if Enron's senior management was really insulated from the truth (i.e. *clueless*) I was going to make certain they knew the truth this time.

As he looked to field another question, I continued.

"I know, but I'm concerned that the value of the asset could be diminished by as much as 50%, and I'm more concerned about the safety of the people who live near the pipeline. I've talked to gas engineers who tell me unchecked CO^2 can degrade the structure of the pipe over a short time, a few years even."

Suddenly I regretted my earlier shot at him about Steve Naeve. I saw a flash of anger that he quickly got under control and knew I had just provoked the second most powerful man at Enron.

"As I said," he said slowly and patronizingly, "and I am sure you know, Enron has numerous safety checks and backups and backups on the backups. We also run pigs [large, barrel-sized devices that traverse a pipeline from the inside; used to monitor the state of the pipe and make necessary repairs] which regularly check internally for any issues. Likewise, helicopters fly low over the pipeline, crossing the entire length to spot any possible exterior problems. You really don't need to concern yourself with it. Who's next?" he said, dismissing me.

"But," I started.

"But nothing, HPL is for sale." He blurted out.

His comment struck me as odd since I didn't think it was common knowledge, but it was obvious he had spoken before he thought out his response. This behavior in the end would ultimately the key to Jeff's undoing at Enron.

Once again, my efforts to blow the whistle had fallen on the deaf ears of an all too arrogant senior executive.

Pursuing the issue any further would have assuredly resulted in what was referred to at Enron as a CLM (Career Limiting Move), and with upcoming performance reviews, the only thing that was likely to rupture at this time would be my career at Enron. At least I had one answer for sure: Jeff Skilling knew what was going on, no question about it. Now my worst fears were confirmed – Enron was everything I had hoped it wasn't. And worse yet, senior management not only knew about the questionable deals, but was arrogant enough to believe if they just "sold" us their story, we would buy it.

The more I got involved in the trading and storage of gas, the more irregularities I saw. While researching the Bammel deal, I had spent time studying the Texas Railroad Commission's Code of Conduct and realized Enron had a problem. As a result of deregulation, pipelines were open for transmission of natural gas to all wholesale customers. The Code of Conduct of the Texas Railroad Commission, the regulatory body for natural gas pipelines in the state of Texas, firmly stipulated there was to be a separation of personnel between those trading natural gas and those shipping, to guarantee fair competition. This was meant to ensure that everyone would be given the same right to capacity, pricing and scheduling.

Every single person involved in the gas trading on the pipelines was well aware of the Code of Conduct, and the requirement they be separated. However, none of them felt the need to stand up when the personnel were regularly commingled, in direct violation of the policy. I mentioned this to Patsy Donald*, a specialist in setting up pipeline facilities or wellheads to ensure they were interconnected to Enron's natural gas pipelines.

"I've noticed we mix personnel, people from trading and transportation. That's a violation of the Code, isn't it?"

"Of course it is. Everyone knows Enron's violating the Code of Conduct, but what can I do about it? I'm not high enough on the food chain to say anything." Then she fixed me with a look that underlined her next words. "And neither are you."

With the dreaded performance reviews looming, I stepped up my efforts to implement the orders given me by Kathy Simpson and Lance Schultz to get rid of Ronnie and Sherlynn. While I didn't relish the role of executioner, I truly felt Ronnie and Sherlynn were excellent candidates for dismissal. I had seen hard workers and goof-offs and they certainly fell into the latter category. Sherlynn, who had not spoken more than a few sentences to me during the first three months as her supervisor, suddenly wanted to take me to lunch. I saw through it as a way of determining her ranking in the upcoming gladiator match. I wanted to say "you should have thought about that a long time ago," but attempting to be a good boss, I actually gave her some constructive criticism to cushion the blow of what was coming.

Kathy took me aside as I prepared my reviews.

"Ronnie? I want him gone. Get rid of that little shit."

I went back to my desk and continued assembling my case against Ronnie and Sherlynn.

"Get rid of people. They gum up the works", quoth Jeff Skilling. That summed up the Performance Review Committee (PRC), otherwise known by its gallows appellation, "Rank and Yank". It was common knowledge that Jeff loved slicing fat from the flanks of Enron and, aside from assets, his next least favorite form of corporate pork was people. Like assets, he viewed people as a necessary evil, which fostered the brutality of the PRC.

Having started the practice in the trading group about six years before I got to Enron, the PRC process was eventually adopted company-wide. Many large companies use a structured review format, encouraging improvement while limiting an environment that might breed complacency. I had seen other such processes, but as I became familiar with Enron's I was surprised by its complexities. More so, I was concerned by its potential for unfairness, and at its worst, absolute corruption.

The creation of the performance assessments allegedly used the following parameters: Customer Relations; Technical Skills; Analysis/Problem Solving; Exemplifies Enron Values; Teamwork; Leadership and Building Business Solutions. Once the assessments were complete and evaluated, one of five ratings was assigned to each employee. At the apex, the best 5% were judged "superior", followed by the next 30% called "excellent", the next 30% labeled "strong", and the 20% faintly damned as "satisfactory".

Finally, the death-row of Enron rankings, the bottom 15% of unfortunates, were split into two categories, one bad, the other worse. The penultimate 10% were branded "needs improvement". This was the "on-deck" circle for those losers about to be dismissed. If you had "issues" you could consider yourself toast. This last ranking automatically numbered your days at Enron, unless you were lucky enough to throw yourself in front of a speeding car to save Ken Lay. On the day your second such "issues" review was rendered, you might as well leave your stuff and flee the building or throw yourself under Ken Lay's car to avoid any further humiliation.

I found it unfair that the company created this bell curve and adhered to it against any humanitarian concerns or acknowledgment of reality. It assumed that only five percent of the employees were superior and that 15% were always verging on failure. There was a cruelty to it but, in the eyes of the company, a cold-hearted logic: keep people off balance.

If you're in the top five percent you want to stay there. In the upper middle of the pack you want to become "superior". Nearer the bottom you want to avoid "needs improvement" and certainly, "issues". And if you're down in that dark, lonely cellar you're going to be terrified and a terrified employee isn't such a bad thing to have. Management takes comfort in knowing the power they hold over their people and revel in the concept that 15% of their staff always has a gun to their heads. Sure, there'll be some attrition – you just know that a certain number of weak sisters will crack and throw in the towel – but most will do *anything* to keep their jobs. Another organization that has found that system supremely motivating is the Mafia.

To begin the process, which took nearly three months, each employee would submit a list of "customer" names, that is, people within or outside the company who could attest to the quality of their work product. Oddly, people could even write self-reviews if they felt they didn't have enough ammo. Even quirkier, if you were of a mind, you could submit an unsolicited review of anyone else in the company; sort of a corporate version of scratching an obscenity about someone on the bathroom wall.

Then, once all the performance reviews were in and the votes were cast, the bosses would hole up in a nearby hotel and the bloodbath would begin. Jammed into sweaty rooms, seated around tables covered in empty coffee cups, stacks of note pads and reams of documentation, one by one, a Human Resources lackey would pull out an employee's file and the manager's comments would fly. The managers would be given a synopsized formal review, an amalgamation of each employee's stack of reviews. Allegedly the evaluations were based upon one's adherence to Enron's high principles, but in practice the survivors and thrivers were those who made the "highest dollar allocation", in other words, profit. The ranking element of the process was called an "auction" and your boss was there to supposedly "bid" for you or stand up on your behalf. A particularly hot employee might be fought over. Slackers and those deemed unpopular were slammed by bad rankings. This step in the process made some sense, but then came the big wrench in the works: Enron's insidious bell curve. While the average age of an Enron employee was 31, the average tenure was 3½ years and turnover from promotions was 20%. Just to stay ahead of the curve the average employee plowed through three or four positions in as little as two years.

This system also pressured managers to fit their people into the impersonal and relentless "preferred distribution" bell curve. With little or no room for exceptions, they now had to conform their findings to fit the percentages of the ranking tiers. If they had too many "superiors" somebody would lose. That meant a diligent worker who might have deserved that all holy "superior" would now to be relegated to "excellent", or worse, a notch below to a mere "strong". Deadlier still, if you were skipping along, enjoying life as a "satisfactory", they might thrust you onto death's doorstep with the feared "needs improvement". Suffice it to say any ranking that plummeted you one lower than your previous assessment gave many people a reason to start a course of antidepressants or switch from beer to bourbon. A reduction in your ranking status would affect your salary, your self-esteem, your standing among your peers and, worst of all, your bonus. Once wounded with an "issues" ranking, like a stricken animal in a herd, other employees would begin to shun you as you might draw the lions. And at Enron no one wanted to be eaten.

Interestingly enough, whistleblowing reports to the Office of the Chairman via Enron's internal hotline, in the months of April and May, concurrent with Enron's semi-annual performance reviews, dropped dramatically. The reports then rose again simultaneously after the completion of reviews in June and December. Employees, who feared retribution at review time, would remain silent until the completion of the review process.

I knew Kathy had re-written reviews to reflect inferior performances for employees who hadn't smooched her fat ass. More likely, negative reviews cropped up when the managers, under pressure to fit the curve, would light into people like sharks did in bloody, chum-rich water. If it was late in the day, they needed to meet their quotas, and if you were unlucky enough to have your file surface, people who didn't even know you would trash you with fervor. But if you made enough money? *Oh yeah, this guy killed his family, knifed his minister, and made threats against the President, but he made a fortune last quarter. Superior? Done.*

Another problem cropped up with the give-and-take of the system. Managers who didn't wield enough power often got their good people thrown under the bus as stronger managers lobbied for and got better evaluations for their prized pupils. Given there were strict quotas, there were only a certain amount of superiors and excellents to go around. Employees not only had to worry about watching their own asses, but working for a weak manager at review time could also cost you.

As the PRC drew near I had a run-in that showed me how vulnerable you could be without friends in high places. One afternoon I received 65 contracts from the Coal Group with a note from the manager of the group that they needed them completely reviewed and analyzed before I went home. I was stunned. Whenever I got contracts to review and analyze, I was always given a reasonable amount of time to turn them around. Kathy Simpson was on a short vacation so I had no one to complain to.

Having no choice, I kicked into overdrive. When I had finished the last of the 65 contracts, I looked up, exhausted, and saw it was a little after 2:30 a.m. I put everything in order, put the contracts near the manager's desk and left him a voicemail. My message to him was simple and by no means rude or disrespectful. In it, I described where he could find the completed contracts and asked, that in the future, if he had that many contracts "I'd really appreciate either extra notice or dole them out to me piece-meal. Thanks."

Despite having worked so late I was still on time the next morning. I went to the manager's desk on the trading floor to find out whether he was satisfied with the results of the project. As I approached him I expected gratitude on his face. What I got was rage. He pointed to a nearby empty conference room.

"Can I see you in here?" he commanded and stomped toward the room. I followed, sick to my stomach that I had somehow done something terribly wrong with the contracts.

We entered the room and he slammed the door. I was badly shaken.

"What the hell do you think you're doing leaving me a message like you did last night? How dare you?" he screamed.

I didn't know what to say. In a split second I recalled my message to him and could think of nothing remotely provocative. "I, uh, I..." I stammered.

He leaned in so close I could feel the heat of his breath on my face. His eyes and mouth were twisted into a mask of fury.

"Do you realize it is review time and this could have a serious impact on the results of your review? Think about it, you goddamn idiot!"

With that he rushed out of the room, leaving me breathless, like I'd just taken a foot to the ribs. I staggered back to my desk trying to make sense of what had just happened and could only conclude that I had just witnessed someone going postal. I had no other explanation. I sat for about ten minutes, trying to gather my thoughts. Was he going to try and get me fired? I could only assume, given how angry he was, that it was possible. Maybe very possible. I went over to Jennifer's desk and sat down. She could tell I was a basket case.

"Oh my God, what's wrong?"

"I don't know. I just got my ass chewed out and I have no idea why. I'm worried I'm gonna get fired."

I told her the story and she picked up her phone. "I'm calling Rebecca. Let's get Jeff in on this."

I stopped her. "Do you honestly think he'd be interested in helping me?"

Jennifer had been sitting next to me at the luncheon the week before. She was surprised and excited that I had confronted Jeff about the corrosive pipeline gas. She laughed. "Yeah, I see your point. I think you'll need to give Jeff time to cool off before you ask any favors."

Yeah, like when Hell freezes over.

We considered the problem for a moment. "Do you have anyone else you can go to?"

"Maggie Francis*, I guess. She's the head of Systems," I answered. Jennifer nodded. "Good. She's the one to help you. She's connected."

On my way to Maggie's office I wondered if Jennifer was right about Maggie Francis. I had met her soon after coming to Enron, and we had struck up a warmer-than-average office friendship. Maggie was a sweetheart and was very patient with all my questions during my first few rookie weeks, but she never struck me as having any clout. As the head of information technology, Maggie's group was responsible for building the integrated systems for Enron's premier trading and settlements system. I sat at her desk for a few minutes and poured my heart out, describing the alarming scene with the head of the Coal group. Maggie listened intently and made some notes. Then she told me she was going to make some calls and to go wait at my desk. I thanked her and left.

That afternoon I received a call from Kathy Simpson's boss, Andrea Converse*, who inquired in detail about the events of the last 24 hours. I recited the events leading up to the nightmare, but her comments were mostly non-committal uh-huhs and hmmms. Before I even finished my story I was performing a mental inventory of how much stuff I needed to pack up should the conversation take an ugly turn and she ask for my resignation. To my surprise it was just the opposite. Andrea was apologetic.

"Lynn, I am so sorry he behaved that way. It's absolutely unacceptable. Don't let him scare you. As a matter of fact, I wonder how he'll like going up against a Managing Director come review time."

And with that she hung up. It was probably a good thing Kathy was on vacation, because she happened to be very close to the caveman who had gone ballistic on me. Fortunately for me, my good friend Maggie Francis knew just which button to push.

During all this I got news that my former mother-in-law, Margaret "Margie" Swenson*, Wayne's mother, had been diagnosed with cancer and was very ill. Although it had not worked out with

Wayne, we still spoke from time to time and I still loved Margie like a mother. I made some hasty travel arrangements and flew up to Springfield, Oregon to visit her. I'm glad I went. My first glimpse of her told me she had a matter of months at best. I spent a weekend visiting and went back to Houston, with the promise I would fly out every several weeks to check up on her.

As the agonizingly long review process began, I submitted the negative reviews of my do-nothing subordinates, Ronnie, the bitter man-child, and Sherlynn, the sullen alcoholic. Before I completed my assessments I did a little soul-searching and asked myself, had I not been given the directive by my bosses to give Ronnie and Sherlynn an "issues" ranking, would I have done so? My answer was, absolutely, *yes*. From the moment I met them and concluded they were merely occupying desk space to pull down a check and added little to the company, they did nothing to dissuade me of the opinion. Ronnie continued to cultivate his Beanie Baby collection, arrange photos of his prized pooches on his desk, and act, even when people were looking, like he was doing nothing to earn his keep. Sherlynn never cut back on her endless personal phone calls, despite knowing I had been assigned to keep an eye on her. They both showed such arrogance and contempt for the system. I happily pummeled them in my evaluation.

The only thing that concerned me was I had also heard rumors that Kathy Simpson had a reputation akin to the "the hangin' judge". She had supposedly eliminated some abnormal number of her staff over the year prior to my joining the group. I also found that Enron's personnel turnover was extraordinarily high by any standard. Enron's massive attrition stemmed from the bi-yearly slaughter of rank and yank and the withering pressure to make money, all cultivated by the underlying mean-spiritedness of Enron's true corporate philosophy.

As I entered my fourth month with the company most of my illusions about Enron's high-mindedness had faded, to be replaced by a far more accurate view – I was working for a company that treasured money above all else. If that sounds naive, allow me to defend myself. I had worked for some huge companies, but I had never been witness to such rampant cynicism and cut-throat attitudes as those bred within Enron. I felt like Pinocchio coming of age in the big, mean city.

To be fair to Ronnie and Sherlynn I had mentioned to them on more than a few occasions my concerns over what I felt their weaknesses would be come review time. Both acknowledged my comments, Sherlynn being more conciliatory than Ronnie, but it was literally in one ear and out the other for both. Since Sherlynn feigned more concern over the way she was perceived, I cut her a little more slack than Ronnie, who acted downright antagonistic toward me when I offered him any criticism. Consequently, I began to ride him a bit more, like trying to break a wild horse. But the more I pushed, the harder he dug in and fired back. It became an unofficial feud between us. I realized Ronnie was a very emotional person and, despite being 30 years of age, he exhibited all the maturity of a spoiled teen. To constantly argue with someone who literally held your fate in their hands was risky at best and suicidal at worst. I'm not a vengeful person, but I began to dislike Ronnie's childish stubbornness more and more. He refused to make any attempt to conform in an environment where conformity equated to keeping one's job. Had it been the television reality show *Survivor,* Ronnie was pissing off the one person deciding whether or not to vote him off the island.

At Kathy's suggestion, I put into operation a plan to step up Ronnie's harassment. Every week he would go through a mini-review of his actions, a sort of confessional, from his comings and goings to his accomplishments during that week. Every Friday, Ronnie was required to place on my desk before quitting time a status report on what he'd been doing. For the first few weeks of this new program Kathy hammered home the point she wanted me to nitpick everything Ronnie did. I hated being made the hall monitor, but Ronnie's lousy attitude and miserable work habits left me no choice.

One morning, Ronnie was late for work by about half an hour and I mentioned it in my report to Kathy. Ronnie was incensed and hotly denied being late. On arrival at work we would all log onto our computers so I checked his log-in time for that day. It clearly showed he was late. Again he denied it. Now it was my word against his so I decided to prove beyond any doubt he had entered the building late.

Enron's security was billed as the highest in corporate America. Every employee was issued a card that electronically identified them when they entered the building and limited access to certain floors. Visitors were given ID cards and if an employee forgot their card they showed their driver's license and were assigned a temporary card for that day's use. Ronnie began claiming I had rigged his log-in time on the computer system to show he was late and I knew I had to scotch this situation or he might turn the tables and leave me in trouble. I contacted the security department to determine exactly what time Ronnie had passed through the security gate with his pass card.

The Enron building had four points of entry into the lobby. To enter from the street, you came in one of two revolving doors, either at one end or in the middle of the building. Then there was an escalator to the parking garage, and another escalator connecting to the labyrinth of tunnels connecting various buildings in downtown Houston. Once inside, to get to the elevator banks, you would pass between columns containing security scanners that would automatically read your badge. You would then be logged into the building.

One step in the procedure, unforeseen as a potential glitch when the system was purchased and installed, was that the scanner took several seconds to reset after each scan in order to read the next person's card. But regardless of the trivial details as to how security performed the actual scans, management had been sold on the state-of-the-art security that allowed them to know exactly who was in their building at any given time.

However, because Enron had grown so quickly, at the beginning and end of the day people jammed through the scanners like cattle to a slaughterhouse. The driven, impatient Enronites were loathe to suffer the wasted seconds as the sluggish electronic readers reset after each entry. So they poured like water through the security stalls, giving the underpaid rent-a-cops fits. With sometimes less than half the badges actually being scanned, the expensive tracking system was haphazard at best.

After three days of having security search their records, sending me a database of absolutely everyone's time entry, we could find no record of Ronnie's entrance into the building on the date in question. I couldn't help but think they can track whether I eat a hamburger or salad in the cafeteria – why can't they track a human being entering the damn building. I realized that Ronnie, being a practiced slacker, and knowing he was under scrutiny, had probably figured out that whenever he was late he could simply herd in with a few people as they crammed past the scanner. If anyone questioned his lateness he would challenge them to "prove it".

After spending far too much time trying to bust Ronnie, and realizing the cloak and dagger description of how I believed he evaded security would only make me look ridiculous, I just dropped it. I had been assigned the task of getting rid of someone, but unlike doing due diligence or vetting a contract, this was emotionally draining. I was glad the PRC was nearly over and, with it, my charge to get rid of Ronnie and Sherlynn.

Once the PRC's findings were made public and the dust settled, I was pleased I had managed to come through my first performance review unscathed. According to Enron, I was "strong". I felt my efforts to rid the group of deadwood would not go unrecognized. They didn't, but by no means in the way I'd expected. The events leading up to the PRC drew me into a web of intrigue and backstabbing I could never have imagined. I was about to deal with forces that had been set in motion long before I came to Enron.

Despite leading the charge to bump Ronnie and Sherlynn out the door, to my dismay they were both still employed after the cuts were made. Kathy and Lance had as much as guaranteed they would be gone, so all I had accomplished was deeply alienating two subordinates. I had also stirred up a hornet's nest. A few days after reviews, Kathy took me aside and dropped her bomb.

"I've heard you're being awfully hard on Ronnie," she said.

I blinked several times as if my ears were playing tricks on me. "What? Too hard? Did I misunderstand you? Didn't you say you wanted him gone?"

Kathy held up her hand. "Yes. Except now he's making waves in Human Resources. He's complaining about your harassment."

"*My* harassment?"

"Uh huh. But don't worry, HR will always side with management. The only thing is, we have to sort of pull back for the time being."

I walked back to my desk like a zombie from *Night of the Living Dead*. Kathy's scheme to get rid of my two subordinates had failed and I was left holding the bag. I now had two enemies sitting next to me and a boss who had turned her back on me.

From that point forward, things began to change in my group. Now Kathy expanded her psychological assault to include me. I didn't understand her about-face and sought out Jennifer's advice. A streetwise tactician, I hoped Jennifer had been with the company long enough to provide some answers. Unfortunately, she had.

"Kathy has a horrible track record with HR," she began, meeting me for drinks after work one night.

"I knew she had some problems with her staff. That I knew," I said.

"What you probably didn't know was how bad they were. She's managed to keep that quiet. The truth is she's had so many run-ins with HR about how she treats her underlings she's been warned a bunch of times to keep her staff together. She must be on thin ice because I've heard HR is scared she's going to piss off the wrong person and create some major legal problems. *Expensive* legal problems. My guess is she used you to help her get rid of Ronnie and Sherlynn so she wouldn't have to get her hands dirty."

As it dawned on me my stomach churned. "And it backfired," I observed. "They're still around and they're blaming me."

"Yeah," agreed Jennifer, "and Kathy doesn't show up on HR's radar."

I cringed. "But I do."

Jennifer shrugged acknowledgment. "Right. And since you're below her you can't afford too many other problems. You've got to watch out from now on."

Jennifer went on to explain that despite Kathy's flawed record and one of the highest turnover rates in the company, she had received regular – and sizable – bonuses. It flew in the face of logic that such chaos would be tolerated, let alone praised, but the results were clear: Kathy was hell on wheels and was well rewarded for her efforts. Her antics would only be seen as a liability when a fat lawsuit outweighed her contributions.

I did some subtle investigating and found that Jennifer's claims were true. Kathy did have a stack of Human Resources complaints against her. Sasha Rice* was an African-American contractor in the group who was studying for her MBA. She apparently didn't kowtow to Kathy's liking, because when Sasha asked Kathy for a little time off to recover from a car accident, Kathy refused. They got into an argument, she was fired and Sasha was currently threatening a lawsuit. Rita Smith* had gotten a severe case of carpal tunnel syndrome and filed a worker's compensation claim. She managed to draw disability only after a vicious fight with Kathy that had to be mediated by Human Resources. I heard that Rita might also be considering a suit.

Just as Kathy was turning up the heat on me, I was also concerned that my attempts to uncover the Bammel scam and the malfeasance with the gas contracts had put me in a different company spotlight. I also wondered how much I'd irritated Jeff Skilling during that luncheon and, if I had, how vindictive was he? I was praying this was all in my mind and I was in no one's crosshairs but Kathy's.

I could feel Kathy growing increasingly frustrated with my attention to detail and desire to offer the most competent risk management analysis I could muster. I had been asked to assess risks and report on them, but more and more I saw that the company didn't really want to know the risks of many of its ventures. Even more troubling was that Enron seemed to be seeking "no win" deals that looked good only at first blush. Due diligence would unravel them, but they made them anyway. I was like a nurse in some horribly corrupt hospital told to keep the monitoring equipment beeping reassuringly even though most of the patients were deceased.

I mentioned my frustrations to Jennifer and she looked at me like I was ten years old.

"Lynn," she laughed, "you've been here long enough. Don't you know that Enron's Vision is 'get the deal done, whatever it takes' and the Values are 'you're only as good as your last deal?'"

A few weeks after the PRC, when I was feeling completely defeated, Kathy called me to her desk. She handed me a sheet of paper. I was shocked to see it was a written warning for my "excessive time" spent on the gas contracts. I was getting slapped on the wrist for doing my job. She fished around on her desk and grabbed another item.

"Because of the PRC, you got this," she said flatly as she handed me another piece of paper. I took it reluctantly, afraid being spared during rank and yank had been an illusion. I looked at the paper fearing it was the addendum to my warning – my pink slip.

I was doubly stunned to see it was a PBA or Personal Best Award for my work on the same gas contracts I had just been warned about. Paper-clipped to it was a check for $500, part of that low-hanging fruit Kathy had promised. Although it only amounted to a single grapefruit and not an entire bunch of bananas, I returned to my desk in a daze, happily holding my ration of fruit. Now it was clear that Enron's left hand didn't know what its right hand was doing, didn't care, or worse, was afraid to know. I had exposed massive fraud within the company, blown the whistle, watched the corruption swept under the rug, received a warning for going too far, then was awarded five-hundred bucks for my efforts. Now I understood that much of what I was attributing to some form of concerted evil within the company had a simpler, less malevolent reason: stupidity.

A few days later, Kathy once again summoned me. When I sat down she handed me a sheet of paper, which appeared to be a schedule for some sort of group therapy session put on by an organization called the American Management Association.

"What's this?" I asked.

"Conflict Resolution," she answered. "Your inability to deal with your hostility toward Ronnie has forced us to sign you up for this."

I was dumbstruck.

"Also," Kathy continued, "you'll be attending a class on sensitivity training. HR figured you could benefit from that, too."

I just stared at her. If I said anything, she would either deny it or call me crazy. The latter would probably be right, since I had believed her in the first place. First, she set me up to take the fall for the botched dismissal of Ronnie and Sherlynn, and now I was being labeled emotionally unstable. The next week I began my series of classes in resolving conflict and "eagerly" looked forward to my one-day seminar on becoming a more sensitive person.

I was on a plane from St. Louis to Houston, returning from sensitivity training, when the man sitting next to me looked over. He appeared to be Indian.

"Who do you work for?"

"Enron."

"Really? Interesting."

"You've heard of the company?"

"Oh yes. I am well connected to the leaders in Nepal and they have been interested in having Enron build a power plant. The problem is they cannot, for political reasons, approach Enron. However, if Enron were to approach the leaders, perhaps through an introduction by myself, they could put a bid in for such a plant."

"Well, then you know that we're building one in India?"

I wanted to feel him out about Enron's ongoing disaster in India (see Chapter 6 for more details).

"Yes, but Nepal is very different. The leaders are interested in using the waters from the Himalayas to generate power. Do you know who I would need to talk with at Enron regarding such a venture?"

"Not really. I'm in the deal compliance division of risk management. But I would be happy to ask Jeff Skilling and let you know. How about if you give me your card and I will e-mail you with the contact?"

He felt around his pockets and came up empty.

"Oh, I'm sorry, I don't have any cards on me, but if you give me one of yours, I will call you and you can give me the name of the individual."

I gave him one of my cards and agreed to make an inquiry with Jeff upon my return to the office. As promised, on Monday morning I sent Jeff an e-mail detailing the meeting and inquiring if Enron would be interested in pursuing the development of a power plant in Nepal. In the back of my mind was the possibility that I would be recognized for bringing a potentially huge asset development opportunity to Enron. Apparently, the point that Jeff hated assets had not hit home hard enough for me. I was expecting a reward while Jeff Skilling probably had asset pushers like me thrown into a secret dungeon in Enron's basement.

Shortly after sending the e-mail, the telephone rang.

"Lynn? Hi, this is Sherri Sera, Jeff Skilling's assistant. The e-mail you sent to Jeff was encrypted. Could you resend it to me?"

I was momentarily confused but thought, perhaps for security reasons, e-mails sent to the Office of the Chairman must be automatically encrypted to avoid hackers.

"Oh, I'm sorry," I responded, "Do you want me to un-encrypt it and send it to Jeff again?"

"No, just send it to me. Jeff doesn't use a computer." I was stunned. I thought I had misheard her. "What?" Then, before she could answer I made another assumption. "I'm sorry, so you mean his is being fixed?"

"No, I receive and print all of Jeff's e-mails. Jeff does not have a computer."

I hung up the phone in absolute astonishment. The President and COO of the largest energy trader in the world not only didn't use a computer, he didn't even have one. I thought back to the time I had been on the executive floors. Rebecca Carter definitely had a computer. Andy Fastow certainly had a computer. Ken Lay at least had a computer screen hooked to a terminal. And so did Ken Rice. The traders used computers. Perhaps with Skilling it was a riff on the old corporate axiom that the fancier the briefcase the higher your place on the totem pole, that is until you got to the top and didn't need a briefcase at all. I guess Jeff didn't really need a computer.

Whether Jeff had an aversion to technology, thought the Internet a passing fad, or just had a bad experience with early versions of Windows, I do not know. I do know that he adamantly objected to the development of Enron's online presence. At the direction of Kathy Simpson, Enron had spent over four years, drawn upon untold numbers of Andersen consultants, and spent God knows how many millions to develop an integrated trading system called Sitara. Now Sitara was more than two years behind schedule and completely unreliable.

Meanwhile, unbeknownst to Skilling or the Sitara folks, Louise Kitchen had assembled a team in England and worked with stealth-like secrecy to create an online trading system. Gathering 380 code writers, program designers, and people like me, she got her hands on somewhere between $30 and $40 million of secret funds to complete her "black ops" program. A mere one week before it was ready for launch for beta testing, Jeff was finally told of its existence – 90 days before it was launched.

Despite being blindsided with it, he once again turned to Andy Fastow to pull a rabbit out of his proverbial hat to find the dollars necessary to start an entire business unit in 90 days. EnronOnline was a free, Internet-based, global transaction system, which allowed a number of conveniences for Enron's customers. The primary function was the ability to view real-time prices from Enron's traders and transact trades instantly online.

Prior to EOL, which would quickly become the largest e-commerce site, trades were made utilizing the telephone in one-to-one relationships. Now traders could utilize the power of the Internet to gain access to a variety of commodities simultaneously. At its inception, EOL traded 14 commodities globally in 15 different currencies, offering over 2,100 different products. It was free of charge, easy to use, accessible via the Internet, faster than the traditional channels, and offered real-time pricing information. And more importantly, it was a closed system, providing us a clear view of our opponent's hand in a high-stakes game of liar's poker.

On May 23, 2001, Enron would announce it had completed its millionth transaction via EOL. Unfortunately, like most everything else, the real truth was hidden below the bottom line. While it was true that 60% of Enron's transactions were being done on EnronOnline – 77% of all trades on the electronic trading platform were completed by just one division. Certainly this should have given investors some indication that Enron was less an energy company than a speculative trading firm.

By October, 2001, a little over a month before Enron's implosion, the company had transacted more than 1,600,000 deals with an average in excess of 6,000 transactions a day.

Although the numbers were impressive, it only bolstered Enron's narcissism. While it created the illusion of innovation Enron had hoped for, it may have hastened the company's demise. Along with "real-time" electronic trades came the real-time demand for cash to settle all of these millions of trades. The more Enron promoted EOL, the more energy Enron bought, the more the company had to pay out; hence, the more it had to promote EOL to transact more sales to settle against the purchases. This self-defeating cycle kept Enron's motor running until it literally ran out of gas.

Interestingly enough, despite having "bet the farm" on the future of broadband trading, as of May 11, 2001, two years after EOL announced it was open for broadband business in May, 1999, EBS had performed exactly 0 trades on EOL. Although EBS announced that its first trade was performed on December 2, 1999, and again announced on April 23, 2001, that "Accelerated provisioning of circuits can be arranged through Enron's internet-based platform, www.EnronOnline.com", no one was buying.

Certainly, Enron's promotion of EOL seemed to pronounce Enron's fatal flaws. The combination of Jeff Skilling's blatant overstatements, Ken Lay's insistent denial, stating "[Broadband] could end up being our biggest and fastest-growing business of all," and the natural "spin" of EBS' marketing head, Tom Gros, stating EBS has made "a number of trades", only perpetuated the speed with which Enron would ultimately implode.

While Enron would attempt to convince its investors that through the innovation of EOL, it had somehow gone from a stodgy utility to a reinvented energy risk management company, it was dangerously seductive for the traders. EOL was like giving a Formula One race car to a 16-year old boy expecting him to drive safely. Enron's Risk Assessment and Control Department (RAC) reported – the first six months of 2000, the traders committed 64 "limit violations . . . where no tangible action was taken to adjust commercial personnel views regarding the importance of a risk management framework and risk control environment." In just three days alone between August 29, 2000 and September 1, 2000, Enron's traders exceeded the trading limits set on the risk they could expose the company to by more than $241,037,000 which was reported to the Board of Directors. To put it blatantly, Enron traders were constantly receiving "warnings" for driving under the influence, and yet no one was issuing tickets, taking their licenses away, much less taking the sauce away from them.

Enron wanted everyone to believe that this allowed all customers the same access to Enron's best prices. They also wanted to give the impression that it dramatically streamlined the commodities trading by removing inefficiencies in the marketplace through simplification of the transaction process. The truth was, while it did speed up the process, it also gave Enron a special edge that no one but Enron realized right away – the knowledge of business transacted by its competitors.

By providing pricing information and market data via EOL, Enron appeared to generously offer a useful service to its customers and competition. The real motivation for EOL was that Enron could now more readily see the long and short positions of their competitors. In addition, those outside Enron seeking to emulate the energy giant would assume that if the published prices on EOL were going up, traders at Enron must know something they didn't. This little bit of synergy helped Enron create self-induced volatility from fear and Jeff Skilling understood better than anyone that volatility and fear meant profits.

In 1996, at the behest of companies like Enron, the Financial Accounting Standards Board (FASB) implemented a form of accounting known as mark-to-market or MTM. This allowed Enron to account for and book revenues for the entire value of a contract over the length of that contract at a given point in time, and presumably determine the ongoing value at any future point to evaluate its current risk. It accomplished that by taking into account future pricing, including the anticipated volatility over the term of the contract.

By definition, volatility is the relative rate at which the price of the energy commodity moves up and down. The volatility is found by calculating the annualized standard deviation of the daily change in price. What they were doing was making deals that were based upon long-term outlooks. Some volatility was accounted for but it was within reasonable limits. The gas business had traditional but measured increases, so such accounting made some sense. But when Enron later got into trading power, all Hell broke loose. Such accounting made for very high risk components of Enron's balance sheet.

Enron's downfall would be the exploitation of the very accounting method they had fought for. As revenues were immediately booked, the traders were instantaneously paid huge bonuses – yet no cash to pay the bonuses had actually come in the door. Enron ultimately became as addicted to the illusionary form of generating revenue as the traders were to the real and immediate cash bonuses. Like a heroin dealer and a junkie needing a fix – the traders and the company supported each other's habit.

The mark-to-market accounting was not much different from futures trading on the commodities market. If the market moved the wrong way just a little, not only could you suffer a loss, but unlike stock, you could lose far more than you risked. It was part of the grab and run, scorched-earth mentality at Enron. It was as if Skilling and Fastow knew the volcano would blow and their trick was to stay in its shadow as long as possible while raking in their fortunes.

When Skilling joined Enron, he developed the company's non-regulated merchant/trading business with ECT, in what was dubbed the Gas Bank. There he directed the buying and selling of long-term gas contracts and created the now-famous Risk Books. The Risk Books included the Index Book, which measured exposure to physical delivery at different locations; the Transport Book, which measured pipeline capacities for delivery; the Omnicrom Book, which measured exposure to quantity options; the Basis Book, which measured exposure to gas prices differing across locations; and the Gas Price Book, which measured exposure to gas price changes.

While Enron's stock had risen for six consecutive years, 1997 saw the stock begin to sag, requiring some drastic efforts. Skilling and Fastow instituted a more aggressive use of mark-to-market accounting and, perhaps more importantly, the creation of more than 1,217 trading "books", which they treated like the contents of the Ark of the Covenant. The trading books told the real story of Enron's bottom line. Andy Fastow made it clear to everyone involved, "We don't want anyone to know what's on those books. We don't want to tell anyone where we're making money." Perhaps more accurately, he should have said "We don't want anyone to know we're not making money."

The value Enron placed on the contracts was based upon a reasonable guess called the "forward-curve". The longer the term of the contract, the better the value for Enron (and of course its traders), assuming they could justify the valuation of the forward-curve. The greater the volatility, the greater the potential value, which meant the greater the reported profits. However, when the projected value met reality and prices were less than Enron paid, Enron would then be required to restate the value of the contract over the entire term of the contract to reflect the true value and thus the real risk at that point in time. This scenario would usually result in a loss, because they had inflated the value in the Risk Books.

And Enron was practiced at handling losses. One way of dealing with it would be to take it as a short-term loss. An even less desirable option was transferring the loss to a profitable division. Then there was their "creative" method, sending the loss to an offshore partnership or off-the-balance sheet partnership, like shuffling off a problem child to boarding school. The other way to deal with loss was their best yet, creating price spikes, which would allow Enron to recognize significant gains and justify its forward valuations over the term of the contract. A Vegas whale showed more restraint at wagering than the corporate scions of Ken Lay. This type of hatchet juggling could certainly make big money but it could also, with little warning, spell disaster.

Enron continued to create "new emerging markets" so as to stay one step ahead of those pesky analysts who might challenge Enron's self-proclaimed price-curves. Soon they would be trading water on Planet Mars. And of course, lacking any proof from an actual Martian, who were you to question Enron's pricing. It was innovative alright but hell, water from Mars has never been traded so we will just have to sell them on our story I could hear Skilling's haunting voice say. And, of course, every other company would be green with envy, falling all over themselves to tap into the Martian water market, failing to see the illusion.

Until EOL, Enron could only give a best guess as to the projection of future prices. With Kathy's useless Sitara system, the only other option was the Psychic Friend's Network. Now, by knowing what other players in the market were bidding, Enron could make significant gains. I am by no means an accountant, but while Enron was telling the outside world one story, I was finding a very different story going on inside.

While developing the pricing indices for EnronOnline, Scott Masterson*, a database administrator and designer, asked me to get involved in creating a rates database for EOL. Once completed, no one could ever again say they were clueless when it came to costs. I saw this as an essential part of the maturation process of an already massive corporation. For the first time, Enron would actually know what it took to procure the lemons, squeeze them and what each plastic cup cost.

Scott and I knew, given the vast number of commodities Enron sought to trade, that the development of a single rates database was likely to be a daunting task. What we found far more surprising than the number of commodities Enron traded was that there was absolutely no standardization for the prices they used. While some of the price sources came from published indexes like *Inside FERC* [Federal Energy Regulatory Commission] or *Gas Daily*, ultimately what we found is that the prices established were often simply as agreed upon between Enron's trader and its customer or counterparty. From the weather desk, to the coal desk, to the power desk to the gas desk, not one single person had an established source of data, but a myriad of spreadsheets with macros designed to determine forward price curves. In some instances, data was downloaded from one of the many publications into an archaic database, which the traders would then use to access prices. This was the Chaos Theory of Commodities Trading.

Summer at Enron saw one big party after another. With the arrival of the Summer Associates, or college interns and grads, Enron went all-out to make certain that they left with a lasting impression. Management knew college kids were usually bright and impressionable, and put on the dog so that come decision time they'd be lining up in Human Resources. Enron understood that you needed underlying milk before you could skim the cream, so the more bodies they had to choose from, the better their pickings would be.

Enron's Big Summer Show included parties in Antioch Park just outside the Enron building, with lunch catered by local restaurants and live-music from people like Brian Black, brother of country singer Clint Black. Everything was on Enron's nickel and in the evenings, happy hour was catered at one of the local bars. Because energy operations and trading seemingly printed money for the company, we were treated like royalty.

The savvy college grads knew this and wanted nothing more than to be traders. Many had been witness to Jeff Skilling's rousing speeches about how each trader was worth millions in net revenue for Enron and huge bonuses rained down like manna. Many of those college kids had heard the eye-popping tales of avarice. Company legends abounded of thirty-year-olds signing seven-figure mortgages in River Oaks, or that a trader was slipping if his Porsche Carerra was more than a couple years old. It was well-known that if you had an ego as outsized as Texas you had a damn good chance of strutting down the Yellow Brick Road to Enron's trading floor.

Kathy's retribution for writing my memo regarding Enron's bank fraud, kept her constantly after me, and I found myself spending less time actually working and far too much of my time trying to figure out how to get her off my back. My company agreement prevented me from moving to another group within the first year, so I put on my thinking cap and looked for a solution on how to deal with an increasingly hostile boss and two sworn foes, Sherlynn and Ronnie.

As we all worked on solving the looming Y2K problem, an answer slowly appeared. Enron was still utilizing two systems to administer thousands of gas and power contracts, one of which was not even Y2K compliant. The duplicated efforts seemed senseless to me, given that one set of efforts was soon going to be rendered obsolete. Out of the encroaching Y2K mess I began to see not only potential redemption in the eyes of the company, but a way to distance myself from my enemies.

Though well over a year away, the Y2K situation was quickly becoming a concern. At one second past midnight on December 31, 1999, what the hell was going to happen? It seemed incredible that with all the brain power in the company, not one person fully understood the ramifications of what those two zeros would do to us. No one could predict what would happen when computer systems, some of which were only designed to recognize a two-digit year code, experienced the internal calendars ticking over to 01-01-00. Would the two-digit systems fail? Would the dumb bunny computers think it was 1900? Would they bring down the other systems? Who knew?

By mid-1998, Enron was still heavily reliant on systems that were not Y2K compliant, and there was a frantic push to get our compliant data entered into two separate systems, Synergy and Global Contracts. As we got more involved in the Y2K fix I found that, despite a legal requirement that companies dealing with critical commodities like energy divulge their Y2K exposure, Enron had not fully disclosed how far away they were from complying with Y2K corrections. They never mentioned to anyone that systems supposed to be operational three years earlier were still in the development phase. I knew that modifying our systems to operate after New Year's Eve 1999 was going to require an enormous amount of manpower to comply with the federal mandates. Unless Enron hired a few thousand new people, I saw long hours ahead as the clock ticked down to Y2K. As I wracked my brain for a solution to my own problems I was beginning to see a way to help myself, and the company as well.

Several years before I came to Enron, the legal department developed a system called the "Contracts Database", designed to identify exposure for the Risk Management people. Once installed, with a press of a button anyone in legal could identify Enron's exposure in certain areas. For instance, if an employee needed to locate every contract containing a provision of *force majeure*, which allowed Enron to wiggle out of a contract in the event of an Act of God, the system would find them. Likewise, the system could also identify contracts allowing for the concentration of higher levels of carbon dioxide.

The Contracts Database was a good system, so good in fact it eventually came under the covetous eye of Jeff Skilling. Because Enron had suffered severe losses when deals had been made without contracts to cover their trades, Skilling insisted on an integrated system to track all aspects of a deal. From the point of entry into a deal trading system, all the way to the scheduling of the physical delivery of the commodity, everything would be matched and entered against the contract. All Skilling asked was that the right hand know what the left hand was doing, and the Contracts Database was his answer.

The system had been taken over, restructured, and renamed Global Contracts to accommodate Skilling's trading group. Everything was fine until word got out that it was nowhere near ready to completely replace the current Synergy system, which was not Y2K compliant. Despite having a battalion of Arthur Andersen consultants at their beck and call, the trading group was operating several separate systems to complete their trade logging. One system settled the trades while another scheduled delivery of the commodity, and yet another was used for providing the tax information. There was no redundancy between them and, without a bridge between the two systems, they were incapable of "talking" to each other.

This put Enron in the embarrassing and potentially costly position of doing something like settling a trade and actually *paying* a customer who had bought gas and should have been paying Enron. Additionally, Enron risked further exposure over the stiff penalties that were enforced by various pipelines for having an imbalance between the inventory of gas in the pipeline and the gas being delivered. The right hand didn't even know what the right hand was doing, and with that system, mistakes could happen without much prompting. And with the grab bag of Y2K, many felt the system would simply melt down.

Down on the 25th floor, Emma Toombs's group was responsible for creating the contracts between the traders and the customer, or counterparty, to cover the deals or trades. To ensure that every trade was done as fast as possible for the benefit of the traders and scheduling, contracts had to be set up in the system very quickly, otherwise the trader could not execute the trade and gas could not be scheduled to flow. Deals would then have to be "validated" to ensure that the appropriate contract had been selected to cover it. Whether a trader and counterparty entered into a sale or a purchase agreement, the proper contract was drawn and checked in validation. Deals were then sent on to the "Confirm Desk", which entered them into the system to confirm the transaction.

Once the contract was set up by Emma's group, it would be passed off to my group to provide analysis of the details. Ronnie and Faith were responsible for entering the briefed information into the database for risk management purposes. While Emma's group could knock out their contracts pretty quickly, thus delighting the traders who lived and died over minutes and seconds, our job of identifying all the legal aspects required more time to do properly, and that was not a luxury the trading environment allowed.

In addition to the flaws of using two systems, it also became very apparent to me that Enron had a fundamental flaw in the accounting of their trading group. Over lunch in the cafeteria I would overhear many a cocksure young trader bragging about his million-dollar mortgage or his yacht moored over in Galveston. But what I knew and they didn't was that although the company knew their basis in a trade, they had absolutely no idea what it was costing them to make it. Despite a large in-house accounting staff, the resources of one of the world's foremost accounting firms working right within the building, as well as myriad personnel assigned to administering deals, there was a baffling lack of understanding as to the overall costs of our operation. I had worked for many large companies and in every case we knew what everything cost – every action taken by every employee – and its impact on the balance sheet. I was increasingly amazed that while Enron knew the dietary intake of every employee based on the employee badges scanned in the cafeteria, they had virtually no clue how much a trade cost from deal to settlement and all the costly support in-between. I wondered if the other divisions at Enron were equally lax in identifying their costs.

While VP of Commercial Support for Energy Operations Sally Beck struggled to understand the Swiss cheese accounting Enron was practicing in the trading group, I saw a way to streamline our workload, possibly save the company money, and have the trading group's computers ready to stave off Y2K. Our group was often blamed by Emma's group for their slowness in setting up contracts. After some noodling around the concept, I went to see the database design group and asked if it would be possible to create a streamlined system to facilitate a merger of my group and Emma's group.

After several meetings, the database people concluded I was on to something and they created an outline describing how it could be accomplished. Next on my checklist was rationalizing the merger of both groups. My plan also required getting Emma's group involved in briefing contracts. This made sense from a standpoint of brainpower. Emma and her group members, Elaine Small and Betty Ramsey*, had legal backgrounds. Emma and Elaine were attorneys and Betty was a paralegal, so it was a perfect fit. It gave Emma's group a little more power – which was a selling point to her – but would also expand their duties and, in turn, give them a heavier work load. Balancing out the pros and cons with Kathy would determine who gained power and probably a bigger bonus.

I was feeling particularly proud of myself. Merging Emma's group with ours would reduce redundant efforts in both camps. It would speed up the process for our group, making us look better, it would get contracts scrutinized and into the system more quickly, save money, reduce the potential for a Y2K catastrophe and, best of all for me, take away my responsibility at having to "assassinate" Ronnie and Sherlynn. With the departments merged, the lines of power and duty would shift and they would no longer be reporting to me. Now I had to sell Kathy on the plan.

Since Enron did not allow smoking in the building, smokers would gather in small clusters in the park across the street. I was often taken by the contrast between Rebecca Carter, standing in the full sun, all black chic, her duster length jacket billowing in the breeze as elegant rings of smoke emanated from her lips, and that of the poor chunky monkey, Kathy. There she was, huddled under a shade tree, puffing furtively on a butt, as if some gifted animal handler had coaxed an upper primate into a khaki pantsuit and gotten her hooked on the pleasures of nicotine. As Kathy sucked on a coffin nail, I approached her.

"I've got a great idea. A way to take a lot of the heat off us with the traders," I opened.

Kathy expelled a small cloud of burning carcinogens. "Oh yeah? How?"

I proceeded to lay out my plan, bolstered by the fact I had cleared it with the computer people who would have to pull it off. Kathy nodded and voiced no dissent. After my five-minute presentation, I could see she was impressed. I had done my homework and left no room for error. Except I didn't factor in one critical element that was the substrate Enron was built on. I didn't because I hadn't fully grasped it yet.

Everything at Enron was a zero-sum game. From the simplest accord between two fellow employees to multi-million dollar gas trades, there was always a winner and always a loser. The business cliché win/win was nonexistent within the tower at 1400 Smith Street. In the culture of Enron, it was never anything but war, from the microcosmic to the macrocosmic. Kathy loved my idea so much that as we walked back into the building her little wheels were whirring full speed to figure out a way to steal it then turn it against me.

To my surprise, Kathy announced a few days later that we would indeed be merging the two groups. I was very pleased someone had listened to me, but at the same time the announcement left me with a feeling of apprehension. When Kathy informed me of the move, she not only didn't thank me for my brilliant suggestion, but made it sound like the decision had been her idea. She told me as if it had been in the works for some time and essentially underplayed its importance. Although I had planned on asking whether my suggestion would land me a bonus, or at the very least another Personal Best Award, her attitude caused me to shelve the question.

Once the move was complete, I experienced two immediate changes, one good, one bad. Happily, Ronnie and Sherlynn were no longer in my charge. Unhappily, not only didn't I physically escape them, the playing field had now been leveled, giving them increased power to undermine me. My sworn enemies were still sitting next to me, but we were now reporting to the same boss, which made us peers in the pecking order. The hapless trusty, I had been thrown back in the prison population.

Now that I had a new political landscape to deal with, I sized up my opponents. Ronnie and Sherlynn were givens – enemies. Faith Randall was solidly on my side, but her stock was about to slip. Faith's only flaw, at least in Kathy Simpson's jaundiced eyes, was that she was black. I had gleaned from subtle caustic comments by Kathy over the six months I had known her that she was never going to be a supporter of the Rainbow Coalition. With the shakeups in the groups, Faith was no longer under my supervision – and protection – and not long after, Kathy's henchmen, Yolanda Floyd* and Marguerite Flores*, managed to put enough pressure on that dear, sweet, hardworking woman to get her to quit.

I had no bone to pick with Emma's underling Elaine Small, but apparently she did with me. When I was interviewed for the first position at Enron, Kathy felt I was overqualified and gave the job to Elaine. She was a lawyer and it bothered her that, at least in the eyes of Enron, I was more qualified and was a rank above her. I never understood her animosity toward me, but when colleagues, as well as my friend and recruiter Mary Rye, filled me in it all made some sick sense. I did my best to avoid Elaine.

I could not avoid Emma Toombs and that's where I had one of my biggest hurdles. Emma was Kathy's lackey, and although my suggestion would likely bring each of them extra dough come bonus-time, Emma resented the extra work and, more so, loathed the notion that someone from another group had come up with such a clever plan. In fact, Emma and Kathy were so envious that I had hatched the merger idea, they simply began calling it their own.

A few weeks after the move, I pulled Jennifer aside. Jennifer could at least give me a temperature reading, if not good advice. I explained that I was not only being robbed of my credit for merging the groups, but the whole thing had backfired.

"What should I do?"

Jennifer shrugged. "Not much you can do. Just watch them. Truth is, you don't have any real friends in your new group."

I developed eyes in the back of my head. Aside from trying to do my job, now I had to worry about getting snake-bit any time I dropped my guard. And my work was hardly consolation. My current task was all part of Enron's big shell game, a creative financing scheme intended to pull the wool over investors' and auditors' eyes and to create a falsely-inflated bottom line for the benefit of Wall Street.

CHAPTER FIVE

Because of inherent limitations in any system of internal control, errors or irregularities may occur and not be detected.

Arthur Andersen, LLP., Enron Auditors
from Enron's 2000 Annual Report

WHAT WILL YOU DO TO CHANGE THE WORLD TODAY?

Every quarter, approximately 10,000 gas contracts were moved or "assigned" from, for instance, HPL Resources to HPL. In three months, they would be moved back or to another entity under Enron's control. To the outside financial world, the result looked like Enron was selling a fabulous volume of gas contracts then generating that many more and selling them too. Truth was, it was happening mostly in-house. Enron had created so many subsidiaries it was easy to transfer assets around and make it look like commerce. This was where the right and left hands were actually informed: the right would pass to the left and the left would pass it back like three-card Monty on a street corner in Mid-town Manhattan, except the marks were everyone from Wall Street to Main Street, including teachers' and firemens' funds.

And Enron didn't stop at shuffling contracts – they loved shuffling people, too. Having been at Enron for six months, I was beginning to question the wisdom of moving people around so often. Not counting the move I caused with the merger idea, my department of five had been relocated on the same floor four times. Ultimately, in the year-and-a-half I spent in the trading department, my group was moved seven times. What I found baffling was the necessity of moving us, which try as I might to understand, I could find no good reason for. It was not only disruptive and disorienting, it was expensive.

Whenever we were to be moved, we were given a few days' notice. On Friday we would pack the contents of our desks into boxes before we left work, and over the weekend a crew would move everything, from the desks, credenzas, file cabinets, chairs, computers and lamps, to the waste baskets. I found that, like everything else at Enron, the crews doing the moving were compensated in a princely fashion. The price tag for moving one desk one time was $2,000. So every time our department moved it cost not only ten grand to move us, but another ten to move the people we switched with. Twenty-thousand down the drain and, on top of it all, we had to find a new route to the bathroom.

And our department was hardly unique. This constant musical chairs within Enron got so out of control that the company commissioned a survey of all employees. On the survey the questions included *How many times have you moved in the last six months?* and *Are the moves affecting your ability to do your job?* Well, duh. In my three years at Enron I was moved more than twelve times.

With the year-end deadline closing in and more projects cropping up almost daily, I was becoming physically and emotionally exhausted. Although I had been warned, between moving the gas contracts around and trying to input data on the Y2K fix, I was putting in excessive hours, weekends included, sometimes racking up more than 90 hours in 7 days. Unfortunately, I was also carrying 10 credit hours at the university. It was company policy to pay for any work-related education and I had signed up for the course before my office hours had gotten out of control.

Because of the hours required to meet Emma's demands, I was unable to start my studies until at least 8:00 p.m. Rather than drive home and begin my studies after dinner at 9:00 p.m., I would often study at work and use my computer for research, leaving the office around 11:30 p.m. I assumed that because the company was paying for each of the $3,000 executive classes, and since it was entirely work related, utilizing the computer after hours would be acceptable.

One Friday evening, after work hours, I spent more than 5 hours online doing research. By 1:30 a.m. I had completed my thesis to hand in to class the next morning. On Monday morning, Emma called me into her office and angrily thrust a printout at me.

"This is a computer activity log. What in the world were you doing online until almost 2:00 a.m. Friday? This is clearly a violation of company policy."

I was shocked. I had been spied on. "I was doing research for the business class I signed up for." Then I added for emphasis, "The class the company wanted me to take and is also paying for?"

Emma's mind was made up and I was insolent in trying to introduce any pesky facts – I could have been answering Ken Lay's fan mail for all she cared. "I'm going to look into what sites you were browsing. If it's anything not business-related we're going to talk again. Understand?"

I nodded and turned to leave.

"We'll be watching you," she added.

After that first official run-in with Emma, a new weapon was added to the arsenal to drum me out of the group. I met my new nemesis, a lowly contractor in the group named Hilda Gaither*. A self-proclaimed "fag-hag", who sought out the company of gay men, it was no surprise that Hilda and Ronnie were buddies. She was also a confidante of Emma's. Popped from the mold adjacent to Kathy's in the evolutionary scale, Hilda was stout, with ham-hock arms, a moon face and loud red hair. She also had a penchant for popping Vicodan like Tic-Tacs. Once I became acquainted with the magnitude of her habit, I was astounded that she could refrain from drooling, let alone do her job. But I soon discovered not to take her lightly or to underestimate her cunning.

As a contractor, Hilda was just another vulture waiting for a casualty among the regular staff so she could swoop in. Hilda understood that to achieve full employment status, and to obtain that treasure trove of benefits received only by vested members in the church of Enron, someone needed to get bumped off. On Enron's zero-sum battlefield I was standing between her and that golden chalice. It also didn't hurt that I had been mean to her pal, Mr. Beanie Baby.

As soon as Hilda figured out I was despised in the department, at least by Ronnie and Sherlynn, she quickly made it her job to keep constant tabs on what I was doing. Although our cubicles were next to each other, my back was to her so I didn't always notice her watching me. Barely five feet tall, Hilda had to work hard to peer over the padded cubicle wall. I would often turn to see her doughy chin squished on the dividing wall between us as her beady eyes focused on my computer screen, trying to determine what conspiracy I was currently engaged in.

As time passed, I heard from several trusted sources that I was now the primary target in the cross-hairs of Kathy's rifle scope. She had several reasons to want me gone. First, my aborted attempt to broom Ronnie and Sherlynn had left an awkward situation: an assassination attempt must always be followed by retribution. Human Resources had received too many complaints and Kathy was not about to take any more heat from them. I had been the fall guy from the get-go and my merger plan posed a potential embarrassment. Now that Kathy and Emma had seized credit, it could make them look bad if the truth got out. They weren't sure how connected I was to the higher ups and, since I wasn't supposed to know they had grabbed credit for the merger, they feared I might accidentally mention to the wrong person that it had been my idea. But most importantly, I had targeted her in writing as the maestro of the cover-up of the bank fraud.

As they turned up the pressure on me I began to ponder quitting. I had been a valued member of the senior executive team at Ralston Purina. There I had felt a part of something despite making less money than I was now. But was money enough to compensate for being thrown into this pit? What compensation was worth constantly watching my back while these angry, venom-spitting vipers circled, just looking for the chance to sink their fangs into my soft underbelly?

I sat down one night and put a pencil on the financial ramifications of leaving Enron. Since the chaos with Brian and Jimmy and the bankruptcy, money and security had become even bigger issues for me. When I took a look at the picture, my heart sank as I realized Enron was a golden cage.

Enron's All Employee Stock Option Program (AESOP) began in 1994. It allowed employees to benefit from additional compensation by giving them stock at a price set at the end of the first calendar year of their employment. The options were based on an annual rate of 2% of their salary for each full year remaining in the program. Employees who had been in for the entire seven years, between the end of 1994 through 2000, would have received a total of 14% of their annual salary as of December 31, 1994. The strike price would be established at that time, based upon a formula of the weighted average of Enron's stock price. However, options would only vest at 50% on June 30th of each year, after the employee had been with the company an entire year. The remaining 50% would vest the following June.

I started in March 1998, and received a total of 5% of my annual salary for the following three years (1% for 1998, 2% for 1999, and 2% for 2000). My strike price was established on December 31, 1998 at $57.0625. This amounted to 465 shares of Enron stock for a value of $26,534.06, if I had chosen to purchase the stock when it was fully vested. For every dollar that the stock went up, I would receive an additional $465. Although it was the rule, my strike price wasn't established until nearly eight months after coming to Enron. The difference between the stock value when I began and where it was on December 31, 1998 made me feel like I'd already lost more than $16,000. There wasn't anything I could do about it, but it was agony having to watch the stock climb before my strike price was set.

I tried desperately not to think about the money I had lost. I was in enough misery, working alongside Ronnie and Sherlynn, reporting to Emma, and being harassed by Kathy and her loud-mouthed Rottweiler, Hilda. I continued to look at the upside and focus on the vesting of these options. On June 30, 1999, my first 50% or $13,295.56 would vest. I would earn anything over the $13,295.56 should I choose to cash in the options. The remaining 50%, or an additional $13,238.50, would not vest until the following year on June 30, 2000.

In late 1999, before I cashed in any shares of stock, all Enron employees received an added bonus when Skilling decided the stock, now in the high $80s, should be split. This gave all program participants twice the number of shares at one-half the strike price. Now I had 930 shares of stock at a strike price of $28.5313. Skilling's promise that Enron's stock would once again reach the high $80s or even $100, implied a potential jackpot for me. If the stock reached $98.53, I would receive nearly $91,632.90 in a little over two years and would net an additional $65,000 in income. As my income continued to rise, albeit slowly, I realized I didn't have to love the people I worked with, I just needed to survive. With a base salary now in the low $70s, plus $65,000 in vested options, and perhaps a bonus or two with a few pieces of low-hanging fruit tossed in, I could make a solid $150,000 in 1999 or 2000. It was a lot of "ifs" but they seemed within reach. All this was in addition to my investment in Enron's 401(k), which was growing faster than I could count my money.

If I reinvested some of my salary back into Enron stock at the discounted price offered employees, within ten years I saw I could realistically be worth around seven figures. Not bad for a single woman who had suffered some major setbacks, both personally and financially. After a long weekend of weighing my options, I decided to stick it out. What was frighteningly beyond my control was: who among my enemies might strike the fatal blow to ruin those plans?

By mid-December, we were in another round of rank and yank. To add to our stress, everyone in my group was told that despite company policy, we could not carry over more than one week of vacation and we would not be allowed to take any vacation time during the Christmas holidays. If you had vacation time accumulated and had not used it by then, tough luck. It was crunch time and the group was once again playing the game of musical contracts, assigning gas contracts from one subsidiary to another to give the illusion of commerce before the tax opportunities vanished on January 1st.

I had been flying to Springfield, Oregon nearly every month for the past five months to spend time with Margie Swenson, my ailing former mother-in-law. I planned to see her in mid-January after taking some time for myself, when I got a phone call from my former husband, Wayne. He told me she had taken a bad turn and the doctors weren't sure she'd even make it to the new year. Distraught that the end had come and I would miss holding her hand one last time, I approached Emma.

"I have a family member near death. I need to be with her. I'd like some time off. I could take it under medical leave," I said, trying to limit details to Emma's prying.

Emma glanced up from her paperwork with a look of irritation. "Who?"

I didn't know what she meant. "Who?" I repeated.

She rolled her eyes condescendingly. "Who's dying?"

I couldn't believe her callousness. "My former mother-in-law."

She looked incredulous. "Your ex-mother-in-law? You've gotta be kidding! Absolutely not."

I took a deep breath. "Look, Emma, we're very, very close. She's more like a mother to me. I've been flying to Oregon every month or so since she got sick. She probably won't make it more than a week or two. I really need to be with her."

Emma shrugged. "Well, just be happy you saw her those other times. You can't go. If I let you go everybody will want to go and that's out of the question."

"Not 'everybody' has a family member dying," I said bitterly.

"Yeah, well, she isn't exactly still family, now is she?"

I stormed away, angry and hurt that she could be so cruel. That night I decided I would either quit or risk my stock options with an early transfer. Enron frowned upon anyone moving from their initial group within one year. The fine could be losing your stock options, but Emma's behavior was so hurtful and mean-spirited, I resolved to risk it. At that point only half of my shares would vest in a few months so my loss wouldn't be that great, but I didn't want to lose anything if I could help it.

Another problem was that I was suffering from increasing pain in my hands. Despite weekly massages, working with my head glued to a computer screen so much, my hands ached at night for hours. I worried I was getting a debilitating disease, but my research online told me my symptoms didn't quite match those of arthritis or any other bone or joint malaise. What my symptoms did match was carpal tunnel syndrome, a numbness and pain in the fingers caused by pressure on a nerve in the wrist. I soaked my hands at night in warm water and tried to pare down the amount of time on the computer. I decided that after the first of the year, I would get it checked by a doctor.

I began a campaign in earnest to find a new job. I scanned the intranet bulletin board listing job openings within Enron. I also started a very discreet search for anything outside the company. I sent out a few résumés, but I was careful to inform prospective employers they absolutely could not contact my current company. I told myself if I found something really good I would walk away from a potentially secure future. Yet if Emma, Kathy, and the other goons in the department were successful in knocking me off, what secure future was there?

A week before Christmas, I saw my opportunity for the perfect escape, and best of all it was in my old stomping grounds. I found a job listing within Enron's Portland General Electric as the Legal Administrator, overseeing the management of their legal department. With more than 18 years' legal experience, including administering multi-million dollar annual budgets and managing large outsourcing projects, I was the ideal candidate for the position. The only glitch was that I would need Emma's approval to even interview for the job since I had not met the company's tenure requirement of at least one year in your initial group. The other problem was that since the offer closed in a few days, it would require leaving Houston on December 22nd to interview on the 23rd. Since Emma had banned me from visiting my dying former in-law, I didn't expect her to be open minded.

"Absolutely not," was her reply to my request.

Then I found a way around Emma the Scrooge. Since Enron actually gave employees Christmas Eve off, and PGE did not, I made arrangements to interview on that day. Since I was highly qualified, and was doing it on my day off, it would have made her look bad if she banned me from taking the interview. She grudgingly gave in for the good of Enron.

Since Christmas Eve was on a Thursday, I flew out on Wednesday, had my interview, and returned to Houston the Monday after Christmas. By the end of the month I suspected the job in Portland wasn't going to happen. In the course of investigating each applicant they would speak to their immediate supervisor. I assumed Emma wouldn't miss an opportunity to stick a knife in me. What I couldn't understand was that, if she and the others had such a problem with me, why didn't she say everything she could to get rid of me? My only conclusion was that, in the world of Enron, hurting a fellow employee was almost as important as making money, and certainly took precedence over solving a problem.

After the last rank and yank I had slipped to a tepid "satisfactory", so I began applying for legal positions within Houston and back in the Northwest. I would search the want ads late at night, each day expanding my search farther and farther, beyond my set standards, just to escape my tormentors. When I found a job that interested me, I would prepare a specialized resume and send it out over the group's fax machine after hours. Although I was using company equipment for personal reasons – a no-no – I rationalized that specific use.

I had been hearing for some time that Enron intended to provide every employee with a Compaq Pentium III computer for home use. The company graciously stated that the computers were not intended to encourage employees to work at home, but were to be considered personal gifts. In the event an employee left Enron within three years of receiving their computer, the company would expect reimbursement. It was no small chunk of change to provide 19,000 employees with the latest PC's as gifts. Given that, in my mind, sending a fax locally, albeit for personal use, caused no skin off anybody's nose, particularly since it was sent after hours.

I started using my lunch hours to customize my resume for different jobs. One afternoon while everyone was out, I turned and was surprised to find Hilda back from lunch. As she leered over the divider wall at my computer screen, I hit "print" and moved quickly toward the shared printer to retrieve my revised resume. As I did, Hilda got her lumbering frame in gear and, after two or three steps, I realized we were in a race to the printer. I tried to pretend I didn't notice, but as I stepped up my pace, her fat little limbs were suddenly pumping with the speed of a cartoon character. I reached the printer first with a momentary sense of relief and grabbed the sheaf of papers in the printer bin, only to be startled as Hilda's pudgy fingers seized them away from me.

"Gimme those!" she yelled.

Shocked, I hesitated for a second then grabbed them back. "No, you gimme! They're mine."

The tug of war had begun. She locked her blubbery meat hooks on them and pulled hard enough to crumple the paper.

All over the trading group, heads popped up from carrels to see Enron's version of the WWF. While I certainly didn't want her to discover my resume, suddenly my resentment of her welled and I just wanted to see her defeated. She represented the forces of blind evil, an angry little stub of a woman who had conjured a hatred of me because I had a job she wanted and yet clearly wasn't qualified for. Yanking at the papers, it dawned on me that Emma had probably dangled the carrot of full employment in front of Hilda's big lips if she could only devise a way to nail me. As Hilda shifted her considerable weight to get a better purchase on the papers, I remembered a scene from an episode of *Kung Fu* and actually pushed the papers toward her. This threw her off balance and, like a mongoose, I snatched the papers away and headed to my desk.

"That's my stuff!" she screamed, thrusting herself in my path.

I decided to use reverse psychology. "What are you hiding, Hilda? I won't tell."

Her face got beet red. "Me? I'm not hiding anything!"

On the fly I sifted through the papers, found mine, and passed the rest to her. She grabbed them so hard they went flying. As she stooped to gather them I continued to my desk. That afternoon word got around about the big screaming match. Emma called me in.

"What on Earth was going on here during lunch?"

"I don't know. It was incredibly unprofessional. Hilda just went nuts when I was trying to get my printouts."

"What were you printing?" she asked. A very suspicious question given the nature of the conflict. I looked oblivious. "A report. I don't know what got into her." As I turned to leave I figured I'd beat Emma to the punch and lowered my voice. "If I were you I'd keep an eye on Hilda. I think she's up to something."

Emma stood dumbfounded and I walked away. Had I been on the trading floor I thought, had I been able to lift her pudgy little body, I could have thrown her across the room the way traders threw their computer monitors and no one would have uttered a word.

Near the end of that day I discovered the company had gone outside to fill the PGE slot in Portland. Enron usually promoted from within and, with my seemingly perfect qualifications, sabotage was my educated guess. That was the last straw. I decided no amount of stock options were worth the mind games I was being forced to endure. I decided to step up my job hunt. But first I composed a short thank you note to the general counsel with whom I had interviewed. Even though I didn't get the job, I thought a little goodwill building might help me with future openings there and, who knows? Perhaps, I might someday find out the real reason I wasn't hired.

That evening I faxed the thank you note to Portland. After the note was scanned and sent, I placed it back in my desk in an unmarked folder. The next morning as I sat down at my desk, my phone rang.

"Would you come here?" said Emma, sounding like a schoolmarm about to discipline an unruly student. I went to her desk. She took a deep breath for effect and handed me an envelope.

"What's this?" I asked. "Open it," she commanded.

Inside the envelope was the note I had faxed the night before. At first I was perplexed, then angry. Someone had obviously rifled through my desk.

"Someone put this on my desk anonymously. It appears to have been faxed from the *company* fax machine," she sneered. "If you have an explanation, I'd like to hear it."

I was fed up but mostly surprised. It was apparent that this was the work of her little mole, Hilda. Having stymied her earlier she sought revenge, but this was the best she could come up with. I smiled to myself that I had faxed a number of resumes and notes to businesses unrelated to Enron, which apparently went unnoticed. I usually took them home at night, but there were a few incriminating pieces of evidence around had Hilda been a little more diligent – and smarter – in her rifling. It seemed idiotic that Emma was calling me on the carpet for something that was actually job-related. Unless she had other evidence, which I doubted, I felt she had a weak hand and was bluffing. I dug in.

"Explanation? For what?" I asked innocently.

"That! That note! You're using company time and equipment to handle personal business. It's not job-related. That's grounds for dismissal."

I kept my cool.

"Well, Emma," I began slowly, "maybe you're right. Let's see... Uh, I sent a letter to PGE regarding my interview there. Last year Enron bought PGE so PGE is, in essence, Enron. So to recap, I sent a thank you note to the general counsel of an Enron subsidiary regarding a position that was open there. A position *within* the company. Call me crazy, Emma, but how is that not job related?"

Emma's narrow eyes blazed in anger. I had never spoken to her with such impertinence, but I was tired of being kicked around. Plus, they hadn't discovered the truly damning evidence, my numerous resumes and cover letters to every legal and gas-related company in the greater Houston area. Now *that* was against company policy. But screw her, because she didn't have a clue.

"Don't ever do it again," she grated, and went back to her paperwork.

I smiled and walked away.

Later that day I went to Human Resources and sat down with Rosemary Plimpton*, someone I trusted and had good dealings with in the past. I explained the fax situation and being chastised by Emma for using the fax to send a note to PGE. I offered to reimburse the company for their loss.

Rosemary scoffed, "I think the company has better things to do than dock their employees ten cents for long distance, especially since it was company business."

I also told her about the politics in the group and how I feared Emma had given Hilda an order to undermine me. And that some of that had come from Kathy in retaliation. Rosemary knew all about the problems in the group from numerous complaints about Kathy and Emma. As we parted, Rosemary patted my shoulder. "And don't worry about Hilda."

I was certain the last two run-ins with Emma had earned me a death sentence. Unless something miraculous happened, I was certain Emma and her minions would come up with some way to be rid of me. It was six months until my first block of stock vested and I was worried they could rob me of it. I soon found a solution to my fears of being summarily fired, but it came from a place I never expected.

Shortly after the rather violent printer run-in with Hilda, I had a series of vicious migraine headaches and then my hands went completely numb. Frightened, I called my doctors, who set up a battery of tests, including an MRI and CAT scan. I waited for the results, assuming they would diagnose my symptoms as stress-related and tell me to take some time off. I fantasized about spending a weekend in a spa but was saving the last of my vacation time to spend with my former mother-in-law, Margie.

I hadn't spent any time analyzing Rosemary Plimpton's comment regarding Hilda, but the day after all my tests, I realized she had been hinting at something she couldn't directly tell me. Hilda was ordered to Human Resources after committing an offense, by no means her first, which was unrelated to me. As a contract employee she was not blessed with the same level of protection – or tolerance – that a fully-vested employee was. She was warned to curb "certain behavioral patterns" and was then given the big, wet slap in the face: she would *never* become a full employee. If she saw Jeff Skilling choking on a hotdog at a company picnic she could forget giving him a Heimlich for all the good it would do her. Hilda would never be allowed to pass those pearly gates of full Enron investiture.

She was furious when she returned to her desk. As she ranted about being "screwed over by Enron", she worked herself into an increasing frenzy. Soon she was throwing things and screaming that someone had glued her desk drawers shut. Sadly, the poor dear had been pushed 'round the bend. Emma had to intervene before someone got brained with a paperweight or Hilda leaped through a window in a fit of insanity. Though I do not derive pleasure from the suffering of others, I was in such a *Lord of the Flies* environment, I couldn't help but feel a little warm and fuzzy when I watched Hilda go berserk.

The next week she was moved away by Human Resources for the "welfare of the group". Hilda's next assignment was a menial filing gig somewhere deep in the bowels of the building.

A few days later, the doctors' verdict was in and I was staggered. I was suffering from a debilitating case of Carpal Tunnel Syndrome. My online research never indicated how severe, or serious, CTS could be. My doctors informed me it was so bad I would need to file for worker's comp. Within the bad news came a faint ray of light. According to strictly enforced labor laws, I would likely be protected from any future harassment by Kathy as long as I stayed at work. But I also knew how Kathy and Emma had handled the last person in the group stricken with CTS who ended up with a worker's comp claim. They fired her.

Rita Smith had been hired for one of the two positions I originally interviewed for in early 1998. She came to Enron as a contract administrator. For reasons I never divined, almost immediately after joining the group, Rita was targeted by Kathy for elimination. When she discovered she was not long for the job, she was suddenly "stricken" with a case of Carpal Tunnel Syndrome. Rita filed a worker's comp claim, which was denied, based upon her short time on the job. In a fight for her survival, Rita then filed a disability claim, which thwarted Kathy from firing her while, according to regulations, it was "being reviewed".

Angered she might be saddled with an employee she didn't like, Kathy got together with Emma and schemed how to get rid of her. Because our groups had not yet merged, I had been privy to Emma and Kathy's scheming during our management meetings. Kathy's worst case scenario was if Rita got her claim approved. She would then have six months of income under the company's short term disability policy, after which time she could come back to work for one day and file a new claim. In that event, Kathy planned to wait it out and fire Rita the moment her claim expired. Although she crossed her fingers, Rita's claim would be denied, it was approved. Then Kathy got an even more unpleasant surprise. She was told that not only couldn't she fire Rita for six months, she had to carry Rita on her payroll while she recuperated. Kathy was outraged.

Knowing she could not discharge Rita during that six-month period without cause, and since Rita was unable to work, Kathy had no cause for firing her. When she learned that, under loopholes in the plan, Rita could return for one day of work at the end of the six months and literally file a new short term disability claim, she seethed with anger. At that point, she resolved that within that one-day window she would rid herself of her burden and damn the potential consequences. A rumor was floating around that, if true, was particularly ironic. Supposedly Kathy was receiving somewhere on the order of $1,000 a week through a disability claim of her own for a back injury that occurred while lifting something extremely heavy during an office move. My guess: her feet.

I'll never know whether Rita planned on filing another disability claim because within an hour of her return after spending six months on the company dole, Kathy offered her a blindfold, a cigarette and ended the suspense. Now that I faced a similar situation, I had Rita's fate in mind as I cautiously approached how I would go about filing a claim.

On January 14, 1999, I filed my worker's comp claim and immediately informed Emma that I would be retaining an attorney as I didn't much trust her and wanted to be fairly represented in the matter. She and Kathy knew I was aware of Rita's situation and was not going to let the same thing happen to me. Ultimately, after multiple tests, a determination was made by my doctor, and corroborated by Enron's doctor, that I had suffered a permanent 8% impairment of my hands.

As soon as my claim was accepted, I was given two weeks off to rest my hands and de-stress. I flew to my family's home in the Northwest to recuperate and spend some time with Margie, who was not expected to live long. The moment I returned the retaliations began again. Elaine Small began referring to me as "Rita, Jr.", even in meetings. She was hoping to make it my official nickname by using it as often as possible. Ronnie managed to find and frame a news photo of a crying Tonya Harding, obviously as homage to my figure skating days. I mentioned these incidents to Emma, but since she was likely the reason behind them, she gave my complaints little attention. I rose above the silliness and concentrated on the Y2K fix and prepping for the next round of "musical gas contracts".

I returned home early one evening in February to find a message from Wayne. Margie's doctors weren't giving her more than a few hours to live. I called Wayne to tell him I was coming, then phoned the airline and made a reservation for the first flight out the next morning. After that, I called Emma's voicemail and left a tearful message. Wayne met me at the airport the next morning and broke the news that Margie had died while I was enroute. He had watched her peacefully pass away at home. Now there was a funeral to plan so I phoned Emma again, but this time I couldn't get her voicemail. It turned out Enron was overhauling the system so I phoned my backup, Dana Reasoner, and left a message. Dana had given me a lot of advice since coming to Enron and I asked her if she would explain my situation to Emma since I was unable to reach her voicemail. I also asked her to tell Emma that I would be taking a week off as vacation. A few days later, on the afternoon of the funeral, I received a call. It was Emma.

"I hope you have an amazing excuse for being AWOL." Her voice was cold.

I was taken aback. "Didn't Dana tell you?"

"Tell me what? I assume by your actions you no longer work for Enron."

Dana and I were bonded in our contempt for Emma and Kathy, but until that moment it hadn't occurred to me that Dana might stab me in the back. In a split second I put the scenario together. I knew Dana had been having problems with Emma and Kathy. If Dana's job happened to be on the line, she would have a motive for not getting my message to Emma. If you could get the wolves to attack another member of the pack, it always took heat off the rest for a while. Dana had been with the company for 14 years and risked losing a lot if she were fired. On top of that, she was a single woman in the process of applying for adoption. For that reason alone, she could not afford to lose her job. It was a month or so until I was able to confront Dana and confirm my suspicions. She had moved to another group and had nothing to lose, so she was coldly candid. She calmly explained that I was indeed a sacrificial lamb, given up in the hopes of protecting her money and her future baby. Given our dog-eat-dog environment, I didn't hold it against her when I found out. But my immediate problem was Emma.

After explaining my situation and how I had relayed my message through Dana, due to Enron's faulty voicemail, I hoped she would give me the benefit of the doubt and let it drop. Clearly it was an excusable mix-up, but Emma was undeterred in her desire to prosecute me. I told her I'd be back at the beginning of the next week to which she said, "You'd better," and hung up.

Over the next week, as I grieved over Margie's death, I worried about whether I would even have a job when I returned. However, given the fact that I was on workers' comp, I knew Emma would use any opportunity to discharge me if I did not follow every little protocol. But I also knew the reverse was true.

Before I returned, I contacted Human Resources to determine what my benefits were under the Family Medical Leave Act. They informed me that because I was no longer married to Margie's son Wayne, I would not qualify. If I had, I would have been given 12 weeks off, fully paid in accordance with Enron's FMLA policy. This would have carried me through March, leaving me just three months before the vesting period on my stock options. I knew Emma would be made aware that my status would not qualify under the FMLA.

This situation made me so miserable and seemed so unfair. I sat down with Wayne and discussed the notion of remarrying him rather than return to work. At first it seemed like a great idea. I could get paid, stay away from that viper pit, and wait until my stock options vested. But after talking it over with him, we both agreed it was not a viable idea. Though the thought of walking back into my group sickened me, I screwed up my courage and decided to go back and face the music.

Expecting World War III, I returned to an anticlimax. Emma apparently got word she couldn't fire me simply out of spite, but she did refuse to chalk up my trip under personal time and docked my paycheck for the entire week. Other than that, the next month was uneventful. By now I concluded my relationship with Enron was just like the ones I had with most men: up and down, mostly down, and always unpredictable.

On April Fools' Day, 1999, at around 2:30 p.m., Kathy called me into her office. I didn't know what to think when I saw the big smile on her face.

"Lynn," she said, with phony warmth, "I wanted to know how you're feeling?"

Kathy hadn't said two words to me in the last four months. I was very wary. Kathy was like a computer virus and could decimate you without warning.

"I know you're not happy in this group," she continued, pretending a little too hard to feel my pain. "You know, you're a valued employee, and because of your abilities I want to transfer you to Brenda Herod's group on the trading floor. But you know I just can't do that unless you get well."

Brenda Herod headed up the Texas desk for the trading of natural gas. Under any other circumstances, I would have jumped at the chance to work for her. But plain as day, I saw the light bulb glowing above Kathy's little pinhead. As a "protected" employee, under the terms of my worker's comp claim, she knew a fly swatter wasn't going to work so she transparently tried honey. I smiled at her and wondered *how dumb do you think I am, lady?* She was right, I was miserable, but I wasn't going to be taken in by her two-bit con. If I took the bait and proclaimed my health to be restored, she would assert my claim was invalid and immediately fire me.

I shrugged philosophically. "That would be great, Kathy." Her eyes lit up. "But too bad I can't. I have a serious disability. Maybe someday when I'm better I can take you up on that offer. Thanks so much."

Around that time, my doctor informed me it was unlikely that I would see any further improvement in my hands. As I did a lot of freelance writing on the side, I found it terribly disturbing that I would be unable to use a keyboard with the same vigor as before. Computer voice recognition software was just being introduced and I bought some for my home computer. To the irritation of those in my work group, my desk was modified to enable me to work with reduced pain.

After a routine exam of my hands, my doctor made a surprising suggestion.

"I think I've come up with a way to relieve some of the pain and numbness you're suffering. Have you ever considered breast reduction surgery?"

I had never considered that a problem, but he firmly believed that my condition was being exacerbated by the pressure of my bra straps digging into my shoulders, causing substantially greater numbness in my hands. After consulting with other physicians it was concluded that such a surgery would benefit me in a lot of ways, including relieving the migraine headaches. On April 8, I told Emma I needed to take time off for surgery. As it was none of her business, I did not inform her specifically what the surgery was. She said she would get back to me. Nearly a week passed and, not having heard anything, I approached her again.

"Emma, I need an answer in order to schedule the surgery."

"I'll review the issue and get back to you," she said. "But I'll have you know, you'll probably have to delay this surgery because of the demands on the group."

Emma was simply being vindictive. I was still on a limited workload and contributed little toward reducing the demands on the group. She also didn't bother to ask how urgent my surgery was. After pressing me, I finally told her that I would be having breast reduction surgery to which she scoffed, "You want time off for that? You've got to be kidding."

"No," I said patiently, "I'm having a lot of problems and it might give me some relief." I added, "It also might help me get off this worker's comp claim," hoping that would be what she wanted to hear. Apparently, my suffering was a bigger reward.

"No," she said, shaking her head, "this isn't critical. I mean, it's not as if you'll die if you don't get it. Wait until we get the contracts assigned for this quarter. Late June would work better. Then you can take a few days off for your surgery."

The next week brought the annual Multiple Sclerosis charity bike ride, the Houston to Austin MS150. I had participated in it the previous two years, once as a rider and the last year as a driver of one of the "sag" wagons, a support vehicle for tired riders. Given the pains in my wrists, riding was out of the question. I signed up once again to drive a sag wagon and made arrangements to loan my bike to another Enron employee. As usual, Jeff Skilling beat out the other 700 Enron participants, raising the most money for the event and boasting to anyone who would listen about how he had done absolutely no training for the 175-mile bike ride. He reveled in the acknowledgment of his financial contributions and basked in the adulation he received for being in such good shape. It was, as usual, a rewarding experience for everyone, with warm camaraderie and money raised for a great charity.

I came in on Monday still jazzed about the ride. My supreme sunburn from the stint in the sag wagon caused several people to inquire how I'd gotten so toasted. I told them how much money we'd raised and that they should participate the next year. Later that morning Emma came by my desk. She was uncharacteristically friendly.

"Quite a sunburn, huh? Someone said you were in the MS150."

"I was. It was great."

"I didn't know you cycled."

My radar came on. Emma was fishing for information to use against me. I decided to mislead her a bit.

"Yeah, I've been riding for 10 years. This is my third MS150 in a row," I answered, with a big smile. I neglected to mention that I hadn't actually ridden a bike.

"Oh, and as usual, Skilling raised the most money," I added with a knowing snicker.

Emma chuckled wryly. "I heard."

I figured the trap was set and if she were to snatch the cheese she deserved to get her fingers snapped. It would take a week or so before I would hear the big "thwack".

On the morning of Friday, April 23, I suffered a severe bout of pain in my right wrist. I tried to work, but the pain increased to the point where by mid-morning, I needed to go to the hospital for a shot of cortisone. During my last exam, the Enron doctor gave me a shot of the anti-inflammatory in my left wrist. However, my right wrist was now in excruciating pain. After waiting six hours in the emergency room, I was told that physicians do not give injections of cortisone in the hospital because of the probability of airborne bacteria causing infections. They gave me some heavy-duty painkillers and I left.

Between rest and medication, by the time I returned to work on Monday, my hand was merely aching. Emma approached my desk.

"Rather than taking Friday as a sick leave day, since you've already used up your quota, I'm going to mark that down as a discretionary holiday. That is, unless you want to take the day unpaid."

Discretionary holidays were two extra days a year given to employees to use whenever they chose. I thought about it for a while and concluded that since I had received the injury on the job, I shouldn't be docked for my own discretionary time. In my opinion, it fell under the purview of a sick day, and charging me a discretionary day was unfair. At the end of the day when everyone else had left, I phoned Emma's voicemail and told her that I would like to schedule a meeting to discuss the situation. A week later, having heard nothing from her, I took my concerns to Ann Hartsell* and Sandra Rossi* of the Human Resources department. They overrode Emma and reinstated my original use of a sick day. Over the previous five or six months I had spent more time covering my ass than getting any work done.

All of the executives received an invitation to attend an elective two-day seminar called "Inside Enron" designed as an introduction into Enron's puzzle of business units. Finally, I thought, I'll get some answers. Despite my huge reservations about Enron's practices, I guessed the company was actually making money somewhere. I hoped this seminar would unveil the magic.

The conference was packed. I assumed many were people like me, desperate to get away from their group for a couple of days, or they simply wondered what Enron actually did. Since I had been unable to uncover the reason the company's stock was climbing – I didn't count moving contracts between subsidiaries or performing other financial sleight of hand – I wanted to learn as much as I could. When we took our first break, after learning nothing substantive, I struck up a conversation with a vice president in Origination named Gil Godwin*. We had met while attending a management conference the previous year. Gil was quite the wheeler-dealer, having put together a very large deal for Enron to purchase and administer all of the gas contracts for Brooklyn Union Gas (BUG).

"I've been here a little over a year, Gil," I said. "Just exactly what does Enron do? How do we make money? I mean, did you ever consider the cost of back office support when you did a deal to see if it was profitable?"

Gil laughed. "Hell no, we never consider that."

Gil had a sarcastic wit, but I assumed he actually knew what made the company tick. There had to be a deep, dark secret as to Enron's liquidity and I figured I just hadn't been savvy enough to discern it.

I laughed with him. "C'mon, tell me the truth, how does this company make money?"

He suddenly looked serious and shook his head. "Honestly? I really don't know." Then he added, with a slightly more serious tone, "Lynn, I have no idea how or even if we make any money. But just try and find someone who does."

The two days at the seminar were so relaxing I decided to extend it a few more and headed to La Costa Resort & Country Club near San Diego to meet a couple of girlfriends. While most of the time was spent by the pool or at the world-renowned spa, a celebrity golf tournament was in progress so we took the opportunity to walk the course and watch the tournament.

After several pleasant days away from the snake pit, I returned to find new controversy brewing. I knew Emma and Kathy had been actively trying to build a case against me, but this time they went too far. Emma had indeed grabbed for the cheese in my mousetrap. My physician called and told me the Enron worker's comp investigator had come by his office. Apparently, they were "investigating allegations of fraud being brought by your supervisor".

"You've got to be kidding?" I said.

I went to see Ann Hartsell in Human Resources. Ann's face was grave as she informed me of Emma's first allegation, that I had ridden my bike in the MS150. This was clearly in violation of the limits of my claim and made me liable for fraud charges. Ann was pale as she explained I might not only have to reimburse the company, I might be prosecuted and end up in jail. Then she told me of Emma's assertion that during my trip to La Costa I had spent most of the time on the links, honing my short game. As Ann rattled off Emma's recitation of my crimes, I started giggling. Soon I was laughing uncontrollably. Ann wasn't sure if I had lost my mind.

"I drove a sag wagon in the bike ride," I began, trying to catch my breath. "And as for playing golf? Sorry, I was too busy getting massages and facials to play golf. Although I did ride a golf cart one day about a hundred yards. Does that qualify?"

Ann exhaled noticeably. "So none of this is true?"

I shook my head, barely able to contain myself. I knew this would backfire on Emma, and to a lesser extent on Kathy, which would add heat to Emma. This latest embarrassment proved too much for her. I believe that despite Emma's animus toward me, some of it must have come from Kathy. Just as I had been directed to move against Ronnie and Sherlynn, so had Emma been given an edict to get rid of me. She had made life hard for me for no good reason, because unlike Ronnie and Sherlynn who were clearly goof-offs, I was a hard worker. But business is business, and I think Emma got just as tired of trying to railroad me as I had with Ronnie and Sherlynn.

A few days after the HR meeting, I was going over contracts with Grace Irwin*, an attorney I had befriended in the legal department. We took a break and chatted. Grace was an interesting character, very well traveled, owned a successful coffee bar, and ran in some pretty elite cliques, counting John F. Kennedy Jr. as one of her close friends. After a little girl talk, we circled back to Enron.

"Did you hear Emma's moving to the Asset Group?"

I hoped she wasn't just playing with me. The Asset Group was the entity that managed HPL. "What?" I said with disbelief.

Grace nodded. "She's made the deal. And I don't think Kathy knows yet."

I relished the moment. Emma had been Kathy's golden girl, and now she was bailing on her boss without even a by-your-leave. I knew this would not bode well for Kathy who lost more employees than Jeff Skilling lost hair down the shower drain.

"When is she leaving?"

"Maybe next month, more like July, I think. You'll still have to put up with her for a while, but something tells me she'll be a lot more manageable."

And she was. She no longer hammered on me for my excused absences to visit the doctor. Ronnie still harbored great animosity toward me, but I didn't have to deal with him very often. It was like the big black cloud was now only dark gray and I could feel a slight easing of tension in the group.

Although I continued to work every day during my worker's comp claim, my duties had been decreased, as a matter of law. For instance, I was allowed to use the computer only for ten minutes at a time before being required to rest for five minutes. One day during one of my mini-breaks Kathy called me into her office.

"How you doing?" she asked.

"Fine."

Despite the mountain of medical evidence from doctors, both mine and Enron's, and the massive workload I had been shouldering prior to the problems, Kathy really thought I was faking it. I thought about Kathy's own $1,000-a-week claim and wondered if she wasn't seeing herself in me. I was hoping we wouldn't go through the same illegal line of questioning we had in April when she tried baiting me with a trading job to "expose" my fakery. She surprised me.

"Since you're really prevented from operating at full capacity in the group, quite frankly, you're not much good to me. There's someone who may be documenting the history of Enron and I've heard he needs some help. If you want you can contact him." She held out a piece of paper with a name and number. "If you're interested, I can loan you out."

Norm Gomez* was the Director of Public Policy Analysis and Ken Lay's speechwriter. Norm was in the process of creating a group to document the history of Enron. In April 1999, Norm had met with Joe Pratt, Cullen Professor of History and Business at the University of Houston, to begin this process. Professor Pratt specialized in energy history. He knew what other energy companies were doing and was involved in documenting their histories. At the time, he was compiling the history of Amoco, as well as working with Shell on a corporate history project.

During our first meeting, an excited Norm Gomez told me that "Enron's history could be the first really good book as far as corporate histories go." According to Gomez's conversations with Professor Pratt, as outlined in an April 16, 1999 memo that he provided to me, Pratt stated that "Enron has the characters (Lay and Skilling in particular) and lots of action around well-defined themes." Pratt also mentioned Enron's "regulatory entrepreneurship". He also suggested that an "autobiography by Lay could be done relatively quickly, assuming Ken makes it a priority".

Gomez said research on the corporate history could begin immediately with oral interviews. The overall project could be released in a year or two after Ken's autobiography, because "so much of Enron's history is currently in the making." Gomez saw the project as an opportunity to "make many deserving Enron employees a footnote to history!" I saw it as a completely different and enjoyable way to spend my days at Enron, at least until my hands got better. It would also afford me a chance to satisfy some of my journalistic desires.

"We can hold down the costs by doing the history internally," he said. "We looked into it and a top ghostwriter for Ken would cost a couple of hundred thousand dollars, and it would take up a lot of Ken's time too. So what we're thinking is an alternative approach. We have Ken record his recollections, using mostly travel time, and in no time we'll have a lot of great material. I think this is particularly recommended, since Ken is very quotable and the book should be in his voice."

Gomez told me Professor Pratt indicated "an interest in working on the autobiography at an advisory level at a nominal fee, because of his respect for Ken." The professor also sold Gomez on his interest and commitment to the project by saying he had "taken plane rides with many CEO's, just to get questions answered."

Gomez said he was "very bullish" on the idea of a series of books "with the grand corporate history coming at the end". My meeting with Norm Gomez lasted about an hour and by the end he was convinced that, with my legal background, as well as writing skills, I would be a prime candidate to work on the history project.

I had done research into the company before coming to work there, but now I had many more questions and hoped this project would not only give me an enjoyable job, but afford me a chance to answer them. I began at once, diving into my research by utilizing both internal as well as external resources. I soon learned that the foundation for the practices I had witnessed in the short time I had been at Enron had been laid years before.

The company history project was a nice diversion. I felt it was makework while the powers above tried to decide what to do with me. In late May, Norm notified me that the company history project had been put on hold. He assured me that when he got a green light he would call me. I let Kathy know. The next day she called me over.

"Okay, I'm going to send you through an executive analysis program called the Birkman Career Assessment. They'll analyze your strengths and weaknesses and help us figure out a place for you that'll make everybody happy."

I was skeptical, assuming it was just another ploy by Kathy to find a way to get rid of me. But after asking around, I was told the Birkman evaluation was something Enron did regularly for upper management and no one seemed to have been dismissed because of it. In fact, people generally benefited from it. I think Kathy had been frustrated in trying to manage me and the Birkman evaluation might provide her with an official way to shuffle me off to some other group without reflecting badly on her. With the history project dead and me back in her hair, Kathy desperately wanted to unload me on someone else.

After completing the questionnaire online, I met with Birkman consultant Tom Hopwood on June 9, 1999. As soon as we got through the pleasantries, Hopwood shocked me.

"By all accounts Lynn, your profile represents exactly what Enron is looking for in its executives," he began. "You are the type that should be very successful here. But you won't be. Ever."

"What do you mean?" I assumed I had fallen right into Kathy's trap. Hopwood would give me a bad rating, I'd be looked at as a problem employee and given my walking papers. I braced for what was to come next. Then Mr. Hopwood gave me an even bigger surprise: honesty.

"I've been working with Enron for some time and I can tell you won't do well here. And the reason? Number one, Enron isn't who they represent themselves to be. Enron's practices, in regards to their employees, flies in the face of their so-called Vision and Values. But perhaps more importantly, at least in your case, is number two. According to your profile, you're careful, focused, low-key, and team-minded. You're most comfortable when the people around you are friendly, give you plenty to do, are direct with you, objective, rational, and give you clear-cut decisions to make."

I nodded eagerly. Nail on the head.

"Yet..." he continued ominously, "after reviewing the reports by your bosses, Kathy and Emma, I have concluded you are working with people who are incapable of providing you with an environment that would allow you to accomplish your goals. In essence, you and your supervisors are diametrically opposed in your thinking. It's almost as if they are trying to cause you to fail."

Almost?! I think my mouth was hanging open. I never expected to get any truth from this session, let alone the brutal, unvarnished version. It was exactly what I wanted to hear.

"Therefore," he continued, "I would suggest you consider finding a new position within Enron." That wasn't just music to my ears, it was a symphony. I wasn't crazy. I almost cried, hearing from an objective stranger, one paid for by the company, that it was not my fault. Whether she planned it or not, this was the single most valuable thing Kathy Simpson ever did for me.

Either as a result of the Birkman Study, Kathy's throwing up her hands at trying to railroad me, or just plain guilt, she offered me an opportunity to work on a very high-profile project. My former crush, Ken Rice, of the JCPenney button-downs and CEO of ECT, had recently assembled a group of experts and asked how much it would cost to transport gas from Houston to the City Gate in Chicago. The point of entry for natural gas into any city is called the City Gate. It is where very large interstate and intrastate pipelines interconnect with the pipelines that feed a city.

That seemed like a reasonable question, given Enron's profits varied depending upon the costs of each deal. Although I had marveled for some time that costs didn't seem to be part of the Enron equation, Ken seemed to agree. The other probing questions Ken posed to his panel of experts were "How does Enron know that shipping on a particular pipeline is the most cost effective?" and "What if we were to do a swap whereby we would buy gas at the Henry Hub and swap with someone who was buying, say, in New York?" He followed that with, "How would our method of shipping and the costs associated therewith compare to the swapped price?"

To my amazement, this situation, spun to look like sheer MBA brilliance by Jeff Skilling, was the basis for Enron's entire business plan and the content of Enron's entire risk books. On a quarterly basis, Jeff would dish up the flavor-of-the-month story, designed to sell the analysts. It always included a detailed plan, clearly defining how Enron would make its money. Through a variety of purchase and delivery points, based upon an integrated grid of energy options, Enron would buy in one location and if more profitable, sell the commodity through transmission somewhere else.

While Skilling speculated that 80 to 90% of Enron's competitors bought and sold gas at the same location, making a pittance on the spread between the bid and ask price, Enron had a significant competitive advantage. For instance, if Enron purchased electricity at one location and swapped it for natural gas to sell to someone else at another location or, let's say, a customer needed gas in Illinois but there was an outage prohibiting delivery in the most direct route, we could re-route the gas in a matter of hours from another location, always knowing the most expeditious and cost-effective means. The problem was, I was hearing loud whispers that Enron had no idea where the most profitable route was. The upshot was, as I suspected, Enron was telling fairytales and Wall Street was listening with a goofy grin on its face.

Clearly, Ken Rice's inquiries reflected his concerns about Enron's proclivity to ignore costs. Apparently he had a death wish and wanted to know how much his group was really making. Ken's brain trust put on their thinking caps and pondered his requests. After three days, the Ph.D.s working on the project reached their decision: they had no idea. Maybe, to be more fair, their failure is better described as an impasse, because no two of them could agree on a formula. One expert opined that one cost was correct while another claimed their rate was the key.

From this Gordian knot of gas economics was born the Rates Database project. It would be a database housed in an independent yet integrated server that would contain the entire pricing schedules for every commodity that Enron currently dealt in or would offer in the future. It would offer anyone interested the cost basis for of all of Enron's business, from extraction to transportation.

It was decided that a group of insiders – with practical, not theoretical, experience working in the energy business – would be charged with creating a practical yardstick for measuring our costs. The previous year, Sally Beck, the Senior Managing Director of Energy Operations, oversaw a cost analysis of what it was costing Enron to do a trade. When the dust settled, considering the amount of back office support in the equation, it was determined we weren't making a lot of money. This was a crushing blow to bulls in the company, because it meant that despite five years of system development post J-Block, Enron was no more efficient in making money – or dodging loss.

Consequently, the creation of shell partnerships and off-the-balance sheet financings would have to increase to make up for the massive inefficiencies. Like a game of 52 Pick-Up, at year's end, debt scattered to Hell and back over Enron's empire would be gathered so that the accountants could reconcile how much had been lost with how much the company would actually reveal, or hide, as loss. Because no one had an accurate read on what costs they were incurring with a given transaction, every deal was contributing to a potential accounting black hole – where do you cut costs if you don't know where your costs are coming from, and what roles are vital to the trades? Although Enron kept growing and growing, it wasn't substance, but rather like a shadow on a wall when you walk farther from the light source – sure it kept getting bigger, but there was nothing there.

I was excited for several reasons. The history project had been fun and a diversion from the horrors of my department. The EOL Rates Database project was not only a chance to continue doing something really interesting, it also represented a chance to finally make a name for myself at Enron. This was the problem that had never been cracked. And for that reason I found myself likening the job to being a test pilot – I would either fly high and be a hero, or crash and burn. Before I agreed to be part of the project, I spent a few days worrying about the big questions: did Enron really want to know their costs and, if so, could it not hurt our bottom line? I really never considered that these shenanigans could topple such a massive company, but I didn't really have a handle on the full depth of the deceit.

Perhaps it was also a way to be temporarily free of Kathy, so I signed on to the project. This would be more telling than anything I had worked on to date. As hard as it is to understand, relative to the pricing of Enron's trades, there was absolutely no structure. While there were indices on which contracts and trades were based, when it came to the more obscure or innovative deals, there was no way to tell the most efficient pricing.

Picture a grocery store. Two customers fill their baskets with identical merchandise and head to separate cashiers. At check-stand one the customer pays thirty-two dollars. At check-stand two the other customer pays fourteen dollars. Imagine now, in this theoretical store, that the managers have no idea what even a box of cereal costs. The cost of lights, heat and rent are also mysteries to the owners. There is better accounting at lemonade stands. This store is run on the Chaos System of Economics. It's Enron.

As I interviewed traders of the various products Enron bought and sold, I learned in detail about the numerous indices available and what various traders would use to price their trades. In the fast-paced environment of energy trading – like stock brokerage – often the traders were literally flying by the seat of their pants. After speaking to a dozen or so of the top traders in gas, electricity and weather, I concluded they were virtually making it up as they went along. No one used a uniform methodology to reconcile their costs against their gains. All this from the leading risk management company.

As I watched MSNBC or CNN's Market Watch shows and heard them carry on so glowingly about Enron, I had to laugh. Had they known what I assumed, they would have been completely mortified. In the end I would be completely ignorant to the fact they had known. Even more astounding was that Enron was in the position to manage other companies' risks. I thought it was both hilarious and tragic that no one was managing ours.

One Friday evening I arrived home and turned on MSNBC. A leading analyst for the Janus Fund was crowing about different stocks he recommended.

"Well, I really like Enron." he said to the anchor.

The man's apparent certainty about Enron's future grabbed my attention. Janus was Enron's single largest institutional shareholder.

The guy went on about Enron and how impressed he was. I knew Skilling loved hearing good news from the analysts, since he worked so hard to snow them. Although he was a con man I didn't think a little brown-nosing would hurt me, especially after I had publicly embarrassed him over his pipelines and their bad gas.

I picked up the phone and dialed Jeff's line at Enron. I got his voicemail and reported what I had heard. I congratulated him, hoping it would prompt a return call. I ended the message saying he could call Jennifer Wellsley for a copy of the transcript through Dow Jones Interactive, since she was now managing the subscription service, which included access to over 6,500 publications and television transcripts. Then I called Jennifer as a courtesy to give her a heads up that he might be calling to request the transcript.

On Saturday morning, I received a telephone call from Jennifer at home. The second she opened her mouth I realized she was furious. "Lynn, this is Jennifer. What the hell did you say to Jeff in his voicemail message?"

I told her about the analyst. "I thought Jeff might be interested."

"That is really not cool to take advantage of my personal relationship with Jeff and Rebecca to further your professional career." I was taken aback. Jennifer was obviously desperate to cling to what she thought was her little piece of turf.

"I'm sorry Jennifer, I didn't see any harm. Don't be so sensitive."

"Well, Jeff and Rebecca are my friends, not yours, and I would appreciate it if you'd remember that." And with that she hung up. She didn't know I had e-mailed Jeff when I had been solicited by the businessman from Nepal. The call reminded me that in the environment we were in, there really were no friends.

With the EOL Rates Database project, I was away from Kathy. Not only did I not have to see her daily, I didn't even report to her. Even better, because I had managed to survive this long, as soon as this project was over I would be free to interview for any position I chose. I just wondered how easy, or hard, Kathy might make that process.

A few days later, a group of seven put together an informal lunch for me before my surgery. Despite not being invited, Kathy tagged along – to the dismay of most, as she was strongly disliked. During a lull in the conversation, she blurted out, "So what gossip have you heard lately?" For a second or two I visualized myself saying, *"Well, for one you dumb bunny, your main girl has put a knife between your shoulder blades and is moving to Assets",* but I resisted the temptation. The conversation slid into the usual mundane stuff and I was glad I hadn't torpedoed Emma. As much as I loathed her, I knew it was her news and she would spring it on Kathy eventually. But I sure would like to have been a fly on the wall.

In our monthly newsletter, *Enron Business,* we were asked to vote on who we would most like to come speak to Enron employees. Hands down, the winner was Jack Welch, then CEO of General Electric. However, Jeff Skilling had veto power.

"Absolutely not," Jeff said. "The guy's an idiot."

Mr. Welch was immediately stricken from the list. We were then asked to cast our votes on a much more important matter – "Should Jeff Skilling keep his new beard?"

Soon, the television monitors in the elevators were beaming his hirsute mug and glistening head – urging us to cast our votes. It was an inspired ploy, causing everyone to forget about one of the preeminent corporate leaders in America by distracting us with Jeff's facial hair. I'm certain Jeff's motivation was to protect the minds of his troops from the poisonous ideas of Jack Welch.

CHAPTER SIX

If you can't lie your way out,
you don't deserve to be in this business.

Rebecca Mark, Chief Executive Officer
Azurix

WATERWORLD

Enron loved beautiful people and Rebecca Mark was the corporate poster girl for perfection. At nearly six feet, she was the quintessential alpha female, the head lioness with a luxurious mane of gold cascading over sinewy shoulders. "Mark the Shark" had just been ranked number 14 on *Fortune's* list of the fifty most powerful women. Harvard educated, strikingly attractive, and with a net worth containing too many zeros, Rebecca was the woman the distaff class at Enron sought to emulate. And for those of us who dutifully showed up every day to perform our tasks, a sighting of the elusive powerhouse created buzz over Cobb salads in the company cafeteria.

Rarely seen around corporate headquarters, the click-clacking of her four-inch stilettos on the granite of Enron's lobby signaled an opportunity to glimpse this magnetic entity. Rebecca, at a gym-buffed forty-four, was a mythic corporate paladin who traveled the world making larger-than-life deals with no mere individuals or companies, but rather kings and countries. Rebecca understood the creation of grand assets and her specialty was as big as they get: pipelines and power plants. Rumor had it she might change her wardrobe up to six times in a day to emit the correct vibe for a specific presentation or meeting. I admit I was in awe of the Chairman of Enron International (EI). Although we had not yet met, the stage for our encounter had been set some years before.

In 1993, newly-elected Bolivian president Gonzalo Sanchez de Lozada promised his people he would come up with a way to reduce their landlocked country's dependence on the cocaine trade. The promise was somewhat disingenuous as many countrymen earned good money from the harvesting of coca. But he knew the rest of the world, and particularly US politicians, would hear the word and flock to help, particularly if there was easy money to be had. Sanchez de Lozada announced sweeping plans to privatize 50 percent of all national companies through capital investments by foreign corporations. Beginning with the airlines, they would move to the energy sector, first with hydroelectric power, the country's number one energy source, then ultimately to the natural gas and oil companies. Sanchez de Lozada was particularly keen on developing a way to increase his oil production as well as get his natural gas to neighbors Brazil and Argentina.

While praised for his efforts, the Bolivian government would not allow Sanchez de Lozado's proposed full ownership by foreign investors, so they offered 50% of each company to the highest bidder. It was essentially a partnership arrangement whereby Bolivia would get an injection of capital, and cash-rich foreign firms could swoop in and take advantage of Bolivia's abundant natural resources. As a sop to the poor – which was pretty much everyone – monies paid into the capitalization would be used to develop Bolivia's first universal pension plan.

Opportunity beckoned, and Ken Lay prepared to send his warrior princess into the fray. Having spent much of her life readying for this move, Rebecca Mark was primed to jump into the international sandbox.

Born Rebecca Pulliam in 1955, she was the second of four children from Kirksville, Missouri. I had read stories of her running around the farm with a machete, and could now see how that training aided her, whether it was blazing trails through cornfields or business. She joined Enron in 1982, after spending six years in the banking industry at First City National Bank of Houston. Then she worked at gas firm Continental Resources' treasury department. In 1985, Ken Lay's Houston Natural Gas snatched the gas outfitter up, and the father-daughter relationship was born. She began climbing the ladder by sheer luck and determination, often declaring that the international project development she headed was 90% education and 10% deal making. And education it was. Paired with her mentor, John Wing, they negotiated the billion-dollar power plant in Teeside, England that resulted in the J-Block disaster. I knew enough about their styles to see that while Skilling thrived on blunt force confrontation, Rebecca utilized her degree in psychology to mentally outmaneuver people.

In 1991, she was named chairman of Enron Development Corp. and charged with pursuing international markets. When EDC was sold to pay for the damage caused by those two rogue New York oil traders, Enron International was created and Rebecca was later put in charge. To fund Enron's pursuit of the Bolivian pie, as well as raise capital to pursue other infrastructure projects abroad, Enron Global Power & Pipelines LLC was formed in November 1994. The initial public offering of 8.7 million shares, or 48 percent of EGP&P shares, was priced at $24 per share. The offering netted more than $218 million to Enron. The initial assets of the new development company would include Enron's interest in two power plants in the Philippines, a power plant in Guatemala, and a 4,000-mile pipeline system in Argentina.

While everyone else was playing by the rules and dutifully bidding for 50% ownership, Enron had a different plan. In order to ensure its position, Enron agreed to jack up its bid in exchange for a 55% ownership and first right of refusal on any other pipeline that touched Bolivian soil en route to Brazil, including Argentina and Peru. When the leaders of the national oil company, Yacimentos Petroliferos Fiscales Bolivianos (YPFB), discovered they would be in the minority position, they went nuts, organizing strikes and accusing Bolivia's state of accepting bribes from Enron.

In an incident on March 22, 1996, that would later be echoed in India, Bolivia's army, fearing that angered YPFB employees would sabotage the project, took control of the natural gas facilities and refineries. When the 23 other foreign companies heard of the deceit, they leaped at Enron's throat. To placate them, Enron conceded Shell a portion of the concession and retained a mere 42% ownership stake. Enron understood the risks of dealing with South America.

In 1985 the Peruvian army seized $400 million worth of assets from Enron's exploration and development unit, EOG, and nationalized them. Enron knew they were playing with fire in Latin America, but the potential rewards were just too big to overlook.

With Enron's problems momentarily behind them, the news in 1995 that large stores of natural gas had been discovered in north and southwest Bolivia put Rebecca on the map. The prospect of a Bolivia-to-Brazil pipeline loomed and, by 1996, geologists reported that Bolivia was sitting on at least 7.2 trillion cubic feet in natural gas reserves, which many expected would rise dramatically once exploration was expanded. The Bolivia-Brazil pipeline, built primarily by Enron, was a 36" pipe that was 2,100 miles long, and owned 60% by the Bolivian government, at least for that portion of pipeline inside its borders. On the other side of the border, inside Brazil, the Bolivian government owned 20% with Brazil taking 60% within its own borders and 20% inside Bolivia.

By 1996, Bolivia's trillions of cubic feet of natural gas reserves had cemented Rebecca's spot as an international business player, and even more so, as a force to be reckoned with inside Enron. Rebecca's rise did not go unnoticed by Jeff Skilling. Stories of their tumultuous relationship included well-known anecdotes of past sexual liaisons. Rumors about the pair resounded well outside the glass walls of 1400 Smith Street and 3 Allen Center, Enron's international headquarters. One of Rebecca's bold visions was to create an Enron-owned natural gas pipeline grid in Latin America similar to that in the United States. In Jeff's baleful eyes, Rebecca had to be stopped and he knew just where her Achilles Heel was.

As a player at that rarified level, Rebecca got there by taking many chances. And in keeping with the perils of risk taking, she had also made a number of mistakes, some bordering on colossal. Desiring to make her mark as flamboyantly and quickly as possible, she looked for high visibility projects that could be home runs for Enron. With the Bolivian deal under way, Rebecca began negotiations with Israel to build and operate a $600 million Israeli section of pipeline, bringing gas from Egypt. In June 1995, Rebecca made a secret trip to Israel to discuss two gas import ventures in which Enron was interested. The visit came as a result of the Energy Minister Gonen

Segev's announcement that private companies would be allowed to participate in the building and operating of Israel's domestic pipeline for distributing imported natural gas.

While Enron had made a verbal handshake with the state-owned Petroleum Services as to its participation in the project, Segev's predecessor, Moshe Shahal, had opposed the involvement of outside companies. Because Enron had a pending deal with Qatar that required it to conclude its supply contracts to move liquefied natural gas (LNG) by August 1995, a bigger scheme was hatched. Since Rebecca wanted to create assets, a liquid natural gas plant was a damn big asset and fit right in with all that wonderful gas she was planning on transporting. What if Enron created a partnership wherein LNG was exported from Qatar to Israel? Then what if the Israelis built a 2,000 megawatt (MW) power-generating plant fueled by the LNG? It was a big, bold plan, but it was imperative that Rebecca convince Israel to sign on the dotted line, and sign fast.

Rebecca told the Israeli Energy Minister that she wanted to announce the arrangement at the upcoming regional economic conference in Amman, Jordan. However, the Israelis would not be pressured and her request was denied. Instead, Segev agreed to sign, but only on the contingency that Enron would accept the risk in the event they were unable to acquire the LNG from Qatar. In effect, Enron would guarantee Israel service even if it required Enron to go outside Qatar. Because Enron was not in a position to offer such huge guarantees, Rebecca realized she would have to find another source for Israel.

Meanwhile, with Jordan willing to step up to the plate, Rebecca began to look at the Jordanian Red Sea port of Aqaba for building the $300 million LNG terminal. While Enron now pushed for the Jordanian port, Israel still wanted the plant and preferred its own Red Sea port of Elat. According to Rebecca, lack of space there made it unfeasible. Besides, Jordan was willing to do whatever was necessary for Enron to build the plant to reduce its own dependence on Iraq. With Rebecca unable to find a guaranteed source providing for an adequate supply of LNG, in September 1996, Israel informed Enron they no longer considered their agreement to negotiate with Qatar for Israel's natural gas supplies to be exclusive. The October

1995 agreement had given Enron 180 days to finalize its deal with Qatar, but Rebecca had been unable to negotiate the terms, which would include the gasification plant in Aqaba, Jordan for LNG to be shipped by pipeline to Israel. Qatar was angry with Israeli officials over their decision, but the fact was that gas from Qatar was priced 50% higher than what could be had from Egypt.

Then came another problem for Rebecca's rising star. Enron decided to cancel its plans for the LNG plant. With gas reserves 14 times what the US consumed in a year, Rebecca knew Qatar had become a major source of LNG for India. In 1997, Enron got the go-ahead to expand its LNG processing terminal in India to handle the five million metric tons on behalf of Qatar. Since the mid-'90s, Rebecca had been steering a mammoth deal to construct a 2,015 MW power plant in India. The plant was to be located in the small coastal city of Dabhol, about a hundred miles south of Bombay on the Arabian Sea. In 1993, Enron's proposal to build the enormous power plant was cleared by the Sharad Pawar government. At $2.5 billion, the plant would be the biggest foreign investment in India. To pull it off, Enron had formed a joint venture with two other multinational Goliaths, Bechtel and GE Capital Corp. The project would be backed by the US government, secured by international loans, and paid off on a sliding-rate scale of fractions of American dollars per kilowatt hour. By 2017, the plant would be paid off and billing 30 cents a kWh, versus the bargain 4.3 cents, to be charged at the time the plant was scheduled for completion in early 1999.

On the face of it, the deal seemed terrific for both the builders and the users, except the due diligence people apparently missed one thing – 4.3 cents per kWh was still way too much for the impoverished people of the vast, urbanized state of Maharashtra. There, an office worker's pitiful monthly take home of thirty dollars would get you a decent rib-eye back in one of Houston's better steak joints.

Rebecca had been traveling back and forth to Bombay since 1995. Her missions were not only to make sure the construction project was proceeding, but to wine and dine high ranking members of the Pawar government. Laden with sackfuls of Enron cash earmarked to "Educate the Locals" (at least according to the official corporate line-listed budget item), the truth was the money was no more going to the locals to teach them the virtues of harnessing megawatts than it was to explain crop circles in rural England. The dough was strictly employed to grease the wheels of Indian politics and Rebecca was the bagman.

Her payoffs kept the project nicely on track and all looked well until the locals in Dabhol became enraged at what they saw as oppression by a government bent on selling their birthright in the name of privatization, and even more emotional, the growing rape of their environment. The good people of Dabhol understood all too well that the rest of Maharashtra would benefit greatly from such a facility and they would be the ones picking up the costs. One day they got fed up and attacked the construction site. In addition to the pumps, equipment and office furnishings that were damaged or destroyed, most of the 1,500 construction workers were also hurt in the assault. It was a black eye for the project and the beginning of huge headaches for the Dabhol Power Company.

On November 1, 1995, another event helped sour Ken Lay's active participation in the project. Lay and Rebecca were in Bombay to meet with a number of important people, not the least of whom was Manohar Joshi, state Chief Minister. They left Joshi cooling his heels and never showed. Although the official excuse they gave was they "got tied up in Bombay's traffic", the upshot was that they blew off Joshi to hook up with the real local power broker, Shiv-Sena leader Bal Thackeray. Joshi was furious, "highly insulted", and announced that their behavior was "an affront to the office of Chief Minister". Perhaps Mr. Joshi was merely holding out for more money, but he refused to reschedule the meeting and Rebecca publicly admitted she was "in grief" over it. After that, Lay stayed in Houston and Rebecca was on her own with the Indians.

When the Enron-friendly Pawar faction lost the election to the environmentally-leaning Shiv-Sena-BJP alliance, who won on a ticket promising the ouster of the evil Enron, Rebecca's big adventure really began going bad. In addition to the Indian political winds changing, her other large power deals, one also in India and another in Croatia, were not going well. Rumors were rampant around 1400 Smith Street that Rebecca had botched some of the terms of all three deals, thus compromising Enron's position. It was beginning to look more and more like the Dabhol Power Company would never be able to spark a light bulb, so Lay and Skilling decided that Rebecca should concentrate on more US-based programs.

Having conquered the oil and gas world, she was infuriated by the notion that a resource as valuable as water was literally going down the drain – to the average bonehead it was simply a medium to boil potatoes in. Rebecca, in turn, saw a $400 billion industry that Enron should have a piece of. Between late 1997 and September 1998, she hammered so hard on Chairman Ken Lay about cornering the world's fresh water supply, he eventually began to share her vision and decided to get Enron's feet wet with the acquisition of Britain's Wessex Water.

In the summer of 1998, Enron purchased Wessex Water in an all-cash deal for $2.2 billion. While those of us inside Enron clearly realized this was Rebecca's new venture, her name was never mentioned in the press release, although neither was Jeff Skilling's.

Ken Lay said, "The development, ownership and operation of water infrastructure is a logical extension of Enron's expertise developed in the worldwide energy business."

Everyone in the company knew he meant that a glass of water from your faucet was money in Enron's pocket.

"Currently," Ken continued, "there are only a handful of large private sector companies operating in the $400 billion worldwide water market. There are tremendous opportunities for future growth as the water industry moves toward privatization and consolidation. In order to be successful in this global market, players must have water and wastewater operating experience, financial strength, and project development expertise, including capital-raising ability."

England and Wales had privatized their water and wastewater functions in 1989 and Wessex Water was responsible for providing water service to a population of approximately 1.1 million, utilizing an infrastructure consisting of 131 treatment plants, 320 pumping stations, 340 storage reservoirs and more than 6,800 miles of water mains.

Additionally, Wessex provided wastewater services to an area with a population of approximately 2.5 million through its infrastructure of 1,300 pumping stations, 360 sewage treatment plants and 9,320 miles of sewers. Wessex's other business activities included UK Waste, a joint venture with Waste Management International, which provided waste collection, disposal and recycling services nationwide, and SC Technology, which sold and operated sludge drying plants.

The purchase of flagship business Wessex was intended to grab a portion of that multi-billion dollar global water market through privatization. Initially, Enron's ownership interest would be through a company created by Andy Fastow called the Atlantic Water Trust, a joint venture between Enron, which held 50%, while institutional investors would hold the other 50%. However, the Bridging Agreement allowing Enron to fund the operations of the new water company was so prohibitive and costly that whoever took over the company would be paddling upstream from the get go.

Momentarily sidetracked with the problems in India, Rebecca seemed to be back on her way up the corporate ladder. With deals in England, Guatemala, the Dominican Republic, the Philippines, China and Colombia, Rebecca was becoming a seasoned pro at dealing with foreign crises. Now with the explosive resolution to the India debacle, including the financial guarantee by the India government, Rebecca was promoted to Chairman of EI in May, 1998.

Her enormously lucrative employment contract called for a monthly salary of $59,166.67, which equated to a yearly salary of $710,000. Added to that was her 1998 bonus, which equaled 1% of EI's after-tax net income, or $1.7 million. This was up from the paltry $185,000 she was given in 1997. Her 1998 compensation also included a bonus of $3,344,021 for projects not yet completed, as well as 1,281,059 shares of Enron stock as options – in exchange for the forfeiture of her EI stock options – and the forgiveness of a $995,000 loan and interest accrued, as well as a portion of another $2.5 million loan. It was great to be the queen, but things were about to change.

With Enron's stock now trading at over $52, investment analysts were beginning to take note of the energy giant and Rebecca used this to her advantage. Spinning as fast as she could manage, she boldly portrayed the India project "a tremendous success by any standards". Meanwhile, she was negotiating even more international deals, including the 551 MW oil and gas project on the island of Sardinia in Italy, and a 478 MW natural gas combined-cycle power plant in Marmara Ereglisi, Turkey. An overloaded Rebecca agreed to turn over the Turkish deal to the trustworthy hands of Joseph Sutton, EI's president.

Joe Sutton had certainly made his mark in India and earned the promotion. According to the Indian-born doctor based in Houston who had helped grease the skids for Enron's intro to the India government, Joe Sutton had spent more than 300 days a year on the ground in India. While news reported that it was Rebecca who had turned the India deal around, it had actually been Sutton.

I knew that Rebecca had taken a lot of heat over her tactics in India. I have now been to Mumbai (Bombay), India at the invitation of the same business men who entertained Rebecca to give a keynote speech. They have confirmed as I suspected, Rebecca could not have gotten the Dabhol project approved or completed without paying bribes to the Indian government and have confirmed the payoffs. While clearly against the Foreign Corrupt Practices Act, according to the Indians, when in India, you must do as the Indians do, which requires nothing less than situational ethics.

Rebecca said that some days the 20% import duty on equipment could be 30% or more depending upon what the customs inspector wanted it to be. I also heard the fabled story that Rebecca reprimanded an employee who had gotten off Enron's corporate jet in Sao Paulo without his visa and was questioned by authorities. She berated him, saying, "If you can't lie your way out, you don't deserve to be in this business."

One failure can wipe out a portfolio of successes. Soon after the acquisition of Wessex, Rebecca Mark's image as Enron's golden girl began to slip. When the Wessex purchase was announced, analysts not only started questioning the company's sanity, but speculation arose that Mark the Shark was not long for Enron. It wasn't just the apparent misdirection of heading Enron into a market that was nowhere near primed for private takeover. The problems in India and elsewhere contributed to the bad marks on her report card. And with embarrassments and mistakes here and there, it certainly didn't help that her chief rival was on the rise.

Back in 1996, Jeff Skilling, in addition to his duties as ECT's Chairman, had been elevated to the role of Chief Operating Officer and President of Enron. This upset Rebecca's apple cart as it shifted more power to Jeff, who by this time seemed to be making boatloads of money out of thin air. This stood in stark contrast to Rebecca's style, which was capital-intensive projects. Ken Lay looked at Rebecca and Jeff as his overachieving children and when he compared them he couldn't help but be impressed by his "son's" wild success. Meanwhile, his "daughter" had created mixed blessings for the "family" business.

It didn't help Rebecca that her raison d'etre was big, big assets, a philosophy wholly at loggerheads with new COO Jeff's view of assets as being an overly costly means to an end. Though Rebecca returned from India chastened but intact, the fuse was lit to blow her out the door and brother Jeff's match was still smoking.

No mere darling to Ken Lay, Rebecca's savvy, intellect, drive, and gaming skills represented a real threat to Jeff Skilling in his quest to one day seize Ken's throne when he faded into retirement. Consequently, Skilling had identified Rebecca as a target and had been honing a knife for her since he came on board. It was common knowledge that Skilling's enemies disappeared from corporate headquarters with alarming regularity, but getting rid of Rebecca presented a particularly knotty problem for him. Now, after the debacle in India, Skilling could feel his size 9 Gucci on her throat.

Rebecca's problems gave Skilling what he thought was enough ammo to seal her fate, but Ken Lay stood in his way. Lay rationalized it would be an embarrassment to Enron to terminate such a marquee player, despite her screwing up, so he decided the next best punishment was to promote her. His decision was also influenced by Rebecca's assurances that the minute the door hit her in the ass, she'd be hanging Enron's dirty laundry on the clothesline for all the neighborhood – including the SEC and Justice Department – to see. Father Ken had to find daughter Rebecca a new room within the Enron family home.

With Rebecca's corporate life in limbo, Ken Lay decided the next step was to give Rebecca a new challenge. A Shark needs to swim so it was natural she take over the water empire she helped found. Thus Enron's new water division was born and christened "Azurix", a fusion of the words azure, for the color blue, and radix, which was Greek for the root or point of origin. Rebecca announced in March 1999 that she would soon offer shares in Azurix to the public.

Enlisting the services of Merrill Lynch, Azurix would fly under the ticker symbol AZX. With her new charge came a warning from Ken Lay: this venture will not be an anchor on Enron's business and your little boat will have to float on its own. Through sheer force of will, Rebecca knew she would make the company not only work, but skyrocket. Joe Sutton was named Rebecca's replacement as CEO of EI and watchdog of the $20 billion worth of projects that had contributed to 17% of Enron's gross operating profits in 1997.

Meanwhile, the stress my position in Contract Administration was causing had me at wits' end. Although the assaults by Kathy and Emma and their troops had subsided, the damage had been done. I was coping, but I felt like a nervous breakdown was just under the surface. Between having to watch my back every second, as well as the physical injury the job had caused, I was ready for a big change. If I was going to stay at Enron and reap the full benefits of my stock options, short of just quitting and forfeiting them along with any unemployment, I needed to change my relationship with the company. I had to escape my department and those around me. Having witnessed, then covered up bank fraud at Kathy's behest, I yearned to cleanse myself.

Quitting would have been a bitter pill, considering the value of my stock options was climbing dramatically. Yet I was powerless to liquidate since none of it was vested. I had to do something worthwhile, recreate myself again as a productive person. The aborted project to document the history of Enron, then working on the EOL Rates Database, had reminded me there was hope for fulfilling work within the company. But I was tired of uncovering this conspiracy and that malfeasance. I needed something fresh. I prayed hard and hoped. And I hung in there. I had faith something good would come to me. Little did I know that the much-beleaguered Rebecca Mark would soon become my savior.

Sometime in March, about the time Azurix was coming to life, I received a call from Don Black*. He told me he was a vice president and worked directly under Rebecca. I had been hearing about Rebecca from the time I arrived at Peterson Consulting. While assisting Ben Redford* on international bids on behalf of El Paso Energy, we had competed directly against Enron in the Bolivia to Brazil pipeline bid. Don told me they were in the process of forming Enron's new water division and things were "very exciting". I sent my resume to him at the request of Nora Thompson*, Assistant Corporate Secretary for Azurix. Nora had worked for Pamela James and came highly recommended. I interviewed with Don but heard nothing further from him. Although I kept an eye on Azurix, I decided not to hold my breath and went back to making escape plans.

Because of the ugly noises Wall Street and many of the stock pundits were making regarding Enron's apparent insanity at leaping into the water biz, Rebecca decided a little salesmanship on the home front was in order. I attended her presentation to explain to employees just what in the world Enron was doing in water. Many of us saw the little skit as a practice run for the "road show" the Azurix executives knew they would need to drum up interest in Enron's latest venture.

About that time, Azurix suffered a minor setback and slight of its character when attempting to bid on a contract in Sofia, Bulgaria. Told it was too inexperienced to bid, the reaction at Azurix was utter disbelief. No one – but no one – had ever called Enron inexperienced, and it was shocking that anyone would consider any entity associated with Enron as such. But the reverberations of this slam on Enron's water-baby were short-lived.

In May 1999, Azurix showed it was no Fastow shell company when it was awarded the water and wastewater concessions covering two regions in Buenos Aires, Argentina. The 30-year concession covered the large industrial city of Bahia Blanca, population 430,000 and the industrial center of La Plata, population 1,520,000. For this, Azurix paid $438.6 million. While it was the first major contract won by Azurix, it would be followed by a number of other successful bids. What many did not know at the time was that Azurix paid dearly for the rights – as much as ten-fold more than other bidders. Possibly worse, Azurix would later find that the plumbing was bad – the water concession's infrastructure was more or less shot. The wheels at Azurix missed something even a first-time homebuyer gets – an inspection. But, regardless of the wisdom of its first deals, Azurix was clearly alive and kicking.

In early June of 1999, Enron made a company-wide announcement that Azurix would bow with an IPO about ten days later. With Enron's stock now reaching into the low $80s, Azurix was bound to benefit from the halo effect and climb nearly as fast as its powerful parent. With the IPO price set at $19, a shock even to Rebecca, many at Enron loaded up on Azurix when employees were privately offered the stock just prior to its debut with the big brokerages.

With his company about to go public, Don Black needed bodies, so he sought to secure his turf in a land grab of employees. Don put out the word that Azurix was the hot place to be and to come on over and get in on the action. Priced at $19 per share, Azurix would offer 36.6 million shares and expected to raise $654 million. After deducting the underwriting costs, Azurix expected to net $305 million, with the balance of any "over-allotment option" going to the Atlantic Water Trust, another one of Fastow's off-the-balance sheet partnerships. Ken Lay's edict that Azurix must float on its own echoed through the halls. Yet despite the order from Enron to change Azurix's letterhead by deleting the wording "an Enron company" and leaving Azurix on its own, emotions were heady that Azurix could just be the next big thing.

The IPO vacuumed more than $700 million into the coffers of Azurix, or should I say, Enron. According to documents filed with the SEC, Enron retained only 34% of Azurix. The truth was Enron held just over 63% of the water stock, making Azurix far more thinly traded than it appeared. A fact we were instructed to keep quiet. Despite losing some ground from her fabulous 1998 compensation package as Vice Chairman of EI, the new head of Azurix was still able to feed her twin pre-teen sons. With the award of 2,000,000 stock options at a strike price of $16.72, Rebecca stood to make a steamer trunk full of cash. Assuming the value of the stock rose 10%

per year, Rebecca could find herself with a $36 million windfall come tax time. Not bad for a farm girl from Missouri.

In June, 1999, I got another call from Don Black. "Lynn," he said, "things are heating up over here. I'm putting together the International Bid Team for Azurix. You interested?"

Heh, heh. Yeah, Don.

Azurix's offices were located in the same building as Enron International, at 3 Allen Center on Allen Street. It was across Antioch Park from the main Enron building and the two structures were connected by a glass-enclosed skywalk. While waiting in the lobby to meet with Don, I got my first up-close glimpse of the glamorous Ms. Mark. Confidently striding through the lobby, my eyes went to the dazzlingly long gams, then to the large Louis Vuitton briefcase. Breezing past, the Shark glanced my way and flashed a jaw-load of pearly whites. I remembered how the international lawyers at El Paso Energy would bitterly curse her as she beat them at their own game time and again. While I had read the seemingly accurate descriptions of a "tall, willowy blonde with a soft-spoken professional manner", I also knew this girl hadn't gotten where she was on sheer charm and looks. I knew Mark the Shark had no doubt come by her nickname honestly.

Don Black met me in the lobby and directed me back to his office. Don was a hyper, effeminate little ferret with a fixation on micro management. He was also "self-appointed as Rebecca's quality control person". His desk and credenza were out of a Staples ad, with every paper neatly stacked one on top of the other, giving a view of the issues at hand by simply glancing across the desk.

"I've been with Rebecca since her days at Enron International, and absolutely nothing goes out of this office without my reviewing it first. Nothing."

As he spoke I got the impression he was a fanatic about details. After the carelessness over at Enron, I thought it would be a refreshing break.

"I want you on board here, Lynn. What I'm offering you is a power-player position. You'll be assisting in the bid process on development. I'm talking about both international and domestic assets, as well as other projects for Azurix. We're a start-up and we've got a lot of money, but we need to spend money to make money. Asset acquisition is on our front burner."

After alluding to his offer, Don continued droning on mostly about who he was and why he was so important. The way he spoke of himself, and his indispensability, he made it sound like he let Rebecca do the heavy lifting while he was the one who really kept the place together. Regardless of Don's delusions, I believed this would be a great opportunity to apply my corporate development skills in the international arena.

As I left his office and walked back to my own, I realized I knew very little about Azurix's game plan. He had gone on and on about Azurix's lofty goals but never gave me a definitive idea of my specific responsibilities or where he and Rebecca planned to take their new company. Despite Don's sizzling rhetoric, I didn't smell much steak. However, I still considered it the best opportunity I'd had since coming to Enron. It was a new division and the possibilities seemed sky-high. I also wondered how the dynamics of a woman at the top would change things. Enron was a male-dominated company and the pressures on people like Kathy Simpson and Emma Toombs were generated from above. With a woman running the show, I hoped that would change. Although I knew little about the job Don was offering, I sent him a thank you note for the interview.

Rebecca went on the road to convince analysts of Enron's ability to swim in the privatization of the global water industry. In the meantime, Azurix continued to acquire assets at elevated prices right and left, beginning with the purchase of a position in a consortium paying $150 million for a 70% stake in Obras Sanitarias de Mendoza in Argentina. The Mendoza project followed an earlier purchase of a 49.9% stake in a water concession in Cancun, Mexico. The Cancun deal cost $13.5 million, but also required an assumption of $25 million in financial commitments to upgrade the water system, as well as build a new waste-treatment plant to serve the resort areas of Cancun and Isla Mujeres. When I heard about that, my first thought was silly but ominous: *Don't drink the water in Mexico.*

Initially, Azurix's business plan was a three-pronged approach. Asset Ownership and Management consisted of the acquisitions, concessions and BDOOs (build, design, own, and operate), BDOs (build, design, operate), BOTs (build, own, and transfer), and BOOs (build, own, and operate). Next was Azurix Services, which included municipal and industrial O&M (operation and maintenance), residuals management and underground infrastructure development. This was Azurix's attempt at providing outsourcing of water and wastewater services. The last was Resource Development and Management amounting to the exploration for water, extraction, transportation and storage.

The company's publicly-stated goals included selling private or public equity in Azurix at a premium, winning two or more major concessions/projects, and investing capital of $500 million or more. Additionally, Azurix claimed it intended to acquire or develop businesses to establish itself in the municipal and industrial water and wastewater services market while achieving the net income target of $92 million. To do this, Azurix planned to rely upon intellectual capital by recruiting from both within and outside Enron with a focus on proven results and teamwork. Using this powerful brain trust, they would leverage off of proven industry leaders in water, gas and electricity. Furthermore, personnel from EI and ECT possessed advanced skills in development, operations, commercial and merchant functions. Between Enron's company-wide financial talent and Wessex's technical skills, it was a sure winner. To stimulate growth and encourage innovation, Azurix would create an entrepreneurial compensation package for building new business. This was the bill of goods Azurix sold investment analysts who took Azurix stock public under the IPO.

The truth was, few at Azurix had any water experience, except perhaps Dan Branson* from California who headed up the associate/analyst program. Dan was a major surfer dude who impressed everyone with tales of his gnarly water feats hangin' ten and shootin' the pipeline. In a nutshell, at Azurix's core, it was the dimly-sighted leading the blind. Already heading into its second quarter, Azurix announced a net income of $20.2 million and earnings per diluted share of $0.19. The operating results excluded $6.8 million, or $0.06 per diluted share, and an after-tax, non-recurring charge related to refinancing a portion of the company's long-term debt and paying for the free Ding Dongs and roasted peanuts crammed in the filing cabinets for the employees to chow down on.

Meanwhile, over at Enron, with the stock at an all-time high, it was expatriate Rebecca who led the charge and unloaded $21.7 million worth of her own ENE. Jeff Skilling had managed to get rid of Vice Chairman Ken Harrison and now only Becky stood in his way once Ken Lay stepped down. Or so he thought. Ken Lay liked what Jeff Skilling, the businessman, had done for his stock value, but he took a dim view of Jeff Skilling, the person. He threw a wrench in Jeff's scheme by appointing Rebecca to succeed Ken Harrison as Vice Chairman of Enron Corp. She also knew if her former lover took over for Ken, there's no way she would ever find herself under him again so she had a clause in her contract allowing her to exit on golden wings were Jeff to be appointed CEO of Enron.

With Azurix shakily under steam, Chairman Rebecca continued Don's efforts to staff her new firm. Analysts assumed and even reported that she would be peopling the offices with the best and the brightest in the water industry. They were wrong. It was a $700 million frat party and Rebecca was bringing in her friends to get a taste of the cake. Included on her guest list was Janet Charles*, former VP of Corporate Communications for Ken Lay; Janet's husband, Ray*, named Managing Director of Azurix Human Resources; and Amanda Martin, then president of one of Enron's North American business groups. In the best tradition of nepotism, Ken Lay's daughter, Elizabeth, also came on board.

A native South African, Amanda was a fascinating case. Her business acumen should not have gotten her past the secretarial pool yet here she was, a president making $550,000 a year. But Amanda was stunningly attractive and a weasel of the first order. The scuttlebutt was that paramour Ken Rice once boasted he had transformed her from "a K-Mart girl" into the capped-tooth, saline-breasted goddess she now was.

I had seen Amanda here and there, and although she was a friend of Jennifer's our paths had never crossed. One day she passed by my desk. Smiling, she stopped and held out a hand.

"Lynn? Amanda Martin. Jennifer said you had joined us."

We shook hands.

"Jennifer has told me all about you," I said with a smile.

"Well, that can't be good."

"It was," I lied. "Jennifer really likes you."

"I just saw her. She's heading out of town. She's going to the King Ranch. I'm headed to my own ranch."

"Oh really?" I instantly tried to gauge what kind of money it took to own "vacation" property.

"Yeah, my family's moved out from South Africa. My sis brought her fucking dog. Goddamn thing mauled my dog the other day. They've bloody well taken over my place. I had to remind my sister who pays the fucking mortgage."

I was slightly taken aback by her language but plunged on with our conversation, which was very comfortable despite colorful descriptions that would embarrass a sailor. Amanda was clearly a confident woman, probably encouraged by her elevated status within Enron. Consequently, when she blared obscenities around the office, causing heads to pop up to determine the source, she casually took note but didn't break stride. Sort of *I'm Amanda Martin and you can just go fuck yourself if you don't like my fucking language*. That we were in the middle of the Bible Belt, surrounded by faint-hearted conservatives who just might swoon over such verbal degeneration, mattered not a whit to her.

Because Enron was always more about who you knew than what you knew, after Amanda left, a colleague approached me.

"You and Amanda must be good friends," she said. "What's she like? She seems like a tough cookie."

I shrugged. "I don't know."

"Well you two are friends, right?"

"Not really. Until this moment, I'd never met her."

The woman was stunned.

The next time I saw Amanda was in her office, brushing her long blonde hair, gazing at her reflection in the mirrored closet door.

By the time the hiring frenzy died down at Azurix, less than ten percent of the staff had any water experience save for what they drank or showered in. About a month after the IPO, I saw my opportunity and requested a transfer. Wanting to distance myself from the chronic misdeeds in my division, I felt Azurix would be a fresh start, as well as a chance to learn from the legendary Rebecca Mark.

In July, 1999, with my stock options 50% vested, I transferred to Azurix as a member of the International Bid Team. It was my responsibility to prepare the necessary documentation, that is, due diligence, for bids on water projects. I was to analyze the risks of the elements of each deal to determine their upsides and downsides. Then I would assist in preparing the lengthy bid documents that were kept under lock and key in the vault.

The atmosphere at Azurix could not have been more different from Enron's legal department. There was an air of confidence, perhaps even invincibility. Trading water was foreign turf, not only for Azurix, but for the private sector as well. Prior to this venture, water traders were governments, either nations or states, and utilities. We were blazing new trails, but we were up to the task, buoyed somewhat by the heady success of Enron and our seeming Jack-of-all-trades *Zeitgeist.* Had we been a burger chain we would have believed we could build airplanes. And our boss, Rebecca, had also just been appointed a member of Enron Corp's board of directors. That feather in her cap gave her even more cachet value around the office and also placed her one step closer to succeeding Ken Lay when he stepped down. Of course, Jeff Skilling would have a few words about that.

Part of the reason we had such an overweening sense of ability came from the proximity to our illustrious leader. Now that I had finally met and dealt with Rebecca, I was even more impressed and inspired. I would sometimes pass by her spacious office to see her vainly wielding a hairbrush through her lavish locks as she cemented a deal on the phone, or dictated a memo that would alter people's lives forever. I thought of Amanda Martin and had to conclude that quite possibly the secret to success at Enron, at least for a woman, was excessive hair combing.

I couldn't help but watch in awe as Rebecca walked, seeing those tightly-corded calf muscles rippling, the product of iron-willed dedication and a few zillion reps on a Stairmaster. She lived a much larger life than most, having *two*, count 'em, *two* homes in some of Houston's most expensive and exclusive neighborhoods.

The one she actually lived in was in ultra-pricey River Oaks. The one she entertained in was in lavish Tanglewood. I knew Ken Lay had several homes, but since I was working directly for Rebecca, it made it all the more real and glamorous.

To see her in action was a sight to behold. She also had what I believe was the secret behind most exceptionally successful people: fearlessness and a mild sociopathy. Perhaps it was just abject narcissism, but whatever the analysis, Rebecca took what she wanted with little or no regard for anyone or anything. She instilled confidence in me, but in the back of my mind I sensed that the moral void causing the rest of Enron to rot from the head down had probably infected her as well. Yet I was so deliriously happy to be away from Kathy and the vipers, I put it out of my mind, hoping I was wrong.

Initially, what Don Black promised had sounded intensely exciting. I would be flitting between exotic nations, a polished aluminum briefcase chained to my wrist, filled with bids for wonderful projects designed to deliver a bright future to the world's underprivileged. I would be like a James Bond of commerce. Unfortunately, once I was assigned my desk and figured out where the ladies room was, I had to scramble to find work.

For the first two months, Don gave me absolutely nothing to do. As I spent my days trying to appear busy, I looked around and sized up our lavish offices, the world tours our execs were embarking on, the walls of filing cabinets filled with snacks supplied by the company, and I calculated that Azurix's ferocious burn rate had to be exceeding that of most dot-coms. While struggling to pin Don down to discuss upcoming projects, scary murmurings were heard around the office. The chat was how the short burst of big-budget bidding that had established Azurix's first few months was coming to an end. Perhaps even more critical was the disappearance of our free Cheetos and espresso.

Just when I was wondering if I would ever have anything to do, a young woman approached me.

"Are you Lynn?"

She was in her late twenties and about four months pregnant.

"Yes."

"I'm Duleane Schneider*."

"It's nice to meet you. What can I do for you?"

"Do you know where we got these numbers?"

She held out something that looked like an offering memorandum, a marketing tool generally used to hook potential investors. As she pointed to the text, I read it aloud.

"'Azurix estimates that the global water industry has total annual revenues of approximately $300 billion. We estimate that over $600 billion will be spent on worldwide water and wastewater infrastructure over the next decade.'"

"I have no idea where we got these numbers, but I'd be happy to find out."

I went to work to determine their origin and found they had become gospel, according to Azurix, and appeared in every piece of company literature. In fact, more recent documents reflected an even more optimistic outlook and now showed annual revenue estimates to be between $350 and $400 billion.

While searching Westlaw, a premier legal database, I got a break. The World Bank was credited with the numbers Azurix was using. After making at least five calls to various people, including the author of the World Bank's white paper, no one had a clue as to the factual basis that $600 billion would be spent in the next decade on worldwide water and wastewater infrastructure.

It wasn't bank fraud, but it certainly appeared to be a phenomenal example of misrepresentation. Azurix had been using the figures to dupe analysts who used them to set the price for Azurix's public offering. I was dazzled that the number had apparently been pulled out of thin air. I was also curious why it was being questioned only now. If nothing purportedly went out of the office without Don Black's stamp of approval, then the omnipotent Mr. Black had to know the numbers were a falsehood.

I called Duleane and relayed the information I found. We both agreed it would have to be removed from the memorandum before more people were sucked in by Azurix's financial hyperbole. I smiled, listening to Duleane denounce the lies. *Finally, someone who is ethical.* Unfortunately, Duleane was only an Associate. My smile faded as I faced the reality that we were just pawns with little chance of righting such a wrong in this den of thieves. Had we tried, we would have been shut down, just as Kathy had thrown a blanket over my attempt to shine a light on the Bammel scam. I sighed and wished Duleane well with her newly-revised memorandum.

It was around this time that I was driving with Lori Cortez looking at real estate investments when we happened upon the Ripcord Bar. I nearly threw her through the front window of the car, as I slammed on my brakes.

"What's wrong?" asked Lori.

"Remember that e-mail I got? About the AIDS-ridden dildo?"

"Oh Gawd, yes! Why?"

I pointed at the bar. "The return address on the e-mail said 'Ripcord Houston.'"

"Well, sweetie, that's a hard-core gay bar."

I squinted hard and made out the tag line under the big Ripcord sign: ***Houston's Premier Leather Bar***

I knew it. Not that it was gay bar, but it was now obvious that either Ronnie Jones or Hilda Gaither had sent the poisonous e-mail, hoping some foul, "AIDS-ridden dildo" would somehow fall from the heavens and smite me. It seemed far too coincidental that Ronnie was gay, Hilda was a self-described "fag-hag", and Ripcord was a gay bar. Now I had more evidence for the HR people who were supposedly looking into the poisonous e-mail that threatened my life.

With Don Black hovering as the ever-present control freak protecting Rebecca's interests, I was so bored; I debated whether it would be inappropriate for an executive to paint her nails at her desk. Don literally refused to give me any specific responsibilities and also forbade me from being redeployed to another group. I knew he was fearful that, in light of cutting expenses to make more cash available for international acquisitions, if he started letting people go back to Enron it could open the floodgates for losing his entire staff. And that would certainly mean a pink slip for Black. So he continued to bury his nose further up Rebecca's butt while I began scavenging for other work within the group.

My opportunity for actually working came in the form of Ed Reams*, a charming man in his early 50s. He was a close personal friend of Rebecca's who had been hired as a vice president in Resource Development. Don was delighted to cover my salary with his staff budget and I was excited to finally have something to do.

I began with two projects for Ed, which managed to keep me busy, and would hopefully keep me from being redeployed back to Enron. The first project involved assessing closed military bases for water which might exist on the site. I was to look at the feasibility of acquiring them in a bid. The other project concerned researching the possibility of actually transporting water from Alaska to the coast of California. Many people had eyed Alaska's pristine water for years, but how to get it south – if the Alaskans' would allow it – was the big question. I figured if anyone was going to propose a wacky scheme like that it was Azurix.

I eventually became aware of turmoil brewing between Wessex Water personnel and Azurix corporate headquarters. By the pugnacious, arrogant demeanor of the Wessex people, you would have thought Wessex actually purchased Azurix, rather than the other way around. In an effort to fully integrate the two work forces, Wessex began sending their British personnel to work in Azurix's headquarters. I hadn't really paid much attention to them until I had a run-in with Clement Rogers*. While Clement was apparently a bigwig in the organizational structure of Wessex Water, to me he was just another Limey who had crossed the Pond to show everyone that Wessex was the only reason Azurix existed.

Clement stormed in, trying to dictate my work load as he had with his large staff back in Bath. At first I politely resisted, telling him I was working on projects for Ed Reams. But Clement was not going to be patronized by some "underling" and continued pressuring me to take assignments and to report to him. I started ignoring him, which sent him into a rage on more than one occasion. The lack of cohesion within the hierarchy of Azurix caused power voids, and a pushy narcissist like Rogers saw weakness and attacked. I appealed to Don Black to call off Rogers, but all he did was pull his head back in his shell and pretend it hadn't happened. Clement Rogers, as a manager, mistakenly felt he outranked VP Ed Reams, but I continued to "disobey" him by working on Ed's projects. Finally, Rogers blinked and recruited someone who would listen to him, a woman from Human Resources named Tami Sue Johnson*.

It was about this time that I began to notice Jennifer's boss, Sullivan Graas, making frequent visits to the Azurix offices. I wondered what he wanted from Enron's bastard step-child. I knew he and Amanda were good friends, but his high level of interest just didn't add up. He was meeting too often for it to be social, so I called Jennifer and asked what was up. Jennifer and Sully's relationship, which had never been on solid footing, had diminished even more by this time and Jennifer didn't know what was going on.

"I'll give Amanda a call and find out," she said.

She called back a little later.

"Amanda's not talking. She wouldn't budge. There's something going on."

After my own investigation, I discovered that Sully was meeting with Amanda to make his bid for a position at Azurix, which, of course, would come with a promotion. The irony was that Sully was pressing Jennifer to complete a project, which, she would eventually learn, was solely intended to get him his new position at Azurix. With the results of her work in hand, he would appear to have all of the expertise necessary to create Azurix's new intranet and Internet sites.

When Jennifer found out she was being played, she not only saw it as unethical that he had utilized personnel from ECT to do Azurix work, she was particularly pissed that her nemesis had used her to get himself a better job. Jennifer stormed into Sully's office and demanded to know what was going on. Without missing a beat, Sully called HR and asked them to come down. She thought it seemed strange that, almost on cue, someone from HR was available to meet with them.

Sully's histrionics seemed right out of a bad movie.

"I don't like where your accusations are going, Jennifer Wellsley!" he protested loudly enough for nearby "witnesses" to overhear. Jennifer was indignant over his response to her accusation that he used her work for his personal gain. She was even more angry that he was now making her out to be the bad guy in this little drama. After HR intervened she went back to her desk and immediately called and asked me to meet her. I walked over to the Enron building and we went in the Starbuck's Café, reserved only for Enron employees. Jennifer was near tears.

Human Resources had slapped her on the wrist for cornering a boss. In Enron's robotic world, employees couldn't express anger over outrageous indignities perpetrated by other employees because first, emotions were against company policy, and second, outrageous indignities perpetrated by other employees just didn't happen. It seemed like Sully had finally found his opportunity to make Jennifer look bad, knowing all along that if HR ruled against him, he had a job offer with Azurix and could simply walk away and tell them to kiss his ass. Lucky for Sully HR sided with him.

Apparently Sully loathed Jennifer so much he spent an exorbitant amount of time devising ways to get rid of her. But no matter what he came up with, as long as Gary Donohue was in a position of power over him, it was completely useless. Of course, Sully never stopped to consider that he and Jennifer had the same qualifications for their respective positions – none. In typical Enron fashion – it was not what you knew but who you knew that guaranteed you continued employment with the energy giant.

Not knowing whether he would be taken into the Azurix fold, Sully wanted to at least rid himself of Jennifer if he was destined to stay at Enron. He finally concocted the perfect plan to get her out of his hair. He would throw both Jennifer and her knight in shining armor under the bus. Sully went to the legal department with evidence that Gary and Jennifer were having an affair. He claimed he never would have mentioned it, but it had become "a distraction for the group." Sully agreed to provide sworn testimony, believing that Legal would simply have Jennifer reassigned. The last thing he expected was what actually happened – they fired Gary Donohue.

After his "get Jennifer" plan backfired, Sully refocused on what Rebecca dubbed "Azurix's future in the e-commerce market". Azurix was already being criticized by analysts and Skilling, so it needed the appearance of being a cutting-edge company with up-to-the-moment tools to market its wares. The primary objective of the new e-Commerce Group was to develop a Web portal where water treatment facilities could order chemicals and other related products – kind of like a big pool products supply for utilities. Azurix's stated goal for the e-Commerce Group was to provide one-stop shopping. The unstated goal was to take some of the heat away from the street where nervous investors and pesky analysts were continually asking why Enron had stepped outside its core business and was now playing with water. It was hoped that the e-Commerce Group would begin to brand Azurix the "innovative offspring" of Enron, rather than a well-heeled, dilettante stepchild.

A few weeks later, Sully Graas officially came over from Enron to head development of the new intranet, as well as assist with the implementation of Azurix's e-commerce water trading platform. Sully brought along Elizabeth Wright with a promise of bringing underling Colleen Lawrence over as soon as possible. This would leave Jennifer behind at ECT to fend for herself and finally rid Sully of his albatross. After Colleen complained that Jennifer was taking out her frustrations on her, Sully made quick arrangements to have Colleen moved over.

Although the new e-Commerce Group was the dream of his boss Rebecca, Don was uneasy because he didn't really understand it. The moment the group was organized and Sully's assistant had put paperclips in his desk, Don summoned him to his office.

"Everything in this office," he said with his fist tapping the desk, "will be run through me, including content for the intranet. I supervise *everything.*"

While Don offered Sully his complete support, it wasn't really an option: Don was merely insinuating himself into Sully's arena. Don's concern was that Sully might do something without his approval and he wanted to be ready to instantly disclaim any misdoings. While Don Black was a thorn in everyone's side, he was, by far, hardest on Sully. I had an ugly suspicion that much of Don's treatment pivoted on the fact Sully was black.

But Sully had friends in high places, namely his South African buddy Amanda Martin, who outranked Don, so Don's antagonism rolled off his back with grace. Sully was also aware that Don managed to get Wessex Brit Clement Rogers working "undercover" for him to try and dictate the direction of the e-commerce project.

But Sully was ahead of Don and, while he let Clement and Don play out their puppet master fantasy, they actually had little influence on the direction of the intranet and the e-Commerce Group.

I developed a good working relationship with Sully at ECT, and with my work for Ed Reams winding down, Sully recruited me for his intranet adventure. When I had first applied to Sully's group back at ECT, he tarred me with the same stick as Jennifer. In time he realized we were hardly joined at the hip, and in fact saw that we were very different. So Sully and I developed an arm's-length friendship.

After he'd been at Azurix about a month, Sully called me into his office. From the bottom drawer of the file cabinet, he pulled out my resume and my book on sports motivation, which I had given him nearly a year before.

"It's been a long time. Things have changed between us," he said.

I nodded. "Yes, they have."

"I want you to come over to my group. I'll get the necessary approvals for it and I'll talk to Don."

Azurix had not been quite what I expected. Sully's offer was exciting, giving me what appeared to be my first real project since coming over. And it beat the hell out of working for Kathy. Up to that point, Azurix had been a sort of bizzaro, reverse-world version of Enron, from terror to boredom in one easy leap. But aside from a lack of things to do, a dark specter loomed on the horizon that made me glad I had finally found a home. The rumor mill was already making morbid predictions about Azurix's future and envisioning mass layoffs in the offing. Sully's offer seemed like a lifesaver, but there was one catch.

"You'll have to end your relationship with Jennifer Wellsley," he stated emphatically.

I swallowed hard, not believing what I had just heard.

"I require complete loyalty here," he continued. "And I know you and Jennifer are close friends. I know I ask a lot, but I'm offering a lot."

I shook my head and thought *Who are you, the Godfather? What does our friendship have to do with this job?*

"Lynn, everyone in this company is on thin ice, from the day we begin to the day we leave. Any one of us can take a fall with the slightest push. Jennifer hates me. I hate Jennifer. If you tell her something, she might be able to use it against me. I cannot let that happen."

"Okay," I countered, "how 'bout I just not tell her anything?"

"Not good enough," he said firmly. "Some day you'll slip. And I'll pay the price."

Sully and I parried for another five minutes or so then went on to another subject. I never agreed to his outrageous demand and he never pressed me for an answer. We just let it drop for the moment. But I knew it would become an issue if I took the position. I wanted the job, but the price was already climbing out of sight. The conversation that followed with Don Black didn't help.

"I'm telling you, e-commerce is going nowhere. Hard assets will be the only thing that keeps Azurix afloat." Don's eyes narrowed, his jaw clenched.

We weren't three minutes into discussing my move when he fired both barrels. I was very surprised he would unveil such contempt for Sully's contribution to Azurix. I also wondered whether Azurix had been saddled with this e-commerce scam by Jeff Skilling. Enron owned most of Azurix, and when it got down to, as Montana sheep ranchers call it, "nut-cuttin' time", Enron called the shots and perhaps made e-commerce a smoke screen to protect Azurix from the harsh critics of the financial world.

"But I think the e-Commerce Group is a good idea," I countered. Don shrugged. "Assets are a good idea. This whole Internet, dot-com thing is a bubble. I think it's smoke in the wind and I don't want to be pulled down by this thing when it fails."

First Sully orders me to dump a friend, and now Don Black was telling me the entire group was doomed. *What does a girl have to do to get a good job around this place?* Don may have been right in the end, but before he bailed from Azurix with a very fat severance package a year later, he ironically begged to manage the e-Commerce Group versus being laid off.

At first I was technically "on loan" to Sully, but within a month I was absorbed into the e-Commerce Group as an official member. Not long after I started, Sully called me into his office.

He pointed at his laptop. "There's something wrong with it."

I was well-known around the office for being extremely proficient with computers. Sully periodically asked for minor assistance because all of his technical support disappeared with the layoffs. Though it wasn't part of my job, I was happy to help him.

"What's wrong with it?"

"It's too slow. Whenever I try to call things up or operate online, it's like swimming through motor oil. And it's always freezing up on me."

"Have you defragged your hard drive recently?"

He looked clueless.

"How about scan disk? Did you try running that?"

More raised eyebrows. He obviously had no idea what I was talking about.

I sighed. "Okay, give me a few minutes and I'll see if I can figure out what's wrong."

He left for a meeting and I sat down and started trouble-shooting. I pulled up his temporary files, and discovered *Wet N Wild Teens.com*, *All Over Her Face.com*, and *LewdNudes.com.* I was perplexed. While the first one had some aquatic connotation, the latter two didn't really sound like sites associated with the water industry. As I explored his files I found his hard drive jam-packed with salacious material that was probably illegal in at least Kentucky and Alabama, if not Texas. Only then did I recall that Sully spent an inordinate amount of time with his office door closed. I knew that when he had been assigned the laptop, the files had been completely cleaned. After scraping the porn out of his computer, it ran about ten times faster. I didn't mention what I had found and Sully probably had no idea that computers recorded all of your Internet activity.

During this period, I began noticing a hulking, slickly groomed man frequenting the offices. A colleague mentioned he was Rebecca's fiancé, Michael Jusbasche [pronounced juice-bosh]. Jusbasche was several inches over six feet, broad shouldered, and sporting a look that could have come from the union of Elvis Presley and Wayne

Newton. I assumed Jusbasche was there merely to see his beloved, but I soon found I was wrong.

Azurix's Internet portal, to buy and sell chemicals for water treatment plants, was to be called "ChemicalDesk.com". This would complement Azurix's plans for WaterDesk.com, their site concerning business assets. Not long after finding out who Michael Jusbasche was, I discovered that Azurix was currently engaged in talks regarding a partnership between Azurix and his company, Coastal Products & Chemicals. The new entity would be owned by both Azurix and Jusbasche's company. What no one at Azurix knew – save for one person – was that while Jusbasche and Azurix advanced in good faith toward a partnership, Jusbasche was making some secret plans of his own.

Azurix forged ahead with plans for their two new Internet entities, ChemicalDesk.com and WaterDesk.com, and I was asked to formally register the two domain names in August. When I did a search, to my surprise, I found that both names were taken. It struck me as odd that a company as big as Azurix wouldn't at least have checked for availability. I went to Sully.

"I can't get the names. Someone has them."

Sully looked perplexed. "I thought they were available. That's why we took them. Are you sure?"

"Yes."

Sully shook his head. "Then we may have to buy them from whoever owns them because this thing is in the works. I mean a lot of time and effort has gone into this and they're already doing PR and such."

I went back and double-checked. They were taken. I did a quick search to see who owned them. The domain holder was a company called Coastal Products & Chemicals. They had registered the names on July 8, 1999, more than a month earlier. Then I remembered that Coastal Products & Chemicals was owned by none other than Michael Jusbasche. I was stunned. It didn't make any sense. Why had Rebecca Mark's fiancé grabbed the rights to the names? Was this part of their partnership agreement with Azurix? Was it an honest mistake? I soon found out when someone told me Azurix was no longer considering a partnership with the Bolivian expatriate. Discussions with Mr. Jusbasche broke off in August, 1999. Apparently the falling out didn't faze Jusbasche who decided to ensure locking up the entire ChemicalDesk branding by registering ChemicalDesk.*net* on September 13, 1999.

With the price of Azurix stock dropping quickly, the first round of layoffs came with Ken Lay's approval in September, 1999, just three months after the IPO. When the layoffs began, Sully assumed his gang was untouchable. When the icy finger of fate reached out and touched the administrative assistant who had been with Sully for a number of years, he was furious. He took his beef to friend Amanda Martin who said there was nothing she could do. That really stuck in Sully's craw and he continued to complain.

The overall boss of the e-Commerce Group was Chris Wasden, Rebecca's strategic advisor. Due to the behind-the-scenes stress at Azurix, there was growing tension between Chris and Rebecca. Soon Chris was no longer advising Rebecca on strategic matters, but was put in charge of developing the entire e-commerce platform. Despite his diminished value with Rebecca, Amanda was not about to bother Chris with trying to rehire Sully's assistant. Sully would have to live with her. Besides, Amanda knew Sully had a reputation as a whiner and that's how she categorized his demands to reinstate his little helper.

Enron then ordered Azurix to restate its business plan. From that point forward it would label itself a "risk management" company in the water industry. Throughout the ranks at Azurix, the combination of the falling stock and impending peril had the rats in the cages rebelling. The pressure was even a little too much for the head of our group, Chris Wasden. Chris began throwing temper tantrums. The thought of building a business that was clearly headed for destruction was driving him to the brink of madness. Chris, his assistant, Tad Whalen*, and another exec, Mel Heiman*, started talking mutiny. When word got back to Sully that he was not invited to participate, he was enraged. Once again, he ran to Amanda. He felt he had as big a bone to pick with the e-Commerce Group as anyone. All of senior management felt they had been sold a bill of goods after being enticed away from Enron to take a cruise on a sinking ship.

In September 1999, Azurix turned its pockets inside out, fished all the coins out of the sofa and purchased AMX Acqua Management for $55 million in cash and stock. The Latin American water company based in Rio de Janeiro was responsible for drilling over 1,000 wells throughout the region. While Rebecca touted that Brazil represented one of the best opportunities for water investments, Walter Kirchberger of Paine Webber clearly stated that the deal was "not a huge event". The street agreed and Azurix shares fell another ¼ to $15-3/8 with the news.

The AMX acquisition was followed by acquisition of the German engineering company Lurgi Bamag for $30 million. Never mind that Azurix was in the middle of laying off its entire engineering staff in Houston, someone felt the necessity to acquire a German engineering firm. Even the media began commenting on the move, saying "acquisitions and joint agreements fail to buoy a sinking stock price". With yet another acquisition of a 49% ownership interest in a 2,500 liter per second, $25 million municipal wastewater treatment plant being built in the city of Leon, Mexico, the powers at Azurix were praying the rebound would soon begin.

In October, despite Azurix's stock falling like Niagara, Rebecca was named for the second year in a row as one of *Fortune's* 50 Most Powerful Women. Although she had dropped from number 14 to 29th, apparently no one at *Fortune* had done their due diligence. It was kind of like lauding the Captain of the Exxon Valdez for his great seamanship. The press also played up the fact that 110 of the positions in Azurix, equaling 40%, were held by women. No one seemed to care that few had any water experience whatsoever.

By November, 1999, Azurix stock was way underwater at around $5, after being issued at $19.00 less than six months earlier. With the stock tanking so far, everyone left at Azurix was wondering how long we could stay afloat. The holidays were upon us, but few at Azurix felt like celebrating. In a twist of gallows humor, the band scheduled to perform for the Enron holiday concert practiced in Azurix's conference room. It was reminiscent of that famous scene from the deck of the Titanic as the stalwart musicians played "Nearer My God To Thee", even as the frigid water lapped at their ankles. Few of us found the juxtaposition amusing.

My personal life was actually improving dramatically. Doug Brewer, a man who had been my date to a couple of high school dances had come back into my life. In the time since high school, I had remained extremely close to Doug and his family. My senior year of high school I had actually lived with his family when my own family was forced to relocate, as my father expanded his company through an acquisition of a Portland-based business; and Doug's oldest daughter had been the flower girl in my first wedding. Doug understood the drama I had been through in my own life when, after 15 years of marriage, Doug's wife suddenly ended up pregnant with another man's child after having a series of affairs. The court awarded Doug primary custody of the kids, the family home, and she was ordered to pay child support. He had been devastated and I was a sympathetic ear. But four years had passed and a deep friendship had blossomed. In 1999, that friendship would turn to romance.

As Doug and I began to discuss the logistics of our love affair that had us bouncing between Houston and the Pacific Northwest, even Enron and Azurix couldn't dim the joy I felt over seeing Doug in a whole new light after all those years.

Sitting at Colleen Lawrence's desk one day just before Christmas, talking about the future, I commented, "I just can't believe how fast this company went under."

Colleen shook her head. "The only thing that surprises me any more, Lynn, is that you're surprised."

One senior manager did manage to find a lifeboat and escaped back to Enron. After an apparent disagreement with Rebecca over financial reporting, Azurix CFO Rodney Gray walked out the door and high-tailed it back down the block to 1400 Smith Street. Many of us wished it would be that easy for us to flee. Though we all went through the motions, clearly, when the CFO resigns, the handwriting is on the wall and it was simply a matter of time before Azurix crumbled.

With the walls tumbling down around her ears, Rebecca had admittedly been distracted by her love life. After being married in a small civil ceremony in November 1999, Rebecca promised everyone involved that Azurix was still viable and come the new-year, she would put all of her efforts into making it go. I found it odd that with all the problems the company faced, one of the main topics of conversation that Christmas concerned construction of an elaborate stairwell, which would connect the 9th and 10th floors of the office. I guess the bosses figured bad news didn't travel fast enough in an elevator.

Azurix's fabulous Christmas bash gave no indication the company was spinning down a giant toilet. While Rebecca's "party" home was used strictly for entertaining, she was completing construction on yet another mansion in River Oaks. As we arrived, our cars were shuttled away by valets. The vast Mediterranean-style house had been redecorated into a Victorian manor, with the lake-sized pool covered to accommodate the long guest list. While a Victorian Santa Claus entertained the children, my fiancé Doug and I wandered through the crowd of gowns and tuxes, amused at the show of excess. After we made the rounds we found a quiet corner in the study to scan the massive bookshelves. Rebecca dropped in, said hello, then handed us a thick album of pictures from her wedding and photos of her Spanish-style ranch in Taos.

By January 2000, the Y2K menace was over, more or less a non-event for Enron. Few problems were detected, despite the company's massive yet unpublicized failure to get their systems "Y2K compliant". Even better, Enron was reporting an astounding 700% return to shareholders over the past decade. Meanwhile, the Houston Chronicle was nosing around Azurix and reporting that the company brass claimed politics were to blame for the recent loss of critical bids. They noted that AG Edwards analyst Tim Winter saw Azurix fighting a losing battle with French water heavyweights Vivendi and Suez Lyonnaise. He also acknowledged the French were looking long term and skittish US investors wanted a much shorter-term return. Truth be known, Azurix needed nearly instant financial gratification. At that point Azurix was really just a paper tiger, with paper in shorter and shorter supply by the day.

Azurix stock had momentarily bounced back up to $7.00, but it was hardly cause for celebration. Institutional investors had already begun running for cover from Azurix. The largest shareholder in Enron, the Janus Fund, had held the second largest share until they liquidated in September, 1999. But the analysts in Azurix's corner were still lobbying hard.

Debra Coy of Schwab Capital Markets encouraged buyers, saying, "The bottom line is that it's a good buy." In her opinion, the assets alone made Azurix's stock worth $12 to $13 per share. But when I heard Jason Selch from Wanger Asset Management exclaim "This management team has experience in fixing problems," I almost fell out of my chair. Perhaps if he'd said *This team, though wildly incompetent with water, is practiced at creating massive problems overseas then fixing them with large bribes,* I might have nodded in accord. On the other hand I was beginning to see the parallels between international power markets and large-scale cesspools.

Around this time, the results of a big bid came in and Azurix lost. But losing the bid wasn't the news – it was how they lost it. Monroe County, Florida put out a proposal request to water pros for a wastewater management plan for the Keys. A number of big dogs in water responded and Azurix was one of them. Apparently someone at Azurix failed to acknowledge the difference between gallons and liters so Azurix's bid was nearly four times the other bids, equivalent to the amount a gallon is larger than a liter.

With such boneheaded moves Azurix's stock value continued to sink, causing Rebecca's net worth to take a dive of almost $15 million on paper. With another round of layoffs imminent, morale was low and getting worse. Word spread that all the Wessex Brits were soon to be expelled from the Colonies, or at least Texas. The irascible Clement Rogers, who had recently sent for his family and furniture now had to make a hurried call and stop the move. His next call was to the reservation desk at British Airways.

One of the main topics of discussion was how long Azurix would last. Some were giving us weeks, while others thought that even though the patient was brain dead, the heart would continue beating until summer. I hated to venture a guess. It all seemed too negative. But I was also kicking myself for having climbed aboard a distressed vessel. It had all looked so good less than a year before. Now I just prayed that when Azurix went under, Enron would send lifeboats for some of us.

As whispered speculation continued on the demise of the company, I focused on my duties, among which was to check the availability and the registration of Internet domain names for Azurix. Around Thursday, January 13, 2000, a meeting was held with Rebecca Mark and the e-Commerce Group to decide on a list of names for the "water storage/trading platform". Unable to attend the meeting, one of my colleagues, Paul Mason*, gave me the list of names they had decided on. The next day I checked for availability and found that only three of the names weren't registered. They included Waterswap.com, Watervault.com, and the dark horse candidate, Waterport.com. The latter immediately caused some rethinking when Paul said the name aloud to an exec who hadn't been privy to the meeting.

"Say what?" he exclaimed, "Watersports? Are you nuts? Why not Goldenshowers.com?"

I couldn't help but think that Sully Graas might have had that very site on his computer when I cleaned out the "sewage". We deleted Waterport.com as a contender to avoid any confusion with "Watersports.com". I told Paul that only two were available for registration and that the others were owned by third parties. He said he would check with Rebecca to determine what she wanted to do.

Later that evening, Friday, January 14, Paul instructed me to register the two available names: Waterswap.com and Watervault.com. It was late so I told him I would do it first thing on Monday. Come Monday morning, January 17, I sat down at my desk and logged on to the registration site. To my surprise, I found they had been taken. I was wise to the ways of Enron by now and nothing really surprised me. I did some research and when the results came up, I sat back and stared at the screen.

Jusbasche's company had registered them under his other stolen domain name, ChemicalDesk.com on Sunday. I decided to keep my mouth shut, fearing if I revealed my discovery I would be fired. Three days later, on Thursday, January 20, 2000, a memo with the seven names from the original meeting was sent to all Azurix employees asking them to vote on which ones they liked.

A week later, around January 27, after the votes had been tabulated, I informed Paul that the two companies chosen were not available and we would have to pick another name. No one questioned who had bought the names. I remained silent because Michael Jusbasche was the CEO's husband. On Friday evening, January 28, Paul told me he had spoken with Rebecca and they had decided on a new name, Water2Water.com.

To my surprise, Rebecca had already made a public announcement regarding her intentions to operate a water trading platform called Water2Water.com. The site would be designed to provide farmers a flexible and guaranteed supply of water from Azurix. Giving farmers the option of swapping water in years when there was a tremendous demand would generate greater revenues by temporarily allowing one farmer to allocate their water to another – sort of a water clearinghouse. Additionally, the site would offer detailed weather information, crop and commodity prices, soil moisture content, local and crop specific news, as well as classified ads, legislative news and answers to common questions about water transfers. The portal would be a one-stop shopping point for those involved in the agricultural water industry.

"What we're after is the creation of a market." Rebecca told ABC's Evening News. This included Azurix's stake in a major underground water-storage facility in Madera County, California. While gas and electricity suppliers were familiar with "wheeling" product around, making unused capacity available to others, it was something that had never been heard of in the water industry.

What was apparent to me was that Azurix had absolutely no business plan. It seemed now that Azurix was simply doing whatever it could to sustain itself. Rebecca and company were obviously trying to regain Azurix's stock value by creating new tools that would be seen as innovative simply because they were the genetic offspring of Enron. While her acquisitions and new concepts were supposed to be high voltage jolts on the defibrillator paddles, the stock price did not respond.

Paul asked me on a Friday to register the domain name Water2Water.com. I wasn't surprised when I found such an obscure name was still available. After breathing a sigh of relief that Jusbasche hadn't yet gotten his greasy mitts on it, I told Paul I would register it first thing Monday. That Monday, January 31, I logged on, and to my utter dismay I found I had been foiled again by that pesky Bolivian, Señor Jusbasche. Like Whack-A-Mole, the amusement park game where you wield a mallet and attempt to hit the mechanical mole as it pops up from one of a dozen or so holes, I felt like I was swinging the big mallet at Jusbasche, but his furry head was always one hole ahead of me. Once again, over the weekend, he had registered the proposed name.

I couldn't believe that Jusbasche and his ripped-off domain, ChemicalDesk.com, were getting away with these antics. As silly as it was, I was growing increasingly frustrated with what I saw as an ongoing criminal enterprise. It seemed that Rebecca Mark was blatantly breaching her corporate responsibility for confidentiality by telling her husband what amounted to trade secrets. And Jusbasche's actions were even more despicable. I assumed his theft included the plan to sell the domain names back to Azurix. But I guess Rebecca was feeling desperate now that she was down to her last forty or fifty million. Having elevated her to the status of a business deity, I desperately hoped she would surprise me, and in the end I would find she had nothing to do with the actions of her nefarious husband. But I wasn't holding my breath.

While all this domain name comedy was playing out, Azurix had gotten a number of major public relations firms involved in the hunt to capture its business. One New York agency obviously wanted it very badly. The exec in charge of Azurix's marketing, an Irishman named Tad Whalen, got a rather ominous gift in the mail: an ice pick. A cryptic note informed Tad that two days hence he would find out what it all meant. Tad happened to be called out of town on the day in question, and around lunchtime, several well-dressed young men arrived with a huge ice sculpture. Imbedded in the sculpture, which resembled a picture frame, was an envelope containing the nature and amount of the PR firm's bid. Since Tad was gone the thing sat around for quite a while and began melting. After a big enough puddle had accumulated, someone fetched Chris Wasden, as he was the highest ranking Azurix boss, and he chiseled out the bid. Despite its own innovation, the PR firm did not get the Azurix account.

CHAPTER SEVEN

I'm not supposed to do this, but it's a great way to make a lot of money at the end of the day when everyone is desperate for power.

Jeff Richter, Senior Specialist
California Power Trader – West Desk
Enron Power Marketing

POWER TENDS TO CORRUPT

I was in yet another nightmare job and seriously considered leaving. The problem was a moratorium had been placed on Azurix employees returning to Enron because Azurix's stock was in the tank. Coming out of the box at around $19.00, AZX stock was now, at about $4.00, worth hardly more than a pack of smokes. Because of this drastic decline in value, to prevent a run on the job bank at Enron, it was agreed that no Azurix employees would be able to return to Enron in the foreseeable future. I thought of the poor souls on the Titanic, looking ten miles across the icy waters to the steamer California, sitting maddening still, unaware of the terrible drama nearby. I had retained my Enron stock options with the move to Azurix, but if I left the company now it would mean I would lose the last 50% of my options, which had yet to vest. And that was a pretty nest egg I could ill afford to throw away. With Enron's stock in the stratosphere, I decided to grin and bear it. That resolve lasted all of one day when I realized I could no longer work for a company where the top executive was no better than a grifter, albeit a very impressive grifter with great hair.

Frustrated, I needed to tell someone and I trusted Sully enough to talk to him. Notwithstanding his predilection for porn and his early distrust of me, Sully and I had become friends. He fascinated me with stories of being a political prisoner and how the South African government had seized all of his assets and forced him into exile, separating him from his wife and children for two years. He had given me great advice when I bought my Jaguar and always seemed ready to lend a sympathetic, even fatherly, ear. Sully always arrived at work around 7:30 a.m., so I came in early and peeked around his office door.

"Sully, you got a minute?"

"Sure Lynn, what is it?"

I closed the door.

"I've discovered something I need to talk to you about."

His face remained impassive. I expected him to have a bigger reaction. I repeated my statement as if he hadn't heard it the first time.

"Here." I slid the single sheet of paper across his desk.

"What's this?" Sully asked in his usual inquisitive manner.

"My letter of resignation. Sully, this is serious enough that I'm quitting."

He nodded. Sully rarely let his face betray his emotions.

"Tell me why you want to quit."

Sully was well-liked at Enron, but not highly respected for his knowledge. His strength was in his connections and probably no one knew that better than he. I think he believed he had done an excellent job of fooling most of the people most of the time, but because he had moved up the ranks on friendship and not merit, he was in a precarious position. Though a real politician, practiced at jumping hurdles and skirting pitfalls, I was uncertain how Sully would take the news of Jusbasche's maneuvers. He was good, but telling the CEO her husband was a crook would be problematic at best. There was also the very high likelihood Rebecca knew all about it.

I began talking, laying out my sordid story of trying to register the domain names and then having Michael Jusbasche swoop in and grab them. As it unfolded, Sully's eyes widened then his face filled with glee. I did not expect such a reaction. As I set one paper after another in front of him, my evidence of Jusbasche's crimes, and apparently Rebecca's espionage, he read and stacked them neatly on his desk. When I finished he turned and looked out the window for a few moments.

"You don't want to resign. You'll lose your stock options. I have a plan I've been working on, but I've been waiting to tell you. Ken Rice wants me to go to EBS [Enron Broadband Services] to work for the Chairman's office. I want to take you and Colleen and Elizabeth with me, but I need to get over there and get settled. Once I do, we can get you back there without any of you losing any shares."

"I don't know, Sully. You know my family is in the Northwest and I've been thinking very seriously about moving back there. I'm just so frustrated."

Enron's policy of no disaffections from Azurix was supposed to be hard and fast to prevent a mass exodus. There were probably exceptions, but I didn't hold out much hope, despite Sully's connections. Then Sully's advice was particularly insightful.

"Lynn, remember, frustration is one's belief that they have no personal power to correct the situation. Therefore, it is a useless waste of one's personal energy. We would be better served using that energy to correct the situation than simply being frustrated."

What he threw me next was a complete curveball.

"What if I could get you a job trading power in Portland?"

My eyes lit up. I knew how revered traders were inside Enron. This would be the equivalent of a kid from the ghetto being drafted into the NBA. There was no such thing as a trader who just scraped by. Traders were rich.

"Absolutely!" I exclaimed. "Tell me you're not joking."

He shook his head then pointed to my paper trail of evidence against Jusbasche.

"May I make copies of these? This is exactly what I needed to justify my leaving."

Now I realized why Sully had been so excited. As always, Enron was a zero-sum game: a winner, a loser. What I didn't know, and Sully did, was that Amanda Martin was growing increasingly frustrated and Sully was about to channel her negative energy.

Apparently, Amanda had lately been feeling like Cinderella, forced to mop floors at Azurix while her buddy Rebecca Mark got to go to the ball. I had seen the two light-heartedly spar from time to time. When a particularly grueling business trip came up and

Amanda didn't want to go, she berated Rebecca, "You should be going because you're old and haggard anyway."

To which Rebecca stabbed back, "Unlike *some people,* I've been traveling the past ten years building this goddamn company!"

And with that, she demanded Amanda take the trip. The two reminded me of Alexis and Krystle Carrington from *Dynasty*, women with far more money than class or good sense, who were constantly engaged in trashy cat-fights. Sully knew the little piece of dirt I had uncovered was plutonium in the hands of Rebecca's arch enemy, Jeff Skilling. And Amanda Martin, Sully's pipeline to Skilling, was in a foul mood over her lot at Azurix.

A few hours later my phone rang. I saw Sully's name on the caller ID. Our offices were separated by only a few cubicle walls and when he wanted to talk he either signaled or just walked over.

"Can you come in here?" he said in a hushed, mysterious tone.

It was now mid-afternoon and he had been coming and going since our talk.

"Come in, close the door," he said urgently, his eyes fixed on his computer screen. He never looked up, imparting an air of importance. "You must keep this very confidential. I went to Mandy and spoke with her about the situation. I wanted to give her the benefit of my notice since we're friends."

"What about Rebecca?"

"I have a meeting with her on Saturday."

Sully never worked more than his mandated 40 hours and Saturdays were absolutely unheard of. He finally looked up.

"Okay. I have spoken with Jeff Richter in Portland. I originally hired Jeff to be a Lotus Notes developer when he was a math teacher and wanted to get out of teaching. I took a chance on him, so he owes me. He is now in Portland as a power trader. He's expecting your call. He'll invite you to come out and sit on his desk for a week to see whether this is something you want to do."

"Okay."

Sully fixed me with intense black eyes. "Lynn, don't wait. Call him right away."

He said it with such conviction, I figured there was something he couldn't tell me, but I knew I should pick up my cue. I immediately returned to my desk and dialed Jeff Richter's number.

"Enron, this is Jeff."

"Jeff, this is Lynn. Sullivan Graas told me to..."

"Lynn," he said, abruptly cutting me off. "Call me tonight at home. Here's my number."

I copied down his number. His terse behavior gave me the impression we were either doing something wrong or he was impossibly busy. That evening, when I called he told me he hadn't wanted to talk because his calls, like all of the traders were recorded for legal reasons.

His first question, "So why do you want to leave Azurix?" had me stammering for a second as I tried to figure out what version of my story to tell.

"Let me just say," I said, choosing my words carefully, "there are some things going on here that may not be kosher and I think it's best if I leave. Besides, I'm from the Northwest."

There was a pause and I heard a slight snicker. "Sully and I are pretty good friends. I have an idea what's going on."

For a moment I felt like a fool in playing it close to the vest. Sully trusted Jeff and had obviously spilled some of the beans.

"Yeah, it's ugly. I just want to get as far away from this mess as I can. I have a feeling things are about to come crashing down and I don't want to have anything hit me on the head."

Jeff and I hit it off and ended up speaking for two-and-a-half hours. It was decided that I would come out to Portland to check out the trading desk. As a courtesy, Jeff offered to let me stay with him for the week or so it would take to fully understand the business. He ended our conversation with, "Think about it over the weekend, and let me know if it's something you're interested in."

On Monday I went to Sully to express my gratitude and told him about our lengthy conversation.

"Jeff offered to let me stay with him. He was very nice, but I wanted to see what you thought about the appropriateness of it."

Whether it was Enron or even Azurix, travel and lodging for executives was first-class and always paid for. I had thought about

Jeff's offer over the weekend and my radar began signaling that his motives might be less than pure. Sully knew the guy and would tell me what he thought.

He shook his head. "Don't even think about it. Jeff has always had a problem with women. He really wants a girlfriend, but the ones he's interested in never seem to be interested in him."

That settled it. I would go out to Portland, but I would politely decline Jeff's "hospitality". I had seen more than enough women sleeping their way to the top at Enron. I was not about to go down that road no matter how bad I wanted out of Azurix. Sully and I spoke about the trading position then moved on to the subject that had been gnawing at me all weekend.

"So tell me, how did your meeting go with Rebecca? Did you tell her about her husband stealing trade names? Did she even act surprised?"

Sully glanced around, even though no one was within earshot.

"I'm dying to know what she said."

Sully smirked. "She said she asked him to help her!"

"She what?" I screeched.

Sully had just confirmed what I had feared: Rebecca knew everything. But what was more she was arrogant enough to admit it as though what she had done was perfectly legal.

"Oh please. She has a whole company to do that stuff."

"Yes she does."

"But why would he register them in his name if he was "helping" her? That amounts to espionage. Did she say how much she paid Michael to buy the names back?" I added wryly.

"I didn't ask her."

We laughed about it for a moment then he got serious. "Forget Rebecca. We both have to get out of here. I just want you to focus on your trip to Portland and learning the power business. There is a fortune to be made."

That's what I was banking on.

In early February, 2000, I flew out to Portland to sit on Enron's West Power Trading Desk for a crash course in California power trading. After my fiancé agreed it would not be a good idea to stay with Jeff, I made arrangements to stay with a cousin in a small town outside Portland. For the next five days, I agreed to a boot camp of sorts. I would rise every morning at 3:00 a.m. and submit myself to learning the ropes of trading power. I was to arrive at the office at around 4:15 a.m. to begin the day. Jeff would roll in at 4:30 a.m. and the trading would begin at 5:00 a.m. sharp.

I was told that once trading began it was total chaos so I decided I would try to ask most of my questions between 4:30 and 5:00 a.m., while Jeff reviewed his "positions" from the day before. Then he would sign on to EOL, Enron's premier Internet trading platform, and begin setting the prices for the first trades of the day. He told me that at exactly 5:00 a.m., the phones would begin singing like bells and whistles on the slots at the Mirage. Within seconds every trader would be foraging like crazed, hungry chipmunks looking to stuff their cheeks with as many nuts as possible. I couldn't wait.

As with the deregulation of natural gas, Enron managed to use its government connections once again to help them deregulate the electricity business. When the first George Bush was President of the United States, part of the legacy created out of his friendship with Ken Lay was the passing of the Energy Policy Act of 1992. This was a landmark decision that forced utilities to allow wholesale power marketers access to their transmission grids. Deregulation of retail electricity would be left up to the individual states. In 1994, Enron traded its first electrons on the wholesale market. Over the next three years, 250 more corporations would register as power marketers with the Federal Energy Regulatory Commission (FERC).

Prior to deregulation, there were three primary aspects to the energy business: (1) the generation of power; (2) the transmission of power; and (3) the delivery of power to the customer. While power generation required ownership of assets – which Jeff Skilling loathed – with deregulation, the transmission of power was opened up to marketers like Enron. Such traders were free to bid for the power generated, then sell it to utilities delivering the power, and the only assets they required were a phone and a computer.

In 1996, Enron announced it would merge with Portland General Electric, a successful, low-cost electric utility company in the Pacific Northwest. With the ownership of approximately 5,000 MW of generating capacity and more than 38,000 miles of natural-gas pipeline worldwide, Enron would be a "full service" energy company, offering integrated solutions for wholesale and retail natural gas and electricity customers.

The truth was that with the purchase of PGE, Enron would now have unlimited access to two crucial elements of the power business in the West, the power traders and the Bonneville Power Administration (BPA). The BPA was an energy colossus, generating 40% of the power consumed in Washington, Oregon, Idaho and western Montana. With more than 29 hydroelectric dams on the Columbia and Snake Rivers, the BPA was the single largest source of American energy. But perhaps even more important to Enron was the information and relationships PGE and its traders had developed. At face value, Enron was now in a position to become the largest trader of electricity in the world. But more chilling, the people at the top of Enron's pyramid were just beginning to understand they had a mega-billion dollar tiger by the tail. And if ethics were not a problem, the only way they could possibly make more money was if they got locked in the U.S. Mint.

Buying PGE turned out to offer an embarrassment of riches. Perhaps more important than the BPA, would be Enron's access to the king of consumption–California. With its heavy technology sector and massive industrial power consumption, California was growing increasingly dependent on foreign sources for its power.

If the wheels at Enron understood one thing only, it was that the way to make money in the energy market was to create volatility. Just like oil companies claiming an event in the Middle East on Tuesday affects gas prices in Dubuque on Thursday, so too could power traders reap fortunes when they manufactured volatility. But instead of a bombing in Haifa or Amman, it was usually a hot summer that set traders and buyers into frenzies.

Enron knew that if it could create extreme volatility, the State of California would be dependent upon the energy giant to relieve its pain. Enron took a page from the Saudis' book, squeeze the West (in Enron's case, the western US), who would kick and scream but ultimately pay. Enron understood that if holding oil hostage worked for the Kingdom, why couldn't they do the same with electricity?

Liberal California had also been one of the first states seeking to deregulate the retail electricity market. Their idea was designed to allow its 31 million residential electric consumers a voice in choosing their area's electricity provider, like a long-distance telephone company. From 1995 to March, 1998, California worked on retail deregulation and enacted the legislation necessary to move the structure of the state's electricity market from one that was dominated by monopoly utilities to one subject to market forces. Of course the utilities remained responsible for meeting the electricity needs of their customers. However, the new legislation required the three, previously regulated utilities, Pacific Gas & Electric Co., Southern California Edison, and San Diego Gas & Electric, to sell much of the electricity they generated to private companies.

With the new law, the state created the California Power Exchange (CalPX or PX) and the Independent System Operator (ISO). The PX was the primary marketplace for the purchase and sale of wholesale electricity while the ISO managed the electricity transmission grid. This required maintaining the balance in the energy market between supply and demand, the purchase of "emergency power" through "ancillary services", as well as managing the flow of electricity over the transmission lines.

Through the PX and ISO, marketers, like Enron, and the generators of electricity, bid for and scheduled the amounts of electricity for delivery to their wholesale and retail customers (also known as the "load"). The markets, operated by the PX were the "day-ahead market" where electricity for the following day was bought and sold, and the "day-of market" for electricity to be delivered the same day was bought and sold. In addition, the ISO bought and sold power through the "real-time" market to correct any potential imbalances between supply and demand for each operating hour.

When California announced in April 1998, it would open up both the retail and wholesale markets to competition, Enron saw a partial victory. Prices for retail electricity would be capped at 1996 prices, while wholesale prices would be auctioned online through the California Power Exchange (CalPX). In a centralized power exchange, buyers and sellers would engage in a computer-based auction that established market-clearing prices within the state of California.

When Enron closed the PGE deal for $3.2 billion in July, 1997, the utility had approximately 30 wholesale power traders on staff. By early 1998, Houston had relocated 35 traders to Portland and created the "West Power Trading Desk", which would compete against the "Central" and "East" desks for recognition as the dominant trading force within Enron.

By the time I arrived in Portland, there were approximately 100 traders who worked literally 24/7 to trade electricity. While there were rumors that once the trading floor was up and running, corporate would move the entire operation back to Houston, senior management knew the Portland office ran the show and no such move would ever take place. Portland was the "A" team, trading electricity in 11 western states. It was the dominant force west of Colorado, based upon their longstanding relationships with other power marketers.

My first morning as a rookie power trader was the hardest. When I was a Young Life counselor, I remember my favorite girls, Faye Rodgers and Emily Fraker, referred to the "Butt-crack of Dawn". I firmly believe that awakening at 3:00 a.m. is harder on the human system than spending a month in orbit. As I dragged out of bed, probably three hours shy of a refreshing night's sleep, I was already beginning to wonder if I had taken Azurix for granted. Although I had lived and worked in Portland for 8 years, the scene heading into downtown at 3:45 a.m. was eerie. If this was to be the career choice I decided upon, I worried my schedule would be so unsociable I might have tons of money and no friends to share a life with.

I parked and arrived at the elevator just as a woman in her mid-30s shuffled up, carrying a half-dozen bags of groceries. We smiled at each other.

"Can I help you?"

"Sure" she said. "Can you hold the elevator door open while I get the last bag?"

I held the door open while she quickly loaded it.

"What floor?" I asked, offering to push the button.

"Three. Please."

The trading floor.

I wondered why she was schlepping six bags of groceries to the trading floor at 4:00 a.m. I got off the elevator and held the door again while she pulled out the last of the bags. Despite wanting to help her, I realized it would not look good to be seen carrying groceries on my first day at my "new job". I changed the subject.

"Do you know where I can find Jeff Richter?"

"Sure." She pointed at an empty row of desks. "But it doesn't look like he's here yet."

I was irritated he had gotten me to come in so early yet hadn't shown himself. The thought crossed my mind that I was the target of some initiation into the fraternity of traders, like Hell Week. I pictured the traders laughing uproariously, throwing down Ben Franklins like Monopoly money, wagering on what ridiculous time I would show up. Then I realized no one but Jeff Richter probably knew I was coming. And why would Belden, obviously a guy with more money than Croesus, care about me?

I found a vacant desk and watched as one glassy-eyed man after another filed in. Soon the row of desks was nearly filled and a soft, sleepy buzz wafted over the room. Decked out in my suit I was surprised at how prep-casual they were all dressed. The woman from the elevator dutifully unloaded her groceries, laying out a kingly spread of food on tables overlooking the Willamette River. I realized the grocery lady's sole function was locating every conceivable portable breakfast nosh for the traders. I also noted that she and I were the only women in sight.

I sat there, sizing up each male figure to determine whether I could fit into this arcane environment. It wasn't yet dawn and already these men were cracking their knuckles for battle. They were a cult of energy vampires who ate by moonlight. I went over to the food table, grabbed a bagel and tried to make out the outline of the river below. I met some of my "fellow" traders then returned to my desk and began looking through my Palm Pilot.

"Lynn? Hi, I'm Jeff. Did you find a place to park okay?" I turned to find a young man right off the cover of *Cycle Magazine*.

"I never think about it," he continued, "because I ride my bike to and from work."

He was carrying a bike helmet and still had on his cycling clothes. During our marathon phone call, he told me he cycled 65 blocks each way to work, but the impact hadn't hit me until that moment. I too had cycled quite a few miles in my day, but I wouldn't think of such an insane ride on the dark, nippy, wet streets of Portland. But Oregon was a health conscious state, as well as the home of Nike. It was also the only state where assisted suicide was legal.

"Have you met Earl Phillips*? Earl does our power scheduling."
"Yes, we just met."

"Okay, I'm going to change, grab some food and we'll get started."

Jeff changed into khaki pants and a t-shirt then circled the spread and gathered his munchies. I sipped my coffee and reflected that Portlanders and Seattleites had one thing in common: appreciation for a great cup o' Joe. Jeff walked past, signaling me to follow him to his desk. We sat down and he took a slug off his orange juice.

"So, how much do you know about California power markets?"

I took a moment to mentally organize what I had learned, then began my recitation.

"Since there is currently no easy way to actually store electricity, production and consumption must occur at virtually the same time, requiring a fine balance between the two."

I went on to tell him what he already knew, that minute-by-minute, loads must be balanced based upon the factors that affect each power generator, including scheduled outages for maintenance; how fast a generator can ramp up for increased usage like at night when air-conditioners go on, which is impacted by the age and efficiency of the infrastructure of the power plant; and then of course, the unexpected. Without the proper balance, power failures occur, which can be devastating for the consumer. Ergo, the popularity of Enron's trademark "risk management".

I also knew the transmission system, consisting of the interconnecting power lines that carried electricity into, through, and out of California was then managed by the Independent System Operator (ISO). Power lines of course varied in the physical distance they covered, as well as the electricity capacity they could handle. To balance the transmission of electricity between supply and demand, schedules were submitted by both the utilities as well as the energy marketers, like Enron, to the ISO. Along with the type of electricity (i.e., firm transmission or non-firm transmission), the amount, points of origin and delivery were then sent to the ISO. Like a giant Rubik's cube, the ISO would then match all of the information to make certain all pieces created a discernable picture.

Then, depending upon the demand and schedules submitted to the ISO by the marketers and utilities, congestion could result when the total amount of electricity scheduled and the direction of the flow of electricity exceeded the available capacity on a power line. When congestion occurred, the ISO would assess a "congestion management fee" which allowed the ISO to generate the funds necessary to then pay marketers or utilities to reduce their demand and thus relieve the congestion. Congestion could be relieved in two ways – either reducing the amount of electricity or reversing the direction of the flow of electricity away from the congestion.

The ISO then made the additional power it had gained through the Congestion Management Market, or CMM, available through an "ancillary services auction". There were basically three forms of power that could be ordered and created. The first was "spinning reserves", which was additional capacity that could be dispatched within minutes. Then "non-spinning reserves" could be brought up to speed within ten minutes, and finally "replacement reserves" could be generated and contributed to the grid within an hour. Power marketers would bid on these "ancillary services" to ensure they could meet the demands of their customers when necessary.

In the event, after bribing marketers and utilities to forego their claim to the "gold", there was still an insufficient amount of electricity available to meet the demands, the ISO would be forced to go outside California to buy power which was known as "out of market" (OOM) electricity. Although California had price caps of $250 per MWh on any power generated inside the state, anything generated outside California was fair game and in Enron's world of a zero-sum game – this would mean the score would always be Enron "1" California "0". Enron knew that by congesting the lines artificially, not only would they be paid a handsome fee for "relieving the congestion", they could "import" power into California when the ISO came calling.

As I recited these brief details of how the power market worked in much of the western US, Jeff began logging onto his computer. Two wide flat screen monitors spanned his desk. On each appeared the logo for EnronOnline. I recalled working on the indices developed for the pricing of the commodities for EOL. That had been more than a year before and, until that moment, I wasn't sure they had even been implemented. There were rumors flying that it was unlikely EOL would ever be fully launched because of Jeff Skilling's refusal to support the concept of online trading. That hadn't particularly surprised me when I remembered Jeff Skilling didn't even have a computer.

Now I was about to see first-hand the value of the data contained within EOL. I would also observe just how autonomously the Portland office ran from Houston. Most of these traders were born and raised in Portland and wanted little or nothing to do with Houston.

As 5:00 a.m. closed in on us, Jeff's demeanor changed. The metamorphosis had begun. From the gentle cyclist who looked like he donated to Greenpeace, I was beginning to see gills, the upright dorsal fin, and three rows of teeth. I noticed the other men in the room shifting about, putting on their game faces, cutting the unnecessary chatter, as if the Gipper was about to enter the locker room and lead them in a prayer to beat Army. The change in the room's atmosphere was actually intimidating, like a bomb was about to go off and every man knew it.

"Okay," said Jeff, his jaw set matter-of-factly, "straight up five, the phones are going to start ringing. I'll get on the line and you'll be on the extension. You'll pick up the phone, but don't say a word because every call is tape-recorded. You'll take down the order. Part of the process will be for you to grasp the lingo and the codes used between the traders."

He gestured to the desk next to his. I sat and eyed my phone like it was a rattlesnake.

"When you hear someone say 100 at 5, it means 100 megawatt hours at $25 because we can see the last bid was $25 per megawatt hour. As it raises to $25.25 you will hear him say 100 at $5.25 and when it goes to say, $30, you will hear the trader say 100 at 3. Understand so far?"

I nodded.

I watched as Jeff clicked the prices on the screen like baiting a hook. Screw the Rates Database, I could see already there was no rhyme or reason to how he set the prices. I watched the second hand sweep the large white-faced clock nearby, as the morning bidding frenzy grew nearer. Kick-off time was mere moments away. "You write down on this form the orders I take over the phone as they come in. That's how we keep track of them. EOL takes care of the online bids and then Earl will schedule the power for both my desk and Sean Crandall's desk."

"Who's Sean?"

"Sean Crandall trades in the Pacific Northwest at COB, California-Oregon Border. And John Forney, that's him over there, he oversees and trades real-time."

I looked at both men – obviously the "A" team. Sean, to my left, the high school quarterback, while Forney, sitting across from me, looked a bit more like the captain of the tennis team.

"Enron owns the firm transmission rights between the deals Sean does and the deals I do, which allow us to dominate the market. Since I trade south, I watch to see what Sean is doing and set my price accordingly. If Sean does a lot of business it means the line is going to be packed, which is great for us."

In 1999, the California ISO developed firm transmission rights to "hedge" against congestion risk. The firm transmission rights were auctioned in November 1999, for the period February 2000 through March 2001, which meant that the ability to guarantee an uninterrupted delivery of power would be held by only a few players in the market. The firm transmission rights were bi-lateral, meaning there were imports and exports for each zone. With over 30 rounds of bidding between 28 market participants, $41 million was generated for transmission owners as compensation for the congestion usage charge. That revenue was to be paid in the event a transmission line became congested. Enron, or any other broker, would be rewarded for reducing congestion. The trick was to create congestion, then get paid to solve it. Kind of like a fireman who sets fires then gets paid to put them out.

I had been studying Enron's trades and revenue for the grid and, by my calculations, Enron had paid nearly $10 million for the firm transmission rights through California's power grid to cover trades for a period of 14 months. By dominating 62% of the firm transmission rights in Path 26 between northern and southern California, Jeff was right that this zone, which had just come on line February 1, was key to his business. There was a finite capacity to the lines, and when demand grew, so did the price.

"If the congestion is too much in any zone, we can sell the power back to California to relieve the congestion, which generates additional income." Jeff said.

The investment in the firm transmission rights sounded similar to the investment Jeff Skilling described when Enron had purchased the exclusive rights to every turbine that General Electric could make in the next two years to tie up the market for Enron Energy Services. Enron would buy the turbines for EES's asset-monetization through outsourcing. Simply put, they would buy the turbines from GE and lease them back to an outsourcing customer. By cornering the inventory of turbines, Skilling figured he could dominate the world market in power generation.

At exactly 5:00 a.m., every phone on the trading floor lit up. As the room exploded, the rush of testosterone in that first 15 seconds was so powerful I feared I would grow facial hair. Jeff took the orders and I wrote frantically to keep up with him. Meanwhile, Earl Phillips, the scheduling coordinator, sat beside me working on spreadsheets that would be used to send the trades to the ISO. From television and movies I had seen the madness of the New York Stock Exchange's trading floor and this was just how I imagined it. Men screamed and shouted numbers and obscure codes. The volume and tenacity of the ringing phones was a track for some underground music project. Occasionally one trader would yell across to another looking for a price on a particular territory of generation.

In a matter of a few minutes I had taken no less than 20 orders for trades, praying that what I had written down was correct, as information sent to the ISO had to balance. For every transaction, the instructions given by the buyer and seller to the ISO had to match so the ISO knew where the power should be sent. And unlike the stock market, which took moments, this was damn near instantaneous.

Once he got into the flow of the day, I watched as Jeff began raising prices on EOL, fishing to see who would bite. I was mesmerized as he inched his profits up a little at a time, knowing full well that a tiny bump translated to huge sums of money. By 9:30 a.m., trading slowed and Earl Phillips kicked into overdrive. Translating the deals made that morning, Earl identified Enron's purchases and sales and dropped them into a Lotus spreadsheet to be sent to the CalPX and the ISO. Although Ken Lay had said "price caps distort the market," the PX established wholesale prices for the day-ahead and day-of markets, and capped them at $2,500 per MWh. Meanwhile, the ISO established the same day, real-time or spot market for short-term power, that which is under one hour of use, and capped that at $750 per MWh, which had been raised from $250 MWh on September 30, 1999. Meanwhile, retail price for the end consumer was capped at approximately 6.4¢ per kWh.

As Earl gathered all of the data from the various traders for California, I could see their anxiety growing over the balance as Sean and Jeff maximized the use of Enron's firm transmission rights in Zone 26. This was not simply a matter of entering data, it was an exceptionally fine tightrope act. They were trying to hit that happy, and rich, medium between too much and just enough to make the most money.

At 9:55 a.m. everyone began shouting, "Hurry up, Earl!"

Earl was sweating heavily. I could feel my blood pressure rising with the tension in the room. I realized what everyone else knew: if Earl missed the 10:00 a.m. deadline for transmitting the loads,

Enron had significant exposure as they'd already agreed to sell firm transmission. It was simply unacceptable to call your customer back and say "Oh gee sorry, we seemed to have screwed up and missed the deadline." The intensity of the screams got louder and louder as the clock passed 9:58 a.m. Beads of sweat were turning to small rivers on Earl's forehead when he realized the load was not balancing. With literally seconds to spare, he plugged in one more number and I watched as the macro worked its magic.

"GOT IT!" Earl screamed, transmitting his information across the wires.

Suddenly the eye of the hurricane arrived, bringing an instant calm. As if on cue, Jeff and the other brokers dropped what they were doing and sauntered casually over to the food table to graze while I was left to wonder what the hell had just happened. For the next hour, Jeff explained to me the process of buying and selling power and the scheduling of power for delivery.

"If we pack the line with congestion, when the ISO comes back with the results of our transmission bids, we are more likely to get our capacity that we bid, or at least a large portion of it. The ISO will then let us know how much power we actually get and how to adjust our schedules. This is why I always go long in my position and sell it to another desk if necessary."

As my heart rate slowed slightly, Jeff informed me at approximately 10:15 a.m. that he and the other traders would be in a "fundies" meeting for 15 minutes. During the meeting the traders would discuss the fundamental things such as the regional weather with Enron's staff meteorologists, the flow rates of the dams operated by the Bonneville Power Administration and, most importantly, the positions they had all taken. Jeff excused himself and I took the opportunity to visit with Dr. Stress, Earl Phillips.

Earl's career at Enron began with Northern Natural Gas. He had an accounting background and told me his goal was to eventually trade power, but admitted that scheduling, however manic and heart-attack inducing, had been exceptionally beneficial to him. Earl explained that at 11:00 a.m., the ISO would come back with either the green light to go ahead and schedule the flow of power or ask Enron to modify its schedules. Then the traders would once again open the bidding to buy or sell more power based upon power allocations from the ISO. Power would be traded around the clock on the day-ahead market through CalPX. But we were into that golden, money-minting zone right now.

Jeff and the other traders broke from their meeting and reconvened around his desk at 10:45. After a few announcements, they returned to their own desks and Jeff informed me of the results of their meeting. They had quickly determined where the scheduled outages would be, and the fact that the run off from the snowmelt in the mountains was likely to be less than anticipated, which would probably mean a decrease in hydropower. It all added up to an increase in prices. Music to their ears.

At 10:58 a.m., the traders were screaming at Earl again. It amazed me how Louise Kitchen had managed to secretly appropriate a king's ransom to create EOL, and yet the archaic spreadsheet Earl used to schedule the power was not without its bugs. One slip and... *poof.* Gone.

"Do we have it yet, Earl?" yelled Sean Crandall, a well-chewed coffee stirrer hanging from his lip. The young trader had a deceptive boyish charm, because when fully spooled-up, it was clear how he could dominate the California/Oregon Border. At 11:05 a.m. there was still no response from the ISO.

"Are you sure you were balanced Earl?" another trader asked. 11:15 a.m. came and went. As the anxiety mounted, Sean got on the phone with one of his power trading cronies to see if he'd heard anything from the great and powerful Wizard of Oz, the ISO.

The balancing act between short and long was critical. If a trader sold lots of power but had insufficient supply, he was short. If he couldn't find enough buyers for his abundant supply, which, allow me to reiterate, had a very short life span, it could induce ulcers trying to maintain that equilibrium. Although I witnessed no heart attacks, and most of the traders looked young and fit, this type of insane pressure cooker could not possibly be good for one's health. I remembered my concern that morning about having money but being lonely, and revised it to *What good's the money if you're dead?*

At 11:25 a.m., a message popped up on the screens, confirming the bids for power. The room relaxed for three seconds with a collective sigh then went back to work. The phones immediately started ringing. Five seconds later, Jeff and I, as his trusty scribe, were back doing deals for both the spot market as well as the "balance of the month". All the while, Jeff continued clicking his mouse on EOL to increase the spread between the Bid and Ask price for power. He was *printing* money.

When we got through with that burst of trading I asked Jeff what seemed a logical question, based upon my experience with the Rates Database.

"How can you personally control the pricing? Aren't there other people out there trading? Don't you follow some standard pricing indices?"

Jeff's knowing-look left me feeling patronized and naive. "With EOL, we're the only ones that can see who's buying and selling. It lets us perfectly gauge our position compared to other market players."

"There just doesn't seem to be any rhyme or reason about what's being bought or sold and how you're balancing the two. Plus, how do you know if you've extended beyond your risk limit?"

The risk limit had purportedly been set by the company to keep traders from getting out of control.

"If I need to, I'll call Houston and sell if I'm long or buy if I'm short. They'll do the same thing with the East desk or even with Sean. Because EOL is a closed system, we can and do sell between desks and nobody outside Enron can tell. They simply can see we are trading large volumes. Or we can offer a "choice" to a counterparty, which basically sets the price of our bid and ask at the same price. The order from Tim is to keep the market liquid that way and keep our volumes elevated – even if we buy and sell the same amount of power back and forth between the same parties. It's a balance between being long and short and keeping the market liquid."

"What do you mean keep a market liquid?"

"We have to keep the volumes moving – if we are not selling or buying power – we're not making any money and the market will dry up. That's why sometimes we will sell back and forth with the same counterparty at the same price – just to keep the volumes up."

"Isn't that misleading?"

"Everyone does it so no one's being misled. Meanwhile, with each trade, as I watch the market, I raise the price. And because our counterparties can see on EOL that the price is going up, they assume we know something they don't and they start to panic. It's great to be Enron."

"So with EOL, you more or less control the market?"

"I'd say more. The best thing that ever happened to Enron was EOL. It gives a picture of the whole market, what everybody's doing, and it's extremely responsive. Instead of a market snapshot, it's more like a movie camera."

I just had to ask. "But you're governed by tariffs, aren't you?" I was referring to the guidelines or laws established by the states to regulate the system.

Jeff smiled like the cat that ate the canary. "Sure, but we leave those details up to Legal, and so far no one has stopped us. Not to say Tim Belden would even listen. Besides, Houston leaves us alone because we're so damn profitable."

At 1:00 p.m., the action came to a grinding halt as the market closed. Now it was time to gear up for the day-ahead market. Enron would soon be notified what it would be paid for relieving the congestion on the line. I turned to Jeff.

"Explain again what happened relative to the demand on the transmission line. It happened so fast."

"Okay, the power generators hold back power saying that there is going to be unscheduled maintenance or even scheduled maintenance, which makes the supply side short. So what we do is schedule more power than we really need because then, when the schedule comes out, we have a surplus. Because the price set by the ISO is based upon the highest price bid, and supply is first given to those who have firm transmission rights, and then to the bidder requesting the highest volume, our job is to win the bid every time. Look, the ISO's in this to make money too. We're just playing the game. We can then sell that surplus for a profit to those who need it, or if we've created congestion, which means there's more demand than supply, we get paid a rebate of sorts to sell the power back. Because we have firm transmission rights we're in a premium place since Enron paid for these rebates up front."

In fact, Tim Belden was creating congestion alright – scheduling power beyond the physical transmission capacity of the lines. Belden's motto was if the line is capable of transmitting 10,000 MWh – we'll schedule 60,000. The archaic scheduling system Belden was exploiting was unable to identify the error and Belden simply sat back and raked in the cash rebates.

"So how does Sean come in?"

"Well, sometimes Sean does the same thing, which creates higher prices in NP15. Then I'll reduce the power I purchase in the south and we get paid a fee for shifting the load from north to south."

"I'm not sure I follow."

"California caps their prices. We'll buy power there at a low price, export it somewhere unregulated, then re-buy it. Next, we raise the rate and sell it back to California for a profit. I'm not supposed to do this, but it's a great way to make a lot of money at the end of the day when everyone, including the State of California is desperate for power."

That evening, walking to my car, I started thinking about how I came to work for Enron. I was actually wondering about the concept of Karma. If Karma existed, then what had I done to deserve bouncing from one corrupt division to the next? I didn't think it was possible, but the power traders demonstrated the worst business ethics I had seen since I began. And that was saying a lot. I drove home to my cousin's and decided that trading power was not for me, even if it meant coming back to the bosom of my family and a town I loved.

I knew the trades that Jeff and Sean and the other guys were making would negatively impact the price consumers paid for power but why should they care – they were making a killing. FERC was a toothless-tiger at that time and I knew Enron had the thirty pieces of silver to buy Washington. I knew index prices were set by publications like *Bloomberg* and *Inside FERC*. Later, back in Houston, I put it all together. The traders would take calls from the *Bloomberg* reps late in the day and go over their trading volumes. *Bloomberg* would then issue the prices as if it had some official stamp, but the truth was the fox was simply telling the farmer his chickens were all safe and snuggly in the henhouse. Knowing what I did about Enron, it's absurd to think they would share trade secrets with anyone. Of course I didn't begrudge Enron earning back the $10 million it had paid for the firm transmission rights, but they didn't seem to care that there were ways to do it honestly.

We're printing money.

That sentence now rang in my head. The words uttered by Kathy Simpson as she entered our staff meeting in late June 1998, when power in the Midwest was trading for as much as $10,000 per MWh. Although it was reported to be $7,500, I knew that Enron had sold a few MWh's at nearly the $10,000 mark. This was the same power they had bought for a mere *thirty five dollars* per MWh two days prior to June 25, 1998. The result of their unbridled greed put companies out of business and caused at least four heat-related deaths. This wasn't just thievery; in some cases, it was downright murder. Of course, Enron was printing money. Tim Belden would ultimately describe Jeff's "value" to the West Desk power trading operations, in a conversation, recorded like all conversations, "Well, he . . . ah, actually he makes between one and two (million) a day, which never shows up on any curve shift. He just fucks California... He steals money from California to the tune of about a million dollars a day." When asked to clarify his statement, Belden said "OK, he, um, he arbitrages (yeah, uh, yeah – that's it – he arbitrages) the California market to the tune of a million bucks or two a day." Of course, the caller wants to know "Will that every stop?" Belden, in his infinite wisdom, realizes that eventually all good things must come to an end and tells the caller "Yeah." The response was perhaps as disheartening as Belden's own strategy – "Maybe we can put him in a special purpose vehicle" (referring to one of Andy Fastow's good ol' off-the-balance sheet partnerships).

Listening to Jeff Richter for the next four days as he described the intricacies of power trading, and how the power generators were holding back power, I watched as another Enron cash cow, their Federal Emissions business, also skyrocketed. One morning, as I walked from the parking garage to the trading office, I bumped into the woman responsible for deal compliance for the trading of emissions certificates. She gave me a quick education in her business.

I was surprised to learn that power generating entities, particularly when operating at full capacity, were responsible for creating more air pollution than any other industry. In order to stay below the mandatory levels established by the government, they were offered incentives by the feds. If a power producer kept their emissions down they were given allowances or certificates that had a monetary value. Sort of like a get-out-of-jail-free card in Monopoly, except these cards were worth real money.

In 1990, with the Clean Air Act, the Environmental Protection Agency established a cap and trade program that permitted power generators to trade or transfer these emission allowances as an alternative to pollution control equipment solutions. Thus, a new arena of commerce was born with the accumulation and trading of certificates. Enron emerged as the leading trader of emissions certificates, with particular expertise in nitrous oxide (NO) and sulfur dioxide (SO^2). So, at the same time Enron was creating a significant demand for power generation, they were creating an increasing demand for emissions certificates by power generators.

If one plant was clean enough to get an emissions certificate, Enron saw a need and filled it by hooking them up with a dirty plant that needed that special dispensation. Enron would essentially give the polluter a call and as much as say *"You gotta problem? How much money do you have?"* A dirty power generator could then crank out loads of power, knowing they could pollute pretty much all they wanted, by simply buying their way to compliance with a certificate from Enron. With such a wonderful device for polluters available, the price of the certificates rose sharply above their initial value, making the cost almost, but not completely prohibitive for some power generators to purchase. For some, the certificates were not even enough, and because of their level of pollution, they were required by law to scale back the generation of power or face significant fines. But regardless of those dirty few, Enron had pioneered, then monopolized a whole new form of commerce: making money off pollution.

I'm sure it was obvious to Jeff Richter that by day three of boot camp this soldier was not marching to the beat of Enron's West Power Trading Desk. That's when he turned me over to the Director of Trading, Tim Belden. While I had carefully calculated appearing somewhat thick in Jeff's presence, to rule out any possibility of being offered a position, at Jeff's request, I agreed to meet with Tim. Although Belden sat no more than three feet from his golden boy, Sean Crandall, he and I had only exchanged terse hellos. I felt he had worked awfully hard to let me know I was not important enough to waste idle chatter on.

Wednesday afternoon Tim and I met in a small conference room for my "formal interview". I watched him carefully over the week, secretive as he was, often requesting Jeff call him on his cell phone to avoid the recorded lines on the trading floor, as though he was hiding something. To say I didn't trust Belden was an understatement. Behind his boyish looks was someone who was truly too smart for his own good. As he laid out what he was looking for in a trader, I glazed over, more interested in what had brought a guy like Tim Belden to trading power.

A graduate of the University of California at Berkley, Belden had been with Portland General Electric until asked to head the trading floor for the West Power Trading division of Enron. He was intense and pathologically confident, a guy who measured his ranking on the great Cosmic hierarchy by his outsized paychecks and whom he had outfoxed that day. Whether or not he ever had the specific thought, there were entire provinces in third world countries whose GDP couldn't match the dollar output of one Tim Belden. He wore his superiority on the sleeve of his Oxford shirt. Belden and his gang were pulling the worsted wool over a lot of people's eyes, fooling the system and reaping fortunes in the process. Heart-killing stress or not, it was damn fun, and like every other successful Enron exec, there was more than a mild touch of sociopathy.

After rattling on for a bit about how his department was the place to be, he finally focused on me.

"So tell me Lynn, what are your thoughts so far?"

"It's quite a different business then Azurix." I wanted to say *Yeah, Azurix is corrupt but stupid. You guys have elevated corruption to an art form.* But I didn't.

"Are you interested in one of the three positions I have open trading power?"

I had the distinct impression he was jerking my chain now. I had long since realized this office was a boy's club.

"I'm thinking about it." I didn't want the job, but I'd learned to always keep my options open until the last possible moment. While my family lived in the Northwest and I was engaged to a man who lived near Olympia, I wanted to be certain I didn't make the wrong move.

Belden sensed my reluctance and it probably irritated him that I didn't jump at a job that would put me in the top one tenth of one percent of wage earners. The next question was his way of pulling the lever and dropping me through the floor.

"Assuming you were interested in the position, can you tell me what the square root of 363,000 is?"

I had been asked some odd questions in interviews, but this was a long way from anything I had ever heard. I assumed he was joking, so my answer was accordingly flippant.

"Not right off the top of my head, Tim, but can I get back to you on that?"

"Well you must have some idea. Is it 100?"

The interrogation spotlight hit me full face with a thousand watts.

"No."

He wasn't joking. I mentally kicked myself because my radar had warned me he was a jerk and I had still fallen into his little trap.

"Is it 200? A 1000?"

"No."

My face flushed as his shark jaws locked and he shook his head to tear off more flesh.

"So tell me, how would you figure it out, Lynn?" he pressed as hard as he could to humiliate me. Now I was becoming incensed by his belligerence. It wasn't enough to realize that the West Power

Trading Desk was as crooked as the rest of Enron; now I had some pompous blow-hard trying to spank me for not kissing his ass and begging for a job that meant swindling most of the western United States.

"Well, I would take my calculator and put in 363,000 and then push that little button with the check mark on it. How would you figure it, Tim? In your head?" As it came out, I couldn't believe how snippy it sounded, but I had cracked.

"Well, Lynn, if you are going to be a trader, you need to know that, *in your head*, and I can assure you, those traders out there? Each one of them can tell me exactly what the square root of 363,000 is."

"Well, as I said, I am considering my options, and if I was interested in trading, I would take that into account. That is, learning square roots."

Tim cared far less about my math skills than he did to see whether I would be willing to play by the "rules". Obviously, my willingness to challenge his absurd question with a snide answer clearly disqualified me for such a position. The pall over the room signaled the natural finish to our meeting. We shook hands and agreed we would get back to each other. *Not*. I departed the conference room and returned to the desk next to Jeff.

"How did it go?" Jeff asked, as Sean Crandall leaned out and looked down the aisle to hear my response.

"Well, he wanted to know what the square root of 363,000 was. I didn't know off the top of my head so I guess he must have thought I was a real dipstick."

I had no more than uttered that last syllable, when every trader scrambled for their calculators to figure out the square root of 363,000. After several seconds, Sean smugly shouted the winning answer.

"Six oh two point four nine four!"

Nothing like precision. The other traders quietly put their calculators away as if it never happened.

At the end of the week, Jeff and I went to dinner at an Ethiopian restaurant I had discovered some years earlier. After we settled in at our table and dispensed with small talk, he put it to me point blank, "So why exactly are you leaving Azurix? Other than the obvious," he said, referring to Azurix's drastically diminished stock value and stories of layoffs and widespread strife within. This inferred Sully hadn't told him about Rebecca's little problem; her husband the domain thief. I soft-sold my reasons for wanting out and we changed the subject. He never bothered to ask why I didn't want to become a power trader – he had long since divined that. Then he moved on to an interesting subject I had often wondered about: my boss, Sullivan Graas.

"Have you ever wondered what exactly Sully knows? I mean don't get me wrong, Sully's a great guy, but he finesses his way around questions and has great people working for him. He obviously hasn't gotten where he is based on his knowledge. Believe me, I am extremely appreciative of what he did for me by giving me a job at Enron, but it became obvious pretty quickly that he really didn't know much."

As we left the restaurant and said our goodbyes I walked to my car thinking about what extremely valuable and sensitive information Sully Graas had – and who he had it on.

My week in Portland was a wake-up call. I had witnessed a new, more sinister face of Enron. The Enron I had come to know was certainly dishonest, but it was bogged down in infighting and petty politics. As I pointed out, Enron's right and left hands seemed to operate independently at times. Enron Houston's criminal enterprises were carefully contrived, but at times there was an almost Keystone Kops incompetence, despite the bravado and show of arrogance. But after spending time with the Portland power trading department, I came away with a whole new respect for Enron's game of deceit. These guys were steely-eyed pros and they controlled a world so arcane as to be nearly incomprehensible to almost everyone on the outside, and apparently, even to some on the inside, including the governmental agency charged with monitoring them.

I watched as traders used a combination of complex knowledge and brass balls to manipulate prices, steal power, create false crises, and, by the simple act of average citizens twisting their home thermostat, dishonestly separate them from their money. During my time on the desk I got an education watching Enron executives engage in what I saw as unethical, if not illegal, trade practices.As Jeff described Grandma Millie taking it in the shorts at the hands of

Enron's power plays, I realized Enron was buying power in the state of California at the $250 per MWh price cap set by FERC, moving that power outside the state where there were no price caps. Then by causing artificial congestion on the transmission lines, Enron would be paid by California through the ISO to relieve the very congestion they were creating. At the same time, Enron was directing the generators to take power plants "off line" causing an energy crises, requiring the ISO to go outside California to buy enough power to supply Grandma Millie with air conditioning. The thing no one realized was Enron was selling the same electrons they had bought for $250 per MWh from California to itself at huge inflationary rates by claiming the power was "generated" outside California and thus not subject to price caps.

Skilling's haunting words came back to me – 90% of our competitors buy and sell power at the same location – but there's no money in that he would say. Enron had proven its flexibility to analysts and they had actually bought our story. We had a network of energy which allowed us to buy in one location and then sell in another location – I just never assumed he was implying we should steal Grandma Millie's car, paint it and then sell it back to her hoping she wouldn't notice it was her car in the first place.

Enron by now had an entire list of "friends of Enron" who would agree to serve as partners in Fastow's phony "off-the-balance sheet" partnerships. However, despite Enron's efforts to hide their debt, the credit rating agencies wanted something more – cash flow. So Skilling, in typical Skilling fashion said you want money – we'll *print money*. This kept the pressure off until the investment analysts began to ask the simple question – how is Enron making money? Unfortunately, as quickly as those on the trading floor could print the money, Houston was spending it.

Shortly after I left the trading floor, I learned that even Enron was investigating its own trading operations in Portland in August, 2000. Of course, I couldn't help but assume the investigation had been at the urging of the Houston trading floor feeling as though they were getting beaten at their own game. Although amazed by the results of their investigation, no one at Enron was quite ready to turn off the spigot.

California took the brunt of Enron's power plays because that's where the money was. Also, California's price caps gave Enron a Wild-West mentality, because that meant they had a supply of cheap power they could broker for fat profits. Tim Belden called it "Megawatt Laundering", while Richter referred to it as a Ricochet strategy, Forney referred to it as Ping Pong. Enron would take power from the California energy market through the PX and schedule it to flow out of California then "park" it, and then sell it back to the ISO during one of its many emergency states during an OOM call. Reassuring the ISO that the power was "generated" outside California, Forney then sought payment from the ISO under the Congestion Management Market program, which was wired to Enron, setting Forney up for an indictment for criminal wire fraud.

Meanwhile, Richter, Belden, and Forney created a loop of power transmission that once outside California could not be tracked by the ISO. When congestion occurred, one of the ways to be paid for relieving congestion by the ISO was to move power in the opposite direction of the congestion. For instance, in the summertime, when air conditioners are running overtime in southern California, Enron could agree, for a "fee", to "reroute" their power out of the congested zone. Once outside the scope of view of the ISO, Forney could simply move the power around in an endless circle getting paid to relieve congestion, only to move it outside California and then back in at a higher price. On the trading floor, Belden and Richter referred to it as Forney's Loop while those working with Forney referred to it as Death Star; however, once Forney became nervous that the ISO might catch on to his scheme, the name was changed to "Cuddly Bear".

How did they get away with all this? They didn't, at least not in the long run.Of course, virtually all of the traders, myself included, have been deposed by countless governmental organizations. Although like every good crook, Belden and Richter kept a keen eye on their back and each other's. When that eventually failed and the Feds were breathing down their neck, they did the next best thing – threw John Forney under the bus stating he was the mastermind behind all of the schemes. Truth was, numerous people knew about the schemes, including Skilling, but most, including Skilling, felt powerless to turn out the lights on the trading operation.

Today, when asked by a Washington Post reporter recently about the personalities of the power traders, I couldn't help but reflect on Jeff Richter – wondering how he had gotten so wrapped up in this behavior that was so foreign to his Midwestern roots. I doubted, had Jeff not worked at Enron, he'd ever taken this path to self-destruction. Tim Belden, on the other hand, had a sinister mind and given the opportunity to face him once again, I'd be the one asking the questions this time. For starters: "*So tell me, what is the square root of your jail cell?*" Meanwhile John Forney had come by his criminal mind honestly, transferred direct to Portland from the trading floor in Houston where they wrote the book on "printing money".

The thought has certainly crossed my mind, had I actually accepted the position trading power as Jeff's understudy then perhaps I too would've been caught up in the crimes. And, like Belden when asked why he committed the crimes, I would've likely said, as he did, "because I was trying to make money for Enron." But back then my exposure to the trading desk was more than I could handle and it almost made Azurix look good. I headed back to Houston knowing I needed an out and prayed Sully could help.

CHAPTER EIGHT

How can we have profits when we don't have any products?

Susan Forsythe*, Manager,
Enron Broadband Services

RIDING THE LIGHT

On Monday, I returned to the office feeling defeated. I sat down and poured over what had landed on my desk during my absence. When Sully got in we chatted briefly. He told me he was moving back to the main building at 1400 Smith Street and Enron Broadband Services (EBS). It was a good move.

"Can you take me with you?" I asked.

"I'm working on it." He changed the subject. "How was Portland?" I always had the feeling that Sully usually knew the answer before he asked it.

"I, uh, I'm really not interested." I quickly weighed telling him the details but decided it was more than he needed to know. Plus, he was friends with Jeff Richter and, if he really wanted the lowdown, he could call Jeff. Trying to expose the trading schemes in Portland would be a fool's errand. Sully was an astute political operator, but it was almost a given he would have no idea what I was talking about if I tried explaining the complicated shenanigans at the West Power Trading Desk. Sadly, I also knew that anyone in a position to be able to take action most likely condoned it. At the end of our meeting Sully told me to bide my time and wait until he saw an opportunity to bring me over to EBS. He promised to get me out of Azurix.

Two weeks passed and Sully still had no lifeline arranged. Although I had been repulsed and deeply disappointed by Rebecca's behavior with the URLs, I put the matter behind me. Until Sully could rescue me I still had a job writing the content for both Azurix's intranet site, which was entitled Oasis, as well as their public Internet. Slowly getting back into the rhythm of my daily tasks, I knew throwing myself into a new project might take my mind off things.

It had been a while since writing new content for The Chairman's Page, Rebecca's personal Web page, so I decided to write about her recent speech at Rice University regarding the water industry. It would be a nice, relaxing exercise with no chance for unpleasant surprises, which lately had been far too many.

I called Rebecca's office and set up a meeting a few days later to interview her. Meanwhile, I logged onto Dow Jones Interactive, which was one of Enron's research databases containing over 6,500 publications. Figuring that Rebecca's speech would at least have been covered in the Houston Chronicle, I decided to do my research prior to meeting with her so my questions would be to-the-point. Since she had just gotten married, I decided it would be more efficient to search under the most salient element of her new married name, Rebecca Mark-Jusbasche, than to get a raft of false hits with Rebecca Mark. With that, I typed in the word "Jusbasche" and hit the search key.

The search engine indicated 10 hits. I scrolled down the screen to the beginning and was irritated because I thought I had gotten a false hit on my first story. I quickly scanned the screen.

Shell Oil Sues, Charging Theft of Geological Map.

What's this? I was about to continue scrolling when something caught my eye. The story was dated May 29, 1984. I glanced at the story listed directly above it, dated April 7, 1985.

Bottom Line for Industrial Spy not too threatening with Texas.

My eyes opened a bit wider. I was afraid to click on the link to see what the stories would reveal. I was hoping it was a mistake. I read on. It wasn't.

In 1981, while working as a petroleum engineer at Shell's Western Exploration & Production, Joachim Michael Jusbasche stole valuable geological maps. He then traced them to resell to several companies including Continental Coastal Co., Coastal Associates Inc., and 3C Operating Co., of Texas, as well as Great

Lakes Niagaran Inc. and Malmco, both of Michigan. He was indicted for espionage and pleaded no contest. I read, then reread the stories. Neither a leopard nor a Jusbasche can change his spots and this was further confirmation that the Juice Man's career of espionage and corporate theft had been a long one.

I knew I had to tell someone about this. I immediately picked up the phone to call Janet Charles, Managing Director of Azurix Public Relations, then set it back on its receiver. The sensitivity of this information required that it be personally delivered. Rebecca and Janet had been through the PR ringer over the India debacle and I knew that Janet would appreciate the courtesy of a heads-up over this tidbit. I had noticed Yahoo's online investment message board getting increasing inquiries from Azurix's shareholders over the connection between ChemicalDesk and Azurix. In all likelihood, with Azurix's stock in the tank, investigations would soon begin. If anyone got wind of the link between the felonious principal of ChemicalDesk, the "exchange" of domain names, and the curious involvement of the chairman of Azurix, something very unpleasant and odoriferous would hit the fan. I knew Janet would know how to spin this information.

Janet Charles had come to Enron via its internal audit division. She had climbed the ranks to become Ken Lay's voice at Enron until she was sent over to help Rebecca at Enron International. She was one of the classiest, most professional women I had known there. Janet was now indirectly my boss since Sully had left. I not only owed it to her to share what I had found, but I wanted to make sure someone above me knew about it. Rebecca and Michael had been married only a few months so there had been limited opportunities to associate her with his name and his past. But every day brought the possibility that someone with an axe to grind against Azurix might just discover that the CEO's businessman hubby had more in common with Al Capone than Jack Welch. I headed to Janet's office. She was in and I knocked softly. She glanced up and smiled.

"Hi, Lynn."

"Hi, Janet. Can I speak with you for a moment?"

"Sure. Come on in. Just give me a second while I finish looking over this press release. We have a terrible situation going on in Latin America. Sit down, I'll be right with you."

I sat down and began to rehearse how I was going to share this information with her.

Janet finally looked up. "Okay, what can I do for you?"

In much the same way Sherron Watkins had sat down with Ken Lay, I sat now with Rebecca Mark's confidant and began to explain the crimes that had been committed.

"I think we have a potentially dangerous public relations situation on our hands. I don't know if you're aware of the information I discovered prior to Sully leaving."

"No," she said, leaning forward.

"Rebecca's husband, Michael Jusbasche?"

"Yeah...?"

"While trying to register some URL's for the Internet site, I discovered that someone kept snatching them up the day before I was going to buy them."

"Are you kidding?"

"I did a search of the buyer and in some cases it was ChemicalDesk.com, but in other cases it was an individual...."

"Michael Jusbasche," she finished.

"Yes. And ChemicalDesk is his company. A name, I might add, that he stole from us."

Janet waved her hand. "Could you close the door?"

"When did this happen?" she asked.

"Janet, that's not the problem."

"It isn't?"

"Not by comparison. In doing research for an article on Rebecca's speech at Rice, I did an Internet search."

"Okay…."

"I typed in 'Jusbasche' because her name is hyphenated now, and I wanted to avoid false hits. I got this." I handed her copies of the Web pages detailing Jusbasche's crimes.

"He was indicted in 1984 for stealing exploration maps from Shell."

Janet read them and her eyebrows raised in disbelief.

"Good lord."

"Yeah."

After a few seconds she looked up.

"Tell me again, how did you find out about this?"

"Just a simple search on Dow Jones Interactive."

Janet shook her head. "You know, I never asked Rebecca whether she had done the appropriate background checks on him because I always questioned if she really knew who she was marrying. I just never trusted that guy. Only it wasn't my place to ask her."

I understood. "I know it must be difficult when you reach the level Rebecca has to know who you can trust to love you for who you are and not take advantage of your position. I just thought you should know."

Janet sighed and sat back in her chair. "I appreciate it, Lynn. Let me figure this out and I'll get back to you."

I went back to my desk and called Sully. This was, as they say in the CIA, some very hot intel. I would be offering him valuable information that would keep my stock high in his eyes. Like covering myself with Janet, I also didn't want it to get back to Sully and have him think I knew and hadn't clued him in. Sully was all about what he knew and when he knew it.

"I've got to see you immediately. It's urgent," I said.

"I'm tied up most of the day in meetings. How does 2:30 sound?"

I hung up and immediately received a call from Janet.

"Lynn? This is Janet. Can you come over to my office and walk me through how you found this information again?"

I assumed Janet was not a computer whiz. I could have said *just search "Jusbasche" on the Net*, but I went to her office and described the process, so she could perform the same steps on her computer. She logged onto Dow Jones Interactive, punched in what I told her, and in a few seconds the damning evidence was on her screen.

"Okay, let me talk with Rebecca and I'll get back to you."

I waited patiently until 2:30 for my meeting with Sully. I made the long walk over to the Enron building, from the 9th floor of 3 Allen Center, through the lobby, across the skywalk over Allen

Street, through the parking garage, and down the escalator to the Enron Building.

At Sully's office, I suggested we go somewhere no one could eavesdrop on us. We left the building, crossed to the park and sat down on a bench.

"So what's your big secret?" he asked.

"Remember the domain thefts by Jusbasche?"

He nodded.

"He's had practice. I discovered that back in '84, Jusbasche stole geologic survey maps from Shell and turned around and resold them. He was indicted."

I saw a brief twinkle in Sully's eyes. At that moment, I wasn't sure if he already knew, but he never let on. He also didn't seem too surprised, given the impact of the information. I found out later that he had already shared my revelations about the domain thefts with Ken Rice and Amanda Martin, so it was an absolute certainty that Jeff Skilling also knew at that time. I'm sure 15 minutes after our meeting in the park – if they didn't already know – Rice, Amanda and Skilling knew that Jusbasche had sticky fingers. We switched the subject to escape plans.

"Don't worry Lynn, I am going to get you out of there as soon as possible, but I can't guarantee I can get you transferred to Portland." EBS had a large office in Portland. It would be a dream to keep my stock options and go back home.

"Just see what you can do. I'm taking a long weekend. I have a wedding to attend in Las Vegas."

"Yours?"

"Funny. Believe me, Sully, when Doug and I get married, you'll be first on the list."

I returned to my desk and the phone rang. The caller ID indicated it was Janet Charles. I picked up and answered.

"Lynn, I've talked with Rebecca. We've decided we want to remove the hyphenation from Rebecca's last name on our Internet site. From now on she will once again be known as Rebecca Mark, not Rebecca Mark-Jusbasche. Is that a problem?"

"Not at all. So do you want me to also go back and change all references in prior press releases?"

"No, unfortunately, we can't do that because those are also filed with the SEC. We're stuck with those. Let's just drop any Jusbasche references from here on out. Okay?"

"Okay." With that, I hung up, and turned to my computer to make Rebecca Mark a single woman again.

Upon my return from Las Vegas, I was pleasantly surprised to find a voicemail from someone at EBS's Human Resources department. The message asked me to send an offer letter for my transfer to EBS. Sully did not mention he had been successful in getting me transferred so quickly, particularly given the moratorium against transfers from Azurix to Enron. I called him.

"I had a nice surprise on my voicemail. Thanks."

"I told you I'd get you off that sinking ship."

I was scheduled to transfer from Azurix to EBS to work in the Office of the Chairman, effective March 15, 2000. The chairman was my former crush, Ken Rice, but now I was happily engaged. As Sully worked out the details of my move he called to offer updates.

"I'm trying hard, but I cannot justify moving you out to Portland. I'm going to introduce you to Susan Forsythe next time she's in town. She works for me out there and heads up the Competitive Intelligence Group. If Susan sees a need for you then I can probably get it approved."

The week of March 10 Sully phoned me. "Lynn, Susan Forsythe is in my office and I would like you to come meet with her."

"Ok, I'll be right over." This was the call I had been waiting for.

I had heard horrible things about Susan Forsythe, so when I actually met her I was happily disappointed she was not a witch. A kindly matron who seemed genuinely concerned about those who worked for her, Susan was warm and expressed interest in helping me.

"Sully tells me we need to get you out to Portland. He says not only is your family out there, but you have a young man who'd be interested in seeing more of you."

"That's true. My fiancé Doug is out there. I'd love to be back in Portland but I was scared I'd lose my stock options. I knew there was a freeze on transferring out of Azurix."

Susan winked. "Oh, I think we can get around that. I need you in Portland. When can you be ready to go?"

I felt comfortable enough to make a joke with my new savior. I looked at my watch.

"Uh, how's five minutes?"

I floated back to Azurix and phoned Janet Charles.

"Can I see you Janet?"

"Sure. Come on up."

Janet and I had developed a sort of kinship after I shared my revelation with her. She appreciated my bringing her in on Rebecca's "situation" and I think she saw me in a different light. I knocked on her door.

"Come on in," she said cheerily.

"I have to offer you my letter of resignation. I've got a great opportunity in Portland. I'm going to transfer with EBS out there." She didn't seem surprised. We had spoken enough that she was well aware of my trials and tribulations and understood I wanted stability within Enron.

"Are you sure you want to do that? Because if you are uncertain at all with transferring back to Enron, I have great connections at PGE and can recommend you for a position."

The tone of her voice was ominous, as though she was foreshadowing the demise of EBS. She was certainly in a position to know whether EBS was nothing more than a front. I told her I appreciated her offer, but Sully's offer was a done deal and included a company-paid relocation to Portland. I couldn't pass up the opportunity, as much as I liked her. Janet also understood that EBS was the next hottest thing inside Enron, and what I had been offered was the next best thing to being a trader. I crossed my fingers hoping no one would ask me to commit any crimes.

Within a few days, Sully and I met with the head of Human Resources who explained the grab-bag of goodies I would receive to relocate to Portland.

"The company," he explained, "will make arrangements to pack your things and move you out there. Additionally, since Portland is a little pricier than Houston, you'll receive a cost of living allowance for the difference in housing."

I couldn't quite believe what I was hearing. My dream for some time had been to move back to Portland at just about any cost. Now the company was not only paying for my relocation, they were *overpaying*. I had checked on the cost of professional movers and the quotes ranged from $7,000 to $10,000. To my complete amazement, Enron was now willing to shell out nearly $14,000 to move me simply because I wanted to move home, and on top of that, I was getting a cost of living bump in my salary. The benefits of my relationship with Sully were becoming visible or maybe it was because I knew too much of the corruption, the company thought it would simply buy me off. I was so stunned I just had to open my big mouth.

"Oh, I've already reserved a truck to move myself." Despite having worked at Enron for more than two years, I was misguided enough to think that you should treat the company's money as though it were your own. I certainly wasn't willing to spend $14,000 to move myself, so why should I ask Enron to do something I wasn't willing to do.

"Lynn," Sully said in a paternal tone, "you don't want to do that. If EBS is willing to pay for you to move, you should do it."

"I just didn't want to be any trouble. After all, I feel like Enron is doing me a favor sending me out to Portland."

"No, the company will take care of your needs. We will pack and move you. Do you have a car?"

"Uh, yeah."

"Good. We'll ship that, too."

I think my mouth fell open.

He stood to shake my hand. "Well, if that's it, I'll go make the arrangements and will finalize the offer letter for you. You can pick it up this afternoon in HR."

Sully and I left his office. "I was just about to kick you under the table when you mentioned you were planning on moving yourself. Lynn, always get everything you can from Enron."

When they purchased PGE, Enron did not know it contained a huge vein of gold that would be discovered after e-commerce exploded. Energy companies, seeing the proliferation of the Internet, realized they could ride the wave by utilizing the rights-of-way for their transmission lines and pipelines. Those rights-of-way gave them an avenue for the construction of a fiber optic network for high speed, or in the tech argot, broadband, delivery of content for the Internet. However, under the terms of the Natural Gas Act, which regulated their rights-of-way, it had never been FERC's intention to allow energy companies the right to take possession of landowners' properties for capital markets. But like everything else they conquered, energy companies found their way around the laws by claiming to now be telecommunication companies, providing them with the excuse to capitalize without sanctions from the feds or interference from the landowners.

PGE had created a little-known subsidiary to take advantage of the law and the landowners in the process. On April 1, 1997, PGE's subsidiary, FirstPoint Communications, Inc., filed an application for certification to provide telecommunications service in Oregon as a competitive provider. On August 15, 1997, the Order was granted. This gave PGE the right to abuse the intention of FERC's eminent domain statute, which was intended for public convenience and the necessity of accessibility for power and natural gas providers. Now PGE could use their rights-of-way for the purposes of developing a vast fiber optic network.

Ken Harrison, PGE's Chief Executive Officer, hand picked PGE's Chief Financial Officer, Joe Hirko, to lead the development of the telecommunications network, but Hirko had little interest in heading up the enterprise. While FirstPoint leased enough of the fiber optic cable to pay for the lines before the lines were laid, Skilling was uninterested in the network but had his beady eyes fixed on the revenue. Joe Hirko, and fellow FirstPoint execs Karl Underwood* and Gus Baxter* worked to convince Jeff Skilling to invest in the development of the fiber optic network, but it wasn't until Jeff heard the word "trading" that his ears perked up.

In no time, broadband was catapulted to the top of the Enron's corporate hierarchy. A commodity had been born and the push was on to suck the marrow out of it. A new battle front arose and hundreds of employees were redeployed to assist in creating this new emerging market. But the zeal dimmed slightly when it was discovered that Enron had been dilatory in maintaining its rights-of-way along its natural gas pipelines, so the company moved quickly and quietly to pony up more than $2 million to regain legal possession of those rights. With an entire electric grid and 38,000 miles of natural gas pipeline, Skilling realized Enron's spider web of throughways could allow them to become the force to be reckoned with in capitalizing on this exciting new market. With that goal, Enron Communications was born.

But Skilling and his posse knew that title to rights-of-way alone was only part of the equation. Next would come the part that just killed him: spending money on assets. With their shiny new rights in hand, Enron needed to develop the expensive infrastructure of the fiber optic network. It was a monumental task, and in typical Enron fashion they plunged in headfirst, armed only with their spectacular hubris. They had absolutely no experience or knowledge about fiber optics, let alone any clue as to once built, who would come.

Enron had a brief moment of clarity and hired a consulting firm who promptly told them to stay out of what was shaping up to be a volatile business. The risks were too high they warned. To the optimist, the potential returns could be staggering, but the consultants warned that so could the downside. Skilling was watching companies like growing fiber giant Global Crossing and pining for the new frontier. Enron was stinging over the failure of Azurix, and the parallel was inescapable. With Azurix, Enron had grabbed for the golden goose in an established market they had little knowledge of, and they had been punished.

Now here was a nascent gold mine with pioneers the only players. Despite the seeming wild abandon by VC firms to fund anything having to do with e-commerce, Enron knew too well that Main Street investors might be gun shy if they were to stray once again from their core business. But Skilling and the rest of the Enron senior management would not be stopped. Enron had two things that could get them the knowledge they did not have: cash and innovation. They also revised their opinion that Azurix

– hobbled by thin industry knowledge and little financial support for Rebecca – was a preventable failure. And in his heart, Skilling knew that Enron Communications would have one huge advantage over Azurix: him.

Pharaoh Skilling threw open doors to the treasure vaults and ordered his palace guards to begin hauling out chests brimming with the gold and jewels needed to fund his new quest. They brought in experts by the platoon, recruiting the best and the brightest to steer Enron into the riches of the 21st century. Hiring a multitude of talented individuals with industry knowledge, their only Achilles Heel was that it was such a new business there was no real track record – simply "unlimited" potential. And damn the torpedoes. Skilling had boasted numerous times, "I have never failed at anything, especially business." As Jeff and his high priests assembled their new army, the *Why Ask Why...Ask Why Not* ad campaign, which had once been the clarion call of an innovator, was now simply the fatuous mayday from a ship of fools.

Although Enron Communications reportedly intended to develop one obscure product after another, the only thing the company initially streamed was press releases, although most were nothing more than fabrications. On April 19, 1999, Enron made yet another misrepresentation when it announced its entry into mondo broadband with Enron's Intelligent Network, stating the network had been lit, tested and readied to deliver a series of ePowered applications. Enron's Cinderella was dressed for the ball and now sat down waiting for Prince Charming to find her.

On May 20, 1999, Enron made an announcement that it was ready to move toward trading bandwidth as a commodity. This was just what the investment community was waiting to hear. The only problem was – and nobody pointed this out – the store was open, but there were few customers. But Enron had flashed the card it was known for, trading, and the consensus on Wall Street was this had to be good. Then on December 2, 1999, Jeff Skilling got jiggy with it and proudly announced that Enron had transacted with Global Crossing in its first bandwidth trade. While the press release announced that Global Crossing was the seller of the bandwidth, Enron would remain in a "long" position, buying the bandwidth with absolutely no one to sell it to in order to close its position. GLBX was a seemingly underrated stock. Trading in the low $40s, many wags were predicting it would move steadily upward toward Splitsville. They were all mightily impressed that Global had created a massive fiber network, spanning oceans and continents. Their assets were undeniable. Yet again, the naysayers were rudely pointing out that in spite of their impressively colossal capital outlay, there were few takers on the horizon to zoom data around at the speed of light.

Enron continued to keep the PR machine cranked, not only to herald its entry into the market, but in an attempt to define itself as a real player. However, in January 2000, they realized they had made a mistake in coining their business name. They were not actually a stodgy telephone company offering communications, as their name implied, but were, in reality, a *broadband* company. Thus, in the middle of January, with no press coverage, Enron Communications became Enron Broadband Services. While the newly renamed Enron Broadband Services struggled to convince the world it was a player in the broadband market, they desperately beat the bushes to find a creditworthy customer they could actually sell it to. Enron then announced its partnership with Sun Microsystems, which boosted the stock once again to a seven-month high, closing at $71.625.

Ken Rice surprised everyone inside the company when he said at the January 20, 2000 analyst conference that EBS had developed a "revolutionary network control software that, among other things, allowed the company to provide a differentiated quality of service, dynamic provisioning of bandwidth and usage-based metering and billing." He made it sound like we had a system that was completely operational. And certainly had these features actually existed, they would be a cause for investors to stand up and take note; however, it was nothing more than my Prince Charming weaving a fairy tale. It was known throughout the company that Rice was telling tall tales. I was devastated when I realized not only were his shoes fake Italian knock-offs – so was he.

I knew that Ken Rice had resisted the assignment as co-CEO of Enron Broadband – not because he didn't want to share the title with Joe Hirko but because he was tired of the lies. They had worn him down after 20 years with Enron. Yet Rice continued to reassure investors and analysts that "EBS's fiber-optic network is superior and essentially complete", yet the Broadband Operating System (BOS) had not only not developed beyond the internal development stage, it was not running on EBS's premium fiber optic network the way he claimed it was.

At this point, because of the Wild West venture mentality and the promise of riches beyond the dreams of avarice, the high burn rate (money spent to get a business off the ground) of most Internet startups paled to that of Enron's new EBS. As the money was being incinerated at such an alarming rate, with no income on the foreseeable horizon, EBS began looking at a strategy employed by retailers for many years to establish a market. Loss leaders, that is, significantly reducing the price of a product or simply giving it away, was beginning to look like an attractive marketing option. The question was, could they do this and survive? I had the good fortune of being placed on the most powerful team inside Enron Broadband Services, the Competitive Intelligence Group. It was our job to determine who was doing what in the marketplace and what the actual long-term demand was for broadband. The chilling answer came quickly: little or none.

Susan Forsythe, the woman who brought me aboard, was a 20-year veteran of providing market research for companies in the high technology arena. Having been with Tektronix for most of her career, she had been recruited heavily by CEO Joe Hirko. If the required information existed, Susan knew where to find it. To assist her, Susan brought in Kyle McIntyre*, a former CIA analyst, and Harry Snare*, another competitive intelligence professional with over 20 years in the telecommunications industry. Working closely with these three was the highlight of my career at Enron. I quickly realized that if you really wanted to know what your company was capable of, spend a few hours with the competitive intelligence folks. I had paid dearly for my knowledge of Enron's failings, but these three didn't even need to leave their desks to tell me as much about Enron as I had learned first hand in my two years working there.

The employees that constituted EBS's maiden company, FirstPoint Communications in Portland, worked with a solid business model designed to keep capital and labor costs as low as possible. They knew what Skilling refused to acknowledge, that any sort of revenue seemed to be far off on the horizon. Skilling claimed a market potential of $450 billion by the year 2005. Susan and her group of competitive intelligence specialists tried desperately to make Skilling's predictions work. After running the numbers, they looked long and hard into their crystal ball and realized there was no way such big numbers could be justified. Joe Hirko didn't like what they were saying and put pressure on the group to define the market, and define it so it looked good. That would be Joe Hirko's undoing as he would ultimately be indicted for his stretching of the truth to boast stock value.

Harry, Susan, and Kyle went back to the drawing board, agonized over the future of broadband, and finally proclaimed "there is no market right now". Their doomy findings were like telling a guy who struck oil in 1840 that he was just a hair early for the internal combustion engine. While the three were shouting that the current Internet was a large, unfulfilled bubble, Enron was holding its hands over its ears and muttering loudly to drown out their bad news. *Market? Market? We don't need no stinkin' market* was the prevailing mindset at Enron, exemplified by Skilling's conceit, "We define the market, the market does not define us."

And define he did. During Enron's all-employee meeting in February 2000, Skilling laid out Enron's plan for broadband, saying "there were really only two competitors." One was Duke Energy. The other was Pacific Gas & Electric (PG&E). "Duke is laying people off in this business right now, and PG&E announced last week that they are selling the business. So we are in great shape."

Jeff's carefully calculated spin concealed the obvious, that Enron's competitors had actually listened to their competitive intelligence specialists and recognized there wasn't a current market for broadband. In the end, Skilling deftly attempted to convince everyone the failure of the broadband market "caught him by surprise".

As I settled into my surroundings in Portland, I quickly realized one important difference between Enron Houston and Enron Portland. These people did not share the carnivorous Enron attitude I had come to hate. While the office had the benefits of the corporate conglomerate in Houston, the atmosphere was wholly different. My office overlooked the tranquil Willamette River and a Zen-like peacefulness was the prevailing milieu. The only disturbance in the Force I could detect was a rabid distrust of anything from Houston. I quickly got the feeling that Enron Portland viewed Houston corporate as the toxic, dysfunctional parent and wanted as little as possible interaction with them.

Houston, in turn, was by no means enamored of Portland, seeing its office there as a necessary evil. I immediately picked up on the anti-Houston sentiment and made subtle moves to distance myself from where I had just come from. I also worked hard to insinuate myself into the Portland crowd and let them know I was a believer and could be trusted. From my first few exchanges, I knew I was being scrutinized to determine if I was a Skilling spy sent to harm, not help. It didn't take long to be accepted as having the proper level of distaste for the Houston mob.

Skilling didn't like having such a far-flung outpost, especially one that wielded such weight. But he was painfully aware that Portland was way ahead of Houston on the learning curve when it came to moving broadband. When the time was right, he would need Portland to convince the markets he would not repeat the same mistakes as Azurix. The last thing Skilling wanted was for analysts to start buzzing that Enron had spawned another Azurix, and was yet again venturing into a market where they didn't know squat.

Gus Baxter*, as Vice President of Research Technology, was given the task of developing the network. While Gus was charged with making Enron a powerhouse in broadband, the reality was that he spent most of his time complaining about Enron's lack of understanding of what was needed to actually build a network. But his cries were drowned out by the strained creaking of Enron's stock inching further and further into the sky.

Skilling arrived in Portland on a goodwill mission to inform FirstPoint employees that, despite being promised they would receive EBS stock as part of an IPO for Enron Broadband, it was now not going to happen. After watching Azurix's stock being hammered, the captains of Enron felt the savvy EBS employees might feel that a fistful of EBS stock – regardless of its IPO price – might end up as deep underwater as Azurix's shares. Instead, the employees would be given something of value, in this case, options in actual Enron stock that would vest in June of each year for the next three years. In an agreement outside the regular All Employee Stock Option Program available to the rest of us, FirstPoint employees had a very real chance of getting rich in exchange for being held hostage for the next three years.

But things were not so rosy in the Rose City. Employees in Accounts Payable had done some homework and discovered that Enron's statement of the books had no correlation with the facts. When Skilling dropped his guard and exposed his soft underbelly during a meeting with a large group of employees in Portland, one of them pounced.

"Where are you getting your numbers?" asked an indignant Michelle Robinson*.

Ever Mr. Cool, Jeff's eyes barely flickered when he came back with a decisive, "These are the numbers I was given." As damn smart as Skilling was, he always seemed to know nothing when it was convenient. This time it didn't float.

"No, Mr. Skilling, you weren't because I'm responsible for preparing the numbers," she shouted back.

For the first time I was witnessing first hand someone else willing to stand up and blow the whistle. I felt like it would soon erupt into a scene from the movie Norma Rae with the rest of us shouting behind her as Michelle would hopefully jump up and declare the injustice.

Jeff's face flushed as his mind raced for an excuse, someone to blame, a hole to wriggle through. No good escape presented itself so he changed the subject. It was obvious to everyone that Enron's books were being cooked, and though Michelle was the furious one trying to pin that bug Skilling to the styrofoam, she was not alone in her rage.

Rex Dieter* – one of my all-time favorite Enron employees was growing increasingly frustrated with Enron's manipulation of its numbers. Rex sat behind me, sharing the scenic view of the lazy Willamette below. He was responsible for the financial accounting, and as I grew closer and closer to him, he confided that it was his responsibility to "come up" with the numbers that "worked". Because of this, Rex was feeling incredible pressure.

We were chatting one day when the office had cleared out. I noticed Rex looked frazzled.

"You okay?"

"I honestly don't know where the hell they expect me to come up with the numbers. It just isn't gonna happen. The problem is Hannon's demanding that I 'find it'."

Most of the decent souls in the Portland office did not know what kind of shark tank they were dealing with in Houston. I had seen firsthand the school of man-eaters running the show and had become almost inured to their viciousness. The Portlanders could not even conceive of how low the brass in Houston would sink to achieve their ends. While I didn't think Kevin Hannon would have Rex crucified during lunch, Rex and I knew Hannon could make you beg for death when he verbally eviscerated you in front of a room full of people come budget review time.

Rex shared a story with me about our buddy Sullivan Graas. Rex was in Houston for a budget meeting and Hannon went berserk over some numbers Sully was trying to fob off. Everyone knew that Sully was a political operator and not a numbers guy. Unfortunately for Sully, Hannon didn't care who he knew as he stood up and shrieked at him across the big table.

"Are you a fucking idiot? What the fuck are you thinking, you stupid son-of-a-bitch?" Pulling the numbers out of a hat would be Hannon's undoing as he too would be indicted for his fiction.

Hannon proceeded to ream Sully in such an ugly, grisly fashion the incident became part of Enron folklore. Rex and I were worried. He was trying to make the numbers work but knew it wasn't going to happen. By then, Enron's value was being scrutinized by many who were starting to ask the question – *Where's the beef*? But Jeff Skilling would have none of that negativism as he proclaimed Enron's stock to be undervalued at $90.00. He believed that the Street did not fully appreciate the additional $40.00 that should be given to ENE's stock value for EBS's "superior operating network" but the reality was EBS accounted for no more than $10.00 of Enron's stock value as we had an inflated cost structure and very limited resources. Knowing not far behind Kevin Hannon was Skilling breathing down Hannon's neck, the pressure had just gone up three notches to prove him right.

When no one could pull a rabbit out of a hat to come up with the numbers, Skilling decided to pull the numbers out of his own ass. There it was in black and white. The Company's 2000 Annual Report, Jeff proclaimed Enron's net income had hit a record $1.3 billion. There was just one small problem he failed to notice just a few pages later in the Management Discussions and Andersen's audited financial statement Enron's net income was only $979 million.

This was first hope that I would no longer have to look for ways to blow the whistle. Certainly the financial world would see this blatant effort to mislead investors, wouldn't they? My hopes soon began to fade as I realized Jeff really had sold the world his "story". Enron's stock continued to rise.

It had been the same in May, 1998 when Cornell University graduate students Partho Ghosh, Lori Harris, Jay Krueger, Juan Ocampo, Erik Simpson, and Jay Vaidhyanathan had posted their report on the Internet that stated "the Beneish Model shows that Enron may be manipulating its earnings" and recommended and sell on Enron's stock. No one stood up and took notice.

CHAPTER NINE

Well thank you very much, we appreciate that. Asshole!

Jeff Skilling, Chief Executive Officer,
Enron Corp.

WHAT WILL YOU SAY TO CHANGE ENRON TODAY?

In mid-April 2000, we had our first team meeting to gather both the Houston and Portland members of Sully's team together. As one after another entered the room, I realized Sully had his hands full. Aside from my group, the rest were not the elite shock troops Sully had hoped for and promised to deliver. This assemblage was Hogan's Heroes. Sully had gone far in the company with his connections and ability to read the political tea leaves. With this pack of losers, he'd been neither smart nor lucky and he realized his "gig" of hiding behind bright people while claiming personal credit was nearing its final curtain call.

My team was made up of Susan, Harry, Kyle, and myself. We were the Competitive Intelligence Group, an assembly of specialized professionals belonging to the Society of Competitive Intelligence Professionals (SCIP). Sully made it sound like he had also been heavily recruited by Ken Rice to work out of the Office of the Chairman, but the rest of his group looked like they had been heavily recruited from skid row. Sully was a notorious brown-noser, having reached his pinnacle by schmoozing the cream of senior management, and he would have been embarrassed for any of his high-placed pals to see the rag-tag collection assembled before him.

He kicked off the meeting by having various individuals from other company divisions give short presentations about their department's functions. The marketing department discussed the efforts that were being made to define Enron in the broadband industry. When the table was opened to questions, most that were posed were positively idiotic, thereby reinforcing my contention that many on Sully's team were in over their heads. As the questions droned on – and questioner tried to communicate with questionee – the door opened and in rushed a tall slightly overweight woman in a suit.

"Sorry I'm late," she apologized, although it didn't seem necessary since no one, but Sully, knew who she was. Her frantic entrance gave the transparent impression she was very busy and very important. The truth was, this woman with the unlikely name Vicky Skankho* was Sully's charge only because she had been fobbed off on him and he was feeling charitable. In her mid-to-late forties, Vicky had allegedly worked for the White House Press Corps in some minor capacity many years before. I would later learn that her real qualification was that she had been a flight attendant for Eastern Airlines. In Enron's world that made her perfectly qualified to be a Senior Director – unfortunately she had no one reporting directly to her. This meant she was considered expendable overhead and could easily be furloughed at any time.

A few inches under six feet, she was attractive, if you consider Hillary Clinton as such, but then throw in the manly shoulders of President Bill Clinton's Attorney General, Janet Reno, and see what you've got. I had heard that Vicky's attempt to sleep to the top had failed, and she had just enough on some big cheese that she was thrown this bone to keep her quiet. Sully, the eternal suck up, had offered to take her on but regretted it from the start. Vicky had a reputation for being aggressively ambitious, so it was with reservations that Sully gave her haven. The 411 on Miss Skankho was that while running Enron's Associate and Analyst intern program she had somehow screwed up and was now one inept move away from being escorted from the building. I heard those rumors, but I'd been with Enron long enough to be skeptical. It actually sounded like she was right on track to fail upward. While Enron did not tolerate failure, they seemed to reward *really big failure*. For me, far more important than the direction of her career path, Vicky Skankho would turn out to be the reason I finally left Enron.

Enron's Associate and Analyst program was designed to promote the company to the youth market, and thus being able to explain Enron's innovation to the media and analysts by hiring the best and the brightest. The majority of Enron's first-time hires would come through ECT as a result of extensive recruiting at top colleges and business schools. Enron recruiters would travel to the premier campuses, holding "Super Saturday" gatherings at corporate headquarters in December and January for marathon interviews. During that time, each prospect would interview with six or seven different Enron executives. On the following Monday, mirroring rank and yank, the interviewees would be graded from first to last. Those who passed were asked to work as summer interns. The interns received valuable training and exposure while spending 10 to 12 weeks in one group. They also participated in planned activities to thrust them into networking with other interns and Associates.

An intern is an apprentice, and by their nature, apprentices take positions to learn a particular trade. And because they trade off their willing hearts and minds for the pursuit of knowledge, interns generally work for nothing or very little. Or so I thought. Having always been ready to lend a helping hand to those in need, I rented a room in my home in the summer of 1999 to Didier Baslé*, a senior at the University of Texas. Believing he was a struggling young man, as college students are supposed to be, I offered him the room at the bargain price of $100 per month. Our deal was, in exchange for the low rent, Didier, who was from Lyon, France, would teach me his native tongue. As the summer wore on, I realized Didier was no more going to teach me French than stoop to eating at Luby's Cafeteria, so I inquired about his finances. I assumed the highflying young man had misrepresented his family resources since he seemed to have more money than I did.

"Where do you get all your money?" I asked, point blank.

The 22-year-old looked at me like I was dense. "Enron."

Now I felt dense. "Enron is paying you?" My mind immediately assumed some stipend of a few hundred a month, which was a few hundred more than I had expected.

"Well yes." he replied, unsure how I managed to be employed, given how thick I was. "They pay me twenty-five hundred a month."

I was absolutely speechless. It suddenly hit me. It was the height of the dot-com era and youngsters with absolutely zero business experience were being handed ridiculous sums of money. It was all because the men handing it over to them had the muddled notion that a childhood spent thumbing a Gameboy somehow gave them mystical insights into the coming e-Revolution. Skilling and Lay were merely blindly following their corporate brethren in trying to maintain competition for the illusive intellectual capital of the young. When I thought about it, I got angry that Enron was dumb enough to pay some kid like Didier a third of my salary when I had spent twenty years getting where I was. Worse, he thought he was underpaid.

Didier didn't have time to teach me French because Enron kept him far too busy partying. In a jam-packed summer, Enron put on the dog with these kids, hosting the interns to a non-stop frenzy designed to dazzle, like rushing the best frat. Because Didier had shown enormous restraint in not running out and leasing a Porsche with his bounty, I made every effort to convey him to and from work. This often meant joining Enron's Hitler Youth for one happy hour after another. From tequila shooters off bare bellies to college babes nuzzling Managing Directors with Gold AMEX cards, it was a free flowing environment of Texas-sized buffets and bottomless glasses of hooch. This was a side to Enron that few would ever experience and I could not keep up with. I continued to give him rides to work but soon bowed out of being a spectator at the drink-a-thons.

The governor of Texas, the honorable George W. Bush, Jr., had great concerns about the welfare of interns as well. In a letter dated June 4, 1998, he wrote to his pal Ken Lay, in his function as Chairman of the Governor's Business Council, pleading for help. It seems the heartless Texas Legislature had put caps on the number of employees the state could cover, leaving the hundred or so interns the Governor gave refuge to each year out in the cold. George asked Ken to get the Council (read: Enron) to pony up to help him keep his interns gainfully employed. Interestingly, this request came at a time when Enron was pushing hard for the deregulation of electricity in the State of Texas.

Upon graduation, Enron's interns would vie for positions on the Enron Analyst team. If accepted, they would work for the next three years on six-month rotations from one business group to another. Their beginning salaries would be $50,000, with incremental bonuses. If they made it through the grueling three years, they could apply as an Associate. Once accepted into the Associate program, it was expected that you would attend an ivy-league business school, on a full ride from Enron, and return to a starting salary of $80,000. But that amount paled at the potential ahead, because you would also be given a seat on the trading floor. And everyone knew what that was worth.

Enron loved placing their youth corps, the Associates and Analysts, into positions where non-critical manpower was needed. Enron's corporate wheels knew the Associates and Analysts were ambitious tyros, and looked at them as a futures market in brainpower, but understood their limitations when it came to full-blown corporate combat. Everyone in charge knew that the kids would be great for carrying the golf clubs but weren't quite ready to take on Pebble Beach. Unfortunately, some of the interns had an overblown sense of their abilities, having read *Fortune* since they were Junior Achievers.

With the summer of 2000 quickly approaching, Sully was informed he would be required to hire at least one or two associates. Despite his complaints, he was expected to comply with the corporate directive. Shivik Bessmurian* was Sully's sack of rocks for the summer. Hired to assist with market research, Shivik represented the worst of what the internship program puked up. There was only one thing worse than the arrogance of a trader who'd made it big time, and that was the arrogance displayed by an Associate who had made it big time only in his dreams. Shivik had managed to leap the hurdles and make it into the Associate program, but I could only assume his success generated from someone above who saw in him all of the warmth and people skills of Jeff Skilling. Even Ken Lay once said Skilling didn't have a bone in his body that was not strategic, and he clearly recognized that Skilling would never be able to relate well to most employees. But the junkyard owner's dog isn't there for his kids to play with. And just as Ken described Jeff as having a "fast tongue", so too did Shivik Bessmurian. His impertinence was tolerated until he verbally abused Sully's secretary, Florence Sneeds*.

Harry Snare had been asked to assist Sully in the preparation of a letter pleading to Ken Rice for help in the upcoming budget process. The letter was important because the news Sully had to deliver was not going to please Kevin Hannon. Because of my writing skills, Harry came to me for assistance in preparing the letter. Although Sully said he had been recruited hard by Ken Rice, the honeymoon was over and Sully was now fighting tooth and nail for Ken's support. Sully wanted the letter to be clear: either Ken would support him or he was going to leave Enron.

Sully felt like Ken had left him twisting in the wind and he wanted us to express that in the letter. What baffled me was how oblivious Sully was to the lack of strength in his own position. It was obvious to everyone that Ken had worked to get Sully out of Azurix, not out of respect for Sully, but because Ken's lover Amanda Martin had asked him to. The other half of that story was that Sully wasn't respected at Azurix, and the other members of the e-commerce team didn't want to include him in any of their initiatives.

During a Houston trip to finalize the letter, Harry and I were having an informal meeting in his office when we overheard Shivik approach Florence. At issue was that Sully's door was closed, as it often was during my visits to Houston. Initially, I thought it was Sully's need for privacy to view more porn sites, but as I became familiar with his distressed state of mind, I realized it was his way of keeping the wolves at bay. As a vice president, the pressure to perform was becoming increasingly apparent and the buzz was that Sully wasn't making the grade.

As Harry and I fine tuned Sully's letter, I heard Shivik speak in an angry, elevated voice. "Is he in a meeting?"

"Yes," Florence replied. "I'm sorry, Shivik, but he's not to be disturbed."

"I must talk to him now." Shivik's tone was boiling with derision.

"Not now Shivik."

"You can't talk to me like that!"

"Shivik, please..."

Harry and I were looking at each other in amazement. I went to the door to see if Florence was okay and saw Shivik hurl what appeared to be a stapler across the office. It clattered on the wall and Florence cringed like she was next.

"Tell him I'm here to see him. Now!"

As Shivik moved toward Sully's door, Florence bravely threw her considerable mass in his path.

"You can scream at me, but you're not going in there."

"Yes I am," Shivik shouted and tried to get a purchase on her big gooey arm.

"No you're not!" she yelled, shoving him back.

Shivik backed off for a second, then thrust his face to within two inches of hers. "Don't talk to me that way! I'll have you fired!"

Shivik shook his finger in Florence's face. "You'll pay for this!" Then he spun on his heels and stormed away.

Florence was deeply shaken and I asked how she was.

"I'm okay." But I knew she wasn't, as the tears welled in her eyes.

Shivik's antics could probably be legally construed as assault. Harry and I returned to the task at hand. Within a few hours the letter was finished and I took it to Sully. He read it and pronounced that he was delighted.

"This states my position perfectly. Thank you."

Now that he was in a good mood I thought the timing right to deliver the bad news.

"Sully, I think you might want to talk with Shivik."

"Why?"

"I'm sure Florence would not want me to tell you this, but Shivik got verbally aggressive with her today. They practically got in a fight."

"What?" I could see Sully's ebony complexion flush with anger. He jumped up and went to the door, "Florence? Please come in here a moment."

Florence came to the door and Sully began inquiring about the incident. She was obviously embarrassed that she had been unable to control the situation and was virtually attacked by Shivik. She recounted the story but downplayed Shivik's behavior. On her behalf, I inserted the outrageous details. The veins stood out on Sully's temples and he spoke through clenched teeth.

"Florence? You tell Shivik to come see me immediately."

"He's at lunch, I think, Sully."

"Fine. Never mind, I'll leave him a message. And Florence? If I let him stay, promise me – you won't EVER let him talk that way to you again."

Sully gave her fatherly reassurance that absolutely no one would ever cause her distress again if she was doing her job to protect him. I continued my business in Sully's office and upon finishing our discussion, I approached Florence.

"You alright?"

"Yes, but this isn't the first time Shivik has done this. He makes me so mad. There has never been anyone around. I don't think he realized you were in Harry's office. He attacks me all the time. He's the worst kind of monster."

I didn't dare say to Florence what I was thinking, *Then, I guess he'll do very well at Enron.* If Shivik was a product of the Associate program, I was beginning to understand why Vicky Skankho had developed the reputation she had. She was now given leadership of a group under Sully's purview. After our first team meeting in Houston, Sully's two groups decided it would be a bonding experience if we all went to dinner. Like a cruise director keeping the action going, Vicky decided we should play a game. The rules were each person at the table would share three things about themselves. The trick was, only two of them would be true and the object was to guess which one of the three was the lie.

I don't remember the three things I said, because I didn't trust the group enough to share anything of importance about myself. What fascinated me even more than Susan's shockingly true admission that she had witnessed her mother being murdered, was watching the evil gleam in Vicky's eyes as she stored the information in her head for future ammo against her. While I watched Vicky's body English and her gleeful expression as Susan recounted the horrors of her story, I could see that famous Enron stare, the cold expression of a corporate shark sizing up its prey. In a split second, I realized Vicky was going to make a play for Susan's job and try to take over the Competitive Intelligence Group. The CIG carried respect and weight in the company, two things Vicky lacked. While she had climbed to her position on her knees, the thought of running a supremely legitimate entity like the CIG probably gave her goosebumps.

After we had absorbed Susan's tragic tale, the moment arrived that was Vicky's reason for this little exercise. With relish she described her two truths and one lie.

"Okay, number one, I've been asked out by Bill Clinton."

A murmur arose from the table. Consensus? -- Couldn't be true.

"Number two," she said, making eye contact with everyone and challenging each to believe what came next. "I've been asked out by George W. Bush. The younger one," she joked.

While "Dubyah" was merely running for President at that point, and the idea wasn't as outrageous as being asked out by a man who actually was President, it was almost as hard to believe. Vicky scanned the table triumphantly then moved to her trump card.

"And my third truth is I've been asked out by Dan Rather."

What's the frequency, Kenneth? All three were hard to fathom, and it turned out she had not been hit on by the biggest hound of the three, Bill Clinton. But it was still impressive. And with that, Vicky had accomplished her goal to demonstrate to us hayseeds what powerful circles she ran in. It was also a passive/aggressive way to tell us *stay the hell out of my way.*

I was now in one of two groups that were to give Enron a full view of the market. Market Research, based in Houston was led by Vicky, and my group, Competitive Intelligence, based in Portland was led by Susan. Market Research would get into the heads of consumers and attempt to predict the direction of the products and services offered. Competitive Intelligence sought to divine the moves of the competition before they made them. We also had our own competitive intelligence going within the group – our own spy. Harry Snare was based in Houston and was also an ally, which allowed us an inside view to what was really going on. Not long after our "friendly" little dinner, Harry confirmed my suspicions.

"Vicky is definitely out for Susan's job."

"She's said so?" I asked.

"More or less. She hasn't yet said she's going to get rid of Susan, but it's coming. She really has her eye on Competitive Intelligence."

That Vicky knew little about competitive intelligence was unimportant. She wanted the job like a hunter wants a head on the wall.

Harry was solemn. "I've told Susan to watch her back and I suggest you do the same."

I did my best to stay out of the infighting between the two groups. Keeping to myself, I performed the work assigned to me and began to uncover what seemed to be a terrific opportunity for the development for a profit center for Sully. The timing couldn't be better. Sully was a man under the gun and what I had discovered could make him a star. It could also be seen as found money, especially coming from a group that was considered by corporate as a place where money went in and didn't come out. For the CIG to invent a scheme to generate income was almost unheard of.

During this time, Skilling was telling everyone who would listen, that Enron's entry into the broadband business was a logical extension of its current business. With a straight face he stated that the [broadband] industry was "strikingly similar to the natural gas industry of the mid-1980s". Skilling calmly forecast that the demand for premium broadband delivery services could easily surpass the combined markets for natural gas and electricity. When I heard that, I was unclear as to which future century he was referring. We all thought the market for broadband could be significant some day, but at that particular point in time, when we needed to make money, it wasn't even a blip on the radar. Susan, Harry and Kyle were singing in unison, "There is no market".

More and more, I would hear my three colleagues bitterly hashing over Skilling's public pronouncements about the future of broadband and the profits on the horizon, as if the lack of a current market was their personal failing. Susan was the most vocal critic of Skilling, constantly doing the dance of political suicide while we all watched. Sometimes she would throw up her hands in frustration and utter her mantra, "How can we have any profits when we don't have any products?"

While I was uncomfortable with Susan's boisterous proclamations – knowing that Enron walls have keen hearing – I saw a solution to a problem. Skilling touted Enron's superior intelligent fiber optic network, but as far as I could see, Enron did not appear to be utilizing its Intelligent Network for its own business. When I first heard that I thought it was odd. As I looked into it, I realized it was plain dumb.

I attended the all-employee meetings in late February 2000, where Ken, Jeff and Joe Sutton briefed employees about the operating results of 1999. In Skilling's words "we have a very, very unique strategy in our broadband business. We are positioning ourselves in a way that will be almost identical to where we stand in the wholesale business in natural gas and electricity. So it is a very, very different strategy from what other people are pursuing, but it is a very strong strategy".

All the while Skilling was blithering on that Enron's broadband business model would be the same as the one used to create a liquid market for natural gas and electricity, I knew this could not possibly be the case. The commodities were very different. While trading capacity on a fiber optic network may seem like a similar concept, the commodity traveling over the network is very different from gas or electricity, and to my surprise no one seemed to pick up on this. If customers buy power in Madras, Oregon they don't care whether the electrons deliver were generated in New York or California, as long as the lights go on when they flip the switch. This simple principle was how Enron was able to generate revenue in the natural gas and electricity markets, by the "creative delivery" of the commodity over the pipeline network or power grid.

On the other hand, when it comes to data or video being streamed over a network, the customer needs to know that the spreadsheet they send to their office in Omaha doesn't end up as grandma's recipe for fruit cake. Data put into the network is expected to be the identical data being delivered on the other end. The concept seems simple enough, but it represented the foundation of a problem – and my basis for a solution.

Enron's "business plan of the week" targeted the very high bandwidth application users, or "hogs", as we called them. These were the users who streamed video or engaged in large file transfers, which consume huge quantities of bandwidth. In Enron's other business models, profits were derived by the level of creativity used in the delivery method between point A and point B, and the spread between the purchase and sale of the commodity at different locations. In the broadband scenario, Enron would enter new territory. They would now have to demonstrate that the identical data that originated at point A ended up at point B.

To accomplish this, Enron created "pooling points", or interconnections that would connect various fiber-optic networks together at major cities. In the same way airlines connect at hubs and transfer passengers, so too would the data transfer at the pooling points. The key for Enron was to own the pooling points, creating a monopoly on the information. Then they would know what data was being transferred and by whom, but more importantly, could manipulate the price just as they had with the exclusive rights to firm transmission of electricity in California.

To sell their broadband story, Enron created a paint-by-numbers structure for analysts to sink their teeth into. First, there would be the Intelligent Network, a long-haul fiber-optic network, and the interconnected "pooling points", or switches, which allowed other telecommunication companies to connect to the high-speed highway and transfer data via complex servers provided in a joint alliance with Sun Microsystems. Then there was Content Services, which included the demand streaming of video and content delivery, like movies on demand. Finally, there was Enron's bandwidth trading.

Scurrying to assemble people who had any broadband expertise, in addition to the unproven value of bandwidth, Enron continued to brag that it had the telecommunications industry by the tail. According to Skilling, "You can tell from the response in the stock market that they like the strategy. It makes sense. Now all we have to do is execute it." He might as well have said *See – it's true, because people believe it.* I knew Skilling wasn't buying his own tale when his bluster diminished just enough for him to weakly utter, "I think this is achievable."

So many of Skilling's comments over the years would reveal his conscience of guilt as his statements became a web of deceit so much so that he could no longer tell fact from fiction. Ultimately his story would cause his own demise and he would be left wondering why we weren't buying his proclamation of innocence.

To all of our dismay, Enron pronounced in its 1999 Annual Report that the "market for bandwidth intermediation will grow from $30 billion in 2000 to $95 billion in 2004". Even more alarming was Skilling's crazy claim that the communications bandwidth trading and services industry would represent a $450 billion worldwide market by 2005. The particular detail that drove us nuts was the wholly unproven notion that broadband traffic would be traded at all, let alone become a gargantuan industry. Susan made efforts but had no luck identifying the "analysts" to which Skilling referred. As we tried to figure out the budding broadband market, Skilling was like a loose cannon in the market place, making one bold announcement after another. I was fully expecting him to start claiming broadband was going to cure the common cold and stage-fright.

Sully made a trip to Portland for a joint meeting between Houston and Portland shortly after the team meeting and dinner. The meeting was to be video conferenced, essentially putting the two groups in the same room. Ironically, technical difficulties caused the video feed to fail, leaving us with a standard old phone teleconference. It was hardly auspicious for a company promoting itself as the cutting edge in video streaming technology. As we went around the table to discuss the status of our projects, I took the opportunity to enlighten the Houston crowd about a very valuable collection of talents among my fellow competitive intelligence specialists.

"Having been with the Competitive Intelligence Group for about a month now, I want to share with you some things I have learned. These individuals have particularly specialized knowledge and their talents are much needed in this new market Enron has ventured into. They have far ranging expertise in the telecommunications area. I've learned a lot in my month here, and I believe everyone else can too."

"Why do you say that?" Vicky interjected with an angry hiss.

Sensing trouble, Sully intervened. "Vicky, Lynn has merely made an observation she is sharing with the group."

"It was just a comment, nothing more," I added, realizing there was something going on between the two of them. I knew Vicky had it in for Susan, and I think my praise was like fingernails on a chalkboard.

When the meeting ended, Susan, Kyle, and I headed back to our desks. The second I sat down my phone rang. It was Vicky and she was pissed.

"Lynn, Vicky here. I just have to ask you, what was the basis for your comment about the group being so...what? Brilliant? Why did you say that? Did someone put you up to it?"

I was baffled by her anger.

"I'm sorry, Vicky. What are you talking about? Why would anyone 'put me up' to saying that?"

I had a pretty good idea why she was mad, but I was going to make her work for it. For the next hour I listened as she droned on and on about how Susan Forsythe was not long for the company and that she would be the one who would lead Sully's group as the premier provider of competitive intelligence services. The foundation for her experience in competitive intelligence? – She had once worked for a law firm – *as a recruiter* – and before that as a flight attendant. Even with my 18 years of solid legal experience, I felt I was only just qualified to tackle competitive intelligence at this level. Despite my effort to convince her that Susan, Harry and Kyle possessed rare talent and knowledge, she would not hear any of it. Vicky's cognitive dissonance caused her to embrace the notion that brains and a glib tongue were all the ingredients necessary to excel as a competitive intelligence specialist. I tried to find words that let her off that mental hook.

"Vicky, I have seen first hand that there is an incredible demand for knowledge about this field right now. Even if your group were going to lead the competitive intelligence efforts, I think the amount of time required to overcome the learning curve is not a luxury Sully can afford right now. He's under the gun from Hannon and Ken [Rice], and in turn Skilling, and we don't have time to, quite frankly, break anyone in."

"Are you saying you think I need to be 'broken-in'? I don't have the expertise?"

"I'm sure you're really good at what you do. But right now we should be relying on the talents of this group rather than discarding them because you may not like them personally."

There was silence on the other end of the line as Vicky considered her words.

"Look, Lynn, I have nothing against Susan personally. I just know what is going on in Houston."

After an hour of dancing around it was time to bow out.

"At this moment I'm actually not working on competitive intelligence. I'm looking into a plan to maximize savings when it comes to market data information, so I can't be of much more assistance relative to this. Perhaps you should have a conference call with Susan and Kyle and Harry to clear the air and discuss your issues."

I knew that was a logical thing to do, but it was also the last thing that Vicky would do.

"Maybe I will." Then she picked up on my suggestion that I might be usurping her area with my venture into the market data world. She had no idea what I was doing but whatever it was, she probably wasn't going to like it.

"Shivik, Annette*, Mabel, and I will be the sales people for any services offered by Sully's group. I mean, naturally our customers are going to want to utilize those who they interact with on a regular basis before they'll feel comfortable calling any of you guys out in Portland."

Vicky was beginning to sound like a broken record so we ended the call. I called Sully later and told him of Vicky's reaction and her rambling theme of getting rid of Susan.

"Vicky's *M.O.* will be to grab the territory out from underneath Susan," he said.

After a few minutes of discussion I realized Sully was going to do nothing to prevent that. I knew that from then on, I would not be able to confide in Sully when it came to Susan's welfare. I dared not ask him if he had some axe to grind with her. I assumed Susan was in the rifle scope because it was just politically expedient to let Vicky take her down.

CHAPTER TEN

False words are not only evil in themselves,
but they infect the soul with evil.

Plato

A CROOKED COMPANY WITH A CROOKED E

Apparently my little talk with Vicky about being unqualified had gone in one ear and out the other. Soon after, an e-mail was sent out to a select group of internal customers announcing a change in procedure. Previously, anyone with research requests concerning the broadband service could contact either group, depending upon their query. Now, Vicky directed that anyone with such a request would first go through her group, and any pertinent information would then be funneled to Susan's group. When Susan heard this she hit the ceiling and rightly so. She had been with the Broadband Group from the beginning and had developed relationships with her customers, which Vicky was working hard to undermine.

At Susan's direction, Kyle sent out an e-mail response, saying it would be far more efficient if the system already in place were kept there. This petty tug-of-war was embarrassing but, when made aware of it, Sully refused to get involved. Susan went to CEO Joe Hirko to rally support, but Hirko was in his own fight with co-CEO Ken Rice as to who would emerge from the cage alive. Hirko was an outsider to the upper echelon in Houston, and pressure was mounting for him to move there if he intended to keep his position. Sully told Susan and Vicky to work out their differences. He suggested another conference call to clear the air.

We went into our conference room, linked up with Vicky's group in Houston, and began our discussion. It quickly turned heated, and with no one to play ref, heated turned to ugly. As the bile spilled out we heard über brat Shivik shove his chair back in frustration and shout, "I've had enough of this!" Then he stormed out of the room and we heard the door slam.

"Shivik? Wait, Shivik," wheedled Vicky, as if her spoiled son had just had his PlayStation go dark.

Shortly after that, Sully was in town and we had dinner.

"Vicky's a land-grabber," said Sully over his glass of wine. "She has taken a dislike to Susan and will overthrow her if she can."

"And you'll let this happen?" I asked.

Sully sighed. I knew he always had secrets and I wished, for just one moment, I could have opened his head up like a bank vault and looked inside. I'm sure I would have been amazed at what bits of dirty laundry were stored there.

"There's nothing I can do, really."

I leaned forward. I just wanted to make sure we were clear on our use of words.

"There's nothing you *will* do."

Sully shrugged. *All those secrets....* He changed the subject.

Sully knew my background included heavy contract negotiation experience. "Forget Susan and Vicky. They're my problem. Lynn, you need to establish yourself and develop a business niche that is yours alone. You're smart, you have drive. Don't get bogged down with all the bickering. You have a good chance to finally make a name at Enron."

I listened to Sully then went home and thought long and hard about how I could turn my hazy plan into action that would cause the company to take notice. I knew that Enron bought the services of a number of online information and analyst sites. EBS had shelled out $2 million the previous year to use many services, including Nielsen, Multex, Datacom, Dow Jones Interactive, Faulkner, Thompson Financial, Lexis-Nexus, Westlaw, Dialogue, Juniper, IDC, Gartner, and KMI. Up to that point, only certain departments were allowed access to the information.

Protected by zealously-guarded passwords, use of the sites was highly restricted, not only limiting the potential benefits to a greater number of Enron employees who might use the information to aid the company, but the restrictions also caused potential legal trouble. Vicky decided the passwords were merely hindrances and hollow formalities, and began handing them out like mints at a Mexican restaurant. If any of the vendors got wind of the abuses over at Enron, at best they would sanction the company, and at worst sue us.

After poring over a lot of information, I decided there must be a way to use Enron's name to leverage the purchase of market data for little or nothing and also make it available to all. Many of the contracts for the services entered into by Susan could be combined with the contracts Enron Corp. had in Houston, creating a far more efficient system. I formed what I believed to be a very innovative idea.

Because it was my responsibility to negotiate all contracts for market data on behalf of Enron for the Competitive Intelligence Group, I saw the opportunity to employ what I called cross-marketing. Rather than spending $2,000,000, I saw a way, if we presented it properly, to actually generate as much as $10,000,000 in revenue. Because Jeff Skilling was consistently pounding the business units for financial results, if it worked, I would probably get a medal personally pinned on me by Skilling, and far better, a fat bonus.

My "cross-marketing" seemed simple once I laid it out on paper. All of the vendors, or information sites, loved having Enron as a client. It was like having a movie star as your pal. My plan was to approach them with an offer. In essence, EBS would say, "We'll agree to continue to buy your service if, in exchange, you agree to buy from EBS." We would continue to buy their market data services, and they would agree to stream their market data to all of their clients via Enron's Intelligent Network. Rather than that $2 million unrecoverable operating expense, my group would now be a profit center for the company. At Enron you were only as valuable as your last deal, and I knew a money-making innovation, like this, would get attention.

A few days later I was summoned to Houston on business. After my meetings I sat down with Sully and told him what I had in mind. He was ecstatic. "Lynn, this is a really great idea! I'm very impressed. It's exactly what you needed, like I said." Then he added what bordered on an insult. "Did you come up with this idea on your own?"

"Yes, of course I did." As well as Sully knew me and my ethics, this was, after all, Enron. Stealing ideas and calling them your own was one of those many Vision and Values written in disappearing ink.

"Really?" he exclaimed, his eyes bugged in surprise. I didn't know if it was surprise that it was my idea or surprise I hadn't stolen it. "This is a fabulous idea, Lynn. But I have to warn you. You mustn't share it with anyone. I have already told you Vicky's the worst kind of land-grabber, and she and others will steal it in a second. I absolutely mean it. Do not discuss this with anyone. Please."

I told him there were two problems that might get in our way. EBS didn't seem to actually have a stable network to stream data, and not all of Enron vendors would see the benefit of suddenly having to pay Enron, rather than receive their own revenue. Sully's excitement confirmed I was onto something, but I also tempered my excitement knowing he wasn't always hip to what really made the wheels of Enron turn. This time he surprised me.

"I don't know about the integrity of the network, but I think you're right about having a problem with some of the vendors going for this idea."

I sighed. "I thought that might be a sticking point."

"There's an answer. Go see Gary Wesson* in Global Sourcing."

I had never heard of such a group but took Sully's advice. My plan was based on the vendors understanding the value of calling Enron a client, so I was banking on the idea that this would give me an edge in negotiations. Despite all I had seen in my career at Enron, the company was still deeply respected and viewed worldwide as a leader. I was hoping the vendors would treat Enron like a celebrity at a bar – *Mr. Clooney? This one's on the house*. I was surprised, but happy Enron employed an in-house arm-twister.

The group was called Global Strategic Sourcing and their sole job was to "leverage" the Enron brand. This meant any vendor unwilling to play by Enron's rules would be blacklisted, not only with Enron, but within Enron's sphere of influence, which was considerable. In the Mafia, it's called a protection racket. Global Strategic Sourcing saw my plan as another way to squeeze vendors, and set about implementing it. What this now meant was that rather than paying a vendor $250,000 for a contract for market data, they would now be expected to pay EBS for streaming their content to all of their customers, not just Enron, or they would stand to lose the Enron account, which could potentially mean a loss of over $1,000,000. Any vendor unwilling to swap services would be kicked to the curb. This extortionist's touch was not what I had in mind, but I merely proposed and Enron disposed.

I assumed my idea would now get me some recognition. It did and, in typical Enron fashion, it was not what I expected. When Vicky got wind of my brainstorm her first impulse was probably to wish she'd had it. Her second was to make plans to steal it. Vicky immediately demanded that Mabel Thompson*, a research specialist under her wing, be made responsible for negotiating any and all market data. Mabel was a sullen, pinch-faced crone who seemed like she'd know more about the uses for eye of newt than databases.

During a heated call to me, Vicky asserted, "You couldn't possibly know what the research people need."

Never mind that my group had one of the premier market research specialists in the state of Oregon. Suddenly, I was center stage in one of Vicky's power struggles.

Something Sully once said came back to haunt me. *Lynn, don't you realize people in this company will stab you in the back simply because you have one?*

I phoned Sully after my talk with Vicky.

"But she's stealing my idea," I bleated with a schoolgirl pout.

"I know, I know. I told you not to let her know."

"Well I had to let her know eventually." I was frustrated.

"Vicky is a snake. She's only too willing to engage in this behavior. I don't know what she has against you, but she is threatened by you."

Sully's words were hardly comfort and I was irritated he offered me no protection. I had recently heard that Vicky was expanding her quest for power. Rumor had it Susan's job wasn't enough – she wanted Sully's, too. I had it on good authority that Kevin Hannon's animosity toward Sully likely had its roots with Vicky. I thought the timing was right to reveal what I knew to my friend.

"Sully, listen, if she's doing this to me, what's she doing behind your back?"

Sully paused for a very long moment. My question confirmed what he already suspected. He responded in a very calm voice. "If she thinks she can take my job, let her try."

Meanwhile, Susan was becoming increasingly agitated and vocal about what now appeared to be fraud with Enron's wild misrepresentation of the market demand for broadband. Her concern was that investors had little else to rely on but this bogus picture of Enron's broadband future. She discussed her frustrations with financial accountant Rex Dieter, and the two agreed that the value of their Enron stock options, as FirstPoint employees, was far too valuable to just walk away from. However, not everyone appreciated Susan's candor.

On the other side of the cubicle wall beyond Rex Dieter, sat Dustin Snodgress*, a Gen-X Howdy Doody with bright red hair and a nifty little goatee. He sported the official look of the rising dot-comer who seemed more at home arriving to work on a Vespa instead of a BMW. And yet it was that very look he so carefully cultivated that kept him from being accepted into Enron's premiere, and very tight-assed legal department. Dustin was a contract administrator under the supervision of the General Counsel, Kristina Mordaunt. A close friend of Andy Fastow's, she was as inside the circle as you get. Kristina held a lot of power at Enron. She was so close to Fastow, he even allowed her a super-exclusive taste of one of his fake partnerships.

When Susan questioned Enron's practices, Dustin would scream from behind his cubicle wall, "I don't want to hear that! Remember who I work for."

His implication being that duty would require him to report Susan's acts of sedition to Kristina. His failing was being too stupid to keep his mouth shut about being a mole.

Dustin didn't like me either, perhaps for the simple reason that I reported to Susan. One day, after I had negotiated the terms of a contract, he came over to my desk with eyes ablaze.

"Just what the hell do you think you're doing?" His arms flailed about as if he were signing to a blind man. He continued to berate me.

"I am the only one who can negotiate contracts. From here on out that territory is off limits to you."

That was the first I had heard of it. I lowered my voice in an effort to calm him.

"I'm sorry, Dustin, but I think you're mistaken. I always have and always will negotiate contracts."

As he launched into another diatribe I got up and walked away from my own desk, leaving him sputtering.

"You come back here!" he screamed.

A few minutes later when I returned he came around the divider and leaned in close.

"Do you have a problem with me?" he asked with a sneer.

"Yes I do. You're just too dramatic, running around here with your hands in everybody's face like some bad community theater actor. Just do your job and let me do mine."

I had never been so blunt with a colleague. I had always worked hard at being agreeable, but this guy had punched my buttons one too many times. After nearly three years in the big Cuisinart of Enron, I was in no mood for some punk trying to pee on my fire hydrant. From then on Dustin stayed away from me.

I was beginning to question some of the transactions that Enron Broadband was entering into. I had been watching Andy Fastow's handiwork with alarm for much of my tenure at Enron, pledging assets and claiming profits that the company didn't have, but now he was getting involved in EBS. When I came to EBS I was thrilled to finally be with a division that seemed to have a bright future. But with Fastow's hand of death reaching out, it lent credibility to Susan's claim that EBS was nothing more than smoke and mirrors.

Sully arrived for his usual monthly venture to the Northwest. Houston could be unbearably hot in springtime, but Portland was usually pleasant. Typically, Sully and I would have dinner to discuss the Portland office. As he questioned me about the status of the contract negotiations, I gave him an update.

"How many contracts do we have?" he asked

"Fourteen."

"And what is the expiration date on those contracts if we should want to renegotiate them?"

"They have various dates, but I can provide you with a spreadsheet of the details and whether there are evergreen clauses."

"What kind of clauses?"

"Evergreen. You know, they automatically renew, unless written notification is provided of our intention to cancel the contract."

"Oh, of course."

At that moment I realized the man running the two groups at the "world's largest energy company" was unfamiliar with a term that was standard in the energy industry. Sadly, I wasn't surprised.

"Who signed these contracts when we entered into them?"

Generally, only a select few people were authorized to sign contracts. "Well, Susan signed them because I believe she was the only competitive intelligence person on staff at the time."

What I didn't realize was that Sully was not interested in the terms of the contracts, only who signed them. I later learned that Dustin Snodgress had gone to Kristina Mordaunt complaining that Susan was asking a lot of embarrassing questions. Kristina smelled a traitor and called Sully, demanding that he fire her. Unfortunately for them, even at Enron, you couldn't fire someone for rightly questioning the logic of the company's actions, so the only thing they could get her on was signing contracts they assumed she wasn't authorized to sign. That would be a violation of Enron's Code of Conduct and all they'd need to give her the boot. What they didn't know was that she had been given signing authority by CEO Joe Hirko. Once they discovered that they couldn't justify firing her but they could do the next best thing, they slapped her on the wrist.

Sully immediately flew to Portland, with a letter in hand, formally disciplining Susan for signing contracts without consulting a higher-up. That she had the authority to do so was not mentioned. Sully handed her the letter and started railing, claiming he had grounds to fire her. Susan had been under increasing amounts of stress, which had taken its toll on her mental health. This didn't help.

And wily Vicky Skankho had strongly suspected Susan would eventually crack, given the knowledge she had gained during our first team meeting and subsequent dinner. Vicky's observations of Susan's reactions to her personal tragedy had given her a clear view of Susan's soft underbelly, and at Enron this was the definition of Knowledge Management. On the outside, Susan was a brilliant, passionate research whiz, but deep inside she was a fragile woman living in a state of fear. Vicky saw that immediately and applied pressure right up until Susan took a medical leave for stress.

While Susan was away regaining her strength, I was left to contend with Dustin Snodgress, Vicky Skankho and Mabel Thompson. Kyle and I circled the wagons, huddling together to wait for the axe to fall. Kyle told me Enron had far more intrigue than any he'd seen during his days as a CIA officer. He began looking for another job while I watched Vicky recruit yet another Portlander to act as her spy.

Sylvia Hill* came to work most days with an odd little beanie on her head because it had been at least three days since her hair had the benefit of water and shampoo. Although her husband and child were in Portland, Sylvia wanted more than anything to relocate to Houston where her ailing mother was. Sully made numerous promises to relocate her, but I knew it would never happen. Sylvia was smart enough to kiss the right asses. She aligned herself with Vicky in an attempt to catapult herself from a document specialist to a competitive intelligence specialist. It was also a way to get to Houston.

Right in the middle of Kyle's big job search he was called to teach the entire Houston office everything they had yet to grasp. Suddenly, some Einstein in Houston decided that competitive intelligence was a very specialized field that actually took extensive training. Despite Vicky's low regard for the credentials necessary for becoming a competitive intelligence specialist, her crew was getting slammed in Houston for being the simpletons they were. And because of their failings, CFO Kevin Hannon was not going to approve a budget for these lamebrains until they made a better showing of themselves. Hence the cry for help to Portland, where the real competitive intelligence people were. As soon as he got back from Houston, Kyle took me aside.

"Vicky told me if I wasn't ready to relocate to Houston I'd better start looking for a new job."

"I can't believe she'd say that, given your intelligence background."

Kyle smiled sardonically. "Vicky wants to get rid of intelligence."

We both laughed. The next day Kyle gave his notice.

As Mabel and Vicky continued their brazen attack on the Portland office, I realized it was all about competition and had nothing to do with building a company or performing a job properly. With such an egregious lack of expertise, Sully's true nature was now painfully revealed. With his two qualified people, Kyle and Susan, either gone or incapacitated, Sully was floundering to figure out what to do. His next step was a mistake. He reassigned me so I would be reporting directly to Vicky. I thought of Ronnie Jones, and Kathy Simpson's order that I dispatch him. Now Vicky was about to do the same to me. Stock options or not, I had reached the end of my rope. I would rather have reported to Saddam Hussein than to Vicky Skankho. Within a week, as I laid my plans to quit, Sully reconsidered. With his proximity to Vicky in Houston, he had a clear picture of her plans. He called me.

"Lynn, I made a terrible mistake. Vicky has it in for you and I cannot figure out why, but you do not deserve what she is dishing out. You will now be reporting to me again."

It was a relief, but it was also too little, too late. I had fought to make my name with my concept of cross-marketing but it had already been co-opted and I was ready to abandon it too.

"Okay, that's good. But look, Sully, if Mabel wants the contract administration plan, she can have it. I'm done."

Sully knew that's what Mabel and Vicky had been fighting for, so he was only too willing to give it to them to shut them up. But I knew something none of them knew – it probably wouldn't work. After extensive research, I discovered that Enron's fabulous new Intelligent Network, the guiding light in the broadband field, might just be a fake. Like one of those movie sets where the frontier town looks great until you walk through a door and find it's supported by two-by-fours, so, apparently, was the Intelligent Network.

With the delivery method in question, I wondered about progress on the construction of the much-vaunted fiber optic network, and I thought about Jeff Skilling. Skilling had been telling everyone since day one that Enron was an asset-light company. Of all the things Jeff said, that was one of the few I believed. To get the truth I went to the person I considered the source.

Barbara Riva* was a confidante of Susan Forsythe, and I adored her. Barbara was also in the construction group and had a handle on what was going on with the assembly of the network. We took a walk along the river front to a small Persian coffee house. Our friendship had developed as two kindred souls awash in a sea of adversity. We had also watched with growing revulsion what happened to Susan and wondered who would be next.

I trusted her enough to hit her point blank. "Barbara, Skilling's saying the construction on the network is 75% complete. Is that true?"

"Are you kidding? He won't give us the funds to complete the system, enough to even light it up."

"Are you serious? So how much of the network construction is actually completed?"

Barbara looked around and lowered her voice as she said, "About a third."

It took me a second to process that. "Do you mean to tell me Skilling's telling the whole world that the construction of an 18,000 mile fiber-optic network is almost done and we're only a third complete?"

She nodded. "What's worse, he's completely cut off our funding, which is making me very nervous. I can't afford to lose my job."

It seemed extremely fishy that when Enron used broadband they had to turn to someone else. Either that, or they swapped their "system" in elaborate schemes to generate revenue, like with telecommunications giant Qwest, which was from all indications and ongoing investigations an equally corrupt company at the hands of man named Joe Nacchio.

With the money spigot shut off by Skilling, and construction of the network halted, some spectacular innovation was called for. There was no way Skilling was about to allow the loss of momentum and watch Enron's stock drop because his "broadband" story had a phony ending. At the same time, Qwest Communications, having recently completed their merger with Baby Bell, U.S. West, was having its own problems with its stock down 75%.

Qwest and Enron became strange bedfellows in the botched Blockbuster deal. They each realized that a bit of creative accounting could allow them to realize revenues by swapping capacity through a type of long-term lease on their respective fiber-optic networks. The leases, known as "indefeasible rights of use" (IRU) allowed each company to record the incoming lease as revenue. At a time when it was becoming obvious the Internet bubble had burst, and both companies were laying off employees to stay afloat, they signed an agreement on Sunday, September 30 (the end of a fiscal quarter) for no apparent reason other than to artificially realize combined "revenues" of $500 million. Enron would book $308 million for "dark-fiber" sold to Qwest and Enron would pay $195.5 million for "lit-fiber" bought from Qwest. Each company would exchange checks for $112 million to close the deal. Of course, Enron Broadband was not marketing enough "lit-fiber" to warrant such a deal, nor did Qwest need any more "dark-fiber" since it possessed a glutton of unused fiber.

If Sully was going to turn my idea over to Mabel and Vicky, I decided to warn him that the network it was based upon was nothing like I had originally been told. "I have to tell you, this plan may see nowhere near the revenue generation I proposed."

I figured Vicky and Mabel could run with it and make that embarrassing discovery on their own. It would build character. But I couldn't let Sully walk into the trap. Sully reassigned me to work with the ironically entitled Knowledge Management. Headed by Lou Franklin*, a friend of Vicky's she had recruited from an accounting firm, I knew it might be a touchy situation. My new job was to train all EBS personnel on fully utilizing the market data research. The truth was, training the rank and file to be more effective in their use of research would free up Vicky's group to do more intensive research. But Vicky's fear was that if everybody knew how to do research her group might become obsolete.

Enron Broadband continued to stream one press release after another, mostly lies, and my buddy Rex Dieter promised me that EBS had deals in the works that would turn the current broadband market around. The first would be a video-on-demand deal with Blockbuster where movies would be made available to customers without having to leave the house. I had seen Enron stream the Wimbledon tennis championship live and heard they had come a long way in the development of the network, but rumors persisted that all of the deals reported in the press were virtually given away to create the image that Enron was becoming a real player.

The Blockbuster deal was a huge opportunity for Enron. Ken Lay announced on July 19, 2000, that it was "the most visible example of the power of Enron's broadband applications." The CEO of Blockbuster said the winners "will be determined by marketing expertise and brand strength, resources, innovation and commercial alliances." I took that to mean Blockbuster was not so sure of Enron's power, but hoped that with their trademark marketing wizardry and innovation they would pull it off. It wasn't until two months later, on September 6, 2000, Enron announced it was securing the necessary software for the Blockbuster deal, which was scheduled to be launched in less than 90 days. I wasn't the only one to wonder why Enron had waited so long to get their software in place for such a seemingly important deal. Wasn't that sort of like putting the proverbial cart before the horse?

Then Enron told us they would be offering personal computers to more than 19,000 employees for home use beginning in 2001 and generously included broadband access. I was far less surprised than others when it was announced that the broadband outlet would not be the Intelligent Network. Rather, employees would be given a subsidy for Internet connection "so employees can access high-speed broadband applications." Enron's own broadband service was never mentioned.

I had also heard about a deal with Microsoft where Enron would be the provider for the MSN Internet system, but it never materialized. Instead, I was hearing more and more from Rex Dieter about Andy Fastow's financing schemes, which were keeping Enron Broadband afloat. As Rex tried desperately to come up with the numbers for the 2001 budget, Arthur Andersen sent a young analyst to help him out. While Rex was in Houston, sweating profusely as he tried to explain EBS's situation to those who would listen, the kid from Andersen spent his days surfing the 'Net. No wonder Andersen was able to bill Enron a million dollars a week in fees I thought.

In the course of preparing for my training schedule to familiarize everyone at Enron with using our information services, I met with Sully. We came up with an announcement for a worldwide training schedule that would take me from Portland to Los Angeles to Houston to Denver to New York and on to London, all in a matter of weeks. Coordinating the schedules with the traders and originators in each of the offices would be left up to my Administrative Assistant, Laurie Colbert. Sully agreed to the schedule and signed off on the memo. I then sent it to all employees, stating that I would be traveling to their offices for training, and requesting that they sign up.

As soon as the memo went out, I received a frantic call from Sully.

"Lynn, I am giving you a heads up. Vicky is on the war path. She wants to know why your name is on the memo. I told her that I instructed you to do so, but she thinks you're responsible for this."

"Responsible for what, Sully?"

"For trying to take credit for the training."

"Oh you've got to be kidding. How petty could one get?" I was mad at Sully for not having the spine to stand up to his own underling.

I remembered a comment by Rosemary Plimpton in Human Resources, when she referred to the fact that human behavioral interaction is not isolated – *if a person acts a particular way with one person, at some point they will resort to that same behavior with other people because they get the desired result.* Vicky wasn't worth my time. Others would eventually see through her and deal with her. I just wanted to do my job, which I knew was probably not long for Enron. The Portland office was on its last leg and growing layoffs clearly indicated that all job functions would be moved to Houston. I decided I could not go back there. Unfortunately for corporate, there were still a large number of FirstPoint employees whose stock options had not yet vested and would require two more years of employment. There were rumblings that if the employees were let go, Enron would find itself in a big lawsuit.

As I began laying out the rigorous training schedule, I approached Sully about paying for Doug's trip to London.

"I know the company lets us travel business class to Europe, but I can't justify in my mind the $6,000. Instead, I would like to take Doug with me and have the company pay for the both of us to fly coach. The total would be $1,200, which will save the company $4,800."

"That makes sense," agreed Sully. "Let me check on it and I will let you know."

"Okay, great."

Sully took two weeks to get back to me.

"Sorry Lynn, the company requires that you fly business class so you will be rested when you arrive."

"For $6,000? That's insane."

I was astounded. How could it be they would rather spend $6,000, if I were willing to ride in coach. I took a deep breath. "So they won't pay for Doug to go, but you don't care if he goes with me, right?"

"Oh no, he's welcome to go, but you MUST fly business class."

Sully approved the trip and Doug's accompaniment, but the company wouldn't pay for him. Despite Sully's warning I refused to pay $6,000, and Doug and I sat together, in coach, on the trip to London. The cost to EBS for my ticket was $600.

When I returned from my extensive training schedule I went back to work on both the vendor relations relative to Enron's intranet, and Knowledge Management to integrate the market data services to make them available in a company-wide forum. Vicky continued to whine that there would be no need for her group if everyone in the company could readily access information via the intranet. I also heard that during my absence Vicky complained bitterly in a meeting that I was "flying all over the world while we're back here doing all the work."

I came in one day to find Vicky's plant, Sylvia Hill, helping herself to items in Susan's desk. Although Susan had been on a medical leave of absence since May, the files used by Susan and Kyle were now being boxed up to send to Houston. But going through her personal effects was out of bounds. Sylvia plunged into Susan's belongings as if robbing a grave.

"What are you doing Sylvia?"

"I was told by Vicky to go through Susan's desk and see if there is anything I need to do competitive intelligence." Her tone was snide. I got up and walked over to Susan's desk.

"Susan is on medical leave. She still works here. You cannot do that. How do you know those things are not Susan's personal items?" I snapped back.

"Well, we can reimburse her for them if we need to."

I grabbed a book from Sylvia's claws.

"No, Sylvia. It all stays. If you need something, go through Human Resources."

"Vicky told me to do it."

"I don't care."

Other than still trying to get some satisfaction over the obscene e-mail sent to me back in Houston, I had few opportunities to meet with Human Resources. But I was now going to make my presence known to them on behalf of my absent colleague. Susan had introduced me to Marla Edwards* in Human Resources when, a year after receiving the repulsive email, HR in Houston still had not provided me with an answer as to who was responsible. Marla Edwards had been appalled that such a serious matter had been neglected and came to my aid to try and resolve it. She had also worked with Susan and Sully to try to resolve their situation. I knew well the legal issues relative to what could and could not be done while an employee was on medical leave. I stepped into HR and found Marla.

"Marla, can I talk with you?"

"Sure Lynn, what's going on?"

"Sylvia Hill is upstairs rifling through Susan's personal belongings."

"I'm sure that's okay if she's been instructed to do so."

"So you don't see a problem with it?"

"No. Not as long as she was told by her supervisor."

Something was very clearly wrong here. It was like *Invasion of the Body Snatchers*. Someone had turned Marla Edwards into a pod person. Like nearly everyone at Enron, Marla had to keep a close eye on which way the wind was blowing and it was now blowing from Houston, given Portland's days were numbered. She obviously wanted to keep her job and was simply doing as she was told. I understood. I had done it too.

But by now my attitude left little room for patience. I was rapidly becoming a really disgruntled employee. Nearly four months had gone by since submitting my expenses for the training sessions. I had put a lot of the expenses on my American Express, assuming I would be reimbursed immediately. The company was so sluggish in coming through with my money, I was forced to take out a personal loan to pay the oldest two bills totaling $9,444.14 to avoid taking a negative hit on my credit. They owed me around $14,000.

I e-mailed Sully's secretary, Florence Sneeds, on October 17, 2000, inquiring about the status of the unpaid expenses. She called me when she got the message.

"I submitted them for payment on October 12."

"Holy crap, Florence! I gave them to you months ago. Why did you just send them now? I need the money."

Florence apologized and I hung up the phone, fuming. I sat down and typed out an e-mail. She had made a huge mistake, but I figured I could catch more flies with honey.

Florence,
I know that you have a lot of responsibilities when you include all of the people within the group, and quite frankly, I think you have the hardest job of all of us keeping track of everything, but I REALLY need your help. Unfortunately, I don't have an extra $14,000 sitting around to pay for

> *business travel expenses and since the majority of them have been outstanding since June, July, and August, I really need to get paid on these as quickly as possible*
> *Lynn*

Florence soon phoned to tell me that Accounts Payable was holding the expense reports because I did not have receipts for some five dollar lunches at the Enron cafeteria. All told, the items, for which I didn't have receipts, came to $177.90. For that they were holding up paying my $14,000. Now I was furious because Enron's policy allowed expenses under $75.00 per incident to be paid without a receipt. I doubted Jeff Skilling ever had this sort of Mickey Mouse quibbling when he handed in his expense reports. I called Accounts Payable and discovered Florence had never turned the expense reports in and that AP had a mandatory policy of paying all expense reports within 3 days. I was even more furious and sent an e-mail to Sully and Lou requesting an explanation from Accounts Payable since Florence was claiming my payment had been held up.

My phone rang five minutes later.

"Lynn, Lou. What the hell is going on? You're spewing venom and you've got the people in Accounts Payable really upset, accusing them of not paying your expense reports."

"Look, Lou, Florence told me she submitted them on October 12, and here it is the 18th and they say they still haven't received them. Somebody's lying."

"We're having your expense reports audited because there's a charge for a bottle of wine in New York."

That was the last straw.

"Did you happen to notice there was no expense for a $350.00 per night hotel for four days? I saved you people fourteen hundred bucks and you talk to me about a lousy eighty-dollar bottle of wine I bought my brother as a courtesy for staying at his home? Think again, Lou."

I was incensed with his line of questioning.

"And another thing," he continued in his nasal whine, "there are no hotel charges on a trip to Houston."

"That's right. I used to live there. I stayed with friends because I knew Sully was getting hammered by Kevin Hannon for expenditures. Now you're complaining I haven't charged enough? What else?"

"Well, what about the trip to London? Florence called the rental car company and found out your fiancé went with you," he blurted with a *gotcha* tone.

I paused to get a handle on my anger before answering. "Apparently, Lou, you missed the memo on that one. Doug's trip to London was pre-approved by Sully."

"Regardless, before Sully or I will approve any of these expense reports they will need to be audited."

"You mean then, they have not been submitted to Accounts Payable? So Florence was lying."

"She had questions and was instructed to hold them."

"So she lied to me, leading me to believe they were being taken care of. Do you realize I am personally on the hook for the $14,000 because these are expense reports from June and it's now October? I put these expenses on my corporate AMEX card, for which I'm personally responsible, and now you and your people are giving me the runaround."

"Oh please, don't take this so personally."

"I'm taking it very personally, Lou. This is what's going to happen. I will send a note to Accounts Payable, with a copy to you, and then once they've been approved you will sign off on them, immediately." With that I hung up.

I sent all of my expense reports to Accounts Payable with an explanation requesting that they be audited. Within three days as promised, they had been approved without question, with the exception of London, which would need branch president Steve Elliott's signature.

The expense reports were the final straw in my tumble into that level of Hell called Enron. As soon as I was paid, I would request a severance package and walk away. While my insurance was still in effect I decided to tie up a few last medical things. I was informed after my breast reduction surgery that pre-cancerous cells had been found in the tissue. They told me there would be a relatively high chance I would be diagnosed with breast cancer within my lifetime, and what concerned me was the doctor's admonition that any cancer could be exacerbated by stress. I would not allow Vicky or her pack of jackals to continue to nip at me. Then Sully called to cheer me up with news that Vicky had blown off a very important meeting and for her sins had been "redeployed" to EES. It was the next worst thing to being fired. But for me her reshuffling was too little too late.

With my rigorous travel schedule I had been unable to meet with my surgical oncologist in Portland since my move. I now scheduled an appointment with the head of oncology at the University Medical Center. As he looked at the pathology report, he asked a series of questions, which I answered while he typed away on the keyboard of a handheld computer. Finally, the verdict.

"There is an 86% chance that you will be diagnosed with breast cancer within the next five years. That is, unless the pathologist in Houston misdiagnosed the results. I will order the review of the tissue samples by the pathologist here in Portland and then we will determine what we need to do. In the meantime, reduce whatever stress you can from your life. I know this seems like a big blow, but you should be alright. I do suggest you speak with a counselor."

I drove back to the office in shock. I reached my desk and the tears turned to hysterical crying as I dialed the Employee Assistance Helpline for Enron. I wanted immediate approval from the company to pay for a counselor under our mental health policy. An operator answered.

"I need to get some help!"

"Why don't you tell me what is going on?" she asked sweetly.

I began where I had started three years before. I told her about the bank fraud, the espionage, the manipulation of power prices, the sniping and backbiting, and now the misrepresentations and lying at Enron Broadband Services. In a span of about 15 minutes I had shared the highlights of what you have read in the last few hundred pages.

"A crooked company with the crooked E logo!" I sobbed. "That should have been my first sign that it was going to be a wild ride."

To which she responded, "Ma'am," she said with a sort of odd sympathetic tone in her voice, "inasmuch as our fees are paid by Enron, I can't take your call, you'll have to hire a private lawyer."

I was too stunned to respond. My attempts to blow the whistle outside Enron had failed just as they had inside. I felt utterly defeated as I hung up the phone and began to cry. After a few minutes of composing myself I called Marla Edwards in HR. I shared some of my troubles and my crying hammered home the point I was deeply upset.

"Do you want to take a leave of absence?"

"No. I just want a severance package. I want out."

"Okay, let me see what I can do."

CHAPTER ELEVEN

We were changing the world. We were doing God's work.

Jeff Skilling, Chief Executive Officer,
Enron Corp.

THE END OF ENRON

Doug and I got married on Thursday, November 9, 2000, nearly 23 years to the day after going to our first dance together in high school. On Monday, November 13th, I went to the office, collected my stuff, said goodbye to the few people I cared about and walked out. I got in my car, drove away and didn't look back. On that same day, I received a severance package worth $15,019.23, plus an additional $15,019.23 if I agreed not to sue Enron for what I had seen. The agreement said nothing about assisting class action lawyers in a potential claim on behalf of shareholders who I knew would be damaged when the house of cards came crashing down. I immediately contacted Charlie Gastineau, a class action lawyer to alert him about Enron's corruption. At first anonymously but eventually publicly.

In exchange for the signed severance agreement, Lou consented that I would be paid for my outstanding expense reports. On November 21, I received a check for $9,119.83, which didn't include the trip to London. What became apparent as I called them over the next two months was that Sully had never received the appropriate approval from London prexy Steve Elliott to send me there, which meant my expenses of $3,570.98 might never be paid. But Sully's oversight in obtaining the necessary approval was sadly typical. Marla Edwards made numerous calls to Sully who assured her it was being taken care of.

By year's end I had American Express calling me at home looking for their payment. I informed them that I was no longer with Enron, that my corporate American Express card was no longer active and to get it from Enron. American Express didn't see it that way and kept harassing me. Finally, I threatened Sully that I would contact Steve Elliott directly to explain the situation if the reimbursement was not received forthwith. My final expense reimbursement check for $3,570.98 was issued on January 10, 2001. Still, with late charges of $700 on nearly $14,000 due since summer I demanded Enron pay them. They did so in mid-February, 2001.

Some months after leaving Enron, I did an accounting of my stock options. They had been the primary reason I allowed myself to endure such abuse. The grand tally came to a decent $83,086.70.

By late winter of 2000, I was happily married, living in a new home on ten acres. In a self-imposed witness protection plan, Enron and Azurix seemed like distant nightmares. One day, a few months after I quit, the mail brought me an utter surprise, a check for $1,050 from the restricted stock I was awarded while at Azurix. Believing I had forfeited my options when I left the subsidiary, the money was gravy. I thought about Rebecca Mark and how that poor woman had bailed with only *tens of millions*.

My 401(k), 100% invested in Enron stock, was now worth nearly $30,000, a gain of 379% over three years. I did some quick calculations and, assuming Enron's stock value would plane out at the very least, had no reason to believe that in another three years it wouldn't be worth $113,700, or nearly a half a million dollars in six. Along with many others, I had received Enron's literature about *Money in Motion*, which clearly demonstrated that Enron's stock, even in a worst-case scenario of losing 50% of its value, would still represent a 188% gain, which was far better than any other investment option.

I had promised myself when Ken Lay handed over the helm to Jeff Skilling, I would no longer leave any of my money in Enron stock. But in February, 2001, when the changing of the guard was announced, Enron was still hanging in the $70 and $80 range. With no daily reminder of Enron's stock price glaring at me via the reader board, I settled into my life on our farm in rural Washington with my loving husband and temporarily forgot about stock values.

On March 31, 2001, I checked my retirement account. It had dropped nearly $10,000. It was a bit of shock, given I was used to seeing Enron going up, but I believed it would rebound. The drop in Enron's stock price was gradual from that point forward. I was only distantly interested in anything that Enron did and the mistake was mine for not paying closer attention to what was going on.

In April, 2001, I heard about Enron's now infamous first quarter analyst's conference call. Boston hedge fund manager Richard Grubman was questioning Skilling over Enron's financial condition subsequent to the *Fortune* magazine article by Bethany McLean.

"You're the only financial institution that can't come up with a balance sheet or cash flow statement after earnings," accused Grubman.

To which Mr. Skilling astutely rejoined, "Well thank you very much, we appreciate that. Asshole!" and moved on to the next question. Apparently Mr. Grubman was no longer buying the "story". So much for Enron's first value – *Respect.*

On August 14, 2001, Jeff Skilling, Harvard MBA and perennial winner of Houston's MS150, resigned. He had also recently unloaded $66.9 million worth of his Enron stock. It was at that point I started paying closer attention to Enron again. I knew something wasn't right. Although the news reports said that Jeff had resigned for personal reasons, I knew Jeff and I knew better. My knee-jerk assumption was Jeff had been booted. It was true, according to Ken Lay, the Board of Directors had been unhappy with him for a long time. Most had wondered whether Ken had finally caught wind of Jeff's own effort to dethrone Ken, just as he had done with every vice chairman before him. Perhaps they had finally given him the deadly "issues" ranking and sent him packing.

I had seen Rebecca Mark publicly resign for "personal reasons", knowing full well she had been forced out. Maybe Jeff was no different. Or was he? Jeff was one smart guy, but he was soulless. Not in an Isaac Hayes way, but rather in a won't-go-to-heaven way. He ran the company like he knew it would eventually burn up and his toughest task was predicting when to bail before the flames consumed him and his ill-gotten fortune. As Ken Lay noted, Skilling was consumed by strategy, by winning at any cost.

It was Skilling's strategy that in the end may cost him his freedom. While the rest of the executive team was required to sign Deal Approval Sheets, which we referred to as DASH's, indicating that the deal had a green light. The designated executive would literally put their name on the deal and initial it giving the approval for the next person to sign. I always found it fascinating that Skilling carefully avoided ever signing one – even when asked to by legal counsel, indicative of someone with whose real strategy was to distance himself from the fraud – fraud that could not have been committed without his knowledge and approval.

Also, it's a curious coincidence that Jeff and Rebecca Carter got married. Curious, not because they dated, fell in love, and promised to spend the rest of their lives together, but because a wife cannot testify against a husband. Always strategic. In the end, whether he was fired or resigned matters not nearly as much as the fact that he voluntarily and secretly underwent a lie detector test administered by American International Security Corporation on December 4, 2001, the day immediately following Enron's bankruptcy filing.

Enron's freefall had begun and suddenly my retirement kitty was in jeopardy.

"How low can it go?" I asked Doug rhetorically one evening after checking Enron's falling price online. I had been planning to roll the entire balance over in July, but Enron had sent back the paperwork stating that it needed to be notarized. On September 11, along with everyone else, I was profoundly saddened and riveted to my television. For a while I forgot all about the pettiness and greed at Enron.

By the time I received my notarized copy on September 30, 2001, my 401(k) was worth the same amount as I had originally rolled over into Enron stock. I never received the messages that were purportedly sent to employees notifying them of a "blackout" period, but in a stroke of luck, on October 11, 2001, I requested the balance be removed from Enron's control. Five days later, on October 16, Enron reported a third quarter loss of $618 million, as well as a reduction in shareholder equity to the tune of $1.2 billion. Kudos to Mr. Fastow and his partnership hijinks.

On October 24, 2001, Enron's trustee, The Northern Trust Company issued a check to my new IRA in the amount of $8,214.59, which was rolled over into – you guessed it – Enron stock. Also on that day, Andy Fastow was blown out as Enron's CFO. Was he unhappy because he had fallen off the rank and yank bell curve? I doubt it, given he had pulled more than $30 million out of Enron by way of his fake partnerships alone. By the time I could access funds, my 401(k) was worth a little more than a roundtrip coach ticket to Houston. When I finally cashed out my retirement savings it was worth $1,516.82.

I have heard many stories of employees who spent their entire careers at Enron and were devastated by the collapse, but I take full responsibility for losing my money. I had fair warning. Like many Enron employees, I chose to leave the funds exposed to volatility, the one thing everyone at Enron knew could be dangerous. But as an Enronite I had been hammered from day one on the virtues of volatility. We'd all heard Skilling's song of risk management so many times it began to sound like an anthem.

As fall 2001 came, Enron continued its surprises. November 7th was not a good day for Kristina Mordaunt, the powerhouse attorney from EBS. When the company found out Kristina had invested $5,800 in Southampton Place, one of Andy Fastow's LJM partnership structures, and a month later cashed out with a million bucks, she was history. Security guards were dispatched to the wealthy Ms. Mordaunt's desk and she was escorted to the front door. On November 9, word got out the company had overstated its earnings for the previous five years by $567 million. Ten days later, Enron restated its third-quarter earnings while working desperately to restructure a $650 million obligation that was coming due. Two days later, they reached an agreement to extend the debt payment. Now it was *$690* million. Two days after that, Enron got a three week reprieve on paying off the $690 million.

Meanwhile, Enron was bailing furiously and praying former competitor Dynegy would rescue them. However, on November 29, the Dynegy deal came unglued. Exactly one year before, on

November 29, 2000, Enron's stock peaked at $79. When word of the Dynegy failure got out, the stock closed that day at around fifty-cents. On December 2, 2001, Enron Corp., once the bastion of American energy, stumbled and fell, declaring Chapter 11 bankruptcy. That December 2nd was a Sunday intrigued me. The courts aren't open on Sunday. I cynically wondered if someone conspired to file on a day no one suspected, to give a select few a jump on everyone else to unload stock that would assuredly go down pretty fast with such ominous news.

Enron was made up of people, good and bad alike. In our own ways we all believed we would change the world. While I've related much of the bad that I saw, to be fair, the people of Enron also did a lot of good. Charity was actually a cornerstone of Enron. Perhaps some corporate guilt or an attempt to appear caring got the movement going, but the average folks in the company were the ones that took up the cause and did much of the work. Most contributed time and money for the betterment of others, notwithstanding Jeff Skilling's biking and fund raising. While it's been widely reported that many senior executives walked away with tremendous sums of money, I knew that many at Enron were left hanging out to dry. More than four thousand people were laid off just weeks before Christmas with little or no notice. Although Enron was being vilified in the press daily, I knew there were many in Houston who suddenly couldn't make house and car payments, their salaries gone overnight, along with what they thought were prudent investments in the company they trusted. I also knew there were plenty of recently-released Enron employees who were forced to return Christmas gifts and cancel holiday travel.

After reading about it and watching the savaging Enron took on the evening news, I thought it might be a good idea to speak up for all the people who didn't walk out of Enron with $30 million to $60 million. I put in a call to Cindy Olson – at that time, the highest ranking woman at Enron and the head of Enron's Human Resources. Though we had never met I had heard she was fair-minded. Cindy was taking a lot of heat as Trustee of the 401(k), as well as defending herself in a multitude of lawsuits.

We talked for a while and she cheerfully agreed to assist in whatever way possible. I told her I didn't have a formal plan as yet, but I wanted to help people and if I stirred things up, maybe we could rally support. I began contacting business leaders throughout the Houston community to measure their interest in helping out. I soon found out the movers and shakers in Houston had little interest in truly helping anyone because they believed the situation at Enron was simply a matter of layoffs.

Stymied by the charitable hypocrisy of Houston commerce, I called Cindy back.

"What if we put together a fund-raiser; got some name speakers to come in for sort of a 'day of healing.' I'd really like to see Ken and Linda Lay contribute something financially."

"Absolutely. I'm certain they would be happy to do so," said Cindy, with growing excitement. I knew everyone left at Enron had to be suffering from a bunker mentality and any outside offering to help would be soothing.

"Let me begin some planning from my end and I'll let you know," I said.

I contacted Wendy Burkeen at KHOU-TV and told her my plan. Burkeen's response was harsh.

"Look, these people got what they deserved. They're not victims like those of Tropical Storm Allison. Those people are without homes. These people might miss a payment on their BMW. Sorry, not interested."

Apparently, Wendy Burkeen had never attempted to live on $1,100 a-month unemployment. I then contacted the Houston Mayor's office and spoke with Jorde Tollefsen. Initially, Jorde was willing to provide us with a venue until I mentioned having a fund-raising dinner that included Rudy Guiliani, as a guest speaker.

"Guiliani's highly respected and very popular. I believe he would bring in strong support."

"You've got to be kidding!" he screamed into the phone.

I didn't understand the terrible cord I had just struck with him.

"Rudy Guiliani is not welcome anywhere near this town," he snarled. "And for that matter, we don't want the former President

Bush, we don't want the current President Bush, and we sure as hell don't want the Lays. They all ran anti-election campaigns against Mayor [Lee] Brown in the last election. I will in no way help you if you bring Rudy Guiliani anywhere near this city."

I had the highest expectations the call would go better.

For the next two months, I worked with Cindy Olson to put something together to help the little people at Enron, until it was obvious no one in Houston wanted to discuss either Enron or Ken Lay. The city that had gladly taken millions of dollars of Enron's support was now unwilling to even provide a food bank.

It was too difficult trying to arrange to help people in a hostile town from 1,800 miles away and I finally let go of the idea. But I had a gnawing sense that my business with Enron was not over.

As the scandals of power price manipulation began to erupt in the summer of 2001 in California, I contacted Dave Ross, a well-known local radio show host on the CBS affiliate in Seattle, to blow the whistle. In a single act of courage and conviction, Dave Ross, gave me the freedom to speak publicly on his radio show about the details I had witnessed, both on the trading floor in Portland, as well as in the executive suites in Houston. It was solely at the encouragement of Dave Ross that I ultimately went to the federal government.

Taking Ross's advice, I went to the Chairman of the Energy Commerce Committee, Senator Byron Dorgan (D-North Dakota). I called the Senator's office and spoke with a young man, whom I can only assume was an intern.

Believing I may just have the evidence that would open the investigation into Enron's corrupt dealings wide-open, I said, "I'm a former Enron executive and I have evidence of bank fraud and espionage on the part of Enron. What should I do?"

The youngster gave me their e-mail address and requested that I send the details to the Senator. On Thursday, December 20, 2001, at 11:12 a.m., I sent an e-mail to that address with the provocative subject line: **I have evidence of fraud and espionage on the part of Enron**.

My e-mail read:

> *I am a former Enron employee. I have documentation of corporate fraud, which may even constitute bank fraud as NationsBank was involved. I also have evidence of espionage. What do I do?*

I signed the e-mail with my name, address and phone number. I never received a call or e-mail response from Senator Dorgan's office.

At the same time, I forwarded that e-mail to *CourtTV* and Bill O'Reilly. I received a telephone call from Serena Fong from Catherine Crier's show on CourtTV.

"Would you be willing to tell your story?" she asked.

"Sure, of course."

"Do you mind if we speak with the investigative committees and inform them of what you have?"

"No, that's not a problem."

"Great! I'll be calling you back soon."

She never did.

As Sherron Watkins' name spread to every newspaper on the planet, I realized that legal advice might be necessary. I had been witness to everything from espionage to fraud and was concerned someone in authority might actually care about what I knew. I had watched as author Vanessa Leggett was jailed for not revealing her sources in that Texas murder case, so I called the office of her attorney, Mike DeGeurin.

An associate named Paul Nugent got on the line and I explained my circumstances.

"Did you work for Andrew Fastow?" he asked.

I assumed his question was merely out of curiosity.

"No, but his deals came across my desk. I worked on his off-the-balance sheet partnerships."

He promised to get back to me regarding the matter. He didn't.

Meanwhile, Sherron Watkins had retained her own counsel, Philip Hilder. Figuring Hilder might know what to do, I phoned his office. Mr. Hilder's associate James Ridding patiently listened as I described the sordid events I had been a party to at Enron. Ridding explained that Mr. Hilder had been overwhelmed fielding phone calls the moment word got out who he represented. Ridding wasn't sure when Hilder would be able to get back to me, if at all. That evening, at 10:00 p.m. Houston time, I received a call.

"Lynn, this is Philip Hilder. I understand you have been talking with my associate James Ridding and you have concerns about what you may have witnessed while at Enron. Do you know Sherron Watkins?"

"No. I've heard her name, but I have never personally met her."

"I have reviewed James Ridding's notes and I want to tell you in no uncertain terms, absolutely do not talk to anyone regarding what you know. I mean it, absolutely no one. If anyone asks you, you know nothing. This is extremely important. Do you understand me?"

"Yes." I felt more like a scolded child than a prospective client. I continued. "I was recently in contact with Mike DeGeurin's office and..."

"...and did he happen to tell you that he represents Andy Fastow?" he shouted back.

"No."

"Let me tell you something, Lynn, you're playing with the big boys now. Someone is going to go to jail and I know that because this is my area of specialty, white collar crime."

"Well Philip, I only learned of the crimes after they had been committed."

"I know, but the government doesn't care about that."

"Okay. I've got to tell you I don't have a lot of excess money lying around to pay an attorney."

"Don't worry about that. We'll talk about that later. I'll have James send you a retainer agreement."

"You need to know, I sent Senator Dorgan an e-mail and have written a book proposal."

"Okay. If Senator Dorgan's office calls you, you refer them to me."

"Okay."

"And as far as a book goes? No book at this time. There'll be plenty of time for that next year but nothing right now. No radio shows, no interviews. The media will be showing up at your doorstep and you'll wonder what cave they crawled out of. They don't care about you, all they care about is their interview. Now, I want you to put together a lengthy memo about everything you did and saw while at Enron. And let me caution you, do not save it on your hard drive. Believe it or not they can access your computer. Save it on a floppy and print it out and also fax a copy to me."

"Okay."

"Let me give you my pager and home telephone number in case someone from the government calls you."

I took down his numbers and we hung up. I began worrying about the gravity of the material in my possession. From the time I first felt Enron was going bad I started making copies of critical documents. All told, I probably had about two hundred pages. I had some in my office at home, but the really important ones were in a safe deposit box. As the next week or so went by, I waited for the barrage of television reporters to suddenly show up because they had discovered my memo on the Bammel deal. Worse, I pictured the FBI swarming over my farm, ripping up the floorboards in their quest to hang Lay and Skilling. But nothing happened except a phone call from Philip Hilder.

"Have you been talking to anyone?" His voice had an edge.

"No why?"

"I received a call from a book editor yesterday. He asked if I knew you. Had you and I not talked I would have no idea who you were. Look, I told you no book deals right now. You keep that book proposal under wraps. There'll be plenty of time for stuff like that."

"Okay."

A few days later, Hilder's star client, the unsinkable Miz Watkins, was on the cover of *Time* magazine with rumors of a book deal floating in the air. I realized Hilder was probably negotiating a book deal for his client and didn't want me muddying up the waters. What better way to throw me off the scent than to get my trust and tell me to wait, as there would be "plenty of time for stuff like that." I wondered if there was anyone I could trust.

I informed Mr. Hilder I would no longer require his services. I thought of Carl Neil in Portland as someone who might represent me. Carl and I had worked together in Portland and he was an attorney I respected and trusted. I called Carl and told him what I had been going through. In his paternal manner, Carl said, "In my opinion, since you had advised your supervisors you should be fine." The only glitch was he could not represent me because he had a conflict of interest. Turns out he was representing the Portland office of Arthur Andersen. I considered getting counsel from Japan to avoid any conflicts. Then Carl drove the nails through my wrists.

"I'll put you in touch with a really good attorney named Bob Weaver. He's a former federal prosecutor who now specializes in defending white collar criminals – he actually represented Tonya Harding." That I would once again be compared to Tonya Harding, I politely declined the number.

On Monday, February 17, 2002, I listened intently via the Internet to Sherron Watkins's testimony in the Congressional Hearings to determine just what she knew. I was trying to get an overview on the complex set of circumstances that had caused Enron to fall so far so fast. I certainly had my theories, but I was hoping Sherron might add to them. The audio streamed over my computer and at one hour, 38 minutes and six seconds into the testimony, a recess began. As the testimony came to an end, there was a lull and I continued to work at my desk, while the audio played in the background. A few moments into the recess, I heard the Chairman of the Subcommittee, James C. Greenwood (R-Pennsylvania) say, *"Do you know how Olson knew that Fastow... 'cause you know that that's how Watkins learned that Fastow wanted her fired...from Cindy Olson? Do we know how Olson learned that?"*

He obviously didn't realize the audio was still streaming out over the Internet for whoever wanted to listen. Or record it. I grabbed my recorder and hit the record button. *"Right.... But then how do we think Olson learned that Fastow...?"*

Greenwood's voice was followed by inaudible dialogue from an unidentified person.

Greenwood: *"Fastow told Olson?"*

Now I was intrigued. Greenwood seemed to be planning a strategy for the next round of questions.

"And, umm, no one has asked, no one's brought this out? I'm hoping that somebody can bring this out."

Greenwood was looking for a mouthpiece.

"Is somebody ready to ask these questions? Because Cindy Olson may have perjured herself last week when she denied talking to anybody other than Jeff McMahon."

Now it was making sense. Greenwood seemed interested in setting up Cindy Olson for perjury over her testimony the previous week. Greenwood struggled with the words to form his plan.

"Other than...but she, on her duty...she knows that Fast...she knows that Sherron Watkins has given all this information to Lay."

There were a few inaudible exchanges between Greenwood and the unidentified person, then Greenwood laid his cards on the table.

"Olson betrays the workers this way...she knows that Watkins has all these detailed allegations. Second, the end of August somehow she knows directly or indirectly that Fastow wants Olson to fire her. Fastow wants Watkins fired. He's going to stoop...stoop to the level of skullduggery to have her..."

Someone interrupts and he continues, "*Look, it's the whole case for the workers. Nobody's talked about the workers yet today. Cindy Olson knew all of the information she needed to shut down the company stock fund and start selling off the company stock.*"

Cindy Olson's fiduciary responsibilities as Trustee of Enron's 401(k) made her the guardian angel of the employees' retirement fund. Because of the issues raised by Watkins, Greenwood wanted to hang Cindy Olson for not reading the handwriting on the wall and shutting down the 401(k). What Greenwood failed to acknowledge was that the responsibility for protecting a 401(k) lay primarily with the individual who owned it. As one who lost retirement money I'd be the first to admit that.

Greenwood: *"How did Olson say that she knew that Fastow wanted [Watkins] fired?"*

Greenwood, and whomever he was speaking with, began parsing Olson's testimony to determine how she found out Fastow wanted Watkins fired. When Fastow learned that Sherron Watkins had visited Ken Lay to voice her concerns over the accounting treatments, he schemed to rid himself of the rat and, in typical Enron fashion, demanded that her computer be seized. In the end it was he, not Watkins, who got the boot. Greenwood's attack centered on who knew what and when, and who told who.

Greenwood: *She totally withholds; she withheld all this information. She played dumb."*

A brief, inaudible discussion ensues.

Greenwood: *"Like I said, she has exposure problems. [Olson] said the only people she spoke with about this, about Watkins' concerns, were Jeff McMahon – which she barely admitted – and Ken Lay, about it. So the more that comes out about Cindy...see it's very bizarre, and then what happens is that Watkins goes and sees Olson, and Olson suggests...and the only thing that follows is that Olson encouraged Watkins to talk with Lay. And she set up the meeting. What would be great for the workers is to establish a breach of duty from Olson because she was the trustee...would be to elicit that Lay, that Watkins spoke further with Olson, but further get in some details about how Olson knew that Fastow wanted her fired, communicated it to Ms. Watkins, but try to find out how Olson knew that. All that came out right here – very quickly she says."*

Although his excitable, almost stream-of-consciousness rhetoric barely indicates it, Greenwood assumed that Fastow found out Sherron Watkins had been to visit Lay because Cindy Olson must have tipped him off. Cindy testified she spoke only with Lay and McMahon regarding the matter. Hadn't Greenwood considered the possibility that Lay or McMahon told Fastow about Watkins? Regardless, Greenwood was not going to abandon his attempt to nail Olson.

"Who do I want to ask the question?" asked the Chairman, searching for someone to do his dirty-work. Then in the tape there

was an inaudible question to which he responded, *"I don't know. Anybody who is good. Is there a lawyer who still has questions?"*

But a lawyer would not be enough. This also had to look like a partisan issue.

"No, I mean is there a lawyer on the Democratic side who can understand the two hat thing? Is Markey a lawyer?" (referring to Congressman Edward Markey (D-Massachusetts)) *"I mean I could brief somebody really quickly."*

There's a discussion and someone else speaks. *"I'll go get him."* Greenwood sizes up Watkins as a pawn.

"Okay, just let me say a quick thing in terms of pitching it...it's like Watkins didn't know at the time that Olson wore two hats. All she knew is that [Olson] was an HR person. [Olson] was a trustee. This cost Watkins money."

It's apparent, Greenwood is working hard to sell his concept. I hear him getting frustrated in his attempts to convince the other guy of the importance of getting Olson.

"No trustee! Trustee! She's a fiduciary. She should have shut down the company stock fund."

An unidentified female responds, *"Well, I don't know about that."*

Greenwood: *"Well, I do. I'm a pension lawyer."* Then he laughs. *"This is like our only chance to get this out. Because, she's friends with Lay, trying to get back on the Executive Committee. In her rush, the workers were betrayed. Watkins...but Watkins didn't know at the time of her other role."*

Here, he coaches his interrogator.

"'How do you feel now, Ms. Watkins? When you find out that Cindy Olson had control over the stock fund?' I'm telling you it's a great question – it's a great question. [Olson] had control over the stock fund. Right then you can ask Ms. Watkins, 'If you were a trustee of the stock fund wouldn't you have prevented people from buying more stock?' Provided that the stock was inflated. Cindy Olson knew everything you were saying. Cindy Olson knew that Fastow wanted you fired, was going to seize your computer, which is an admission by conduct that everything you were saying was true. If you were a trustee of the stock fund...that is draped with Enron

stock wouldn't you have started selling or at least stopped buying more stock? How do you feel Ms., now that you know Cindy Olson [was the Trustee]*?"*

I still couldn't determine who Greenwood was talking to but it was obvious his "assassin" was finally on board. *"Yeah, Yeah."*

Greenwood: *"The other thing is, Cindy Olson testified that Watkins was tentative – this ISN'T a tentative woman."*

I had remembered Phillip Hilder's words, "Someone's going to jail."

Greenwood wanted that person to be Cindy Olson.

"But here's the point – this is the problem. Olson was the one who told Watkins that Fastow wants her fired and seizes her computer. Shouldn't that Ms. Watkins have told Miss Olson that everything you were saying was true? Basically, use the burning building analogy. There's a burning building and she was a trustee, she should have run in and saved these peoples' retirement, but she covered it up."

"And Olson knew?" At last I heard the voice of the person

Greenwood nominated to go after Olson.

"Olson knew in August everything. Fastow was trying to fire Watkins." Greenwood laughs. *"Is that the response of a responsible CFO? Somebody who raises accounting questions – you fire her and seize her computer? It's the equivalent of shredding. And Olson had all of the information, she could have literally saved people hundreds of millions of dollars. As trustee of the 401(k) plan. Trustee of the 401(k) plan. Meanwhile she jets around in the company jet with uh, Linda Lay. That's interesting and everybody knows that. They're really buddy buddy with Mrs. Lay, letting her personal, her personal interests...She's tight with Mrs. Lay...flies around on the company jet – get that out. They'd go to Aspen together – that was common knowledge in the company. Trying to get back with the top echelon of the company 'cause Skilling had kicked her out and he was gone. She betrayed the workers."*

Greenwood concludes: *"Here, let me give you the dates: 8/14 Skilling resigns; 8/16 Watkins memo #1; and then Watkins goes to Olson; 8/22 Watkins meets with Lay, and then 8/30 Olson tells Watkins that Fastow wants her fired and wants her computer seized. THIS IS THE POINT. Why isn't Olson selling the stock? (inaudible)*

Because she knows the whole thing is a house of cards. She betrays the employees." Then Greenwood goes in for the close. *"Somehow Olson finds out that Fastow wants Watkins fired. You're the man – the perfect guy to ask this."*

It was my first up close and personal view of a conspiracy. Twenty eight minutes in all, I wondered who Greenwood had gotten to do his dirty work. I listened as he explained the circumstances to some unidentified member of Congress, a man he had recruited to go for Cindy Olson's jugular. I was curious about which Democratic hit-man Greenwood had been proselytizing.

It turned out to be Congressman Bobby Rush, a Democrat from Illinois. Rush was given the floor and he directed his question to Sherron Watkins.

"I want to thank you Mr. Chairman and Mrs. Watkins. It is certainly very pleasing that you are here and your testimony has been forthright and I would say without any kind of a value – in terms of Ms. Temple's testimony [in-house counsel at Arthur Andersen] *– it is diametrically opposed to the kind of testimony that Ms. Temple presented to this committee and it's certainly appreciative by the committee, at least with one member of the committee, and I believe that it's appreciative, that your testimony is appreciative, is appreciated* [corrects himself] *by the American public. On what date did you first speak with Cindy Olson or communicate with her in any way about your concerns about the financial condition of Enron?"*

I could almost hear Greenwood doing a slow burn as Rush botched the attack. But if Greenwood didn't have a pretty good sense he was grasping at straws then I suppose it was a good idea to make someone from the opposition look like a dummy. Rush stepped valiantly into that role. In his zeal to put some scalps on his belt to satisfy the bloodlust against Enron, it's sad Greenwood went after one of the small fish. I suppose he was as afraid of the Skillings and Lays and Fastows as much anyone in Congress who understands the power of their money and friends.

I picked up the phone and called Cindy Olson. As the greeting on Cindy's voicemail began I remembered it was President's Day, which meant Enron was closed – but then so were government offices – or were they? I left her a message to call me immediately, omitting any details until I could speak with her personally. I ran in to town to buy a better tape recorder. The first recording I made was slightly muffled and I wanted the clearest evidence possible. I would re-record the conversation with Greenwood off the Web site when I got home. As I neared my home my cell phone rang. It was Cindy.

"What's going on? Your message scared the hell out of me."

"Cindy, I hate to tell you this, but you're being set up." I explained what I had heard, and told her of my intention to tape it again before someone realized what had gotten out over the Internet.

"I'll forward the tape to you tomorrow via FedEx."

When I got back to my office, after being gone no more than 30 minutes, the Web site was down. At least I had the initial tape. I left a message on Cindy's voicemail telling her that someone had taken the site down between the time I had left my house and returned. The next morning at approximately 10:00 a.m., the Web site finally came up when I logged on. I navigated to the Congressional hearing and searched for the incriminating recording of Congressman Greenwood. It was there, but now 10 minutes were missing from the conversation I had heard the day before.

EPILOGUE

When you make a mistake pass the age of accountability, there is no excuse for it. Only a fool doesn't try to understand and explain to himself why he made the mistakes he made.

William Jefferson Clinton

THE REST OF THE STORY

While the world now knows the leading cast of characters in the disaster film that is Enron, "actors" such as Jeff Skilling, Ken Lay, Andy and Lea Fastow, Rick Causey, Rick Buy, Ben Glisan, Rebecca Mark, and my idol, Ken Rice, rarely has the spotlight focused on the supporting cast. Yet, the tale of Enron could not have been written without so many other willing players, like the employees, the Board of Directors, the auditors, the law firms, the banks, the analysts, the credit-rating agencies, the media, the investors blindly willing to turn over their hard-earned dollars to brokers, and of course, our government. Everyone had their motivations for choosing to support the corruption of Enron.

All 20,000 employees, myself included, chose to look the other way for what we thought would be our own financial benefit. The Board of Directors would later claim they knew nothing. However, in 2001, a presentation was made to the Board of Directors that revealed between 2000 and 2001 there was a 300% increase in whistle-blowing reports via Enron's internal hotline in the Office of the Chairman. In 2001, reports of fraud and misconduct went from 2 reports per month to 2 per day. Of those, 32% were purported criminal acts. Of that 32%, three-quarters were considered acts of fraud.

Meanwhile, we now know the role Arthur Andersen played while receiving more than $1,000,000 per week to look the other way. Although Arthur Andersen claims they were a victim of Enron's fraud, they apparently, at the very least, suspected something fishy was going on when, on two separate occasions, they hired Professor Messod Daniel Beneish from Indiana University to run his earnings manipulation model to determine whether Enron was manipulating its earnings. On both occasions Professor Beneish informed Andersen the evidence showed Enron's earnings were being manipulated. They chose to ignore the evidence. Why? When Andersen's own accountants referred to Enron's use of mark-to-market accounting as "intelligent gambling" one can only assume that Andersen, at best, was an apologist for their client, and at worst, a co-conspirator.

Enron's primary law firm, Vinson and Elkins, also seemed to selectively see what they wanted to see. When asked by Enron to review the off-the-balance sheet partnerships to determine whether they met the legal requirements of Generally Accepted Accounting Principles, they instead spent their time trying to figure out how to constructively discharge Sherron Watkins.

In the meantime, while the banks were keenly aware that Enron was manipulating the numbers they were willing to play both sides. No more than high-profile loan sharks, the biggest banks were willing to loan money in exchange for investment banking business used to hedge Enron's risk in its off-the-balance partnership scheme. In fact it was the banks that enabled Enron to keep afloat with loans from quarter to quarter. While Andy Fastow's crisis management pillaged the company, Skilling stepped in to reassure the banks that he was officially giving Fastow his blessing on these fraudulent transactions. In the end, however, the banks, like any other loan shark, eventually cut Enron off at the flow of dough thus crippling its ability to sustain the charade. The curtain was finally pulled back to reveal there was no Wizard in Oz.

Doing their part in the scam, the analysts from the investment banking firms were ballyhooing Enron's stock. While such "research" should hardly be enough to sustain a bank's enthusiasm for any entity, analysts who positively rated Enron's stock as a "strong buy" were rewarded handsomely for their role in sustaining the lie. Those who refused to support the lie were fired for their dissension by the banks with whom they worked.

Finally, perhaps the biggest outside supporters of the scam were the credit rating agencies that were privately negotiating with Enron in order to falsely keep its credit rating high in order to give Enron access to commercial paper. With banks relying on the strength of Enron's fabricated credit rating, there was a sense that everything was fine. This situation arose because companies rely on their credit rating to give them access to equity required for their very survival. Call it symbiosis or collusion, credit rating agencies are slow to downgrade their ratings out of fear it will cause a run on the bank. When credit is down-graded, companies are suddenly exposed to a "Material Adverse Change" allowing banks to call their loans. When Enron's stock finally crashed through the floor the credit rating agencies had no choice. Investor confidence was gone and Enron's credit had to be down-graded to junk bond status.

Then add in the media and the hype they flagrantly spread in support of Enron's stock – in a mass group-think. They bought Enron's fiction and began spreading the gospel. I have yet to see one journalist admit they did a mediocre job of "investigating" and reporting the facts behind Enron. Rather, they blame Arthur Andersen and Enron for misleading them. Didn't they have enough journalistic savvy to at least check out Enron's audited financials? And had they, would they have possessed the elementary accounting skills to divine the truth behind Enron's bluster?

And we can't forget the investors who, like sheep with cash, blindly turned over their life savings to their brokers, expecting those brokers to protect them. Of course most of the brokers were relying on all of the smoke and mirrors everyone else was. Even the mutual fund industry got in on the act, manipulating the markets through the timing of its trades on behalf of large institutional investors all the while leaving the individual investors in the dark.

Investors are not off the hook in losing their money when you consider there was sufficient evidence–in time to save their bacon – that Enron was manipulating its earnings. In Enron's 2000 shareholder letter, Jeff Skilling proclaimed, "Enron hit a record $1.3

billion in net income." And yet most who bought Enron stock chose to remain invested despite the fact that just a few pages beyond the shareholder letter, Enron's audited financial statements showed the Company's actual net income was only $978 million. Well, it's only three hundred and some million, it's not like it was real money, you say.

And then there was the government. While I realize my view from a rural location in the Pacific Northwest may not be the same as someone in a metropolitan city, we do have access to television and the Internet. While I had never been a proponent of conspiracy theories, after my time at Enron I have come to believe anything is possible when it involves big money and big power. And if someone, or some entity, with a lot of money and power wanted more of both it would be very hard to stop them. The horrific events of September 11, 2001 had been weighing on me when I recalled something from the time I worked on Enron's history project.

Ken Lay had written to then Texas Governor, now U.S. President, George W. Bush, Jr. on April 3, 1997, advising him to befriend Ambassador Sadyq Safaev, Uzbekistan's ambassador. Lay indicated that this would be really good for Enron because they were in the midst of negotiating a joint venture with Uzbekistan and Russia to develop a huge natural gas pipeline in the region. Enron later received funding from the U.S. government in 1998 to perform a feasibility study for moving the vast stores of gas from Russia to the Black Sea. The most efficient path of the 1,040-mile Trans-Caspian Pipeline was to begin near the town of Chardzhou in northern Turkmenistan and extend southeasterly through Afghanistan to an export terminal that would be constructed on the Pakistani coast on the Arabian Sea.

Unfortunately, 440 miles of the proposed pipeline was to cut through the chaotic and hostile nation of Afghanistan. Regarding that little wrinkle, Edward M. Smith, president and CEO of PSG International (PSG is a 50/50 partnership of GE Capital Structured Finance Group and Bechtel), reminded a Senate Subcommittee on East Asian and Pacific Affairs in his testimony on March 3, 1999, "...the success of the Trans-Caspian project is critical to the interests of the United States in the region and that the project will not succeed without the active support and assistance of the United

States Government. That support is required in two areas. The first is in helping to solve geopolitical threats to the project. The second is in providing critical support to the private lenders and investors in the project through the financing and insurance programs of (the Overseas Private Investment Corporation) OPIC...." Mr. Smith further said, "The US government recognizes that it is of great importance that the countries of this energy-rich region remain independent and stable sovereign states."

Meanwhile, after ongoing and futile negotiations with the Taliban since 1995, Unocal's Vice President of International Relations, John J. Maresca, former United States Ambassador to the Organization for Security and Cooperation in Europe (OSCE), was a bit more direct in his testimony before a House subcommittee when he said that (Unocal) "cannot begin construction until an internally recognized Afghanistan government is in place."

It was obvious, despite the urgent requests before the House and Senate by the likes of Unocal, Amoco, and Enron, unless and until something gave the United States enough cause to force a "regime change", the Taliban would remain the governing body in Afghanistan. Thanks to Osama bin Laden, the prayers of the American oil conglomerates were answered on September 11th.

The attack on American soil gave George W. Bush exactly what he needed to rid Afghanistan of its evil force – the Taliban, thereby making way for the construction of the $3.0 Billion Trans-Caspian Pipeline. And on October 7, 2001, the air strikes began leading the way for a "stable government" to be installed.

In little more than 45 days after the air strikes and less than 90 days after the attacks of September 11th, construction on the pipeline that "cannot begin...until an internally recognized Afghanistan government is in place" began on November 27, 2001. The nagging question for me remains – how does any company undertake a construction project of this magnitude that "cannot begin construction until an internally recognized Afghanistan government is in place" unless the company has somehow been given inside information as to when that stable government will be appointed? How does a multi-billion dollar project get approval before it seems there is even a remote chance it can be completed?

On December 5, 2001, one week after the construction commenced, the stable Afghanistan government was put in place at the UN Conference on Afghanistan (the *6 Plus 2 Group*). After nine days of negotiations in a Bonn, Germany hotel, the announcement was made that an "interim government" had been created that "will attempt to govern Afghanistan for six months beginning December 22." And who should lead the newly minted *interim* Afghanistan government – none other than former Unocal consultant Hamid Karzai.

Notwithstanding any real or imagined threats to U.S. security, getting rid of the Taliban and Saddam certainly paved the way for the American energy conglomerates. Recalling that the Prime Minister of Kazakhstan said in July 1998 that he was "actively considering the construction of pipelines via Afghanistan and Iran as viable options as well," can Iran be next on that list of unstable sovereign foreign states that miraculously climb to the top of our enemies list when we want something they have?

The Caspian Basin has enormous reserves of oil and gas. Estimates from the US Energy Information Administration are that proven oil reserves for the region are estimated at 16-32 billion barrels, comparable to those in the United States (22 billion barrels) and North Sea (17 billion barrels). Natural gas reserves are even larger, accounting for almost 2/3 of the hydrocarbon reserves (proved plus possible) in the Caspian region. Based on proven reserves, Kazakhstan, Turkmenistan and Uzbekistan (the same Uzbekistan that Ken Lay wrote George W. Bush about on April 3, 1997), each rank among the world's 20 largest natural gas countries. Proven gas reserves are estimated at 236-337 trillion cubic feet, comparable to North American reserves (300tcf). Massive direct investment in Kazakhstan's oil industry has gradually increased production and the trend is expected to continue. Oil and natural gas production is expected to increase by 75% between 2000 and 2005, according to the Prime Minister of Kazakhstan.

The Trans-Caspian project was significant enough to the Bush Administration that, in the middle of the war in Afghanistan, the White House issued "Fact Sheets" on the project. Interestingly enough, the Bush Administration did not consider the financial annihilation of thousands of investors from the Enron catastrophe nearly as important because they issued no "Fact Sheets" on its significance. Yet, in contrast, many economists claim the fall of Enron was more economically devastating than even September 11th.

Prior to its bankruptcy, Enron operated in 41 countries, had assets purportedly worth $65.5 billion, 21,000 employees and revenues of over $100 billion. It has been estimated that Enron's cover-up to hide over $10 billion in losses cost investors $190 billion dollars and contributed to the loss of more than $9 trillion dollars to our economy.

Even as Enron's fearless leader Ken Lay was publicly promoting Enron stock until the very end, he was privately and vigorously cashing in his own stock – a practice common to upper management at many companies. Living from stock option to stock option, Ken was on the brink of financial disaster himself. All told, Enron directors and senior executives exercised a net option value of more than $116,977,511 between January 1, 2001 and August 31, 2001. As with the rats on the Titanic, Enron's big wheels seemed to have a jump on when to panic than did the rest.

While I myself have reflected on the personal lessons learned from selling my soul, I wonder whether the same is true for the relatively small group of Enron executives who, over a three year period, between October 19, 1998 and November 27, 2001, reaped over $1.071 billion, an average of more than $53 million apiece. While the majority of Enron employees lost their life savings, these senior executives received the following proceeds of stock:

J. Clifford Baxter – $34,734,854
Richard B. Buy – $10,656,595
Richard A. Causey – $13,386,896
James V. Derrick – $12,563,928
Andrew S. Fastow – $33,675,004
Mark A. Frevert – $54,831,220
Ken L. Harrison – $75,416,636

Joseph M. Hirko – $35,168,721
Stanley C. Horton – $47,371,361
Steven J. Kean – $5,166,414
Mark E. Koenig – $9,110,466
Kenneth L. Lay – $184,494,426 (Not bad, Kenny Boy!)
Rebecca P. Mark-Jusbasche – $82,536,737
Michael S. McConnell – $2,506,311
Jeffrey McMahon – $2,739,226
Cindy K. Olson – $6,506,870
Lou L. Pai – $270,276,065 (Wow! Way to go, Lou!)
Kenneth D. Rice – $76,825,145
Jeffrey K. Skilling – $70,687,199
Joseph W. Sutton – $42,231,283

Meanwhile the average payout for board members was $1.5 million over that same 3 year period, for more than $119.5 million in total. Below are the individual payments to Enron's directors:

Robert A. Belfer – $111,941,200
Norman P. Blake, Jr. – $1,705,328
Ronnie C. Chan – $337,200
John H. Duncan – $2,009,700
Joe H. Foy – $1,639,590
Wendy L. Gramm – $278,892
Robert K. Jaedicke – $841,438
Charles A. Lemaistre – $841,768

As of today, 32 defendants have now been criminally charged in connection with the fall of Enron, including accounting firm Arthur Andersen. Although 13 defendants have pleaded guilty or been convicted by a jury, and the total forfeiture has been nearly $200 million, the Justice Department would have you believe the financial recovery has been on behalf of the "victims." Yet despite the announcement of the first of many class action lawsuits filed on behalf of the employees to recover their pensions, Jeff Skilling and Ken Lay are still fighting, claiming they are entitled to their money before the *little guy*. Meanwhile there are still those who feel they are entitled to the life they grew accustomed to inside Enron, like Chief Accounting Officer, Richard Causey, who asked the Court to unfreeze $225,000 of his $6 million in frozen assets for his membership to his country club while awaiting trial. The Court denied his motion.

Perhaps more frightening than Enron's cover-up, is the rotten, morally void corporate culture fostered at Enron, one that exists at far too many other American firms, with the underlying message to those who were willing to heed it that Enron was only the first to fall. We have now seen a long list of companies like Coca-Cola brought to its knees by corruption. And what caused it all? In a morally responsible reinterpretation of the famous words of Gordon Gekko from Oliver Stone's movie, *Wall Street*, greed is <u>*not*</u> good. Greed for power or money or both was what drove Enron, along with many innocent investors' fortunes tied to it, into the abyss. What happened was that greedy men and women, aided by scared men and women like me, damned the costs to snatch what they felt they deserved. Thousands of people, including teachers, firemen, and civil servants, many of whom had never even heard of Enron, lost their life savings, their jobs, their futures.

Enron and the countless number of companies that have been investigated for similar behavior are not an accident; but rather an American tragedy, brought about by the avarice of players failing to care about the consequences of their actions. When we consider that during nearly the same period Ken Lay was unloading his Enron stock options, former IBM chairman Lou Gerstner cashed in $424 million in stock, do we begin to see that Enron did not write the book on grabbing for all you can. Of course in 2002 IBM was caught in its own accounting scandal. The widespread corruption we have witnessed in corporate and financial America stems from our values, our way of life, our desire to win – to be number one. From the cradle we teach our children to excel. For entertainment we strand people on islands to stab each other in the back or elevate anti-heroes who come out on top but are bereft of human values. Enron wasn't just some corporation based in Texas that played fast and loose with other people's money, it was the failure of a system, a microcosm of the system of humanity. Twenty-thousand people came together in a commonality and it went bad. What is at stake is our very way of life. If we are to survive, we must find a way to return compassion, wisdom, and the highest standards of integrity to our corporations.

And to our lives.

As for me, today, I am happily married and have attempted to put the harrowing experience of Enron behind me, and bring about some positive change as a result of my experiences. I know there will always be those who remain critical of my actions and my motives. While, I could have sought my 15 minutes of fame at the height of the Enron story, particularly given that my brother-in-law is an executive at NBC in New York; I chose rather to have 15 years of impact.

Today, I am the founder and Chairman of The Integrity Institute, a non-profit public policy institute which assesses and certifies corporate integrity at the request of organizations and institutional investors for the benefit of their stakeholders.

Since leaving Enron, I have heard countless stories from others who sought to follow their own moral compass or blow a whistle, whether at Enron, or elsewhere inside their own companies. With each and every story I hear, I'm drawn into the fact that while none of us are perfect, our collective imperfections have caused our society to go astray. Behind each and every story of corruption, there are countless numbers of human beings who most times remain faceless.

In 2002, the Sarbanes-Oxley Act (SOX) was passed by Congress in response to the public outcry of stakeholders damaged by greed. Although the new law seeks to curtail the fraudulent practices that were pervasive at Enron and other companies, when we consider that most of the sections of the new law were included as mitigating factors under the Federal Organizational Sentencing Guidelines created in the early 1990s, we have to realize even with all 1107 sections of SOX, we cannot legislate a conscience.

According to AMR Research, compliance with the law will cost Fortune 1000 companies approximately $2.5 billion in 2004. Combine this with the 400% increase in directors and officers insurance rates that many are experiencing, and we begin to understand the high cost of low ethics. However, let us not forget the real cost of compliance – to individuals who simply remain silent – failing to follow their moral compass or refusing to blow the whistle. Enron was full of them – myself included. But today, remaining compliant is more costly under the revised Federal Organizational Sentencing Guidelines.

In Spring 2004, Jamie Olis, a 38-year old mid-level executive at Dynegy, received a 24-year sentence for his role in "Project Alpha", a structured financing deal, not unlike the ones I had seen at Enron. Ironically enough, it was Dynegy who had turned up at the 11th hour offering to save Enron from itself just weeks before its implosion, and yet it was a Dynegy executive that received the first of what is likely to be many stiff penalties under the new post-Enron laws.

As I saw Mr. Olis after his sentencing, I was struck by this image of a man in the prime of his life (in a position not dissimilar from mine at Enron), with his wife, holding their six-month old daughter. I'm sure I'm not the only former employee of a corrupt company who found themselves whispering to themselves, "There but for the grace of God go I."

Before Mr. Olis, there was Betty Vinson, also a mid-level executive, this time at WorldCom. Originally asked by her bosses to make false accounting entries, she protested, but eventually became compliant. Over the next six quarters she continued to make illegal entries, according to her testimony. In the end she would help falsify at least $3.7 billion in profits. Although she complained, and considered quitting, she was soon rationalizing her behavior. In the end, she, along with two others, were indicted, and pleaded guilty to securities fraud.

While both Andy Fastow and Betty Vinson copped guilty pleas and received 10-year prison sentences, there's a bit of injustice when we compare Fastow's $2.4 million salary, $1.8 million in stock-related compensation, and $50 million in "ill-gotten" gains with Ms. Vinson's relatively piddling $80,000 salary. Mr. Olis, whose salary had been $162,000, was not nearly as lucky. Rather than roll over and plead guilty, he rolled the dice, and went to trial only to receive a virtual "death sentence".

While most of us look to hold the CEO or CFO accountable, few of us stop long enough to recognize that without loyal company employees like Mr. Olis, Ms. Vinson, or myself, who become compliant, the massive scams that have been perpetrated in the past decade would not have been possible. Unfortunately, for every senior executive who actively engages in such corruption, there are hundreds, if not thousands of mid-level employees, who, at the very least, become complacent with a culture that demands their compliance.

No employee today has any excuse for not blowing the whistle. Section 301(4) (A) and (B) of Sarbanes-Oxley (SOX), focuses on the receipt, retention and treatment of problems regarding accounting, internal accounting controls, or auditing matters. Publicly traded companies are now required to have a confidential and anonymous reporting tool while Section 806 protects employees of publicly-traded companies who provide evidence of fraud against retaliation. And Section 1107 sets the penalties for those who engage in retaliation against an informant for providing information to law enforcement agencies at a maximum of ten years in prison.

While we can only hope that these provisions provide a sufficient comfort level for employees to report, it does not appear as though it has curbed the corruption. Nearly three years after the implosion of Enron, the Securities and Exchange Commission receives nearly 50,000 whistleblowing reports per month.

APPENDIX I

CHRONOLOGY[1]

1985

07/17/85 – Stockholders of Houston Natural Gas Corporation (HNG) agree to a $2.3 billion merger with InterNorth Inc., forming America's second largest pipeline system and the first nationwide natural gas pipeline network. Management reports it would, in the interim, conduct its business as HNG/InterNorth.

1986

04/10/86 – Stockholders at the annual meeting of HNG/InterNorth approve changing the corporation's name to Enron Corp.

1987

01/25/87 – Enron Corp. reports that its oil trading subsidiary, Enron Oil Corp., lost nearly $1 billion in unauthorized trading. Enron Corp. eventually pays $142 million for violating trading limits.

03/12/87 – Kenneth L. Lay, Chairman and CEO of Enron Corp., testifies before the Senate Subcommittee on Energy Regulation and Conservation.

1988

06/14/88 – Enron Corp. announces it has established a wholly owned subsidiary, Enron UK Ltd. in London, England, where the power industry has been deregulated. Enron Corp.'s corporate strategy shift – to capture unregulated markets in addition to its

[1] *Major Source: Congressional Research Services (Reprinted with Permission).*

regulated pipeline operations – is disclosed to corporate officials at a meeting that becomes known as the "Come to Jesus" meeting.

1989

11/16/89 – Richard Kinder, vice chairman of Enron Corp., announces before the New York Society of Security Analysts, a shift in the psychology of natural gas users away from spot purchases.

1990

07/11/90 – In U.S. Southern District of New York, a former Enron Corp. vice president, who was also secretary and treasurer, is sentenced to 400 hours of community service and required to pay an unspecified amount of restitution to Enron Corp. for fraud. Another former Enron executive was sentenced the previous month to one year plus one day in prison, and fined more than $5 million for the same crime.

07/17/90 – Jeffrey K. Skilling becomes chairman and chief executive officer of Enron Finance Corp., a subsidiary of Enron Corp.

1991

03/19/91 – Forrest E. Hoglund, chairman and president of Enron Oil & Gas Co, testifies before the Texas Railroad Commission.

1992

12/16/92 – Enron Corp. and a consortium acquire Transportadora de Gas del Sur SA, operator of the southern Argentina pipeline system. This is Enron's first presence in South America.

1993

05/06/93 – Enron Corp.'s UK Ltd. power plant begins operation in Teesside, England.

06/30/93 – Enron Capital Corp., a subsidiary of Enron Gas Services Corp. (EGS), and the California Public Employees Retirement System (CalPERS) announce that they have agreed to form the Joint Energy Development Investments Limited Partnership (JEDI). Each contributed $250 million to the partnership.

09/23/93 – Kenneth L. Lay, Chairman and CEO, Enron Corp., testifies before the House Ways and Means Committee, Subcommittee on Trade (testifying on behalf of Greater Houston Partnership).

1994

06/03/94 – Enron Power Marketing and Citizens Power & Light continue negotiating energy commodity deals in which they diminish fluctuations in electricity prices to their customers and link the customer's buy or sell price to the price of another commodity.

06/13/94 – Robert H. Butts becomes vice president and comptroller of Enron Corp.

10/00/94 – Enron Corp. to form new company, Enron Global Power & Pipelines, for developing-nation projects.

1995

01/31/95 – Linda F. Powers, vice president, Global Finance, Enron Development Corp., testifies before the Committee on Appropriations, Subcommittee on Foreign Operations.

02/10/95 – Forrest E. Hoglund, chairman and CEO of Enron Oil & Gas Company, testifies before the House Ways and Means Subcommittee on Trade.

03/07/95 – Rebecca P. Mark, chairman and CEO, Enron Development Corp., testifies before the Senate Committee on Foreign Relations, Subcommittee on Near Eastern and South Asian Affairs.

03/23/95 – Kenneth L. Lay, chairman of Enron Corp., testifies before the House Committee on Appropriations, Subcommittee on Foreign Operations, Export Financing, and Related Programs.

03/30/95 – Linda F. Powers, vice president, Global Finance, Enron Development Corp., testifies before the Senate Committee on Foreign Relations.

04/04/95 – Linda F. Powers, vice president, Global Finance, Enron Development Corp., testifies before the House Committee on International Relations.

12/21/95 – Enron Europe opens trading operations in London.

1996

02/29/96 – Harvey Forest, CEO, Solarex Business Unit of Amoco/Enron Solar, testifies before the House Committee on Appropriations, Subcommittee on Energy and Water Development.

04/23/96 – Ken Dorland, representing Enron Corp., testifies before the House Committee on Ways and Means, Subcommittee on Trade.

05/15/96 – Kenneth L. Lay, chairman and CEO, Enron Corp., testifies before the House Committee on Commerce, Subcommittee on Energy and Power.

06/03/96 – Enron Europe opens an office in Norway, Enron Nordic Energy.

06/27/96 – Andrew N. Hoyle, vice president–marketing, Enron Oil & Gas Company, testifies before the House Committee on Resources, Subcommittee on Energy and Mineral Resources.

10/08/96 – Enron Corp. consortium begins construction of Trakya power project in Turkey.

12/01/96 – Jeffrey K. Skilling becomes president and chief operating officer of Enron Corp.

1997

03/06/97 – Jeffrey Skilling, president and chief operating officer, Enron Corp., testifies before the Senate Committee Energy and Natural Resources

03/16/97 – Linda F. Powers, senior vice president, Global Finance, Enron International, testifies before the House Committee on International Relations, Subcommittee on International Economic Policy and Trade.

03/19/97 – Enron Renewable Energy Corp., a majority-owned subsidiary of Enron Corp., announces that its subsidiary, Zond Corporation, has signed a major contract with MidAmerican Energy Company. This is the largest wind energy supply contract in history.

04/16/97 – Mark Haedicke, general counsel and managing director, Enron Capital and Trade Resources Corp., testifies before the House Committee on Agriculture, Subcommittee on Risk Management and Specialty Crops. (Testifying on behalf of the International Swaps and Derivatives Association - ISDA.)

05/01/97 – Enron Corp. and Amtrak agree to a wholesale pact for purchase of electrical power.

05/09/97 – Jeffrey K. Skilling, president and chief operating officer, Enron Corp., testifies before the House Committee on Commerce, Subcommittee on Energy and Power.

06/04/97 – Enron Corp. and Portland General Corp., a holding company, receive final merger approval from Oregon Public Utility Commission.

07/31/97 – Edmund P. Segner III, executive vice president and chief of staff, Enron, testifies before the House Committee on Resources, Subcommittee on Energy and Natural Resources.

10/13/97 – Mikhail Gorbachev, former president of the Soviet Union, to accept the prestigious Enron Prize for Distinguished Public Service from the James A. Baker III Institute for Public Policy of Rice University.

10/23/97 – Enron Corp. makes an entry into the California electricity market.

1998

01/14/98 – Ralph Hodge, chairman, and David Lewis, vice president, both of Enron Europe, provide testimony before the Trade and Industry Select Committee of the House of Commons.

01/15/98 – Enron Corp. signs a power agreement with Pacific Telesis.

01/19/98 – CalPERS, the nation's largest public pension fund, commits $500 million to a $1 billion partnership (JEDI 2) established with a direct investment vehicle, Enron II. Enron II is the second investment partnership between CalPERS and Enron Corp.

05/20/98 – Mary Joyce, senior director of compensation and benefits, Enron Corp., testifies before the House Committee on

Education and the Workforce, Subcommittee on Oversight and Investigations.

05/20/98 – Elizabeth A. Tilney, senior vice president, advertising, communications and organizational development, Enron Corp., testifies before the House Committee on Education and the Workforce, Subcommittee on Oversight and Investigations.

07/24/98 – Enron Corp. forms Global Water Company. Enron's purchase of Wessex Water (England) provides the basis of Azurix, Enron's United Kingdom water subsidiary.

09/24/98 – Steven J. Kean, senior vice president of government affairs, Enron, testifies before the Senate Committee on Energy and Natural Resources.

1999

01/21/99 – Enron Communications and RealNetworks form an alliance to deliver broadband steering media service.

02/02/99 – Enron Corp. to issue 12 million shares of common stock.

02/03/99 – Rebecca A. McDonald becomes executive managing director of Enron International.

02/03/99 – Tim Rebhorn, commercial director of iron and steel initiatives, Enron International, testifies before the House Committee on Ways and Means, Subcommittee on Trade.

04/07/99 – Houston Astros baseball franchise and Enron Corp. agree to name the major league ballpark "Enron Field," part of a 30-year contract.

04/14/99 – John Hardy, Jr., vice president, project finance, Enron International, testifies before the House Committee on International

Relations, Subcommittee on International Economic Policy and Trade. (Testifying on behalf of the Coalition for Employment through Exports, International Energy Development Council, and the National Foreign Trade Council.)

05/20/99 – Enron Communications announced a plan to commence the trading of bandwidth as a commodity.

07/01/99 – Roger Fragua, manager, American Indian affairs, Enron Corp., testifies before the House Committee on Resources, Subcommittee on Water and Power.

07/01/99 – Enron Corp. promotes Joseph Stutton to vice chairman.

07/13/99 – Ground breaking ceremony for Enron Corp.'s new 40-story office tower in Houston.

07/15/99 – Steven J. Kean, executive vice president, Enron Corp., testifies before the Senate Committee on Energy and Natural Resources. (Testifying on behalf of the Electric Power Supply Association.)

07/20/99 – Enron Corp. and Enron Oil & Gas Company (EOG) announce a transaction to establish EOG as a widely held public company that will be independent of Enron. Under the share exchange agreement, Enron Corp. will exchange 62.27 million of its 82.27 million shares of EOG common stock for EOG's China and India operations. In connection with the exchange, EOG will contribute $600 million in cash to one of EOG's India subsidiaries that will be transferred to Enron. The $600 million will be used to finance international activities.

07/22/99 – Steven J. Kean, executive vice president of Enron Corp., testifies before the House Committee on Commerce, Subcommittee on Energy and Power.

10/21/99 – Nelson Mandela, former president of South Africa, to accept the prestigious Enron Prize for Distinguished Public Service from the James A. Baker III Institute for Public Policy of Rice University.

10/26/99 – Enron Corp. announces the launch of EnronOnline, a global Internet-based transaction system for wholesale energy and other commodities.

11/09/99 – U.S. Treasury releases the Report of the President's Working Group on Financial Markets: "Over the Counter Derivatives Markets and the Commodity Exchange Act."

12/02/99 – Enron Communications announces its first commodity bandwidth trade.

2000

01/10/00 – *Fortune* magazine rates Enron Corp. 24th of its 100 best companies to work for in America.

01/20/00 – Sun Microsystems and Enron Corp. agree to accelerate the adoption of broadband services.

01/20/00 – Enron Corp. hosts its annual equity analyst conference in Houston.

01/20/00 – Kenneth L. Lay, chairman and CEO, highlights Enron's 700% return to shareholders over the past decade.

02/23/00 – Enron Corp. starts Enroncredit.Com, a real-time credit department for business-to-business customers.

03/09/00 – Enron Corp. announces the launch of the first online sulfur dioxide emissions allowance auction. The auction will be accessible through Enron's Internet-based transaction system, EnronOnline.

04/18/00 – First appearance of Raptor, special-purpose entity to remove certain investment losses from Enron Corp.'s books.

05/02/00 – Enron Corp. begins to provide bandwidth products via EnronOnline.

05/16/00 – Enron Corp. with IBM and AOL as investors form an independent company, New Power Company. Headed by H. Eugene Lockhart, New Power will market power and natural gas over the Internet to homes and businesses.

07/19/00 – Blockbuster and Enron Broadband Services announce a 20-year agreement to launch entertainment on-demand service through Enron Intelligent Network.

08/23/00 – Enron's Corp. stock reaches record high of $90.75 a share.

10/05/00 – New Power Company, an energy trading company via the Internet, initial public offering of shares is priced at $21 per share.

12/07/00 – London's Financial Times Energy (FT Energy) names Enron Corp. company of the year.

12/13/00 – Enron Corp. announces that Jeffrey K. Skilling has been elected CEO effective Feb. 12, 2001, assuming this role in addition to those of president and chief operating officer. Kenneth L. Lay will continue to serve as chairman of the board.

12/18/00 – Broadband Services, a wholly-owned subsidiary of Enron Corp., and Blockbuster, Inc., announces it has begun delivering movies via the Blockbuster Entertainment On-Demand service over Enron's broadband network in Seattle, Portland, OR, and Salt Lake City, UT.

2001

01/16/01 – Kenneth L. Lay becomes an adviser on the Administration's transition team on energy.

01/19/01 – Enron Energy Services and Owens-Illinois, Inc. announce a 10-year energy management agreement.

01/30/01 – Enron Corp. announces pricing of 20-year, zero coupon convertible senior debt securities. Gross proceeds of this offering will be $1.25 billion. The securities will carry a 2.125% yield to maturity with an aggregate face value of $1.90 billion, convertible into common stock at an initial premium of 45%.

02/12/01 – Jeffrey K. Skilling becomes CEO of Enron Corp.

03/09/01 – Enron Broadband Services announces that it has terminated its exclusive relationship with Blockbuster, Inc.

04/26/01 – Enron Corp. and Sierra Pacific Resources announce they have agreed to terminate their purchase and sale agreement for Enron's wholly owned electric utility subsidiary Portland General Electric.

05/02/01 – Enron Corp.'s vice chairman, J. Clifford Baxter, resigns.

08/14/01 – Board of Directors for Enron Corp. reports a regular quarterly dividend of $0.125 per share on the corporation's common stock to shareholders. The indicated annual rate is $0.50 per share.

08/14/01 – Jeffrey K. Skilling resigns as Enron Corp.'s president and CEO. He will continue to serve as a consultant to Enron and its board of directors. Kenneth L. Lay, currently Enron's chairman of the board, will assume the additional responsibilities of president and CEO. Sherron Watkins subsequently sends Kenneth L. Lay an unsigned memorandum warning of accounting irregularities and possible scandals to come.

08/28/01 – Enron Corp. promotes Greg Whalley to president and chief operating officer and Mark Frevert to vice chairman.

09/14/01 – Enron Corp. reports that it is donating $1 million to support the relief and recovery efforts arising from the terrorist actions of Sept. 11.

10/16/01 – Enron, during its posting of third quarter earnings, reports its first loss in 4 years.

10/24/01 – Jeff McMahon replaces Andrew Fastow as Enron Corp.'s chief financial officer.

10/31/01 – Enron Corp.'s board of directors appoints a Special Committee, to be chaired by William Powers, Jr., to examine and take any appropriate actions with respect to transactions between Enron and entities connected to related parties. The board also reports that the SEC has opened a formal investigation into certain of the matters that are the subject of current press accounts and that previously were the subject of its informal inquiry.

11/01/01 – Enron Corp. announces that J.P. Morgan and Salomon Smith Barney, Inc. have executed commitment letters to provide $1 billion of secured credit lines supported by Enron's Northern Natural Gas Company and Transwestern Pipeline Company assets.

11/07/01 – Azurix Corp., Enron Corp.'s United Kingdom water subsidiary, announces that it has completed the sale of its wholly owned subsidiaries, Azurix North America Corp. and Azurix Industrial Corp., to American Water Works Company, Inc., which will assume $6.1 million of previous debt.

11/08/01 – Enron Corp. provides additional information about related parties and off-balance sheet transactions and restates earnings for 1997-2001. Enron Corp. announces that it has filed its third quarter 2001 10-Q report with the Securities and Exchange Commission.

11/09/01 – Dynegy Inc. and Enron Corp. agree to a merger.

11/13/01 – Enron Corp. reports that the board of directors has elected Raymond M. Bowen, Jr., executive vice president–finance and treasurer. Mr. Bowen had been serving as chief operating officer of Enron Industrial Markets.

11/28/01 – Dynegy Inc. and Enron Corp. merger agreement dissolves. Enron Corp.'s bonds downgraded to below investment grade, or junk bond status.

11/30/01 – Enron Corp. lays off 1,100 workers in Britain.

12/02/01 – Enron Corp. and 13 of its subsidiaries file voluntary petitions for Chapter 11 reorganization in the U.S. Bankruptcy Court for the Southern District of New York.

12/03/01 – Enron Corp. announces that it has arranged up to $1.5 billion of debtor-in-possession (DIP) financing. The financing, arranged by Citigroup and J.P. Morgan Chase, will be syndicated and is secured by substantially all of the company's assets. Enron Corp. announces the layoff of more than 4,000 company employees.

12/10/01 – SEC chairman, Harvey L. Pitt, delivers speech about Enron Corp.'s collapse.

12/11/01 – The California Public Utilities Commission (PUC) orders an investigation to assess the effects of Enron Corp.'s bankruptcy filing on California customers.

12/13/01 – The SEC announces that on December 12, 2001, it filed a subpoena non-compliance enforcement action in U.S. District Court for the District of Columbia against Andrew S. Fastow, the former chief financial officer of Enron Corp. Pursuant to a subpoena issued on October 31, 2001, Mr. Fastow was obligated to appear for testimony before the SEC staff at 9:30 a.m. on December 12, 2001. Mr. Fastow chose not to appear and instead informed the SEC staff, through counsel, that he would not appear as required by the subpoena.

2002

01/04/02 – Enron Energy Services group wins approval of the U.S. Bankruptcy Court, Southern District of New York, to void nearly 700 contracts to supply power and gas to businesses and local and state government entities throughout the United States.

01/09/02 – U.S. Department of Justice confirms that an Enron-related criminal investigation has begun.

01/10/02 – U.S. Attorney General John Ashcroft and David Ayres, his chief of staff, recuse themselves from the Justice Department's criminal investigation of Enron Corp.

01/10/02 – Arthur Anderson notifies the SEC, the FBI, and several congressional committees that a significant but undetermined number of Enron related electronic and papers documents were destroyed.

01/10/02 – Administration acknowledges that Kenneth L. Lay met with Treasury Secretary last October, regarding concerns of Enron Corp.'s not being able to meet its financial obligations.

01/11/02 – Federal bankruptcy judge Arthur Gonzalez rules that Enron Corp.'s bankruptcy (Chapter 11) case will remain in the state of New York.

01/14/02 – Sale of Enron's energy trading operations to UBS, a Swiss financial service conglomerate is made public.

01/15/02 – New York Stock Exchange suspends trading in Enron Corp. shares.

01/15/02 – Arthur Andersen fires David B. Duncan, lead partner on the Enron Corp. account. Thomas H. Bauer, Debra A. Cash, and Roger D. Willard are placed on administrative leave. Houston-based partners being relieved of management responsibilities are: D. Stephen Goddard, Jr., Michael M. Lowther, Gary B. Goolsby, and Michael C. Odom.

01/17/02 – Enron Corp. fires Arthur Andersen LLP in all capacities.

01/23/02 – Enron Corp. announces that Kenneth L. Lay has resigned as Chairman of the Board and Chief Executive Officer of Enron Corp. Mr. Lay, who will also retire as an Enron employee, will remain on the company's board of directors.

01/24/02 – Price-Waterhouse-Coopers reports that Enron Europe's liabilities are in excess of $1 billion, but a little more than $100 million is anticipated to be generated through settlement of outstanding contracts.

01/25/02 – J. Clifford Baxter, former Enron Corp. vice chairman, is found dead.

01/27/02 – Enron Corp. board names Stephen F. Cooper interim CEO and chief restructuring officer.

01/28/02 – The Severed Enron Employees Coalition files suit in order to recoup losses by participants in Enron Corp.'s bankrupt 401k retirement plan.

01/31/02 – Governor of California requests the U.S. Federal Energy Regulatory Commission to investigate possible energy market manipulation by Enron Corp.

02/01/02 – Enron Corp.'s Special Investigative Committee of the board of directors releases its report, known as the Powers Report.

02/03/02 – Andersen Worldwide, S.C., announces that former Federal Reserve Board Chairman Paul A. Volcker has agreed to chair an Independent Oversight Board (IOB) to work with Arthur Andersen LLP in making fundamental changes in its audit practice.

02/04/02 – Kenneth L. Lay resigns from Enron Corp. board of directors.

02/05/02 – The Enron Europe group, the European bankrupted arm of Enron Corp., has liabilities of more than $2 billion, according to Price-Waterhouse-Coopers.

02/08/02 – UBS Warburg announces today that it has completed the transaction under which it has obtained from Enron Corp. an exclusive license to the technology to operate North American natural gas and power trading operations.

02/11/02 – The former EnronOline, Enron Corp.'s Internet-based transaction system, makes its reappearance as UBS Warburg Energy (UBSWenergy.com). Lawrence Whalley, Enron's former president, assumes the same position with UBS Warburg Energy.

02/13/02 – The Federal Energy Regulatory Commission releases communications of an investigation showing how Enron Corp., through its affiliates, used its market position to distort electric and natural gas markets in the West.

02/18/02 – The Financial Services Authority (United Kingdom) announces an investigation into the role of British bankers who helped Enron Corp. create financing schemes.

02/18/02 – UBS Warburg reports that its bid for Enron Corp.'s North American wholesale electricity and natural gas trading business has been approved by the United States Bankruptcy Court in New York.

02/20/02 – James Derrick, Jr., Enron Corp.'s executive vice president and general counsel, resigns.

02/22/02 – U.S. bankruptcy judge Arthur Gonzales rules on the appointment of an examiner in the Chapter 11 case of Enron North America. The examiner is to be selected by the Office of the U.S. Trustee.

02/22/02 – Thirty-three states ask Judge Arthur Gonzales to block Enron Corp. executives from securing advance money for their legal defense from the bankruptcy estate.

02/27/02 – U.S. bankruptcy judge Arthur Gonzales rules that Enron Corp. executives cannot secure millions of dollars from the company for their legal fees.

03/01/02 – U.S. Treasury provides access to some Enron-related documents via its frequently requested FOIA-processed records on its Web site.

03/06/02 – U.S. bankruptcy judge Arthur Gonzales gives approval for $1,100 for each laid-off Enron employee.

03/11/02 – The Andersen Independent Oversight Board releases a preliminary report on the reform and rebuilding of Arthur Andersen LLP.

03/14/02 – The U.S. Department of Labor announces that State Street Bank and Trust of Boston, Mass., will act as the independent fiduciary for Enron Corp.'s retirement plans.

03/14/02 – Deputy Attorney General, Larry Thompson, holds a news conference regarding the Arthur Andersen indictment.

03/14/02 – House Committee on Ways and Means approves, by a vote of 36-2, H.R. 3669, a bill with provisions affecting employer stock in 401(k) retirement plans.

03/15/02 – The General Services Administration suspends Enron Corp., related entities, several former Enron officials, Arthur

Andersen LLP, and a former Andersen official from conducting new business with the federal government. The suspension is for a period of 12 months for all parties except for Andersen, whose suspension is for the duration of the indictment.

03/15/02 – The Federal Energy Regulatory Commission issues a subpoena to Enron Corp. to produce certain documents on or before 3/29/02.

03/15/02 – Federal Judge Melinda Harmon, U.S. District Court for the Southern District of Texas in Houston, names the University of California as lead plaintiff in a shareholders' class action lawsuit against Enron Corp. senior executives and its former accounting firm, Arthur Andersen LLP.

03/19/02 – House Committee on Education and the Workforce approves, by a vote of 28-19, H.R.3762, a bill with provisions affecting employer stock in 401(k) retirement plans.

The Securities and Exchange Commission announces final plans for completing reviews of auditor independence systems and controls for each of the five largest independent auditing firms.

03/21/02 – Senate Committee on Health, Education, Labor and Pensions approves, by a vote of 11-10, S. 1992, a bill with provisions affecting employer stock in 401(k) retirement plans.

03/22/02 – The Andersen Independent Oversight Board outlines a new framework for the reform and rebuilding of Arthur Andersen LLP as a firm dedicated, first and foremost, to quality auditing.

03/23/02 – Senate Committee on Governmental Affairs issues 29 subpoenas to Enron Corp.; its former auditing firm, Arthur Andersen LLP; and members of the Andersen board going back to 1992.

03/26/02 – Joseph Berardino, Arthur Andersen LLP chief executive, resigns.

03/27/02 – U.S. Trustee overseeing Enron Corp.'s Chapter 11 reorganization appoints a five-member committee, in order that workers will have input into the bankruptcy proceedings.

03/27/02 – New Power Holdings, a proposed Enron Corp. spin-off to Centrica (Britain's largest natural gas supplier), was jeopardized when bankruptcy judge Arthur Gonzalez refused to release Centrica from potential liability for Enron's taxes. The proposed deal would pay Enron $56.5 million for its 44% stake in New Power.

03/27/02 – Chairman of the Senate Committee on Government Affairs seeks information from the current Administration and the Archivist of the United States on all national energy policy communications concerning Enron, since 1992, with the Securities and Exchange Commission, the Commodity Futures Trading Commission, the Federal Energy and Regulatory Commission, the Departments of Labor, Energy, and Commerce, the Export Import Bank, and the Overseas Private Investment Corporation. The Chairman sent letters to members of the Vice President's energy task force, seeking similar information.

04/05/02 – U.S. bankruptcy judge Arthur Gonzales gives approval to make acting Enron chief executive Stephen F. Cooper a full-time employee at $1.32 million in annual salary.

04/08/02 – Arthur Andersen LLP announces a reduction of its U.S. workforce by approximately 7000 positions during the next 2 months.

04/09/02 – David Duncan (Arthur Andersen Global Managing Partner) indicted. Graduated from Texas A & M and then began with Arthur Andersen in 1981. From 1997 until its implosion, Duncan headed the Enron audit team. He has pleaded guilty to obstruction of justice for ordering the destruction of Enron-related documents two days after learning of the federal probe. He is awaiting sentencing and is cooperating with prosecutors.

06/16/02 – Arthur Andersen found guilty by a jury for obstructing the Securities and Exchange Commission's investigation of Enron. The auditing and accounting firm was required to pay the maximum fine of $500,000 and was sentenced to five years probation. The firm has since been disbanded.

08/20/02 – Michael Kopper (Assistant to Andrew Fastow) indicted and pleads guilty. Graduated from Duke University with a degree in economics, as well as a graduate degree from the London School of Economics, he came to Enron in 1994, after working for Toronto Dominion Bank. He and his domestic partner were the major players assisting Andrew Fastow in pulling off the financial schemes. He managed a number of Fastow's partnerships and pleaded guilty to money laundering and wire fraud. He has agreed to assist prosecutors and is awaiting sentencing.

09/12/02 – British Bankers Gary Mulgrew, David Bermingham, and Giles Darby are indicted and charged with seven counts of wire fraud. Each is fighting extradition from London for prosecution for their role in the financial schemes of Andrew Fastow's off-the-balance sheet partnerships. The three previously worked for National Westminster Bank and schemed to defraud the bank out of more than $7 million.

10/14/02 – Timothy Belden (Managing Director of Enron Power Marketing) indicted and pleads guilty to conspiracy to commit wire fraud in connection with manipulating the energy prices in California. He is cooperating with prosecutors and is awaiting sentencing. He agrees to forfeit $2.1 million to be applied to his restitution which shall equal the amount of damages caused by his actions.

11/26/02 – Lawrence Lawyer (low level Enron employee) indicted and pleaded guilty for filing a false tax return that did not report funds he received on one of Andrew Fastow's off-the-balance sheet partnerships called RADR created for the purposes of divesting Enron's interest in wind farms for regulatory purposes. He is awaiting sentencing and has agreed to cooperate with prosecutors.

2003

02/04/03 – Jeffrey Richter (Manager of Enron Power Marketing) indicted and pleaded guilty to one count of conspiracy to commit wire fraud and one count of making a false statement to federal investigators as to his role in the California power crises. He has agreed to cooperate with prosecutors and is awaiting sentencing. He faces up to ten years on the two counts. He has agreed to pay restitution equal to amount of the loss which he caused.

04/29/03 – Ken Rice (Chief Executive Officer of Enron Broadband Services) indicted on charges of conspiracy to commit wire fraud and securities fraud, money laundering and insider trading for overstating the potential of Enron's broadband division. He pleaded guilty in July 2004 to a single count of securities fraud. He is awaiting sentencing for up to 10 years in prison, 3 years supervision, and a $1 million fine or twice the gain or loss. He was also required to forfeit his Telluride home; his wife's platinum, sapphire and diamond necklace, with 16 diamonds, 226 sapphires, and a platinum, sapphire and diamond bracelet with 6.65 carats of sapphires and 1.68 carats of diamonds; his 1995 Ferrari; a 1999 Shelby; and the monetary contents of his numerous bank accounts.

04/29/03 – Kevin Hannon (Chief Operating Officer of Enron Broadband Services) indicted on charges of conspiracy to commit wire fraud, money laundering and insider trading. The charges stem from lies told to investors and the public as to the potential of Enron Broadband Services, as well as the millions made in stock sales when the stock was elevated. He is awaiting trial.

04/29/03 – Rex Shelby (Former Senior Vice President of Engineering and Operations for Enron Broadband Services) indicted on charges of conspiracy to commit wire fraud, money laundering and insider trading. The charges stem from lies told to investors and the public as to the potential of Enron Broadband Services, as well as the millions made in stock sales when the stock was elevated. He is awaiting trial.

04/29/03 – Joe Hirko (Former Co-CEO of Enron Broadband Services) indicted on charges of conspiracy to commit wire fraud, money laundering and insider trading. The charges stem from lies told to investors and the public as to the potential of Enron Broadband Services, as well as the millions made in stock sales when the stock was elevated. He is awaiting trial.

04/29/03 – Kevin Howard (Former Vice President of Finance of Enron Broadband Services) indicted on charges of conspiracy to commit wire fraud, money laundering and making false statements to the FBI. The charges stem from lies told to investors and the public as to the potential of Enron Broadband Services, as well as the millions made in stock sales when the stock was elevated. He is awaiting trial.

04/29/03 – Michael Krautz (Former senior Accounting Director of Enron Broadband Services) indicted on charges of conspiracy to commit wire fraud, money laundering and making false statements to the FBI. The charges stem from lies told to investors and the public as to the potential of Enron Broadband Services, as well as the millions made in stock sales when the stock was elevated. He is awaiting trial.

04/29/03 – F. Scott Yaeger (Former Senior Vice President of Business Development for Enron Broadband Services) indicted on charges of conspiracy to commit wire fraud, money laundering and insider trading. The charges stem from lies told to investors and the public as to the potential of Enron Broadband Services, as well as the millions made in stock sales when the stock was elevated. He is awaiting trial.

04/30/03 – Ben Glisan, Jr. (Treasurer of Enron Corp.) indicted and pleaded guilty in September 2003 to one count of conspiracy to commit wire fraud and securities fraud. He refused to cooperate with prosecutors and was thus the first Enron executive to go to prison and is serving five years. The U.S. Government seized $900,000, plus the $412,000 in taxes he paid on the money. He earned his bachelors, as well as his master's degree from the University of Texas. Prior to joining Enron, he worked for the accounting firm of Coopers & Lybrand in Dallas and then Arthur Andersen in Houston. He joined Enron in 1996 and became treasurer in 2000. As an investor in one of Fastow's off-the-balance sheet partnerships, he earned $1 million from a $5,800 investment. He was fired from Enron in 2002.

04/30/03 – Lea Fastow (Former Assistant Treasurer; wife of Andrew Fastow) indicted. She met Andrew Fastow at Tufts University from which she graduated in 1984. Both worked at Continental Bank in Chicago while they earned their MBAs at Northwestern University. Both then came to Enron where she eventually became the Assistant Treasurer. She left Enron in 1997 when her son was born but remained active in Enron's business, serving as the head of its Art Committee, as well as executive assistant for one of Enron's off-the-balance sheet partnerships. Initially charged with criminal activity, the U.S. Government, out of fear of losing her husband's cooperation in the case, dropped its criminal charges and filed a single tax misdemeanor against her when the judge refused to accept a reduced criminal sentence. She began serving a one year prison sentence in July, 2004. Upon release she will be under one year of supervision.

04/30/03 – Andrew Fastow (Chief Financial Officer of Enron Corp.) indicted and pleaded guilty in January, 2004 to a single charge of conspiracy to commit wire fraud and a single charge of conspiracy to commit securities fraud. He joined Enron in 1990, after earning his MBA from Northwestern University in Chicago. He was fired from Enron on October 24, 2001 when it was discovered he had been involved in a massive scheme to defraud the company. In exchange for his cooperation with prosecutors, he agrees to serve 10 years in prison and forfeit $23.8 million, approximately ½ of his ill-gotten gains, as well as his homes in Galveston and Vermont, along with another $6 million. His agreement coincided with his wife's so that their two young sons would not be without a parent in the family home while the other serves their prison sentence.

05/30/03 – John Forney (Manager of Enron Power Marketing) indicted on 11 counts of conspiracy to commit wire fraud in the illegal trading schemes to manipulated the energy prices in California during the winter of 2000-2001. By creating false congestion, the California grid operates would pay Enron to relieve the artificial congestion. He has pleaded guilty to charges related to the power crises and is awaiting sentencing.

10/29/03 – Dave Delainey (CEO of Enron Energy Services) indicted and pleads guilty of one count of insider trading and agreed to cooperate in the government's case against Enron officials. He has agreed to forfeit $4.2 million, plus pay $3.7 million to the Securities and Exchange Commission. He is charged awaiting sentencing and has agreed to never serve as an officer or director of a publicly-traded company. He admits that he participated in a wide-range of schemes for the purposes of deceiving the public about Enron's financial status. He left Enron in March, 2002.

2004

05/18/04 – Paula Rieker (Director of Investor Relations; Board Secretary; Trustee of the Enron retirement plan) indicted and pleads guilty. She is charged with insider trading for selling Enron based upon her knowledge about Enron's losses attributed to the internet business, as well as failing to protect the retirement funds of Enron employees, and misrepresenting Enron's financial status to the analysts and the public. She pleads guilty and agrees to cooperate with investigators. She is subject to up to 10 years in prison and a $1 million fine. She returns a half a million dollars she received from her sale of the Enron stock.

07/07/04 – Richard Causey (Chief Accounting Officer of Enron Corp.) indicted and charged with 36 counts of conspiracy to commit wire fraud, securities fraud, insider trading, money laundering and making false financial statements. Also named in the indictment is Skilling and Lay. Causey received his master's degree in accounting from the University of Texas. Upon graduating, he was hired by Arthur Andersen. He joined Enron in 1991, and was eventually promoted to Chief Accounting Officer, a position he held until he was fired in 2002.

07/07/04 – Jeffrey Skilling (CEO of Enron Corp.) indicted on 35 counts of insider trading, securities fraud, wire fraud, conspiracy and lying on Enron's financial statements. If convicted, he could face up to 325 years in prison, plus $80 million in fines. He joined Enron in 1990 and became president and chief operating officer in 1997, until he was named CEO in February, 2001 when Ken Lay resigned. He resigned his position on August 14, 2001

07/07/04 – Kenneth Lay (Chairman and CEO of Enron Corp.) indicted on 11 counts of conspiracy to commit wire and securities fraud, perpetrating wire, securities and bank fraud, making false and misleading statements to employees, as well as to banks, analysts and credit-rating agencies for the period between August 14, 2001 and January 23, 2002. Ken Lay became Chairman and CEO of Houston Natural Gas in 1984 until it merged with InterNorth in 1985 forming Enron. He resigned on January 23, 2002.

07/22/04 – Dan Boyle (Former Vice President of Enron's Global Finance group) indicted. He is accused of conspiracy to commit wire fraud and falsifying books, records and accounts. He is also charged with making false statements in a deal involving three floating power plants off the coast of Nigeria. He is accused of a side-agreement deal with Merrill Lynch to hide Enron's losses and is awaiting trial.

07/22/04 – Sheila Kahanek (Senior Director) indicted. She has a degree from the University of Houston and worked as an accountant at Ernest & Young prior to joining Enron in 1998. She worked with Enron's Asia Pacific/Africa/China division. She is accused of trying to cover up her role in the Nigerian barge deal in which Enron and Merrill Lynch had a "handshake" deal. She is also accused of ordering a worker to destroy evidence, as well as conspiracy to commit wire fraud and falsifying books and records. She is awaiting trial with others charged in sham Nigerian Barge deal.

07/22/04 – James Brown (Head of Merrill Lynch's Strategic Asset Lease and Finance Group) indicted and charged with lying to the grand jury as to the promise made by Andrew Fastow to repurchase Nigerian barges sold to Merrill Lynch for the sole purposes of hiding loses. His handwritten notes indicate "reputational risk i.e. aid/abet Enron income stmt manipulation." He is also charged with conspiracy to commit wire fraud, conspiracy to falsify books, records and accounts, as well as perjury and obstruction of justice. He is awaiting trial with others charged in sham Nigerian Barge deal.

07/22/04 – Dan Bayly (Global Head of Investment Banking Division at Merrill Lynch) indicted and charged with conspiracy to commit wire fraud and falsifying books and records, as well as lying to Congress and the SEC regarding the Nigerian Barge deal. He is awaiting trial with the others charged in sham barge deals.

07/22/04 – William Fuhs (Former Vice President of Merrill Lynch) indicted and charged with conspiracy to commit wire fraud and conspiracy to falsify books, records and accounts, as well as making false statements to the FBI and obstructing the investigation in the Nigerian barge deal between Merrill Lynch and Enron. He is awaiting trial with the others charged in the Nigerian barge deals.

07/22/04 – Robert Furst (Managing Director of Merrill Lynch) was indicted and charged with conspiracy to commit wire fraud and conspiracy to falsify books, records and accounts. He is responsible, according to prosecutors for drawing up the plans for Merrill Lynch to temporarily purchase floating power plants off the coast of Nigeria in order to help Enron falsify its financial position. The deal guaranteed Merrill Lynch a 22 percent return on its investment within six months. He is awaiting trial with the others charged in the Nigerian barge deal.

08/25/04 – Mark Koenig (Director of Investor Relations of Enron Corp.) indicted and pleaded guilty to securities fraud in aiding and abetting Enron in its misrepresentations to the analysts and media. Joining Enron as a corporate treasurer in 1985, he was eventually transferred to the investor relations department. He faces up to 10 years in prison and a $1 million fine. He is awaiting sentencing and has agreed to cooperate with prosecutors in U.S. Government's case against Ken Lay, Jeff Skilling and Richard Causey.

APPENDIX II

CRIMINAL CHARGES	
Total (As of September, 2004)	**33**
GUILTY PLEAS	**14**
Ben Glisan Jr. (Treasurer)	5 years in prison
Lea Fastow (Former Asst. Treasurer)	1 year in prison
Andrew Fastow (Chief Financial Officer)	Awaiting sentencing
Michael Kopper (Managing Director)	Awaiting sentencing
Mark Koenig (Investor Relations)	Awaiting sentencing
Paula Rieker (Investor Relations)	Awaiting sentencing
David Duncan (Arthur Andersen)	Awaiting sentencing
Timothy Belden (Head of Power Trading)	Awaiting sentencing
Jeffrey Richter (Power Trader)	Awaiting sentencing
Lawrence Lawyer (low level employee)	Awaiting sentencing
Dave Delainey	Awaiting sentencing
Ken Rice (CEO – Enron Broadband)	Awaiting sentencing
John M. Forney (Power Trader)	Awaiting sentencing
JURY CONVICTION	**1**
Arthur Andersen	Fined
OTHERS CHARGED	**18**
Ken Lay	Awaiting trial
Jeff Skilling	Awaiting trial
Richard Causey	Awaiting trial
Nigerian barge deal	
Dan Boyle (Vice President of Enron Global Finance)	Awaiting trial
Sheila Kahanek (Enron Senior Director)	Awaiting trial
James Brown (Merrill Lynch Strategic Lease Group)	Awaiting trial
Daniel Bayly (Investment Banking Merrill Lynch)	Awaiting trial
William Fuhs (Vice President Merrill Lynch)	Awaiting trial
Robert Furst	Awaiting trial

Broadband division

Joe Hirko	Awaiting trial
Kevin Hannon	Awaiting trial
F. Scott Yeager	Awaiting trial
Rex Shelby	Awaiting trial
Kevin Howard	Awaiting trial
Michael Krautz	Awaiting trial

British bankers

Gary Mulgrew	Fighting extradition
David Bermingham	Fighting extradition
Giles Darby	Fighting extradition

INDEX

A

B

C

D

E

F

G

H

I

J

K

L

M

N

O

P

Q

R

S

T

U

V

W

Y

ABOUT THE AUTHORS

Lynn Brewer is a former Enron executive. In her nearly three years at Enron, she was responsible for Risk Management in Energy Operations, the e-Commerce initiatives for Enron's water subsidiary, and Competitive Intelligence for Enron Broadband Services. During her tenure she witnessed numerous instances of illegal and corrupt dealings, including bank fraud, espionage, power price manipulation and the gross overstatements to the press, public and financial world.

Prior to joining the energy giant, Lynn worked in forensic accounting and spent 18 years as a legal professional in private practice, until she joined Ralston Purina where she worked in Corporate Development for the General Counsel and Chief Financial Officer.

Since leaving Enron, Lynn has become an internationally recognized speaker on the subject of corporate integrity, addressing audiences in South Africa, New Zealand, India, Canada, Venezuela, and the New York Stock Exchange. She provides compelling details into Enron's rise and fall, leaving audiences shocked when they realize how vulnerable they are to becoming the next Enron.

She is the Founder and President of The Integrity Institute, Inc., which independently assesses and certifies corporate integrity at the request of organizations for the benefit of their stakeholders. She holds a Certificate in Business Ethics from Colorado State University and serves on the steering committee for the Open Compliance and Ethics Group. In 2003, she was nominated for the *Women of Influence* Award and in 2004, she was named a *Paul Harris Fellow* by The Rotary Foundation of Rotary International.

Lynn is also the author of *SportsVision: Athletic Excellence through Visualization*, (foreword by Lou Holtz and Mike Ditka), based upon her 15 years as a competitive and professional figure skater, as well as a coach.

Matthew Scott Hansen is the co-author of the bestseller *Andy Kaufman Revealed.* Matt, his wife Stephanie, their two dogs and four cats live in Southern California.

Printed in the United States
41472LVS00004B/108

9 781418 485368